Technically-Write!

RON BLICQ
RGI LEARNING INC.

LISA MORETTO
RGI LEARNING INC.

CANADIAN EIGHTH EDITION

Pearson Canada
Toronto

Library and Archives Canada Cataloguing in Publication

Blicq, Ron S. (Ronald Stanley), 1925–
Technically-write! / Ron Blicq, Lisa Moretto. — Canadian 8th ed.

Includes index.
ISBN 978-0-13-215885-5

1. Technical writing—Textbooks. I. Moretto, Lisa A. II. Title.

T11.B55 2011 808'.0666 C2010-905289-7

ISBN 978-0-13-215885-5

Vice-President, Editorial Director: Gary Bennett
Editor-in-Chief: Ky Pruesse
Acquisitions Editor: David S. LeGallais
Marketing Manager: Loula March
Senior Developmental Editor: Suzanne Schaan
Project Manager: Cheryl Noseworthy
Production Editor: Tara Tovell
Copy Editor: Joe Zingrone
Proofreader: Tara Tovell
Compositor: Nelson Gonzalez
Art Director: Julia Hall
Cover and Interior Designer: Miguel Acevedo
Cover Image: Getty Images

4 5 14

Printed and bound in the USA.

Contents

About the Authors

Ron Blicq and Lisa Moretto are Senior Consultants with RGI Learning Inc., a consulting company specializing in oral and written communication. They teach workshops, based on the Pyramid Method of Writing presented in this book, to audiences all over the world. In 2001 they started delivering their courses on the web, at **www.rgilearning.com.**

Ron is Senior Consultant at RGI's Canadian office. He has extensive experience as a technical writer and editor with the Royal Air Force in Britain and CAE Industries Limited in Canada, and taught technical communication at Red River College from 1967 to 1990. Ron has authored six books with Pearson Education Canada and has written and produced six educational video programs, such as *Sharpening Your Business Communication Skills* and *So, You Have to Give a Talk?* He is a Fellow of the Society for Technical Communication and the Association of Teachers of Technical Writing in the United States, and of the Institute of Scientific and Technical Communicators in Great Britain. He also is a senior life member of the Institute of Electrical and Electronics Engineers Inc. Ron lives in Winnipeg, Manitoba.

Lisa is senior consultant at RGI's United States' office. She has experience as an information developer for IBM in the United States and as a learning products engineer for Hewlett-Packard in Great Britain. Lisa holds a BSc in technical communication from Clarkson University in New York, and an MSc in user interface design from the London Guildhall University in England. Her specialties include developing online interactive information, designing user interfaces, and writing product documentation. She is a senior member of the Society for Technical Communication and a member of the Institute of Electrical and Electronics Engineers Inc. Lisa lives in Rochester, New York, and teaches effective technical communication to engineering students at the Rochester Institute of Technology.

Preface

Not long after you graduate with your university degree or college diploma, you will start having to write business-oriented emails, letters, reports, and possibly technical proposals. This book contains numerous examples of informal and semiformal documents, all based on the unique "pyramid" method for structuring information, a technique that has helped countless technical people overcome "writer's block."

Three factors drive us to incorporate the changes we introduce into each new edition of *Technically-Write!* First, we listen to instructors of technical writing, not only in Canada but also around the world, who tell us what they need in the classroom and what features of the previous edition have worked particularly well for them (see the list of reviewers on the following page). Second, we read what the technical societies are drawing to their members' attention, in particular the Canadian Association of Teachers of Technical Writing, the Society for Technical Communication and the IEEE Professional Communication Society (both in the US), and the Institute of Scientific and Technical Communicators in the UK. Third, we talk to people in the engineering field and technical industries, to determine their specific needs and the changes they are experiencing (the Association of Professional Engineers and Geoscientists of Manitoba has been a consistently fine resource in this regard).

Two other factors, both in the electronics field, also are predominant: (1) the continually evolving use of email for sending letters and reports rather than just as a messaging medium and (2) the rapidly growing worldwide use of handheld communication aids such as the BlackBerry and online forums such as Facebook and Twitter. They are having a major impact on the way new generations are seeing technical communication.

So, what are the major changes in this edition? Primarily, we have

- introduced far more email-based examples of reports and letters (concurrently eliminating almost all references to the interoffice memorandum, which is practically non-existent in most industries),
- tightened up our writing style to reflect the growing use of bulleted subparagraphs adopted as a reporting medium by many industries,
- combined the two chapters dealing with long reports (i.e. semiformal and formal reports) into a single comprehensive chapter,
- moved the section on writing references and bibliography entries to a stand-alone appendix near the end of the book, to make it easier for readers to access, and

- introduced an "objectives" section at the start of each chapter, so you can quickly determine how the chapter will help you when you write and speak in business.

We appreciate the advice and helpful suggestions from users of the book, both teachers and students, and the advice of reviewers. In particular, we thank the following reviewers: Signe B. Gurholt (New Brunswick Community College, Saint John Campus), Michael S. Hume (Centennial College), Erin Robb (Langara College), and Ron Slavik (Mohawk College of Applied Arts and Technology). Their ideas have guided us in preparing this eighth edition. We are also celebrating, for it's 40 years since the first edition of *Technically-Write!* was published!

RB & LM

Supplements

For Students

PEARSON mycanadiantechcommlab™

MyCanadianTechCommLab (www.mycanadiantechcommlab.ca). This state-of-the-art, interactive, and instructive solution for technical communication is designed to be used as a supplement to a traditional lecture course or to completely administer an online course. See the opening pages of this text for details.

Throughout the text, icons highlight material where related activities or samples are available on MyCanadianTechCommLab:

- Explore dozens of **writing samples**, from letters to emails to reports, that model effective communication. Explore
- Practise correcting ineffective communication using interactive **document makeovers**. Feedback guides you to understand problems and find solutions. Practise
- Watch **videos** of professionals from various fields talking about how their writing and speaking are vital components of their success in business and industry. Watch

MyCanadianTechCommLab includes a Pearson eText that gives students access to the text whenever and wherever they have access to the internet. eText pages look exactly like the printed text, offering powerful new functionality for students and instructors. Users can create notes, highlight text in different colours, create bookmarks, zoom, click hyperlinked words and phrases to view definitions, and view in single-page or two-page view. Pearson eText allows for quick navigation to key parts of the eText using a table of contents, and provides a full-text search. The eText may also offer links to associated media files, enabling users to access videos, animations, or other activities as they read.

A student access card for MyCanadianTechCommLab is packaged with every new copy of the text. Access codes can also be purchased through campus bookstores or through the website.

CourseSmart. CourseSmart goes beyond traditional expectations—providing instant, online access to the textbooks and course materials you need at an average savings of 60 percent. With instant access from any computer and the ability to search your text, you'll find the content you need quickly, no matter where you are. And with online tools like highlighting and note-taking, you can save time and study efficiently. See all the benefits at **www.coursesmart.com/students**.

For Instructors

The eighth Canadian edition of *Technically-Write!* is supported by a comprehensive supplements package. Some of these instructor supplements are available for download from a password-protected section of Pearson Education Canada's online catalogue (vig.pearsoned.ca). Navigate to your book's catalogue page to view a list of supplements. See your local sales representative for details and access.

Instructor's Manual. This manual includes additional exercises, teaching tips, and other useful material, based on the authors' extensive teaching and workshop experience. Instructor Notes, with suggestions and answers, are provided for the Additional Projects that are available to students on MyCanadianTechCommLab.

MyTest (www.pearsonmytest.com). MyTest from Pearson Education Canada is a powerful assessment generation program that helps instructors easily create and print quizzes, tests, and exams, as well as homework or practice handouts. Questions and tests can all be authored online, allowing instructors ultimate flexibility and the ability to efficiently manage assessments at any time, from anywhere. MyTest for *Technically-Write!*, 8th edition, includes over 300 questions in multiple-choice, fill-in-the-blank, and true/false format. These questions are also available in Microsoft Word format.

Test Item File. This test bank includes all the questions from the MyTest version in Microsoft Word format.

PowerPoints. PowerPoint presentations cover a variety of topics, including "An Introduction to the Pyramid Method of Writing" and "Writing Plan for a Job Application Letter."

CourseSmart for Instructors. CourseSmart goes beyond traditional expectations—providing instant, online access to the textbooks and course materials you need at a lower cost for students. And even as students save money, you can save time and hassle with a digital eTextbook that allows you to search for the most relevant content at the very moment you need it. Whether it's evaluating textbooks or creating lecture notes to help students with difficult concepts, CourseSmart can make life a little easier. See how when you visit **www.coursesmart.com/instructors**.

Technology Specialists. Pearson's Technology Specialists work with faculty and campus course designers to ensure that Pearson technology products, assessment tools, and online course materials are tailored to meet your specific needs. This highly qualified team is dedicated to helping schools take full advantage of a wide range of educational resources by assisting in the integration of a variety of instructional materials and media formats. Your local Pearson Education sales representative can provide you with more details on this service program.

People as Communicators

We spend many of our waking hours communicating. If we write and speak clearly, efficiently, and persuasively, our messages expedite the transfer of information. But if we write or speak in a disorganized, unconvincing, or uninteresting way, we confuse our readers or listeners and they simply tune out. Similarly, if as listeners we mentally switch off while someone else is speaking, we contribute to information loss.

When you speak directly to someone, your listener has the opportunity to ask questions if he or she does not understand you. But when you write to somebody, that person no longer has this advantage. The results of poor communication soon become apparent, as Cam Collins and Elizabeth Drew found out.

Cam wants to attend an extra-high-voltage (EHV) DC power conference, so in an email to Fred Stokes, his manager, he writes,

> Fred
>
> The EHV conference described in the attached brochure is just the thing we have been looking for. Only last week you and I discussed the shortage of good technical information in this area, and now here is a conference featuring papers on many of the topics we are interested in. The cost is only $495 for registration, which includes a visit to the Freeling Rapids Generating Station. Travel and accommodation will be about $1150 extra. I'm informing you of this early so you can make a decision in time for me to arrange flight bookings and accommodation.
>
> Cam

Fred Stokes was equally enthusiastic and wrote back,

> Cam
>
> Thanks for informing me of the EHV DC power conference. I certainly don't want to miss it. Please make reservations for me as you suggested.
>
> Fred

Cam was the victim of his own carelessness: he failed to communicate clearly that it was *he* who wanted to go to Freeling Rapids!

Elizabeth had a good idea...

Because she communicated inefficiently, Elizabeth did not realize she had missed a golden opportunity to be first with an innovative software technique. Elizabeth's job is to design modifications for her company's equipment and then prepare documentation for implementing the changes. To speed up cross-referencing the drawings to the parts lists, she developed unique software to interface the two programs. It was faster and easier to use than the existing program, effectively reducing her cross-referencing time by 50%.

...it was simple and efficient...

So the next day, she knocked on the engineering manager's (Mr Haddon's) door, convinced he should know about it because she felt the company could patent it. This is how their conversation went:

Elizabeth	**Mr Haddon**
Oh! Mr Haddon! You know how long it takes to do the documentation for a new part...?	
	Yes..s..s..?
The problem is in trying to interface between the graphics computer and the parts list...	
	(*Mr Haddon appeared to be listening politely, but internally he was growing impatient.*)
...It has to be done by hand, you see...	
	Doesn't the drafting department do all that?
Oh, yes! They do. I was just trying to help them...to speed up their work a bit.	
	You're working for the chief draftsman now?
Oh, no! It was just an idea I had—to modify the software we use...	
	I don't remember issuing you a work order...
No. You didn't. I was doing it on my own... (*She meant she was doing it on her own time.*)	
	You mean the I.T. people asked you to do it?
Well—uh—no. Not exactly...	
	But you have been modifying one of our software programs? Without authority?
(*Reluctantly*) Uh-huh.	
	I thought I had made it quite clear to all the staff: No projects are to be undertaken without my approval! (*His tone was cold and abrupt.*)
I wanted to try...	
	That's final!

...but Elizabeth didn't know how to articulate her ideas clearly

Elizabeth's simple suggestion had become lost in a web of misunderstanding. Consequently, her idea lay dormant for two years, until a major software company came out with a comparable program. Elizabeth knew then that perhaps there *had* been potential for her design.

They need to focus their messages

If Cam and Elizabeth had paused to consider what their managers *most needed to hear* from them, they would have focused their messages much more efficiently.

Cam should have started with a request rather than describe background information:

> May I have your approval to attend an EHV DC power conference next month?

Elizabeth should have started with a statement of purpose:

> I have designed a software program that can possibly save us thousands of dollars annually. May I have a few moments to describe it to you?

In business and industry we have to communicate clearly and understand the implications of failing to do so. A poorly worded order that results in the wrong part being supplied to a job site, a weak report that fails to motivate the reader to take the urgent action needed to avoid a costly equipment breakdown, and even an inadequate job application letter and resume that fail to sell an employer on the right person for a prospective job—these all increase the cost of doing business. Such mistakes and misunderstandings can be prevented by more effective communication—communication that is receiver-oriented rather than transmitter-oriented, and conveys messages that are clear, concise, and complete.

Chapter 1
Why Technical People Need to Write Well

Books encouraging scientists, engineers, and technicians to write well have existed for over one hundred years. The authors who wrote those early books were responding to a 1901 report by the Society for the Promotion of Engineering Education (SPEE), which said (in part),

> The writing skills of engineering students are deplorable and need to be addressed by engineering colleges.

Technical communication was not part of a technical student's curriculum back then, but some engineering and English professors quietly began teaching the importance of good writing to their students. Then, later, they parlayed their knowledge into textbooks. The following excerpts show that, all those years ago, the early professors were already saying what today's instructors are emphasizing to their students.

The First Fifty Years

In 1908 T A Rickard, an associate of the Royal School of Mines in London, England, published *A Guide to Technical Writing*,[1] in which he wrote,

> Conscientious writers try to improve their mode of expression by precision of terms, by careful choice of words, and by the arrangement of them so that they become efficient carriers of thought from one mind to another.

Rickard titled one of his chapters "A Plea for Greater Simplicity in the Language of Science," having noticed that technical people tended to write in a long-winded way that was not easy to understand.

In 1922 Karl Owen Thompson, who taught English at the Case School of Applied Science in Cleveland, Ohio, published *Technical Exposition*.[2] In the introduction he commented on the differences between literary and technical writing:

> The study of English at a scientific school has a more directly professional application than it has at an academic college. Instead of courses in literature with their cultural purposes, courses are given that prepare the students for the types of reading and writing that will be required of them after they are graduated from college.... English is more than a tool, it is a part of life itself in its many activities.

In today's global community, Thompson would replace "English" with "language"

At the University of Michigan's College of Engineering, J Raleigh Nelson insisted from 1915 onward that his students write clearly. In 1940 he summed up his thoughts in a book titled *Writing the Technical Report*,[3] in which he wrote:

> In report writing, in particular, there is an increasing demand that the first page or two shall provide a comprehensive idea of the whole report.

This was the first documented reference to what we now refer to as the *executive summary*, which precedes a long report or proposal (see Chapter 5).

Reginald Kapp taught electrical engineering at University College in London. Like Nelson, he insisted his students write well. In 1948 he summed up his thoughts in a pocket-sized reference book titled *The Presentation of Technical Information*,[4] in which he particularly drew attention to the importance of identifying the audience before starting to write:

> You must consider carefully the extent of the reader's knowledge, his range of interests, and...any peculiarities...that might influence his receptivity for the information you have to impart.

Rickard and Kapp strongly stressed the need to identify the audience before starting to write

Similarly, forty years earlier, T A Rickard had written,

> If you describe a stamp-mill to an experienced mill-man, a mining student, or a bishop, you will vary the manner of telling. The most effective will be that which has a sympathetic appreciation of the other fellow's receptiveness. Do not plant carnations in a clay soil, or rice in a sand-heap.[5]

Technical Communication Quarterly
www.attw.org
***Technical Communication Quarterly* is the journal of the Association of Teachers of Technical Writing.**

(These authors were writing books for technical professionals, who were almost entirely male in the early part of the 20th century. They would write very differently today: for example, Rickard would probably change *mill-man* to *mill worker* and *other fellow's* to *other person's*.)

A Change in Style

Tyler G Hicks was a mechanical engineer who taught at Cooper Union School of Engineering in New York. He had written numerous articles and three technical books before turning his attention to engineering writing. In 1959 Hicks wrote *Successful Technical Writing*,[6] which had a refreshing direct style. Here are three examples:

Hicks's writing still sits well with today's readers

> Technical writing always pays off. You never lose when you write a good technical piece.... Good writing is a sure road to professional recognition.

> Talk directly to the reader. Bring him into the discussion. Use the personal pronouns "we" and "you," but with discretion.

> Choose verbs that create active impressions to the reader, and steer clear of the passive voice. You thus give life to your style.

These five writers were very conscious that they were preparing their students to take up important roles in the engineering and technical professions. What they had to say to their students then is just as relevant today.

Although writing styles may have changed, the message remains constant

REFERENCES

1. T A Rickard, *A Guide to Technical Writing* (San Francisco: Mining and Scientific Press, 1908), p 8.
2. Karl Owen Thompson, *Technical Exposition* (New York: Harper & Brothers Publishers, 1922), p vii.
3. J Raleigh Nelson, *Writing the Technical Report* (New York: McGraw-Hill Book Company, 1940), p 39.
4. Reginald O Kapp, *The Presentation of Technical Information* (London: Constable & Company Ltd, 1948), p 20. (Reprinted, with slight revisions, and published by the Institute for Scientific and Technical Communicators, UK, 1998.)
5. Rickard, p 12.
6. Tyler G Hicks, *Successful Technical Writing* (New York: McGraw-Hill Book Company, Inc, 1959), pp 1 and 194.

In 2010, the Kapp book was still in print

Chapter 2
A Technical Person's Approach to Writing

In this chapter you will learn how to

- develop a writing outline in a natural, nontraditional way,
- start writing a letter or report more easily,
- check what you have written for clarity, accuracy, and correct tone, and
- check your words to ensure they meet your reader's needs.

Engineering technologist Dan Skinner has a report to write on an investigation he completed seven weeks ago. He has made several attempts to get started, but never seems to find the right moment: maybe he was interrupted to resolve a problem, or it was too near lunchtime, or a meeting was called. And now he is down to the wire.

Unless Dan is one of those unusual people who can produce only when under pressure, he is in danger of writing an inadequate, hastily prepared report. But if he were to relax a little, instead of worrying that he has to organize himself and his writing task, he would find the physical process of writing a much more pleasant experience. But first he must change his approach.

Simplifying the Approach

The writer's pyramid helps you focus your letters and reports

Throughout this book we will be advising you to *tell your readers right away what they most need or want to know*. This means structuring your writing so that the first paragraph (or, in short documents, the first *sentence*) answers their most urgent question. This reader-oriented style is known as the "pyramid technique." Imagine every letter, email, or report you write is shaped like a pyramid: there is a small piece of essential information, the **Summary Statement**, at the top, supported on a base of details, facts, and evidence, the **Supporting Details**.

Figure 2-1 shows the basic pyramid structure. In later chapters we will show you how to break the supporting details section into smaller compartments to create well-organized documents. For example, in the opening paragraph of his letter report in Figure 2-2 (see page 6), Wes Hillman summarizes what Tina Mactiere most wants to know (whether the training course was a success and what results were achieved). In the

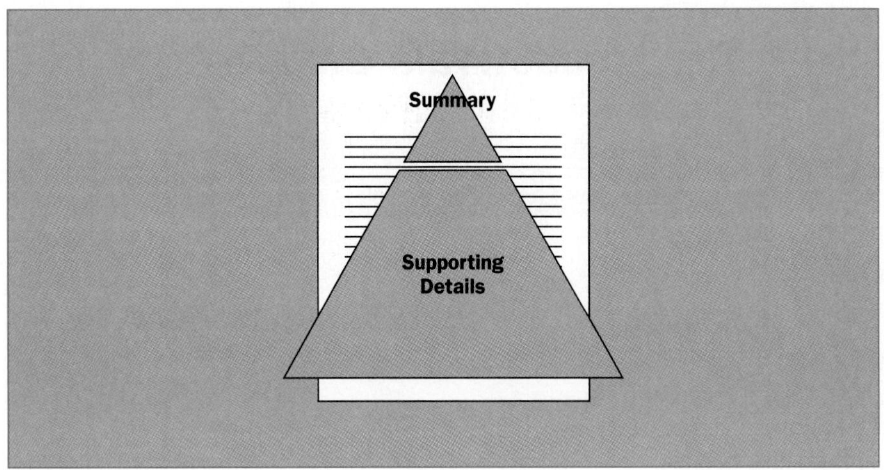

Figure 2-1 The pyramid writing technique.

Society for Technical Communication
www.stc.org
With more than 20 000 members worldwide, STC is the largest professional organization serving the technical communication profession. The society's diverse membership includes writers, editors, illustrators, printers, publishers, educators, students, engineers, and scientists employed in a variety of technological fields.

remainder of the letter he fills in background details, states briefly how the course was run, reports on student participation, and suggests the option of broader training pending student survey results.

Explore

Every document shown in this textbook has been structured using the pyramid technique, which is the simplest, fastest, most effective way to plan and write any document, regardless of its length. If Dan Skinner had known about the pyramid, he would have found it much easier to get started.

Planning the Writing Task

"Disorganize" the writing task!

The word "planning" seems to imply that you must start by thoroughly organizing your information. We disagree. Organizing too precisely or too early in the writing process will slow rather than speed your writing. The key is to organize your information much more simply, by brainstorming in the initial planning stages until you have collected, scrutinized, sorted, grouped, and written the topics into a logical outline that appeals to the reader. These stages are shown in Figure 2-3 (see page 7) and are the steps we recommend you follow.

1. Gather Information

First, assemble all the documents, results of tests, photographs, samples, computer data, specifications, and other supporting material that you will need to write your report. It's essential to gather everything now, because later you won't want to interrupt your writing to look for additional facts and figures.

The Meadowvale Group

Management Consultants
Box 181 – RPO Graydon
Winnipeg MB R3M 3J2

October 16, 2011

Tina B Mactiere, President
Macro Engineering Inc
600 Deepdale Drive
Toronto ON M5W 4R9

Dear Ms Mactiere

Results of Pilot Conflict-Resolution Training

The Conflict-Resolution training we provided for staff of Macro Engineering Inc was completed successfully by 11 of the 12 participants. The average score achieved on the post-test was 72.6%.

Summary (main message)

The training was held on October 7 and was set up in response to an August 12, 2011, enquiry from Mr F Stokes, Manager of Human Resources. (The syllabus is attached.) The purpose was to evaluate the feasibility of extending the training to all Macro Engineering technical and administrative staff. Participants were chosen from different departments to achieve a broad evaluation of the program's suitability. The number of participants was limited to 12 to ensure optimum facilitator–participant interaction.

Supporting Details (all the facts)

The first 90 minutes were used partly to define the terms and definitions that would be referenced during the remainder of the day, and partly to draw specific areas of concern from participants. The balance of the day comprised instruction (30% of the time) and role-playing (70%). At first there was some resistance to role-playing from three participants, but this was overcome quickly when they observed that the role-playing was not threatening. One participant had to withdraw after three hours to deal with an emergency in his department.

There were three forms of course evaluation at the end of the day: a test completed by each participant; an evaluation of the course effectiveness, also completed individually; and a group discussion, coordinated and documented by Gillian Miller, of your department, to determine the suitability of extending the course to other Macro Engineering staff. Results of these evaluations were retained by Ms Miller.

We enjoyed developing and facilitating this pilot course for Macro Engineering staff and, if the survey results show there is the need for broader training, we look forward to providing you with a proposal.

Sincerely

Wesley G Hillman
Course Leader
enc

Figure 2-2 A letter report written using the pyramid technique.

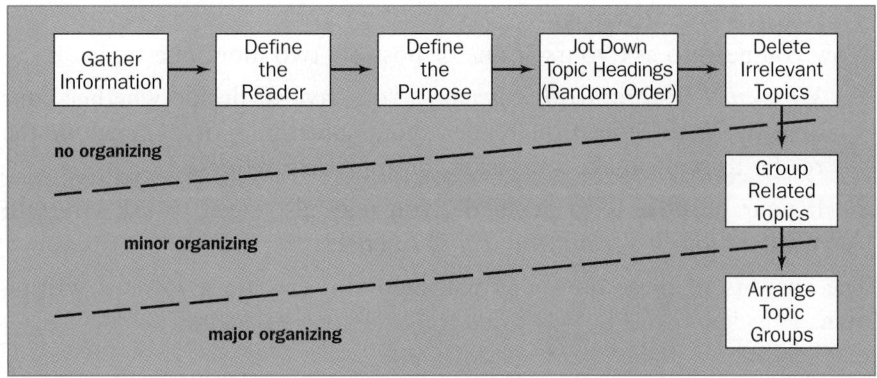

Figure 2-3 The seven planning stages. In practice, these stages can overlap.

2. Define the Reader

Watch

Next, clearly identify your audience. This is probably the most important part of your planning, for if you do not, you will tend to write an unfocused report that misses its mark. Ask yourself six questions:

1. *Who, specifically, is my reader?* If it is someone you know, your task is simplified. But if it is someone you don't know (such as a customer in an out-of-town office), we suggest you try to imagine the type of person who would hold such a position.
2. *Is my reader a technical person?* Knowing this will help you decide whether to use technical terms in your report.
3. *How much does my reader know about the subject I will be describing?* This will give you a starting point, since you won't need to cover information the reader already knows.
4. *What does my reader want to know or expect to be told?* You need to anticipate whether the reader will be receptive or hostile to the information you will be presenting.
5. *Will more than one person read my report?* If so, then repeat questions 2 through 4 for additional readers.
6. *Who is my* ***ultimate*** *reader?* This becomes your *primary* reader: the person who will make a decision or take action after reading your report. Sometimes the ultimate reader is not the person to whom you direct your report, but a secondary reader. For example, you may have to address your report to an executive in another company, yet you know that the person who will use it is an engineer reporting to that executive.

Pay attention to the ultimate reader

Remember that Dan's inability to identify his reader was one of the reasons he had difficulty getting started on his report-writing task.

3. Define the Purpose

Now you need to ask yourself one or possibly two more questions:

Decide: Why am I creating this message?

7. *Why am I writing to this person?* You have to decide whether your objective is to ***inform*** the reader about something, or to ***persuade*** the reader to reply, make a decision, or approve a request.
8. If your purpose is to persuade, you may also need to ask yourself: *What action do I want the reader to take?*

The answers to these questions will help you prepare a *focused* writing plan.

4. Jot Down Topic Headings

Now *brainstorm* your ideas and pieces of information.

Loosen up: Allow yourself to brainstorm

More than likely you have been taught to develop your writing plan in a traditional way, using standard headings such as "Introduction," "Initial Tests," and "Material Resources," and arrange them in a logical, prescribed order. But we suggest you try a different approach:

- We want you to list all the topics you plan to discuss in random order, and make no attempt to arrange the topics or force them into groups. Write only brief headings, not full sentences.
- Now examine each topic to see if it suggests less obvious topics, and write them down (still in random order).
- At this point do not try to decide whether each topic is relevant. If you do, you may stifle your creativity and become too logical and organized.
- Let your list develop randomly, regardless of the importance and eventual position of each topic in your report.

At the end of this session your list should look like Dan's list in Figure 2-4.

5. Delete Irrelevant Topics

Start grouping your topics into compartments

Print a copy to work on and then examine your list of headings. Divide them into two groups:

1. Those that bear directly on the subject.
2. Those that that will be of only marginal interest to your reader.

Delete any topic that is not essential, as Dan has done in Figure 2-5 on page 10.

6. Group Related Topics

Start pulling the pieces together

Now group the remaining headings into "topic areas." Do this by simply coding related topics with the same symbol or letter. In Figure 2-5, letter (A) identifies one group of related topics, letter (B) another group, and so on.

Building OK – needs strengthening
Elevators – too slow, too small
Talk with YoYo – elev mfr (10% discount)
Waiting time too long – 70 sec.
Shaft too small
How enlarge shaft?
    Remove stairs?
Talk with fire inspector
Correspondence – other elev mfrs
Talk with Merrywell – Budget $950 000
Sent out questionnaire
Tenants' preferences –
    Express elev   No stop – 2nd flr
    Executive elev   Faster service
    Prestige elev   No stop – ground flr
    Freight elev
Freight elev – takes up too much space
Shaft only 10.85 × 2.5 m (when modified)
Big freight elev – omit basement
Tenants "OK" small freight elev
    (YoYo "C" – 2.45 m)
YoYo – has office in Montrose
Basement level has loading dock
Service reputation – YoYo?
    – Others?

Figure 2-4 Initial list of topic headings, typed in random order.

Let the initial outline develop naturally, loosely

7. Arrange the Topic Groups

Now you are ready to take your first major organizational step: arrange the groups of information into the most suitable order, first considering which order of presentation will be

- most interesting,
- most logical, and
- simplest to understand.

The result becomes the writing plan for your report (your outline) which should be similar to Dan's, as shown in Figure 2-6 (see page 11).

A final comment about outlining: if you have already developed an outlining method that works well for you, or you are using outlining software successfully, then we suggest you continue as you have been doing. The outlining method suggested here is for people who are seeking a simpler, more creative way to develop outlines than the one they are currently using.

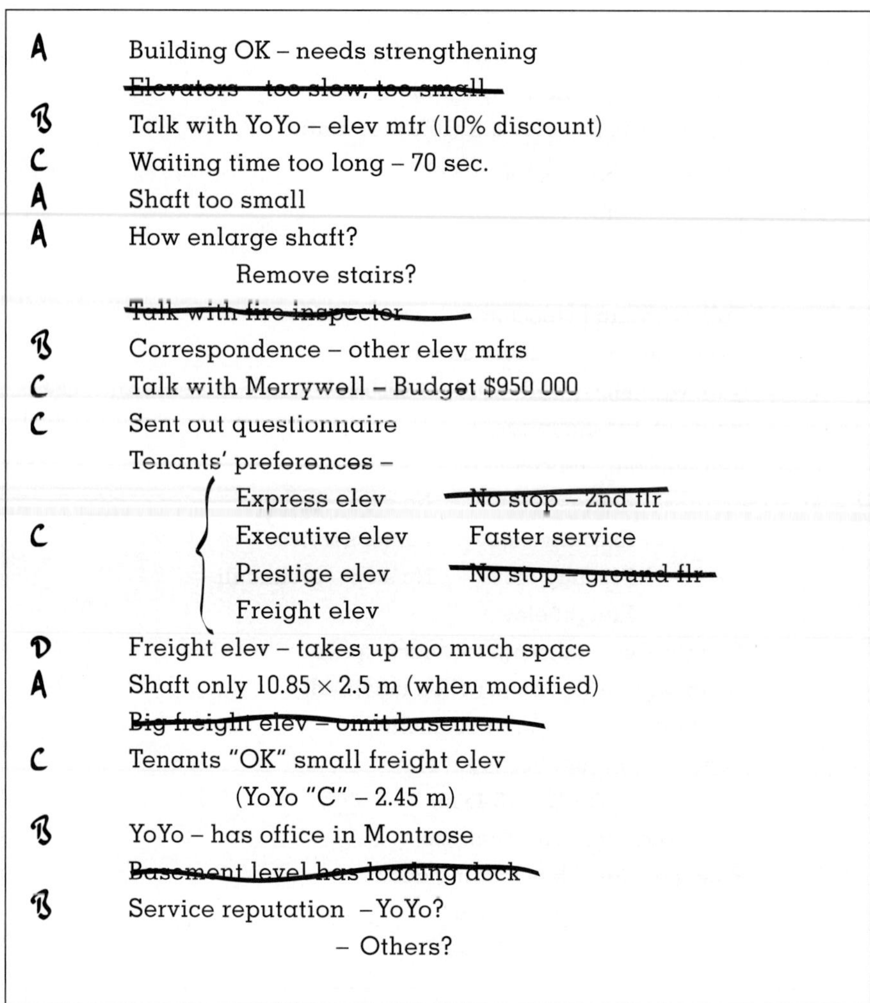

Figure 2-5 The same list of topic headings, but with irrelevant topics deleted and remaining topics coded into subject groups (A–structural implications; B–elevator manufacturers; C–tenants' preferences; D–freight elevator).

Writing the First Draft

Have you ever sat down, ready to write, only to find you don't know where to begin? Or have you experienced the opposite: you have tackled the task enthusiastically only to find, on reading your words, that they don't say what you want to say?

Tips for combatting "writer's block"

To counteract this block, we suggest you start writing at paragraph 2 or somewhere in the middle of your report. Or, if a particular part of your project interests you most, then write that part first. Your interest in and familiarity with the subject will help you write those first few words—and will keep you going once you have started.

Building condition:
    OK – needs strengthening (shaft area)
    Existing elev shaft too small
    Remove adjoining staircase
    Shaft size now 10.85 × 2.5 metres

Tenants' needs:
    Sent out questionnaire
    Identified 5 major requests
    Requests we must meet:
        Cut waiting time: 32 sec (max)
        Handle freight up to 2.3 m long
    Requests we should try to meet:
        Express elev to top 4 floors
        Deluxe models (for prestige)
        Private elev (for executives)

Budget: must be within $950 000

Elevator manufacturers:
        Researched 3
        Only YoYo Co. offers discount
        Only YoYo Co. has Montrose office

Figure 2-6 Topic headings arranged into a writing outline.

Let the final outline evolve from the subject matter...

...rather than force the subject matter into a prescribed pattern

Write without stopping to revise; that comes later

Continuity now becomes essential: don't interrupt the writing process to correct a minor point, write perfect grammar, find exactly the right word, fiddle with page layout, or construct sentences and paragraphs of just the right length. That can be done later, during revision. The important thing is to keep building on your rough draft.

Writing and revising are two entirely separate functions, and they call for different approaches. Writing calls for you to be creative and totally immersed in your subject, so your words tumble out in a constant flow. Revision calls for lucidity and logic, which means you have to reason and query the suitability of your words. Writers who try to correct their work as they write soon become frustrated, because creativity and objectivity are constantly fighting for control.

Taking a Break

Let time "distance" you from your writing

When you have written the final paragraph of your report, resist the temptation to start revising it immediately. By all means pass the draft through a spell-checker, make a back-up copy, and print a copy. But then set them aside and tackle a completely unrelated task.

Reading without a suitable waiting period encourages writers to look at their work through rose-tinted glasses. Sentences you would normally recognize as weak or too wordy appear to be fine. Inaccuracies that under other circumstances you would notice immediately, go unnoticed. Paragraphs that might not be understood by a reader new to the subject will seem clear to you. Your familiarity with your work can blind you to its weaknesses.

The remedy is to wait.

Yet we have a warning: read your report on hard copy, not on screen. Research by many people has shown that you will find up to 30% more points needing attention when you read a printed draft than when you read the same words on screen.

Reading with a Plan

Read all the way through without a pen in your hand

Do your first reading without stopping to make corrections, so you gain an overall impression of the document. The next reading should be slower and more critical, this time with a pen in your hand so you can make changes as you go along.

Checking for Clarity

To check for clarity, search for passages that are vague or ambiguous. If the following paragraph remained uncorrected, it would confuse and annoy a reader:

Confusing!

Muddled Paragraph

When the owners were contacted on April 15, the assistant manager, Mr Pierson, informed the engineer that they were thinking of advertising Lot 36 for sale. He has however reiterated his inability to make a definite decision by requesting his company to confirm their intentions with regard to buying the land within two months, when his boss, Mr Davidson, general manager of the company, will have come back from a business tour in Europe. This will be June 8.

The only facts you can be sure about are that the owners of the land were contacted on April 15 and the general manager will be returning on June 8. The important information about the possible sale of Lot 36 is confusing. The writer was probably trying to say something like this:

Clear!

Revised Paragraph

The engineer spoke to the owners on April 15 to enquire if Lot 36 was for sale. He was informed by Mr Pierson, the assistant manager, that the company was thinking of selling the lot, but that no decision would be made until after June 8, when the

general manager returns from a business tour in Europe.
Mr Pierson suggested that the engineer submit a formal request to purchase the land by that date.

The more complex the topic, the more important it is to write clear paragraphs. Although the paragraph below is quite technical, it would generally be understood even by nontechnical readers:

Technical, but still clear

Clear Paragraph

A sound survey confirmed that the high noise level was caused mainly by the radar equipment blower motors, with a lesser contribution from the air-conditioning equipment. Tests showed that with the radar equipment shut down the ambient noise level at the microphone positions dropped by 10 dB, whereas with the air-conditioning equipment shut down the noise level dropped by 2.5 dB. General clatter and impact noise caused by the movement of furniture and personnel also contributed to the noisy working conditions, but could not be measured other than as sudden sporadic peaks of 2 to 5 dB.

This writer has made sure that

- the topic is clearly stated in the first sentence (the topic sentence),
- the topic is developed adequately by the remaining sentences, and
- no sentence contains information that does not substantiate the topic.

If the paragraphs you write meet these basic requirements, you can feel reasonably sure you have conveyed your message clearly.

Checking for Correct Tone and Style

Explore

How do you know when your writing has the right tone? One of the most difficult aspects of technical writing is establishing a tone that is correct for the reader, suitable for the subject, and comfortable for you, the writer. If you know your subject well and have thoroughly researched your audience, you will most likely set the correct tone.

Finding the Best Writing Level

Keep coming back to your readers: plant yourself in their shoes

If you are writing about a very technical topic, and you know that your reader is an engineer with a thorough understanding of the subject, you can use technical terms and abbreviations. But if you are writing on the same topic for a nontechnical reader who has little knowledge of the subject, you need to write a simplified narrative, explain technical terms, and generally write more informatively.

Adjust the level of writing to suit the reader

For example, when engineer Rita Corrigan wrote the following in a modification report, she knew her readers would be electronics technicians at radar-equipped airfields:

We modified the MTI by installing a K-59 double-decade circuit. This brightened moving targets by 12% and reduced ground clutter by 23%.

But when Rita reported on the same subject to the airport manager, she included more description and eliminated some technical details that might not be meaningful:

> We modified the radar set's Moving Target Indicator by installing a special circuit known as the K-59. This increased the brightness of responses from aircraft and decreased returns from fixed objects on the ground.

Suppose Rita also had to write to the local Chamber of Commerce to describe improvements to the airport's air traffic control system. This time her readers would be entirely nontechnical, so she would have to avoid using *any* technical terms:

> We have modified the airfield radar system to improve its performance, which has helped us to differentiate more clearly between low-flying aircraft and high objects on the ground.

Keeping to the Subject

Technical writing is *functional* writing

You need to convey just the right amount of information for your readers to understand the subject thoroughly. The key is to differentiate between essential "need-to-know" details and inessential "nice-to-know" pieces of information. Use this as your guideline:

- **Need-to-know** details are all the facts and figures, and sometimes your opinions, that the reader must have to make a decision.
- **Nice-to-know** details are all the bits of information that you may find interesting but that the reader does not need to make a decision.

It should be your goal to cover just the right amount of information for your reader to fully understand the subject and the point you are making. Compare the difference between the following descriptions of the same piece of equipment, written for different audiences:

Literary Description	The new cabinet has a rough-textured dove grey finish that reflects the sun's rays in varying hues. Contrary to most instruments of this type, its controls are grouped artistically in one corner, where the deep black of the knobs provides an interesting contrast with the soft grey and white background. A cover plate, hardly noticeable to the layperson's inexperienced eye, conceals a cluster of unsightly adjustment screws that would otherwise mar the overall appearance of the cabinet and would nullify the esthetic appeal of its surprisingly effective design.
Technical Description	The grey cabinet is functional, with the operator's controls grouped at the top right-hand corner where they can be grasped easily with one hand. Subsidiary controls and adjustment screws used by the maintenance crews are grouped at the bottom left-hand corner, beneath a hinged cover plate.

A technical description concentrates on details that are important to the reader (it tells *where* the controls are and *why* they have been so placed), and so maintains an efficient, businesslike tone.

Using Simple Words

To write big words, when smaller words that have the same meaning already exist, will make you sound unnaturally pompous. For example, you would do better to replace "Our design contains ultra sophisticated circuitry" with the much simpler expression, "Our design is very complex." The unnecessary use of big words, when smaller, more recognizable synonyms are available, will cloud your technical writing.

Don't use a 90-cent word when an equally suitable 25-cent word exists

Removing "Fat"

During the editing stage you need to be critical of sentences and paragraphs that are loaded with low-information-content words and expressions that add little or no information. Their removal, or replacement by simpler, more descriptive words, can tighten up a sentence and add to its clarity. Low-information-content words and phrases can be hard to identify because we often see them in other people's writing. Consider this sentence:

> For your information, we have tested your spectrum analyser and are of the opinion that it needs calibration.

The expressions "for your information" and "are of the opinion that" are words of low information content. The first can be deleted, and the second replaced by "consider," so that the sentence now reads:

Weed out unnecessary expressions

> We have tested your spectrum analyser and consider that it needs calibration.

For a list of low-information-content words and wordy expressions, see Tables 11-1 and 11-2 on pages 278 and 279.

Repeating information can also contribute to excessive length:

> We tested the modem to check its compatibility with the server. After completing the modem tests we transmitted messages at low, medium, and high baud rates. The results of the transmission tests showed...

Deleting the repeated words in sentence 2 ("After completing the modem tests") and sentence 3 ("...of the transmission tests...") makes a much tighter paragraph.

> We tested the modem to check its compatibility with the server, and then transmitted messages at low, medium, and high baud rates. The results showed...

Checking for Accuracy

Nothing annoys readers more than discovering they have been given inaccurate information (particularly if they have been using the information before they discover the error). Readers assume you know your facts and have checked that they are correct. If readers discover even a single technical error, they may question your credibility.

Maintain quality control

When transferring technical details from one document to another, you need to check that all the facts, figures, equations, and quantities have been copied correctly. It's too easy to see "421" on the original document and then type it as "412"; often you will not notice the error because "412" *sounds* right.

How many of us have written "there" when we intended to write "their," or "too" when we meant "two"? By all means use your spell-check program, but recognize that it will not identify errors like these.

Revising Your Own Words

When proofreading a letter or report, ask yourself five questions:

1. **Can my readers understand me?**
   Will the person I am writing for be able to read my report all the way through without getting lost?
   What about other readers who might also see my report? Will they understand it?
2. **Is the focus right?**
   Is my report reader-oriented?
   Are the important points clearly visible?
   Have I summarized the main points in an opening statement that the reader will see right away?

Make yourself a checklist, and then *use* it!

3. **Is my information correct?**
   Is it accurate?
   Is it complete?
   Is all of it necessary?
4. **Is my language good?**
   Is it clear, definite, and unambiguous?
   Are there any grammatical, punctuation, or spelling errors?
   Does every paragraph have a topic sentence (preferably at the start of the paragraph)?
   Have I used any big, overblown words where simpler words would do a better job?
   Are there any low-information-content words and phrases?
5. **Have I kept my report as short as possible while still meeting my readers' needs and covering the topic adequately?**

By now your letter or report should be in good shape and you can issue it with confidence. The approach described here does not make report writing a simple task, but it will help you read and revise more efficiently.

ASSIGNMENTS

Exercise 2.1

Describe why the pyramid method of writing will help you become a better presenter of information.

Exercise 2.2

Which do you feel is the better way for you to develop an outline for a report: the organized method or the "random" method? Explain why.

Be comfortable with your writing method

Exercise 2.3

(a) What are the seven stages advocated for planning a report?
(b) Which is the most important stage? Explain why.
(c) Must the stages be followed exactly in the sequence listed?

Exercise 2.4

If several people are likely to read a report, how can you identify which will be your primary reader?

Exercise 2.5

Is it better to write a report without stopping to "clean up" the construction along the way, or to write a page at a time and edit that page before going on to the next? Explain why.

Exercise 2.6

What two factors will help you write more easily, and set the right tone?

Exercise 2.7

From the list of five main questions that you, as a writer, should ask yourself during the revision stage (see the boldface questions on page 16), which do you think is the most important? Explain why.

Chapter 3
Letters and Email

How to Write Business Letters That Get Results
www.bly.com/Pages/documents/File136.doc
Well-known copywriter Robert W Bly provides valuable advice about writing correspondence: "Failure to get to the point, technical jargon, pompous language, misreading the reader—these are the poor stylistic habits that cause others to ignore the letters we send."

In this chapter you will learn how to

- identify and focus your reader's attention on your "main message,"
- arrange the parts of a letter in a logical and coherent sequence,
- differentiate between writing to inform and writing to persuade,
- be clear, concise, and complete in your correspondence,
- adjust the tone of each letter to suit a specific reader, and
- write effective email messages.

A business letter must be focused, well planned, brief, and clear. The pyramid technique will help you achieve this objective.

Using the Pyramid

Figure 3-1 on page 20 shows the basic pyramid. The top part of the pyramid is followed by the supporting details and facts. Your readers will know right away why you are writing to them.

Identifying the Main Message

Readers want to know *right away* what you most need to tell them

When you write pyramid-style, you automatically focus the reader's attention on your main message, which is *what you most want your reader to know and probably do*. It is the first thing your reader sees.

If you begin a letter with background information rather than the main point, your reader will wonder why you are writing. Don McKelvey's letter to Jim Connaught is a typical example of an unfocused message.

Dear Mr Connaught

I refer to our purchase order No. 21438 dated April 26, 2008, for a Vancourt microcopier model 3000, which was installed on May 14. During tests following its installation your technician discovered that some components had been damaged in transit. He ordered replacements and in a letter dated May 20 informed me that they would be shipped to us on May 27 and that he would return here to install them shortly thereafter.

It is now June 10, and I have neither received the parts nor heard from your technician. I would like to know when the replacement parts will be installed and when we can expect to use the microcopier.

Sincerely

Don McKelvey

Jim had to read more than 70 words before he discovered what Don wanted him to do. If Don had written pyramid-style, starting with a main message, Jim would have known immediately why he was reading the email:

Readers don't want to plough through paragraphs of background information before they encounter your main message

Dear Mr Connaught

We are still unable to use the Vancourt 3000 microcopier we purchased from you on April 26, 2008. Please inform me when I can expect it to be in service.

The microcopier was ordered on P.O. 21438 and installed on May 14. During tests, your technician discovered that some components had been damaged in transit. He ordered replacements, then in a letter dated May 20 informed me that they would be shipped to us on May 27, and that he would return here to install them. To date, I have neither received the parts nor heard from your technician.

I am asking you to phone me directly at (204) 493-5555 to tell me when your technician will come to finish the repairs.

Sincerely

Don McKelvey

Getting Started

Finding exactly the right words to put at the top of the pyramid can be difficult. To overcome this block, first key in these six words:

This proven technique will never fail you!

I want to tell you that...

And then finish the sentence with what you *most* want to tell your reader. For example:

Dear Ms Reynaud

I want to tell you that...the environmental data you submitted to us on October 8 will have to be substantiated if it is to be included with the Labrador study.

Then, when your sentence is complete, delete the *I want to tell you that...* expression. What you have left will be a focused opening statement:

Dear Ms Reynaud

The environmental data you submitted to us on October 8 will have to be substantiated if it is to be included with the Labrador study.

Often you can use an opening statement formed just as it stands when you remove the six "hidden" words. However, if the opening statement seems a bit abrupt, you can soften it by inserting a few additional words. For example, in the letter to Ms Reynaud, you might add "I regret that…":

Dear Ms Reynaud

I regret that the environmental data you submitted to us on October 8 will have to be substantiated if it is to be included with the Labrador study.

Figure 3-1 shows that in business letters the main message is more often referred to as the **Summary Statement**. Good news or bad news, you must place the main message right up front.

Practise

Avoiding False Starts

If you do not use the six hidden words to start, you may inadvertently open with an awkward sentence that seems to be going nowhere. For example:

A "dragged out" start

Dear Mr Corvenne

In answer to your enquiry of December 7 concerning erroneous read-outs you are experiencing with your Mark 17 Analyser, and our subsequent telephone conversation of December 18, during which we tried to pinpoint the fault, we have conducted an examination into your problem.

This long, rambling opening does not state the topic early enough. Figure 3-2 contains a list of expressions that can easily cause you to write complicated, unfocused openings. In their place, start with *I want to tell you that…*, which will help you focus your reader's attention on the main message.

The writer's pyramid helps draw attention to the most important information

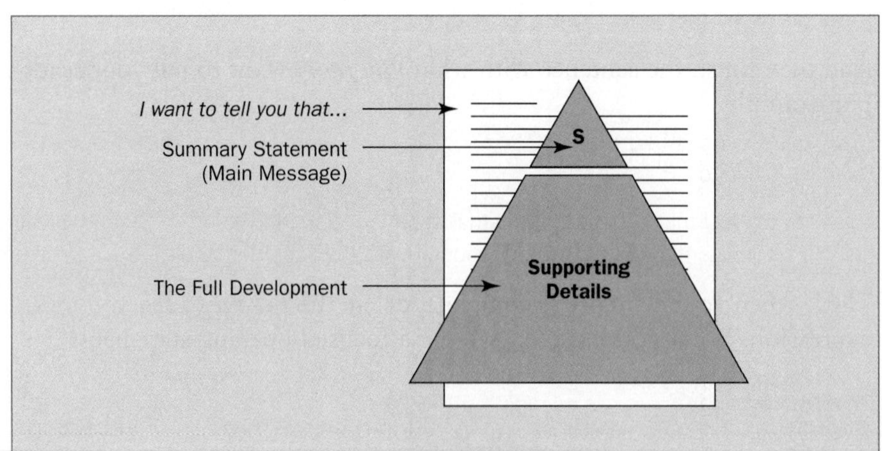

Figure 3-1 Creating a letter's summary statement.

When You Write a Letter...

Never start with a word that ends in "...ing":

Referring...
Replying...

Never start with a phrase that ends with the preposition "to":

With reference to...
In answer to...
Pursuant to...
Due to...

Never start with a redundant expression:

I am writing...
For your information...
This is to inform you...
The purpose of this letter is...
We have received your letter...
Enclosed please find...
Attached herewith...
My name is...

IN OTHER WORDS...

Don't Spin Your Wheels!

Figure 3-2 Avoiding awkward starts.

Try inserting *I want to tell you that...* in front of these openings: it doesn't work!

If the letter referring to the Mark 17 Analyser had started this way, it would have been much more direct:

A direct start

Dear Mr Corvenne

(I want to tell you that...) The problem with your Mark 17 Analyser seems to be in the extrapolator circuit. Following your enquiry of December 7 and your subsequent description of erroneous read-outs, we examined... (etc).

Planning the Letter

Explore

Once you have identified and written the main message, your next step is to select, sort, and arrange the remaining information in a logical order. This information should relate to what you have said in the Summary

Statement and provide evidence of its validity. For example, when Paul Shumeier wrote the following Summary Statement, he realized he would be presenting his reader with costly news:

Dear Mr Larsen

Tests of the environmental monitoring station at Wickens Peak show that 60% of the instruments need to be repaired and recalibrated at a cost of $7265.

He also realized that Mr Larsen would expect the remainder of the letter to tell him why the repairs were necessary, exactly what needed to be done, and how Paul had derived the total cost. To provide this information, Paul had to identify which questions would be in Mr Larsen's mind after he had read the Summary Statement. This meant asking himself six questions, all based on *Who?*, *Where?*, *When?*, *Why?*, *What?*, and *How?*:

Six questions. six answers. The answers provide the facts, forming the body of a letter

Who (was involved)?
Where (did this happen)?
When (did this happen)?
Why (are the repairs necessary)?
What (repairs are needed)?
How (were the costs calculated)?

The answers to these questions become the **Full Development** (or *supporting details*) of the writer's pyramid shown in Figure 3-1. Paul must also determine which facts the reader must have to understand the situation and, if necessary, make a decision. Any inessential, only "nice-to-know," details need to be omitted.

Explore

Opening Up the Pyramid

To help Paul—and you—organize a letter, the lower part of the pyramid is divided into three compartments in Figure 3-3: the **Background**, **Facts**, and **Outcome.**

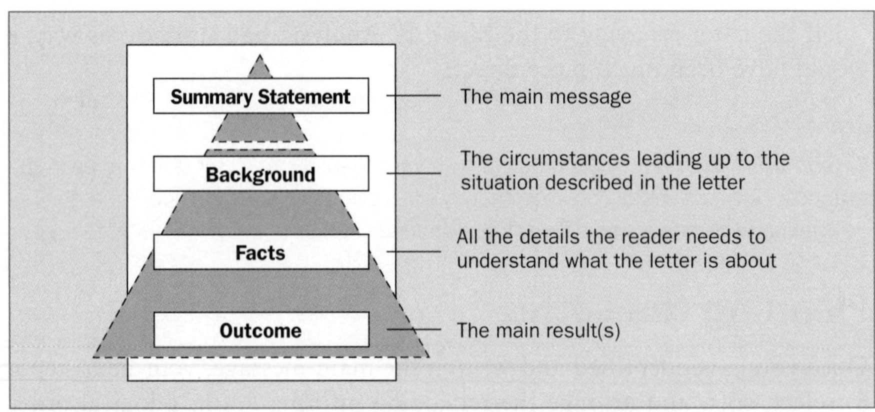

Figure 3-3 Basic writing plan for an informative business letter or email.

The **Background** covers *what* has happened previously, *who* was involved, and, sometimes, *for whom* the work was done and *where* and *when* the event occurred or the facts were gathered. Paul wrote:

A well-developed *background* section leads into direct, uncomplicated details

Our electronics technicians examined the Wickens Peak monitoring station on May 16 and 17, in response to your May 10 request to Patrick Friesen.

The **Facts** expand on the main message by answering the questions *Why? What?* and *How?* Paul wrote,

Most of the damage was caused by a tree northwest of the site that fell onto the station during a storm on April 23 and damaged parts of the roof and north and west walls. Instruments along these walls were impact-damaged and then soaked by rain. Other instruments in the station were affected by moisture.

Use attachments to simplify a letter

Major repairs and recalibration are required for the 16 instruments listed in Attachment 1, which describes the damage and estimated repair cost for each instrument. This work will be done at our Shepperton repair depot for a total cost of $4485. Minor repairs, which can be performed on site, are necessary for the 27 instruments listed in Attachment 2. These on-site repairs will cost $2780.

These two paragraphs provide all the details the reader needs to fully understand the situation. Note how Paul has placed the details in two attachments and summarized only the points of each in the body of his letter (the attachments are not shown here). This avoids cluttering up the middle of his letter with a long list.

The **Outcome** describes the result or any effect the facts have had or will have. It simply sums up the main result:

I have obtained Ms Korton's approval to perform the repairs and a crew was sent in on May 23. They will complete their work by May 31.

Sincerely

Paul Shumeier

But if the reader is expected to take some action, or approve somebody else taking action, then the **Outcome** becomes a *request for action*. If Paul had needed a reply, he could have written this:

Write an *action statement* if you want your reader to act or react

If these repair costs are acceptable, please telephone, fax, or email your approval to me so I can send in our repair crew.

Sincerely

Paul Shumeier

Arranging the body into a **Background–Facts–Outcome/Action** sequence will help form a logical, coherent structure in each of your letters. But before starting, you have to decide whether you are writing to inform or persuade.

Writing to Inform

Letters and emails that purely inform, when no response or action is required, are organized around the basic Summary–Background–Facts–Outcome writing plan shown in Figure 3-3. Kevin Toshak's email to Tina Mactiere, in Figure 3-4, falls into this category.

Another example is a confirmation letter, in which the writer confirms previously made arrangements:

An informative letter *tells* the reader what has been done or what has to be done...

Christine

Summary I am confirming that you will represent both Macro Engineering Inc and H L Winman and Associates at the Materials Handling conference in Montreal on May 15 and 16, 2011, as agreed at

Background the Planning Meeting on March 23. At the conference you will

Facts

- take part in a panel discussion on packaging electronic equipment from 10.00 to 11.15 a.m. on May 15, and
- host a wine-and-cheese reception for delegates from 5:00 to 7:00 p.m. on May 16.

Janet Kominsky is making your travel and hotel reservations, and the catering arrangements for the reception. Anna King will provide brochures from Calgary, and my secretary will make up packages for you to distribute.

Outcome I'll brief you on other details before you leave.

Wayne

...it doesn't expect the reader to respond

Although the basic writing plan has four compartments (see Figure 3-3), you do not have to write exactly four paragraphs. As both Wayne's and Kevin's examples show, you may combine two compartments into a single paragraph, or let one compartment be represented by several paragraphs. It's important, however, to keep the compartments in the correct sequence.

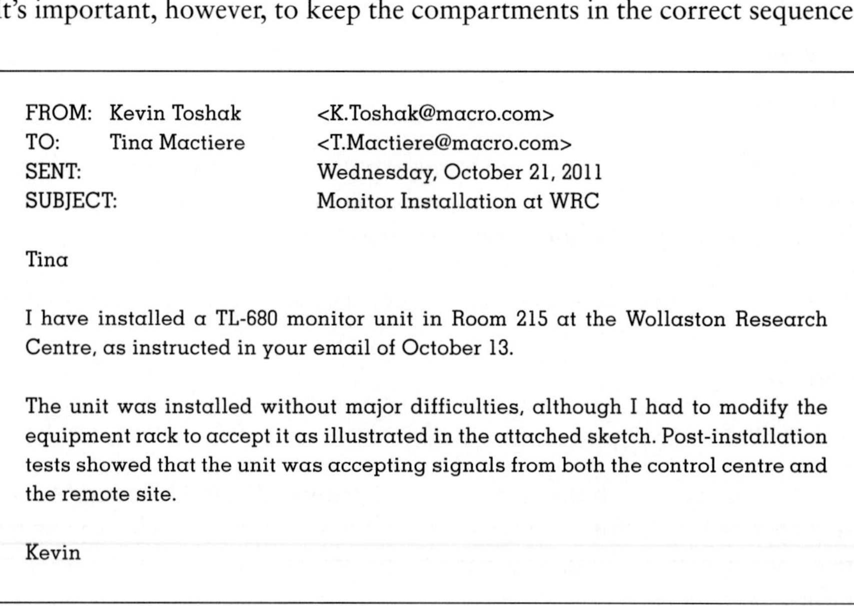

FROM: Kevin Toshak <K.Toshak@macro.com>
TO: Tina Mactiere <T.Mactiere@macro.com>
SENT: Wednesday, October 21, 2011
SUBJECT: Monitor Installation at WRC

Tina

I have installed a TL-680 monitor unit in Room 215 at the Wollaston Research Centre, as instructed in your email of October 13.

The unit was installed without major difficulties, although I had to modify the equipment rack to accept it as illustrated in the attached sketch. Post-installation tests showed that the unit was accepting signals from both the control centre and the remote site.

Kevin

Figure 3-4 An informative email.

Writing to Persuade

In a persuasive letter you expect your reader to respond or take action. Consequently, the writing plan's **Outcome** compartment is renamed **Action**, as shown in Figure 3-5. A request and a complaint are typical examples of persuasive letters or emails, and so is the informal proposal described in Chapter 6.

A persuasive letter *sells* the reader to take some form of action

Making a Request

Many technical people claim that placing the message at the start of a letter is not a problem until they have to ask for something or give the reader bad news. They then tend to lead gently up to the request or negative information.

Explore

Many writers hesitate to open with a request

Bill Kostash has to write to a customer to ask if she will accept a change in the preventive maintenance contracts he has with her company:

Strategies for Writing Persuasive Letters
www.washburn.edu/services/zzcwwctr/persuasive_menu.html
This step-by-step guide covers the purpose of the persuasive letter, prewriting questions for the writer, writing strategies, and revision tips.

June 18, 2011

Dear Ms Nguyen

I am writing with reference to our contract with you for the preventive maintenance services we provide on your RotoMat extruders and shapers. Under the terms of the current contract (No. RE208) dated January 3, 2011, we are required to perform monthly inspection and maintenance "...on the 15th day of each month or, if the 15th falls on a weekend or holiday, on the first working day thereafter."

Bill is off to a bad start. Instead of opening with a summary statement he has inserted all the background details first, so Bea Nguyen does not yet know why he has written to her. He has also opened with one of the expressions listed as an awkward start in Figure 3-2. He continues:

Our problem is that almost all of our clients ask that we perform their maintenance service between the 5th and 25th of each month, to avoid their end-of-month peak

An unfocused, meandering request letter

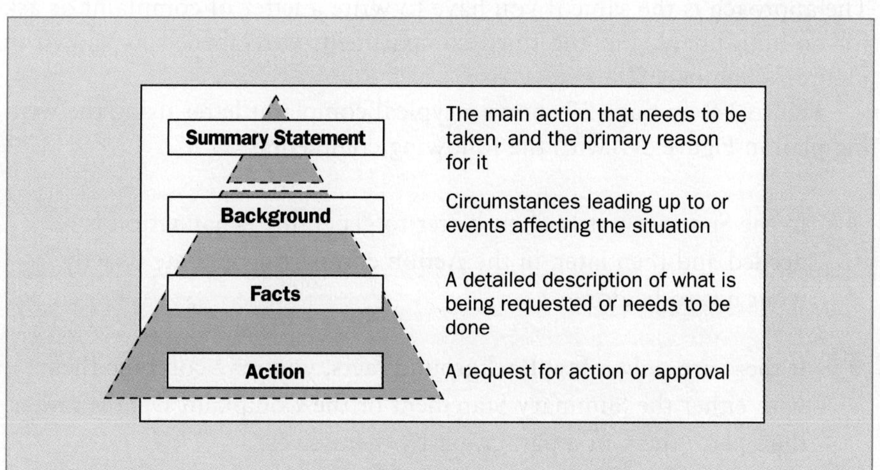

Summary Statement
The main action that needs to be taken, and the primary reason for it
Background
Circumstances leading up to or events affecting the situation
Facts
A detailed description of what is being requested or needs to be done
Action
A request for action or approval

Figure 3-5 Writing plan for a persuasive letter or email.

Except for the last compartment, tell and sell writing plans are similar

accounting periods. This in turn creates difficulties for us, in that our service technicians experience a peak workload for 20 days and then have virtually no work for 10 days.

(Bea Nguyen still does not know why he is writing.)

Consequently, to even out our workload, I am requesting your approval to shift our inspection date from the 15th to the 29th of each month. If you agree to my request, I will send our technician in to service your machine on June 29—a second time this month—rather than create a six-week period between the June and July inspections. Could you let me know by June 25 if this change of date is acceptable?

Sincerely

William J Kostash

Now Bea knows why Bill has written to her—but she had to read a long way to find out.

If Bill had used the writing plan in Figure 3-5 to shape his letter, his request would have been much more effective. The revised letter is shown in Figure 3-6 with the following numbered comments:

1. contains his **Summary Statement** (he states his request and what the effect will be),

Writing with a plan creates a coherent request

2. contains the **Background** (the contract details),
3. contains the **Facts** (it describes the problem), and
4. contains the **Action** statement, in which he mentions *two* actions: what he wants Bea to do (call him) and what he will do (schedule a second visit).

Registering a Complaint

The approach is the same if you have to write a letter of complaint or ask for an adjustment, but the third compartment is relabelled as shown in Figure 3-7 on page 28.

Figure 3-8 on page 29 shows a typical complaint letter using the writing plan in Figure 3-7 with the following comments:

1. In the **Summary**, it is often better to generalize what action is needed and then later, in the Action compartment, state exactly what has to be done.

2. If there are only a few **Background** facts, you may combine them with either the Summary Statement or the Complaint Details rather than place them in a paragraph by themselves.

Mechanical Maintenance Systems Ltd
2120 Cordoba Avenue
London ON N6B 2G6

June 18, 2011

Ms Bea Nguyen
Contracts Administrator
Multiple Industries Limited—Manufacturing Division
18 Commodore Bay
Cambridge ON N1R 5S2

Dear Ms Nguyen

❶ I am requesting your approval to change the date of our monthly preventive maintenance visits to service your RotoMat extruders and shapers to the 29th of each month. This will help spread my technicians' workload more evenly and provide you with better service.

A focused, definite, direct request

❷ Our contract with you is No. RE208 dated January 2, 2011, and it requires that we perform a monthly inspection and maintenance on the 15th day of each month. ❸ Unfortunately, almost all of our clients ask that we perform their maintenance service between the 5th and the 25th. This creates a problem for us in that our service technicians experience a peak workload for 20 days and then have very little work for 10 days.

❹ Could you let me know by June 25 if you can accept the change? Then I will send a technician to your plant on June 29 for a second visit this month, rather than create a six-week space between the June and July inspections.

Sincerely

William J Kostash

William J Kostash
Service Manager

Figure 3-6 A request letter written pyramid-style.

❸ In the **Complaint Details**, describe in chronological order what happened so the reader will understand the reason for your complaint or request for adjustment.

Explore

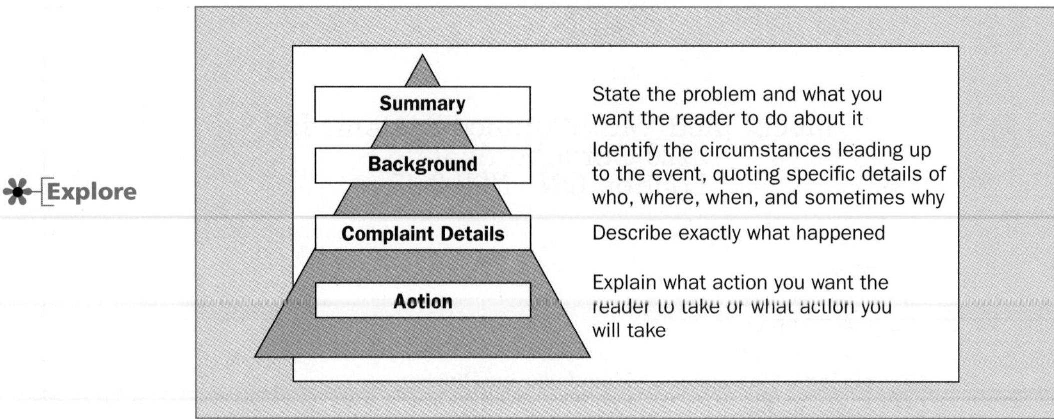

Figure 3-7 Writing plan for a complaint.

4. The **Action Statement** must be strong and confident and specifically identify what action you want the reader to take or, in some cases, what action you will take.

Responding to a Complaint

Figure 3-9 on page 30 shows dual plans for responding to a complaint. If you agree with the complaint and can perform the requested action, you can write a short letter. However, if you disagree with the complaint, you have to provide a detailed description of why you cannot act as requested by the reader.

Creating a Confident Image

Your writing will create an image not only of you but also of your confidence and your competence. Consequently, everything you write must be clear, concise, and complete. We call these the "Three Cs of Effective Communication."

Be Clear

Clarity depends on appearance as well as simplicity of expression

A clear letter conveys information simply and effectively, so that the reader easily understands its message. Writing clearly demands creativity and attention to detail.

Create a Good Visual Impression

The appearance of your letter creates an impression of you and the organization you represent. If a letter is sloppy or contains typos or spelling errors, then your reader will probably imagine you as a careless person working in a disorganized organization. But if a letter is neat and placed

RGI Video Productions
316 St. Mary's Road
Winnipeg MB R2H 1J8

November 10, 2011

Mr K Bruyere
Sales Manager
Professional Image Business Equipment
Suite 100
1675 Mattingly Drive
Winnipeg MB R3J M2C

Dear Mr Bruyere

1 The Nabuchi 700 laptop computer you recently sold me had a defective lithium-ion battery that had to be replaced while I was outside Canada. Consequently I am requesting reimbursement of the expenses I incurred to replace the battery.

2 I bought the computer and a Nabuchi 701PC international power converter from your Willows Mall store on September 4, 2011. (See attached sales invoice No. 14206A.)

The computer worked satisfactorily for the first six weeks, but during that time I had no occasion to use it solely on battery power.

3 On October 25 I left for Europe, first giving the batteries an 18-hour charge as recommended in the operating instructions. While using the computer in flight, after only 35 minutes the low-battery lamp lit up and the screen warned of imminent failure. I recharged the batteries the following day, in Rheims, France, but achieved less than 25 minutes of operating time before the batteries again became fully discharged.

As the Nabuchi line is neither sold nor serviced in France, I had to buy and install a replacement lithium-ion battery (a Mercurio Z7S), which has since worked fine. I have enclosed the defective battery, plus a copy of the sales receipt for the replacement battery I purchased from Lestrange Limitée, Rheims.

4 Please send me a cheque for $244.30, which at the current rate of exchange is the Canadian equivalent of the EUR 123.67 shown on the sales receipt.

Sincerely

Suzanne Dumont, P.Eng
enc 3

Set the scene

...offer the details...

...and end with a firm Action Statement

Figure 3-8 A complaint letter written pyramid-style.

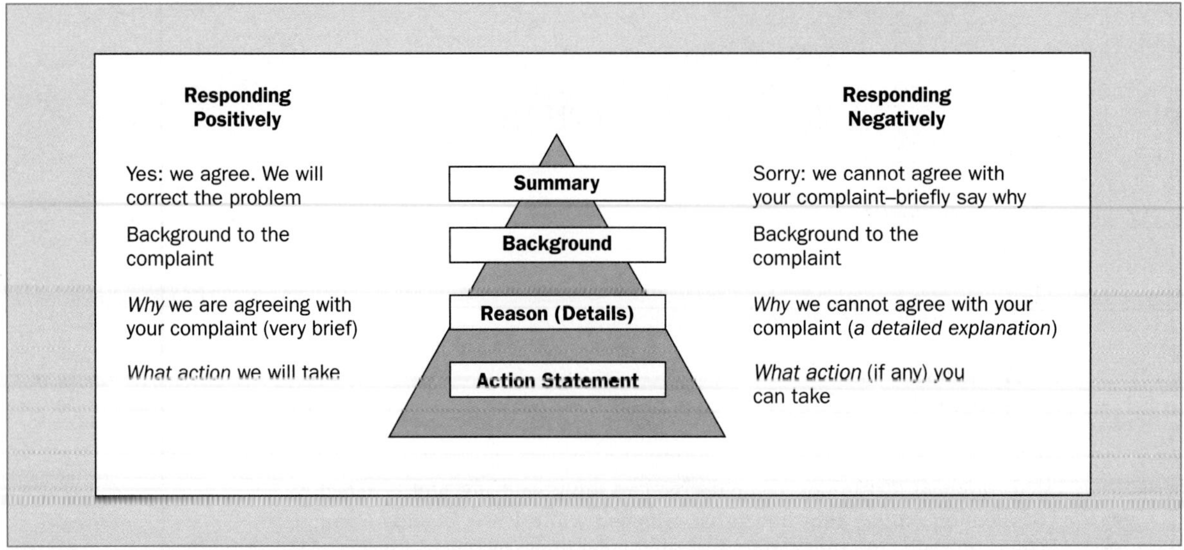

Figure 3-9 Writing plan for responding to a complaint.

Explore

properly on the page, then your reader will imagine a well-organized person working for a quality company.

Develop the Subject Carefully

The key to effective subject development is to present your material logically, progressing gradually from a clear, understood point to one that is more complex. This means developing and consolidating each idea so the reader will fully understand it before proceeding to the next idea. The sections on paragraph unity and coherence in Chapter 11 (see pages 262 to 265) provide examples of clear paragraphs.

Be Concise

For technical business correspondence, concise means writing short letters, short paragraphs, short sentences, and short words.

Explore

The key word here is "short"

Short Letters

A short letter introduces its topic quickly, discusses it in sufficient depth, and then closes with a concluding statement, its length dictated solely by the amount of information that needs to be conveyed. If you have a long (i.e. two- or three-page) letter to write, we suggest you borrow a technique from report writing. Instead of placing all the information in the letter, change the letter into a semiformal report and then summarize the highlights—particularly the purpose and the outcome—into a one-page letter placed at the front of the report (so that the report becomes *an attachment* to the letter, as shown in Figure 3-10).

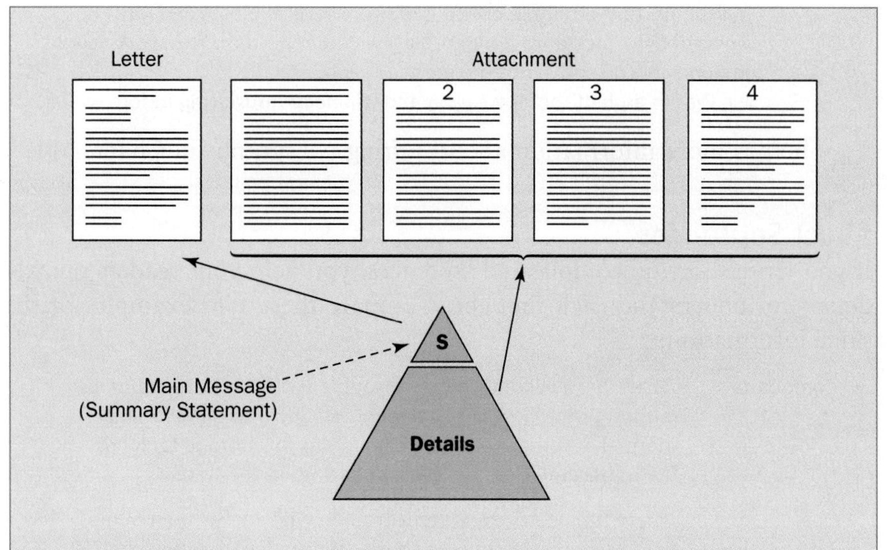

Figure 3-10 A short letter with an attachment is an adaptation of the pyramid method of writing. An example can be seen in Figure 5-4 (page 86).

✱ Explore

If you use this format, refer to the attachment in the letter *and* insert a main conclusion drawn from it:

> During the second week we measured sound levels at various locations in the production area of the plant, at night, during the day, and on weekends. These readings (see attachment) show that a maximum of 55 dB was recorded on weekdays, and 49 dB on weekends. In both cases these peaks were recorded between 5 and 6 p.m.

A short cover letter is like an executive summary (see page 105)

Short Paragraphs

In business and industry, readers want short paragraphs containing easy-to-digest information. To do this let the first sentence of each paragraph introduce one idea, then make sure that all remaining sentences in that paragraph develop the idea adequately and do not introduce any other ideas. This is known as a "topic sentence," which is shown here in italics:

Think of a paragraph as a miniature pyramid

> *We have tested your 15 Vancourt 801 DVD drives and find that 11 require repair and recalibration.* Only minor repairs will be necessary for 6 of these drives, which will be returned to you next week. Of the 5 remaining drives, 3 require major repairs which will take approximately 20 days, and 2 are so badly damaged they will have to be replaced.

If an idea you are developing results in an overly long paragraph, try dividing the information into a short introductory paragraph and a series of subparagraphs:

> My inspection of the monitoring station at Freedom Lake Narrows revealed three areas requiring attention, two immediately and one within three months:
>
> 1. The water stage manometer is recording erratic readouts of water levels. A replacement monitor needs to be flown in immediately so that the existing unit can be returned for service.

Paragraphs that are longer than eight or nine printed lines are too long

2. The tubing to the bubble orifice is worn in several places and must be replaced (30.5 metres of 8 mm tubing will be required). This work should be done concurrently with the monitor replacement.
3. The shack's asphalt roof is wearing and will need resurfacing before winter.

There is more information about writing paragraphs in Chapter 11.

Short Sentences

If you write short, uncomplicated sentences, you help your readers quickly grasp and understand each thought. Compare these two examples of the same information:

Convoluted sentences create the impression that their writer is confused

Complicated	There has been intermittent trouble with the vacuum pumps, although the flow valves and meters seem to be recording normal output, and the 18 cm pipe to the storage tank has twice become clogged, causing backup in the system.
Clear	There has been intermittent trouble with the vacuum pumps, and twice the 18 cm pipe to the storage tank has become clogged and caused backup in the system. The flow valves and meters, however, seem to be recording normal output.

The first example is confusing because it jumps back and forth between what the trouble is and what is working normally. The second example is clear because it uses two sentences to express the two different thoughts.

Short Words

Short words are especially important for readers whose first language is not English.

We have to use many long and complex terms and acronyms in the engineering and scientific fields. To make your information more readable, surround technical terms with simple words. Be aware, too, that in today's global society, many of your readers may read and write English as a foreign language. Long words that are not in the average English speaker's vocabulary may cause confusion and misunderstanding. Chapter 11 has more information about writing for an international audience.

Explore

Be Complete

As a writer, you must evaluate your information and determine what is "need-to-know" and what is "nice-to-know" information. Don't just dump *all* the details you have into your letter or email and expect your reader to sift through it. On the other hand, don't be thin with your details and leave too many unanswered questions with your reader. To find the right balance, ask yourself: "What details does the reader *need* to fully understand the situation or make a decision?"

Be Definite

Know clearly what you want to say *before* you start writing

People who think with their fingers on a keyboard or a pen in their hand sometimes produce indecisive letters that are irritating to read. These writers seem to examine and discard points without really attacking the problem. By the time they have finished a letter, they have decided what they want to say, but it has been at the reader's expense. We call this a "brain dump."

Using the writer's pyramid will help you avoid this trap:

1. Decide exactly what you want to say (i.e. develop your main message).
2. Place the main message right up front (use *I want to tell you that*... to get started).
3. Ask yourself what questions the reader might ask after reading the main message, and then answer those questions in the remaining compartments.

Explore

If you write primarily in the active voice, you will sound even more definite. Active verbs are strong; passive verbs are weak. For example:

Write directly from person to person, and name the "doer"

These passive expressions	*Should be replaced with*
it was our considered opinion	we considered
it is recommended that	I recommend (*or* we recommend)
an investigation was made	we investigated
the outage was caused by a defective transmitter	a defective transmitter caused the outage

For more information on how to use the active voice, see Chapter 11 (page 270).

Adopting a Pleasant Tone

Practise

To achieve the right tone, your correspondence should be businesslike yet friendly. To avoid sounding like a large, bureaucratic organization, try writing the way you speak, in a comfortable, conversational tone, without slang, regional idioms, or humour.

Be careful, though, not to make your correspondence *too* chatty or informal. In business and technical writing you should consistently sound professional because you can never tell when your letter or email may be forwarded to someone else. Here are some suggestions:

Know Your Reader

Reminder: Know who you are writing to!

If you have not identified your reader properly, you may have difficulty setting the correct tone. You need to know your reader's level of technical knowledge and whether he or she is familiar with the topic you are describing. Without this focus you may seem condescending to a knowledgeable reader or overwhelming to a reader who has only limited technical knowledge. If you do not personally know your reader, then identify the *type* of person—or people—who will be reading your words.

Be aware that you may have multiple readers at multiple knowledge levels. If you identify a secondary reader, also identify that person's knowledge level and choose your tone and language appropriately. However, always direct your main message to the primary reader or decision maker.

✓• [Practise

Be Sincere

Care about both your topic and your reader

Sincerity is the gift of making your readers feel that you are personally interested in them and their problems. You convey this by the words you choose and the way you use them. A reader would be unlikely to believe you if you came straight out and said, "I am genuinely interested in your project." The secret is to be so involved and interested that you automatically convey the ring of enthusiasm that would appear in your voice if you were talking about it.

✱-[Explore

Be Human

Too many letters lack humanity. They are written from one company to another, without any indication that there is a human being at the sending end and another at the receiving end.

Do not be afraid to use the personal pronouns, "I," "you," "he," "she," "we," and "they." Let your reader believe you are personally involved by using "I" or "we," and that you know he or she is there by using "you." Contrary to what many of us were told in school, letters may be started in the first person. If you know the reader personally, or you have corresponded with each other before, or if your topic is informal, let a personal touch appear in your letters by using "I" and the reader's first name:

Personalize your letters

Dear Ben

I read your report with interest and agree with all but one of your conclusions.

If you do not know your reader personally and are writing formally as a representative of your company, then use the first person plural and the person's last name:

Dear Mr Wyndam

We read your report with interest and agree with all but one of your conclusions.

✱-[Explore

Avoid Words That Antagonize

In writing, you have only one chance to explain your point. If your reader interprets your words differently from the way you had intended, you don't have the opportunity to rephrase them. You also don't have the benefit of body language, voice inflection, or facial expressions.

Be careful not to use words that imply the reader is wrong, has not tried to understand, or has failed to write clearly to you; otherwise, you may place the reader on the defensive. The following sentences would annoy or antagonize a reader:

You may unknowingly upset or antagonize your reader

> You have failed to include receipts for your expenses.
> *Better:* Please provide receipts to cover your expenses.
>
> We insist that you return the form by November 3.
> *Better:* We request that you return the form by November 3.

Close on a Strong Note

Explore

You may feel you should always end a letter with a polite closing remark, such as: *I look forward to hearing from you at your earliest convenience*, or *Thanking you in advance for your kind cooperation.* In contemporary business correspondence—and particularly in technical correspondence—such closing statements are not only outdated but also weaken your impact on the reader. Today, you should close with a strong, definite statement:

> Please send your comments to me by Friday, January 14.
>
> I will complete the project and deliver my report to you on September 21.

You should resist the temptation to add a polite but uninformative closing remark. Simply sign off with "Regards" or "Sincerely."

Using Business Formats

Explore

There are many opinions about what is the "correct" format for business correspondence. Most popular word-processing packages include templates for writing business letters, memos, faxes, and proposals. Some are good and easy to use; others are less practicable. The example shown in Figure 3-11 on page 36 is the format most frequently used by contemporary technical organizations.

Letter Style

The letter format most commonly used today is the full block (see Figure 3-11). The comments below refer to the circled numbers beside the figure.

Most business letters in North America are written full block style

❶ The trend today is to eliminate all but essential punctuation from the address, salutation, and signature block (more punctuation is used in the US than in Canada). This also is the standard in European countries. The Post Office now requests one space between the city and the province or state, two spaces between the province and the postal code (or the state and the zip code), and no punctuation. The province or state is always printed as two

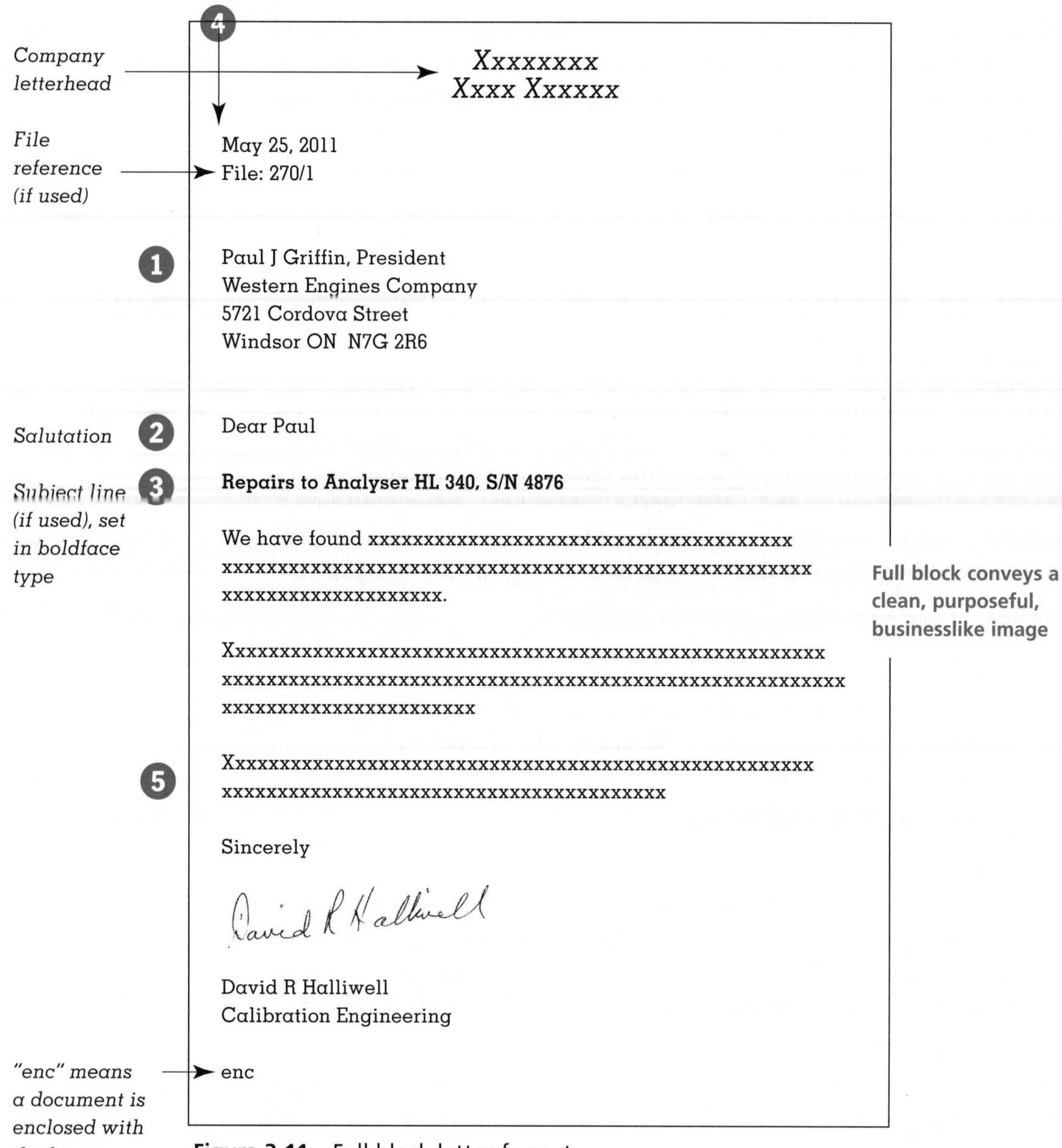

Xxxxxxxx
Xxxx Xxxxxx

May 25, 2011
File: 270/1

Paul J Griffin, President
Western Engines Company
5721 Cordova Street
Windsor ON N7G 2R6

Dear Paul

Repairs to Analyser HL 340, S/N 4876

We have found xxxxxxxxxxxxxxxxxxxxxxxxxxxxxxxxxxxxxx xxxxxxxxxxxxxxxxxxxxxxxxxxxxxxxxxxxxxxxxxxxxxxxxxxxx xxxxxxxxxxxxxxxxxxxxx.

Xxxxxxxxxxxxxxxxxxxxxxxxxxxxxxxxxxxxxxxxxxxxxxxxxxxxx xxxxxxxxxxxxxxxxxxxxxxxxxxxxxxxxxxxxxxxxxxxxxxxxxxxxxxx xxxxxxxxxxxxxxxxxxxxxx

Xxxxxxxxxxxxxxxxxxxxxxxxxxxxxxxxxxxxxxxxxxxxxxxxxxxx xxxxxxxxxxxxxxxxxxxxxxxxxxxxxxxxxxxxxxx

Sincerely

David R Halliwell

David R Halliwell
Calibration Engineering

enc

Figure 3-11 Full block letter format.

capital letters (e.g. "SK" for Saskatchewan), and the postal code or zip code is on the same line as the province or state.

2 Today's trend toward informality encourages writers to use first names in the salutation: "Dear Jack," especially after the first exchange between two people.

Never address a letter to "Dear Sir or Madam" or "To Whom It May Concern." This indicates that you do not know who the recipient is and that the content can't possibly be personalized.

If you don't know a name, address the letter to *the position the person holds:* "Dear Customer Service Manager" or "Dear Human Resources Manager." This allows a mail clerk to direct your letter to the right department.

If you are replying to a letter or email signed by A J Winters, and you don't know if A J is male or female, then write "Dear A J Winters."

3 The subject line should be informative (not just "Production Plan" or "Spectrum Analyser"); it may be preceded by Subject:, Ref:, or Re:. It should be set in boldface and not underlined.

Never refer to the subject line in the body of the letter, as in "The defect is with the above-mentioned product model." This forces your reader to stop and search for information. Repeat the information so your message is clear and easy to read.

4 In the full block format every line starts at the left margin.

5 Close confidently. Most of us were taught in school that we should end a letter with a polite "complimentary close." In business, however, it is better to close with a definite statement that says exactly what action you want the reader to take (for a *persuasive* message), or what action you have taken (for an *informative* message).

These five closing statements are overused, weak, and indefinite:

- Your cooperation in remedying this problem will be greatly appreciated.
- I look forward to hearing from you at your earliest convenience.
- Thanking you in advance for your attention to this matter.
- If we do not hear from you within 21 days we shall consider handing the matter over to another authority.
- Thank you.

These three closing statements create a much stronger impression (of both the writer and what will or has to be done):

- I will call you on May 30 to set up a meeting date.
- Please call me by February 15 and inform me what action you intend to take.
- I need your approval by June 8 if I am to obtain a discount airfare and a reduced conference registration fee.

And then add just one more word: *Regards*, or *Sincerely*.

Writing Electronic Mail

Although it is a fast way to communicate...

The criterion for writing email remains the same as for all other forms of written communication: keep the message brief but clear.

When Mike Toller in Vancouver, BC, opened up a shipment of parts from Carlson Distributors, he found the order was incomplete and contained some items he had not ordered. He made a note of the deficiencies, sat at his keyboard, and typed in this message:

> To: Carlson Distributors, Montreal
>
> Your inv 216875 Oct 19, our P.O. W1634. Short-shipped
> 10 toolsets MKV, 4 801 sockets plus 2 doz mod 280A lathe bits unordered.
> Advise.
>
> M Toller
> Crown Manufacturing, Vancouver

...email needs just as much care and attention as business letters

A Beginner's Guide to Effective Email
www.webfoot.com/advice/email.top.php
This useful guide includes an introduction to email and a discussion about why it differs from ordinary correspondence.

In Montreal, Chantal Goulet puzzled over the message, and then typed this brief reply:

> To: M Toller, Crown Manufacturing, Vancouver
> From: C Goulet, Carlson Distributors, Montreal
>
> The message you sent regarding our invoice 216875 and your P.O. W1634 was difficult to understand. Please explain your concerns.
>
> Chantal Goulet

Mike was surprised: he thought his message was crystal clear. So he again sat at his keyboard and wrote:

What Mike Toller should have written the first time

> To: Chantal Goulet, Carlson Distributors, Montreal
> From: Mike Toller, Crown Manufacturing, Vancouver
>
> My message was quite clear: You short-shipped us 10 toolsets type MKV and 4 No. 801 sockets. You also shipped 2 dozen model 280A lathe bits we did not order. Please ship the missing items and advise how you want the bits returned.
>
> Mike Toller

Chantal replied in six words:

> Mike:
>
> Thanks. I will investigate the situation.
>
> Chantal

If Mike had been more explicit when he wrote his original message, both he and Chantal would have saved time.

Explore

Keep the message short but keep it clear

Email Etiquette

Email is one of the most used and abused tools we have in business, and if we are not careful it can cause problems. In today's global society you will find that you communicate with people by email that you may never meet in person or talk with on the phone. Often the only impression they have of you and your competence is based on the email messages you send. For this reason, we encourage you always to be professional when using email. If you are careless and sloppy, you create an image that you and your organization are careless and sloppy.

Watch

Text messaging from electronic devices such as a BlackBerry or a cellphone is different. You will develop a cryptic language that you know your audience will understand. Yet you should avoid using these shortcuts in your email messages.

There are no established guidelines for writing email, but we can give you some suggestions that will help you be an efficient email communicator. Remember, email does *not* give you a licence to

- write snippets of disconnected information,
- write incorrectly constructed sentences,
- forget about using proper punctuation,
- ignore misspelled words, or
- be abrupt or impolite.

And never use your work email as a forum for telling long stories, anecdotes, or jokes.

Writing Effective Email
http://jerz.setonhill.edu/writing/e-text/e-mail.htm
This document offers 10 tips to help you write effective professional emails. If you want to be taken seriously by professionals, you should know email etiquette.

Adopt the Right Tone

Too often, we hear people say: "It's only email. It's supposed to be casual and quick." That's true. With email you can be less formal in tone but you still need to be professional. You still need to address the recipient and you still need to "sign" your name to the message. Even if you have a signature file attached to every message you should still type your name at the end. Doing so will help humanize this very technical mode of communication.

Inside your small work groups you will develop a more casual style for quick messages. But be aware that email is not a conversation, and short, one-line comments are ineffective if one person leaves the desk area and returns to a string of one-line messages. It takes too long to catch up to the flow of the interactions.

Explore

Use a Specific Subject Line

Because people receive so much email, the subject line must grab their attention. Consider it a mini Summary Statement. It is the first indication to the reader of what your message is about.

Mark Hoylston, an engineering technician responsible for installing a new network at a client site, was writing to his supervisor to explain that there was going to be a delay in the project because they had discovered some additional work that needed to be done. His subject line on the email was simply

Subject: Progress

Because it seemed routine, his supervisor decided to read it later, when she had more time. If Mark had written

Subject: Delay in Project Progress

the word "Delay" would have caught her attention.

Make sure you always use a subject line. Some people forget, or do not realize the importance of using one. In many cases, if message recipients do not recognize your name, they will delete your message without reading it. A specific subject line encourages them to open and read the message. Be aware that many spell checkers don't check the subject line, so you have to check it yourself.

If you have been replying to a message several times, make sure the subject line still reflects the content of the message. You may have to initiate a new message or change the subject line in the reply message.

Write "Pyramid-Style"

You can use the pyramid method for writing email messages, just as you do for ordinary letters:

1. Start with what you most want your reader to know and, if appropriate, what action you want the reader to take.
2. Follow with any background information the reader may need to understand your message, and provide details about any point that may need further explanation.

Check that each message contains *only* the information your reader will need to respond or to act—and no more. Separate the essential "need-to-know" information from the less important "nice-to-know" details. Your email will still have four compartments (Summary, Background, Details, Outcome/Action) but they may be much shorter than they are in a letter format. For example, the Summary and Background may be in the same sentence.

Make sure you have a strong action statement if your email message is a sell message. Too often we hear people complain that their audience is not responding to a message. Usually, it's because they have written a tell message and the audience does not understand that a reply is expected.

If you need to include extensive details, use the email message as the summary and then put the details in a file attachment so your message uses the structure shown in Figure 3-10 on page 31. Your readers will appreciate this since they are not forced to read the entire document; they read the highlights in the email message and turn to the details in the attachment when they need them.

Proofread with Care

Proofread email *very* carefully: the informality of the medium and the speed with which you can write messages tends to invite carelessness. If a message is long or particularly important, we recommend you print a copy of the message and proofread your words on paper. You will catch more of the errors this way than reading them on the screen.

Reread what you have typed, even for a one-sentence reply

Be Cautious

If you are annoyed or irritated by a message you receive, *wait* before replying. Let your irritation cool down. Email is ideal for transmitting facts; it's the wrong medium for sending emotional messages.

Too many people sit at their desk and send email messages when the telephone or a personal visit with someone would be more appropriate. With email, you cannot hear a person's voice and may misinterpret the tone as being aggressive when it wasn't meant to be. A quick phone call can resolve an issue, where a series of emails might escalate it.

Remember that email is not a good medium for conveying confidential information, and it is particularly not a medium for making uncomplimentary remarks about other people. Never put anything in an email that you would feel uncomfortable saying to someone in person. Because email messages can too easily be forwarded or copied to other readers, you have no control over who else may see what you have written. Be just as professional as you are when writing regular letters.

Similarly, be just as sensitive when deciding to copy a message to another person. Be sure that the original sender would want the message distributed to a wider audience.

Tailor the Content

If you are writing to multiple readers, consider sending *two* messages rather than a single all-embracing message. Write

1. a short summary, which you send to readers who are interested only in the main event and the result, and

2. a detailed message, which you send to readers who need all the details.

It may take more of your time to write two messages, but your varying audiences will be more satisfied and will more easily use your information.

Avoid Overloading the System

Limit how many readers receive your message

Be selective when replying to a multiple-reader message. Don't simply click the "Reply All" button rather than taking the time to address your reply only to those readers who need it. If everyone uses the "Reply All" command, the system—and everyone else's inbox—will quickly become overloaded.

Help Identify the Originator

Make sure the originator's name is evident

Write your name at the foot of every message you create, even though your name appears in the "To–From" list at the top or in a signature file. If a recipient decides to forward the message, this will ensure your name is associated with your text. You can still insert a signature file at the bottom of the message which contains information on other ways to contact you. Typically you can include your name, company name, title, phone number, fax number, and website.

When replying to a message, particularly if your reply is going to multiple addressees, copy a line or two from the original message to help put your reply in context. Identify the excerpt by placing a ">" sign before each line, like this:

```
Dan Reitsma wrote on May 12,

> The Society's constitution was last updated in
> 2002 and needs amending.

I agree, but first we need to check how much editing was done by Karen
Ellsberg before she retired in 2006.
```

This reduces the frustration your reader will experience from having to scroll down through all the attached messages (often called the "history" or the "trail").

Avoid Complex Formatting

Use only simple formatting if you are sending messages outside your email system. Bold, italic, and colour formatting may not convert correctly in transmission or may not be available in the recipient's system. If the message is printed on a black and white printer or photocopied, the colour will be lost.

Write short paragraphs and follow each paragraph with a blank line. Avoid creating columns and indenting subparagraphs, because what you see on screen may not be what your readers see. For example, your screen may look like this:

Some email systems do not transmit tables and charts well

Facilities are located as follows:

Facility	Location	Distance
Master Control	Calgary, AB	28.6 km south of transmitter
Remote Site 1	Regina, SK	Downtown
Remote Site 2	Thunder Bay, ON	2.5 km north of university

But your readers may see something like this:

Facilities are located as follows:

Facility Location Distance

Master Control Calgary, AB 28.6 km south of transmitter

Remote Site 1 Regina, SK Downtown

Remote Site 2 Thunder Bay, ON 2.5 km north of university

If you need to format columns, consider sending the information as an attachment to an email message.

Indicate Emphasis with Care

Use upper- and lower-case letters, just as this sentence has been written (not like the one below).

Don't Shout!

> PARAGRAPHS COMPOSED OF ALL CAPITAL LETTERS ARE HARD TO READ. YOU CANNOT EASILY IDENTIFY WHICH ARE THE KEY WORDS.

This may be perceived as if you are shouting or that you are angry. The opposite is also true:

> paragraphs composed of all lower-case letters are hard to read. you cannot easily identify which are the key words.

Don't use decorative backgrounds. They can make your information hard to read and can take up large amounts of computer resources.

In your professional emails there is no room for short, cryptic notations such as *<lol>*, *btw*, *thx*, *B4*, and *cuz*. These conventions should only be used between friends in quick text-messaging communications. If your audience does not understand the notation, you risk misinterpretation or lack of communication.

ASSIGNMENTS

Project 3.1: Write Better Opening Sentences

Each of the examples below is an ineffective opening statement to a letter, memo, or email. Revise each to make it more effective. (Remember that each opening sentence is preceded by *Dear....* Don't be afraid to use the first person, singular or plural, and the active voice. For information about the active voice, see page 270.)

1. Accompanying this memorandum is the revised forecast for the second online documentation phase.
2. The purpose of this letter is to inform you that, on or about March 16, you are scheduled to be transferred to the Waverley Heights office for a period of approximately nine weeks to three months.
3. Enclosed please find three copies of the Lakeland Agreement for your review and to sign and return.
4. Further to my memorandum of January 30, the briefing on interconnection services has currently been rescheduled. It will now take place at 9 a.m. on Friday, March 13, in conference room B.
5. For your information, it is our company's policy to provide a diversified workforce that encourages employment of employees with different ethnic backgrounds and without reference to their colour or sexual orientation.
6. I am writing to inform you that shortly there will be a vacancy on the company's workplace safety committee and am encouraging you to apply.
7. In answer to your enquiry of October 13, it is possible that approval for your Class C operator's licence, if it is to be granted, will occur before the end of the current financial year.
8. With reference to your January 27 letter, we have conducted an extensive examination into your records. The examination shows that, if you will complete the enclosed Form 2710, you will be entitled to a refund.
9. This is to confirm that, in our discussion of April 13, it was mutually agreed that next year you will represent us on the Provincial Environmental Resources Committee.
10. In the matter of changes to product pricing, it is our recommendation that the conditions pertaining to last year's pricing should be extended to the end of the current year.

Project 3.2: A Parking Problem

You work for DigiWeb Inc, where you supervise a team of three technicians who are assembling and testing digital modules for the Department of Defence under government contract DD11-728617. It's a long-term contract that the company values very much. The three technicians are permanent employees and work well with you as a four-technician team that is always on schedule.

Yet, there is a problem with one of the technicians: Lloyd Pomeranski. Rather than rent a company parking space, he parks on the street. This poses a problem because every two hours he has to dash out to a parking meter and insert $2. Each time it takes him between 9 and 12 minutes (you have timed him), during which the other technicians cover for him. An additional irritant is that he is forever going around to other employees, trying to change paper money into $1 or $2 coins. You have tried to persuade him to take a company parking spot, but he just laughs: "Why should I? I save $15 a month this way!"

You asked the area manager what action you should take. "Give Lloyd a warning," he replies. "Tell him his job is in jeopardy if he doesn't smarten up." He tells you to write it on paper and have Lloyd sign that he has read it. "That will make it a legal document," he says. "And be sure to send me a copy."

Information on parking costs:

- A company parking space would cost Lloyd $45 a month.
- Lloyd's street parking, at $1 per hour, amounts to $28 to $30 a month.

Write the notice as a letter. At the bottom, insert this: "I have read and understand the contents." Insert a blank line for Lloyd's signature below the above sentence.

Project 3.3: Resolve a Billing Error

Today you receive a credit card statement covering last month's purchases. There are five entries for expenses you incurred during a business trip between the 10th and 14th of last month:

Item	*Date*	*Vendor/Location*	*Control No.*	*$*
1	10th	St James Motel, Burntwood Lake	0134652	73.90
2	11th	Burntwood Auto Service	0148167	49.44
3	12th	Wapiti Autos Ltd	0203916	624.80
4	14th	Wapiti Inn	0205771	256.50
5	14th	Burntwood Auto Service	0211606	53.63

Items 2, 3, and 5 are for purchasing gasoline for the panel van. But item 3 puzzles you because the van simply would not hold that amount of gas! You do not have your credit card receipts (you sent them to the Accounting Department at head office, with your expense account), but you do have a travel log in which you recorded your gasoline purchases:

11th — 51.02 L @ $0.969/L
12th — 63.17 L @ $0.989/L
14th — 52.63 L @ $1.019/L

You consider that a data entry error must have occurred on the 12th, which put the decimal point in the wrong place in the transaction.

Write to the manager of customer accounts at WindsorCard (Suite 2160 – 24 Hudson Avenue, Toronto, Ontario, M4J 2B5). Explain the situation and ask for credit.

Project 3.4: Commendation for Overtime Work

Assume that today is the 20th of the current month. Two days ago you returned from a field assignment at Weekaskasing Lake, where for three weeks you have been a supervisor working with two technicians installing and testing a remote sensing system for measuring radiation levels. The project had to be completed by the 17th of the month, when it could be linked with similar installations at other sites. But one of the technicians injured his hand on the 8th of the month and had to be sent to a hospital in nearby Wedgley City for minor surgery. This cost four days. Time was tight, and with you and only one technician remaining on site it seemed impossible to meet the completion deadline; in fact, you estimated you would finish two days behind schedule.

You did meet the deadline, however, because the uninjured technician suggested she could work an overtime schedule of four hours per day until the lost time was regained. Now you decide to write a report to Janet Handley, your manager, commending the technician for her willingness to give up her time and keep the project on schedule. Here is some information to draw on:

- You were working on Project Radiation Seventy.
- The technician who worked overtime was Laura Lussier.
- The injured technician was Frederic Morganski.
- Laura worked four 12-hour days to meet the deadline.
- You worked beside her, for the same hours.

Project 3.5: An Improperly Printed Textbook

As a consultant with a firm of consulting engineers you frequently write technical proposals in response to Requests for Proposals (RFPs) issued by major power utilities, different levels of government, and even other consulting firms. This is how your company gets much of its work. Recently, however, you have realized that your firm lacks experience in writing its own RFPs when it needs to hire a contractor to perform certain work, or a consultant with expertise in a field with which your company is not familiar. So you search for information at Locus Books, where you buy an ideal book titled *The RFP Writer's Resource Book*.

Imagine your dismay, however, when one week later you discover that pages 85 through 140 are missing: instead, you have a repeat of pages 29 through 84. But when you return to Locus Books to get a replacement copy, you read a notice on the door saying the property has been requisitioned by the city and is closed permanently. You also find that no other bookseller in your city has that book.

Your only recourse now is to write to the publisher. Use the following information:

- The publisher is Diamond E Books, 28 Northolt Road, Slough, Berks, UK, AJP 2AO.
- The book bears ISBN 3-877614-3-5.
- It was written by Marianne Jackson and Peter Foulds.
- It was published in 2011.
- Locus Books was at 213 Grantley Mall in your city.
- The price you paid was $89.95 + tax (GST and PST, where applicable).

Decide whether you want a refund or a replacement book to be shipped to you. Also decide how you will return the book (costly to ship) or find some other way to show the error.

Project 3.6: Acknowledge a College Award

Assume that you are in the last year of the course you are enrolled in, and that three weeks ago the head of the department told you that you have been chosen as this year's winner of the Inter-Provincial Engineering Association (IPEA) award for "proficiency in technical studies."

Yesterday you attended an awards luncheon with other award winners and representatives of the firms and organizations donating the awards. You sat next to Calvin Reiman, vice-president of the local chapter of the IPEA, who presented the award to you.

Today, write to the president of the local chapter of the IPEA to thank the association for the award. Use these details:

- The president is Marjorie Wiens.
- IPEA's address is 710 Durham Avenue of your city.
- The award is $500 plus a wall plaque inscribed with your name.

Project 3.7: Complain About an Entertainment Centre

Assume that you have recently returned from a holiday in Waverley, some 1200 km from your home, where you visited friends Martin and Joan Lamont. You were impressed with the features of Martin's Nabuchi 98 Portable Entertainment Centre, which looked just like a laptop computer. Joan had given it to Martin at Christmas and bought it from Craven's Discount Centre at 1837 Kelly Street in Waverley. You decided to buy one for yourself.

But you were disappointed to discover that Craven's had sold out, no more were on order, and they were the sole distributor in Waverley. However, Harry Craven, the shop owner, said he still had the demonstrator, which he could sell you for 5% off the regular discount price. You suggested a 15% discount would be more appropriate, but Mr Craven insisted on 5%. He added that he would have his technician give it a good checkover, if you would leave it with him for 48 hours. Two days later you picked it up, paid $759.95, and received Craven's invoice stamped "Paid in Full." The following day you flew home without opening the carton.

When you plugged in the Nabuchi 98, you found the CD player worked but the DVD player would not work. You also discovered there is no local service centre for Nabuchi products, so you took the unit to Modern TV and Radio at 28A Waltham Avenue. When you picked it up three days later, shop manager Jim Williams said it's working fine now and handed you a tiny circuit board.

"There's your problem," he said. "Craven's in Waverley must have replaced the original board, because the name Craven is stamped on this one." He said that whoever inserted the board did not align it properly and bent the pins by forcing it into its socket.

You paid $103.50 for the repair job on Modern's invoice No. 1796. Now write to Harry Craven, tell him what happened, and ask for a refund of $... (you decide how much).

Project 3.8: Request Approval to Attend a Course

Assume that this is the second Monday of the current month, and that for the past four weeks you have been on a field assignment in Quebec City, where you have been conducting an extensive hardware and software installation program for Inter-Provincial Telephones (IPT). You have been assisted by two technicians (Ted McCourt and Carolyn Freedman), and you are now three days ahead of schedule. The task is to be completed by the 12th of next month.

Today, you receive an email with a link to a website from McGill University in Montreal advertising a one-week course. Details are:

Course title:	Managing in a Technological Environment
Course dates:	Monday 5th to Friday 9th of next month
Type of course:	Maximum immersion: 9 a.m. to 5 p.m. daily, plus 7 to 10 p.m. Wednesday evening; approximately 20 hours of home assignments
Cost:	$695; includes materials, books, and lunches, plus a guest speaker from industry at each lunch
Registration:	No later than noon on the 23rd of this month; telephone registrations accepted
No. of participants:	16

You are impressed by the technical standard of the course described on the website and want to attend. (Because of previous assignments, you missed a similar extension department evening course offered by your local university last winter. Your company sponsored four engineers to attend that course, for which the fee was $365 each.)

Write an email to your department head, Dennis Copthorne, in which you

- describe the course (convince him it is a good one),
- ask if you can attend,
- ask if the company will pay the tuition fee plus travel and lodging,
- ask to be spared from the IPT task for one week (be convincing), and
- ask for a quick reply (because time is short).

Assume that Dennis can give you technical and financial approval to attend. Also assume that you have a rental car for the IPT project, which you can use to drive to Montreal, but that $34.95 per day will have to be added to your expenses to reimburse IPT for using the car. The hotel cost in Montreal will be $129 per night.

Project 3.9: Delayed Drilling Equipment

You are a supervisor with Multiple Development Industries Inc (MDI)—a company with offices in both the US and Canada. You are currently supervising the installation of environmental equipment at a new office building in your city. It will be a highly ecological building that will depend on drawing much of its heat and cooling from a geothermal source. This will mean excavating to 152 metres below the ground surface with a special Megablitz 400 drill specially designed for this type of work. Your local office of MDI has arranged to borrow a drill from the MDI Chicago office.

The drill was to be shipped to you on a 6:15 a.m. flight from Chicago on Tuesday of last week. It was then to be used round-the-clock for 48 hours and returned on Friday morning's flight back to Chicago. A special five-person drilling crew from the Chicago office was flown in on the same flight, and a contract for hiring eight local drilling workers was arranged with Morton Installers in your city.

When you met the flight on Tuesday, you discovered that the drilling crew had arrived but the drill had not. A check with the airline revealed (after a four-hour delay) that the drill had been put on the wrong aircraft and was now en route to Seoul, South Korea. It would be Friday before the drill would reach you. Because you now had 13 expensive drillers hanging around with nothing to do, you researched local companies and found you could rent a Megablitz drill immediately for 48 hours at a cost of $23 000. A contract was signed and the work was done on schedule.

Today, you write to the airline to request payment of the difference between the original rental cost and the local rental cost. Write the letter, drawing on the following details:

- The Chicago office of MDI is at 317 Waltham Drive East.

- The Chicago office was renting the drill to your office at a preferred company rate of $2000 a day (for four days). The rental agreement was number MDI 3546.
- The MDI drillers were brought in from Chicago at a cost of $600 each per day. The local drillers cost $200 a day.
- The airline was Remick Airlines, Remick Building, Suite 400, 2320 Albatross Avenue, New York 10012.
- The airline shipping document was number RA213865.
- The rental cost for the Chicago Megablitz was to be based on four days (Tuesday through Friday) = $8000.
- The local company renting a drill to you was Bottner Drilling Equipment Ltd, 1540 James Avenue of your city. The rental invoice from them was BDE3567.

You are writing a letter rather than an email because you want a paper document for legal purposes.

Chapter 4
Short Reports

In this chapter you will learn how to plan and write

- reports that describe an event or incident,
- field trip and field inspection reports,
- project progress (status) and completion reports, and
- industrial and academic laboratory reports.

Short Informal Reports http://jerz.setonhill.edu/writing/technical/reports/index.html This document introduces two basic principles of technical communication—meeting the reader's needs and using the inverted pyramid.

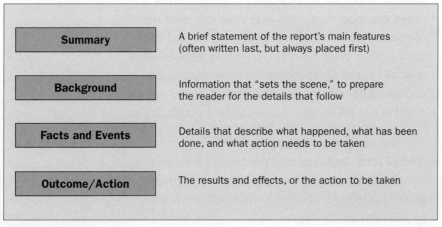

The word *report* may make you think of a long formal document, yet many reports are written as letters or short, informal emails.

There are many types of short reports, all based on the writing plan outlined in Figure 4-1. Each report contains

1. a brief statement describing what the reader most needs to know,
2. a short introduction to the problem or situation,
3. a detailed description of the data, situation, or problem, and what has been done or could be done about it, and
4. a conclusion that sums up the results and possibly recommends what should be done next.

Keep in mind that these pyramids are just templates. You can use them as is or you can adapt them to your particular situation.

The writing plan for basic reports is similar to the plan for business letters

Summary	A brief statement of the report's main features (often written last, but always placed first)
Background	Information that "sets the scene," to prepare the reader for the details that follow
Facts and Events	Details that describe what happened, what has been done, and what action needs to be taken
Outcome/Action	The results and effects, or the action to be taken

Figure 4-1 Basic writing plan for short reports. The plan is modified slightly to suit each situation.

Writing Style

The reports described in this chapter are written in a direct, informative style. Their writers are usually describing events that have already occurred, so they write mostly in the past tense, which helps them to be consistent. They switch to the present tense only if they need to describe something that is currently active, and to the future tense when they have to state what will happen or what has to be done. All three tenses are used in the report shown in Figure 4-2.

	To: Don Gibbon <dgibbon@winman.ab.ca> From: Dan Skinner <dskinner@winman.ab.ca> Date: 24 January 2011 Subject: Carpet problem at KMON-TV	
	Don	
	The indoor/outdoor carpet we installed in KMON-TV has corrected the noise problem but is "pilling" badly. I will examine the carpet with the manufacturer's representative to find the cause.	***Summary***
Past tense	The carpet was installed in the satellite studio control room during the night of January 6–7, to reduce the ambient noise level by 3.6 dB.	***Background***
Mainly past tense *Present tense*	At the station manager's request, I returned to the control room today and checked the carpet's condition. After only about two weeks it has tight little balls of carpet material adhering to its surface. I called the manufacturer's rep, who said that the condition is not unusual and does not mean that the carpet is wearing quickly. He suggested that it may be caused by improper cleaning techniques and probably can be easily corrected. However, our client is not pleased with the carpet's appearance.	***Facts***
Future tense	The manufacturer's rep and I will return to the control room between midnight and 2 a.m. on January 31 to study the carpet-cleaning techniques used by maintenance staff. I will email our findings to you later in the day.	***Outcome***
	Dan	

Figure 4-2 A short report sent via email.

Incident Report

If you are involved in or witness an accident in which equipment is damaged or people are injured, you need to write a report describing what you saw. An incident report informs management and others of what happened and is often kept in a permanent file.

An incident report describes an event

Bob Walton, an engineering technologist with H L Winman and Associates of Edmonton, is on a field trip to Dryden, Ontario. He has been involved in a traffic accident near Brandon, Manitoba, his co-traveller has been injured, and some of his equipment has been damaged. He wants his manager, Jim Perchanski, to send out replacement equipment by air express.

Bob's report is in Figure 4-3 on page 54. The numbered paragraphs below comment on how he wrote it.

1. This is Bob's **Summary**: it takes a main piece of information from each compartment that follows.
2. This is the **Background**: by clearly describing the situation (*who? where? why? when?*) Bob helps Jim more easily understand what happened:
   - Bob establishes where they were, how they happened to be there, in what direction they were travelling, and who else was involved.
   - He itemizes vehicles, licence numbers, and drivers' names in an easy-to-read list.
   - He mentions that he is enclosing a sketch (see Figure 4-4 on page 55).

A well-developed background results in a clear description of the event

3. Because his background information is complete, Bob's **Facts** can be concise. He simply provides a chronological description of what happened from the time the Toyota started to slide until all vehicles stopped moving.
4. In the **Outcome** Bob describes the results of the accident (injuries, damage), what he has done since (rented a van, requested replacement equipment), and the equipment he needs. He closes on a strong note: by describing what is being done about the project.

A test for an effective report: Does the reader have to ask questions? (No questions = a good report)

Bob knows his role is to be an informative but objective (unbiased) reporter. No doubt he has an opinion of who is at fault, but to state it would have injected subjectivity into his report.

When Jim Perchanski reads his email in the morning, he will know immediately what has happened and what action he needs to take.

To: Jim Perchanski <jperchanski@winman.ab.ca>
From: Bob Walton <bwalton@winman.ab.ca>
Date: 17 September 2010
Subject: Traffic Accident at Brandon MB

1 Pete Crandall and I were involved in a multiple-vehicle accident on September 16, which has resulted in injuries to Pete, damage to our van and some of our equipment, and a two-day delay in our inspection of the Sledgers Control project. I need you to ship me replacement equipment, listed below, on Tuesday September 21.

2 The accident occurred at 17:15 on Highway 1, about 5 km west of Brandon, Manitoba. We were travelling east in company panel van TLA 711, on our way to site RJ-17 at Dryden, Ontario. Pete was driving and we were approaching the intersection with Highway 459.

Details of other people involved, and their vehicles, belong in the Background, not the Event

Other vehicles involved in the accident were

- Toyota Tercel, licence 881 FLM, driven by D Varlick
- Ford truck, licence TRB 851, driven by F Zabetts
- Pontiac Grand Am, licence 372 HEK, driven by K Schmitt.

Positions of the vehicles and our panel van immediately before the accident are shown on the attached sketch.

3 As the Toyota attempted a right turn into Highway 459 it skidded into the Ford truck, which was standing at the intersection waiting to enter Highway 1. The impact caused the Toyota's rear end to swing into our lane, where Pete could not prevent our van from colliding with it. This in turn caused the van to slide broadside into the westbound lane, where the Pontiac approaching from the opposite direction collided with its left side.

4 Pete was taken to Brandon General Hospital with a broken left knee and a suspected concussion; he will be there for several days. The panel van was extensively damaged and was towed to Art's Autobody, 1330 Kirby Street, Brandon. The following equipment was damaged or shaken out of calibration:

- 1 Spectrum analyser, HK7741
- 1 Calibrator, Vancourt model 23R
- 24 glass vials, 200 mm long, 50 mm dia

Please ship replacements to Winnipeg on an evening flight on September 20, for me to pick up at the airport on September 21, and email the airline and flight number to me.

I am staying at Hunter's Motel in Brandon (tel 204 453 6671). I have rented a replacement van from Budget and have informed the duty engineer at site RJ-17 that our inspection of the Sledgers Control project will start on Wednesday September 22, two days later than planned.

Bob

Figure 4-3 An email incident report.

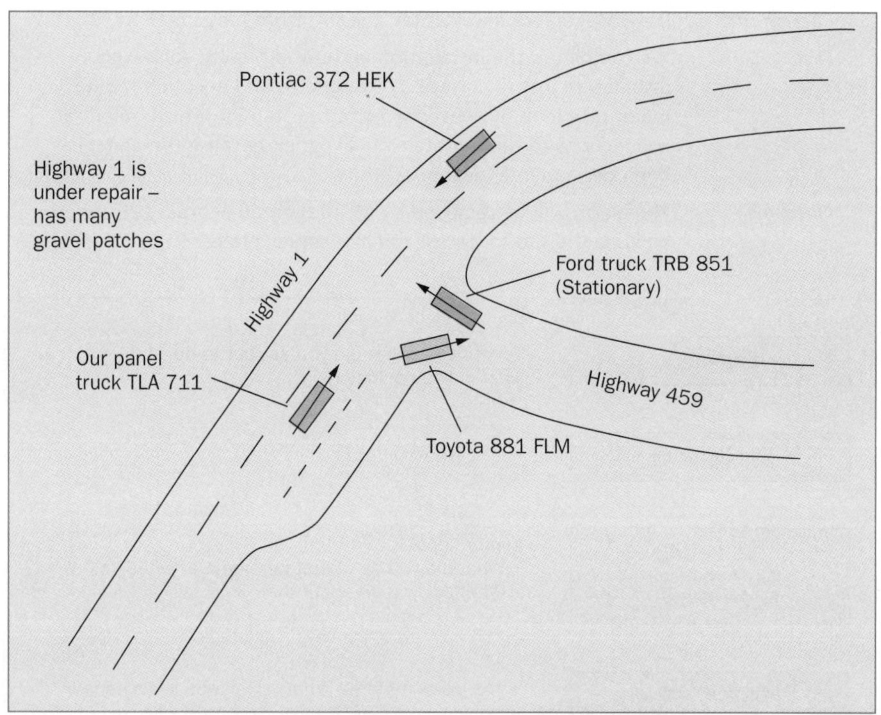

A sketch helps a reader visualize the situation

Figure 4-4 Attachment to Bob Walton's report (Figure 4-3).

Trip Report

When you work offsite, you need to report your activities

Whenever you are involved in an activity or perform work outside your normal working conditions (visiting a client, attending a conference, working remotely) you will be expected to keep your supervisor, manager, or co-workers informed of your activities by writing a short Trip Report.

You may have been absent only a few hours, inspecting cracks in a local water reservoir; you may have spent several days installing and testing a prototype pump at a power station in a nearby community; or you may have been away for two months, overhauling communications equipment at a remote site.

The simplest way to write a trip report is to answer the questions shown in Figure 4-5 on page 56, which, like all examples in this chapter, is a modification of the basic writing plan in Figure 4-1.

Short Trip Reports

Short trip reports do not need headings. A brief narrative following the Summary–Background–Facts–Outcome pattern carries the story:

Summary I have installed a prototype automatic alarm at No. 7 remote monitoring station for a one-month evaluation by the Roper Corporation.

Background	Dave Makepiece and I visited the site from January 15 to 17.
Facts	We completed the installation without difficulty, following installation instruction W27 throughout, and encountered no major problems. However, we omitted step 33, which called for connections to the remote control panel, because the panel has been permanently disconnected.
Outcome	The alarm will be removed by M Tutanne on February 26, when he visits the site to discuss summer survey plans

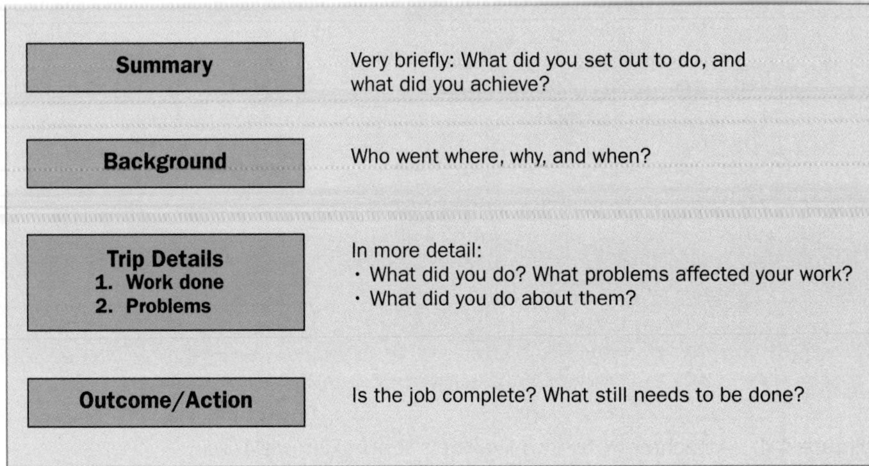

Figure 4-5 Writing plan for a trip report.

In practice, the very short Background can probably be combined with either the Summary or the Facts to form a single paragraph.

Longer Trip Reports

Longer trip reports require headings to help readers identify each compartment. Typical headings might be

- **Summary**
- **Assignment Details** (Background)
- **Work Accomplished** (Facts)
- **Problems Encountered** (Facts)
- **Suggested Follow-up** or **Follow-up Action Required** (Outcome/Action)

You also need to include any problems you experienced

Anna King's instructions to H L Winman and Associates' engineers (see Figure 4-6 on pages 57–58) tell them how to organize their longer trip reports, describe the information that would normally follow each heading, and include excerpts and sample paragraphs.

Except for the Action or Follow-up section, trip reports should be written in the past tense.

H L WINMAN AND ASSOCIATES

475 Lethbridge Trail, Calgary AB T3M 5G1

Guidelines for Writing Longer Trip Reports

Use a standard format for longer trip reports. These instructions suggest how you can organize your information under five main headings: ***Summary; Assignment Details; Work Accomplished; Problems Encountered;*** **and** ***Follow-up Action.*** You may omit the headings from very short reports.

This may look like a model report...

Summary

Make your summary a short opening statement that says what was and was not accomplished. Draw attention to any significant outcomes.

Assignment Details

State the purpose of the trip and include any other information the reader may want to know. If the information is lengthy, use subheadings such as

- Purpose of Trip
- Background
- Project No./Authority
- Personnel Involved
- Person(s) Contacted
- Date(s) of Field Trip

Work Accomplished

Describe the work you did. Present it in chronological order unless more than one project is involved, in which case describe each project separately. Keep it short: don't describe at great length routine work that ran smoothly. Whenever possible, refer to your work instruction or specification, and attach a copy to your report:

...but really it's an instruction

> The manual control was disconnected as described in steps 6 to 13 of modification instruction MI1403, enclosed as Attachment 1.

Go into more detail only if you encountered difficulty, or if work was necessary beyond that anticipated by the job specification:

> At the request of the site maintenance staff, we installed a manual control in the power house as a temporary replacement for a defective GG20 control. I left the parts removed from the panel with Frank Mason, the senior power house engineer, together with instructions for returning the panel to its original configuration.

If parts of the assignment could not be completed, identify them and explain why the work was not done:

1

Figure 4-6 Anna King's instructions for writing longer trip reports also show how a trip report should look.

We had to omit Test No. 46 because the RamSort equipment had been removed.

Problems Encountered

Describe problems in detail. Knowledge of problems you encountered and how you overcame them will be valuable to the engineering or operating departments, which may be able to prevent similar problems elsewhere.

Avoid statements that do not tell the reader what the problem was or how it was overcome. For example,

> Considerable time was spent in trying to mount the miniature control panel. Only by fabricating extra parts were we able to complete step 17.

If this information is to be used by the engineering or operating department, it must be more specific:

> We had difficulty mounting the miniature control panel according to the instructions in step 17. Because the main frame had additional equipment mounted on it, which prevented us from using most of the parts supplied, we had to fabricate a small sheetmetal extension to the main frame and mount it with the miniature panel, as shown in Attachment 2.

Follow-up Action

Tie up any loose ends here. If any work has not been completed, draw attention to it even though you may already have mentioned it under "Work Accomplished." Identify what needs to be done, if possible indicate how and when it should be done, and say whose responsibility it now becomes:

> The manual control mounted as a temporary replacement in the power house is to be removed when a new GG20 control panel is received onsite. This will be done by Frank Mason, with whom I left instructions for doing the work.

The Outcome looks forward, says who will do what

In some cases you may direct follow-up action to someone else in your own or another department:

> The manual control is to be removed from the power house by R Walton, who will visit the site on May 12.

If your report is very long, insert subheadings and use a paragraph numbering system to increase its readability.

Anna King
January 20, 2011

2

Progress or Status Reports

Explore

Progress Reports www.io.com/~hcexres/textbook/progrep.html This document deals with the purpose, timing, format, and organization of progress reports.

Progress or status reports keep managers aware of how well their project groups are doing. Even for a short-term project, management wants to hear how the project is progressing, especially if problems are affecting its schedule. Because delays can have a marked effect on costs, management needs to know about them early.

A progress report may be a one-paragraph statement describing the progress of a simple design task, or it may be a multipage document covering many facets of a large construction project. Regardless of its size, the report should answer the four main questions the reader is likely to ask:

Anticipate your reader's curiosity

1. Will your project be completed on schedule?
2. What progress have you made?
3. Have you had any problems?
4. What are your plans/expectations?

To answer these questions, a progress report can use the standard Summary–Background–Facts–Outcome arrangement (see also Figure 4.7):

Summary	A brief overview of the project schedule, progress made, and plans
Background	The situation at the start of the report period
Facts	Progress made and problems encountered
Outcome	Plans/expectations for the next period and impact on the schedule

In a progress report the writing plan has extended beyond the four basic compartments

Summary	A brief description of the overall situation
Background	Project history (in a short progress report, often combined with the Summary)
Progress	The work that has been done, the problems that have been encountered, and the effect these problems have had on progress
Situation Now	What is currently being done
Future Plans	What will be done to complete the project, and when it will be done

Figure 4-7 Writing plan for a progress report.

Figure 4-8 shows how survey crew chief Pat Fraser used these compartments to write an effective progress report (the numbers below are keyed to parts of the report):

1. The **Summary** tells civil engineering coordinator Karen Woodford how closely the survey project is adhering to schedule, and predicts future progress. This is the information she wants to read first.

2. The **Background** section reminds Karen of the situation at the end of the previous reporting period and predicts what Pat expected to accomplish during this period. Background should always be stated briefly.

The past–present–future structure is equally apparent here

3. The **Facts** (or Discussion) section is broken into two parts:

   - Work done during the period (3a)
   - Problems affecting the project (3b)

   Pat Fraser opens each paragraph of this compartment with a topic sentence (a summary statement) that states the main point of the paragraph in general terms:

   - Dry, clear weather…enabled us to progress faster than anticipated.
   - The electrical fault in the EDM equipment…recurred on May 23.
   - I have had difficulty hiring reliable people to clear brush along the route.

   Pat then describes in more detail what happened, using *facts* (exact dates and position numbers, for example) to support each topic sentence. To prevent the report from becoming too long, Pat attaches the survey results and simply refers to them in the narrative. (Because of their length, they have not been printed with Figure 4-8.)

4. In the **Outcome** paragraph Pat tells Karen what the crew expects to accomplish during the forthcoming period, and even suggests when they might eventually get back on schedule. This final statement clearly supports the opening paragraph, and brings the report to a logical close.

5. Pat types his name at the end of the document to indicate this is the end of the report. This is especially important in a multipage report.

To: Karen Woodford <kwoodford@winman.ab.ca>
From: Pat Fraser <pfraser@winman.ab.ca>
Date: 31 May 2011
Subject: Allardyce Survey Report No. 4

The Allardyce Route survey has progressed well during the May 16 to 31 period. The survey crew has regained two days, and now is only four days behind schedule. We expect to be back on schedule by June 30.

The Summary sums up key features from the report's body

Project plan AR-51 shows we should have surveyed positions 30 to 34 during this period. But, as stated in my May 15 report, we were six days behind schedule at the end of the previous period, having surveyed only as far as position 28. Consequently, we expected to survey only to position 32 by May 31.

Dry, clear weather from May 18 to 23 enabled us to progress faster than anticipated. We reached position 31 on May 23, carried out a terrain analysis for the Catherine Lake diversion scheme on May 24 and 25, resumed surveying on May 26, and reached position 32 at 09:00 on May 29, two days earlier than expected. At end of work on May 31, we were just 300 metres short of position 33. Survey results are attached.

Two problems affected the project during this period:

1. The electrical fault in the EDM equipment, which delayed us several times early in the project, recurred on May 23. I had the unit repaired at Fort Wilson on May 24 and 25, while we conducted the terrain analysis, and it has since worked satisfactorily.
2. I have had difficulty hiring reliable local people to clear brush along the route. Most remain with us for only a few days and then quit, and I then have had to hire replacements. This problem will continue until mid-June, when the college students we interviewed in March will join the crew.

The Facts/Discussion describe any problems that affect the work

We plan to advance to position 37 by June 15, which should place us only two days behind schedule. If we can maintain the same pace, I plan to make up the remaining two days during the June 16 to 30 period.

Pat Fraser

Figure 4-8 A progress report.

Here are some other factors to consider:

Heading titles parallel the pyramid's parts but are more specific

- If a progress report is long, use headings such as these to help readers *see* your organization:

  Adherence to Schedule (This is your summary.)
  Progress During Period (These are your facts; state the background information at the front of the Progress section.)

  Problems Encountered

  Projection for Next Period (This is the outcome.)

- For lengthy progress or problems sections, start with a summarizing statement describing general progress, then write several subparagraphs, each giving details of a particular aspect of the project. For example,

  4. Interior construction work has progressed rapidly but exterior work has been hampered by heavy rain.

     4.1 In the east wing, we constructed all partitions, laid 80% of the floor tiles, and installed 20% of the light fixtures.

     4.2 In the west wing, we laid all remaining floor tiles, installed all light fixtures, bolted down 16 of the 24 benches and connected them to the water supply and drains.

     4.3 Outside, we started landscaping on September 16, but had to abandon the work from September 18 to 23 when heavy rains turned the soil into mud. By the end of the month we had completed only the outer areas of the parking lot.

- Be as brief as possible when describing routine work. Quote specifics rather than generalizations, and place lengthy details in an attachment. If, for example, you are reporting an extensive analysis, in your progress section you might write,

  We analysed 142 samples, 88 (62%) of which met specifications. Results of our analyses are shown in Attachment 1.

  Attachment 1 would contain several pages of data (numbers, quantities, measurements), which, if included as part of the report narrative, would slow the reader down.

- Describe problems, difficulties, and unusual circumstances in depth. State clearly what the problem was, how it affected your project, what measures you took to overcome it, and whether the remedial measures were successful. For example,

Each problem description is shaped like a miniature pyramid

Topic sentence Juvenile vandalism has proven to be a petty but time-consuming problem. On September 3, youths scaled the fence around the materials compound and stole about $300 worth of

Facts	building supplies. On September 16 they started up a front end loader, drove it into the excavation, then got it stuck in the mud and burned out the clutch. To prevent a recurrence, from
Outcome	September 18 I have doubled the night watch and have had the site policed by a patrol dog. There have been no further attempts at vandalism.

- Forewarn management of any situation that, although it may not yet affect your project, could become a future problem:

> 7.1 Unless the strike at Vulcan Steel Works ends shortly, it will soon disrupt our construction program. Our present supply of reinforcing barmats will last until mid-October, after which we must find an alternative source of supply. I have researched other suppliers, but have been warned by union representatives that any attempt to obtain steel elsewhere may result in a walkout at other plants.

Predict potential developments...

Include any warnings at the end of the Facts (problems) section, immediately before the Outcome.

- If your report is lengthy, number your paragraphs and subparagraphs. This can help you refer to a specific part of a previous report:

> The possibility of a shortage of steel mentioned in para 7.1 of my September report was averted when the strike at Vulcan Steel Works ended on October 6.

...and then in a subsequent report describe the outcome

- Maintain continuity between reports. If you introduce a problem that has not been resolved in one report, you should refer to it again in your next report, even though no change may have occurred or it was solved only a day later (see the example in the previous paragraph). You must never simply drop a problem because it no longer applies.
- If management expects you to include project-cost information in your progress report, insert it in three places:

  In the **Summary** comment briefly on how closely you are adhering to projected costs.
  In the **Progress** section give more details of costs, and particularly cost implications of problems.
  In the **Outcome** section indicate future cost trends.

  Costs are usually closely linked with your adherence to schedule: the more you drop behind schedule, the more likely you are to have to report a cost overrun.

Personal Progress Reports

A personal progress report serves two purposes:

1. It keeps management informed of your monthly activities.
2. It can be used to document your progress and help you manage your time.

Most organizations use performance evaluations as a tool to help employees grow in their careers and focus on professional development. Managers or supervisors are asked to review all of their employees' performance and recognize their strengths and areas for improvement. As an employee, it is important that you be involved in this process. It is usually done once a year.

To help your manager understand what activities you have been involved in and what you have achieved, we recommend you write monthly personal progress reports. Set aside thirty minutes on the last day of each month to summarize the main things you did during the month. Follow the writing plan in Figure 4-9.

There is enough detail in Susan's report (see Figure 4-10) for her manager to understand the situation but not too much detail to slow down the reading. If the manager needs more detail, he will ask Susan. However, Susan's report must have enough detail so both she and her manager can understand the points up to a year later when they are working on her annual performance evaluation.

Susan decided to use paragraphs rather than a list so there is more continuity when reading. Notice how each section is a mini-pyramid with a topic sentence as the summary.

If you are writing regular project status reports you don't need to repeat specifics from earlier reports. Remember, this is about what *you* did, not about the project. Susan decided to break her report into topic areas so the manager understands her activities in each area. You can decide how you want to organize your report, but be consistent from month to month.

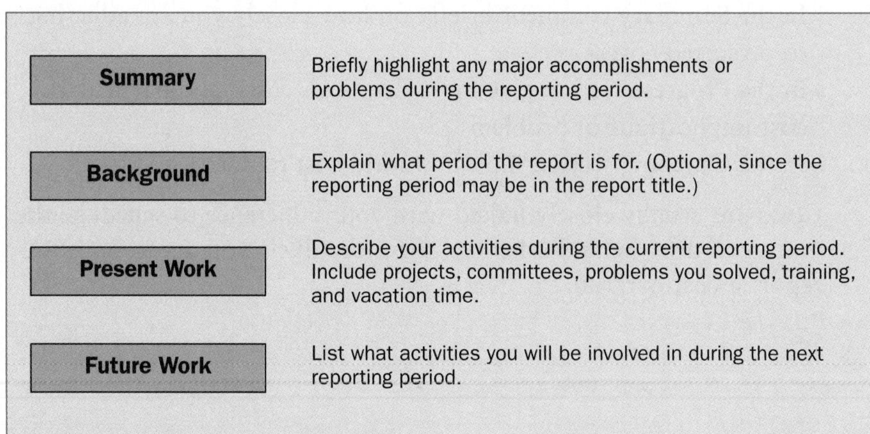

Figure 4-9 Writing plan for a personal progress report.

600 Deepdale Drive, Toronto ON M5W 4R9

Monthly Progress Report for Susan Jenkins
November 1–30, 2010

Summary
Most of my efforts this month were spent diagnosing problems with the CI software. The problems we discovered will need further investigation next month. Although I spent time helping the new intern set up his workstation, it will pay off next month when he is able to help the JCL team begin focus groups for the MarTel project. I was also heavily involved in professional society activities.

Present Work
Centurion Insurance
I completed testing the CI conversion program on two browsers: Mozilla and Internet Explorer. This took longer than I originally estimated because I discovered a problem with the program and had to determine if it was on our end or on the CI platform. Both browsers continue to freeze up immediately after initializing the program. I consulted with the lead technical specialist at CI and we agreed that the code must have not been passing the appropriate parameters. The project is still running two weeks behind schedule.

MarTel Corporation
I worked with the local MarTel account representative to determine who should be involved in the focus group. We determined the demographics and number of participants, the location, and the topics we need to explore.

Intern Orientation
I met several times with Dave Jankowski, the intern from City College. He joined the group this month and will be here for six months. I installed the required software, helped him access the server, and established his passwords. I went over our email guidelines with him so he understands how our team uses email.

Committee Work
I attended the E-learning Administrative Committee meeting in Banff on November 13–14, representing the eastern provinces. We need to stay involved as a firm in what is happening at the national and international level so our computer engineering groups remain competitive.

As the Safety Council representative for our group, I attended a CPR refresher course and met with the other council members to revise our fire evacuation plans.

Future Work
Next month I plan to

- conduct a line item code review of the CI conversion program with the technical specialist to determine any bugs that may be causing the freeze problems,
- monitor the progress of the MarTel focus group,
- supervise the intern's activities,
- prepare a proposal to present a paper at the IEEE Computer Society annual conference,
- investigate adding client testimonials to our website, and
- update all engineer resumes on the company server.

Figure 4-10 A personal progress report.

Project Completion Reports

It's mostly the Facts compartment that gets expanded and relabelled

A project completion report may be the only report evolving from a short project, or the last in a series of progress reports concerning a lengthy project. Thus the Summary–Background–Facts–Outcome arrangement shown in Figure 4-1 can be adhered to fairly closely, with the Facts section being separated into two compartments labelled **Project Highlights** and **Exceptions** (see Figure 4-11). The Exceptions section draws attention to deviations from the original project plan.

The project completion report emailed by Jack Binscarth at the end of his analysis of oil samples for Cantor Petroleums shows the five writing compartments (see Figure 4-12). In a short report like this it's acceptable to combine two, or sometimes more, writing compartments into a single paragraph. In Jack's report, paragraph 1 contains both the **Summary** and the **Background**, and paragraph 2 contains both the **Project Highlights** and the **Exceptions**.

Inspection Reports

An inspection report is an extended trip report

An inspection can range from a quick check of a small building to assess its suitability as a temporary storage centre to a full-scale examination of an airline's aircraft, avionics equipment, repair facilities, and maintenance methods. In both cases the inspectors report their findings in an inspection report:

- The building inspector's report is brief: it states that the building either is or is not suitable, and gives reasons why.
- The airline inspector's report is lengthy: it describes in detail the condition of every aspect of the airline's operations and lists every deficiency (i.e. conditions that must be corrected).

Explore

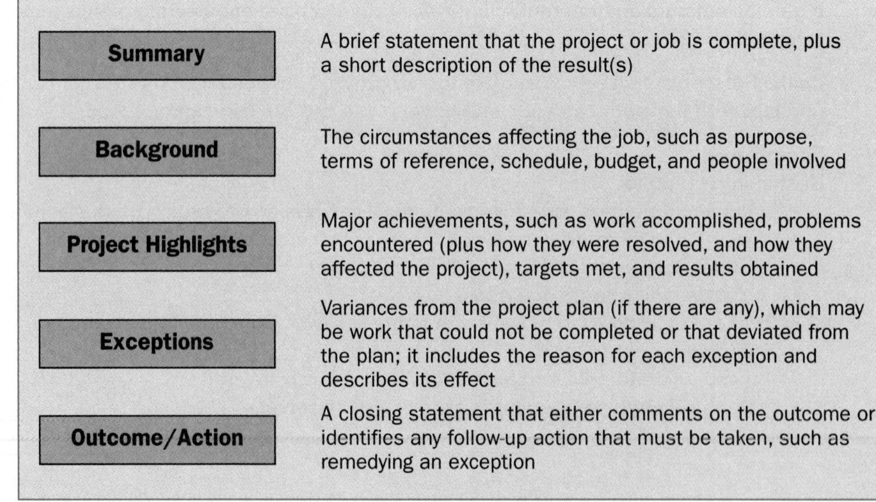

Summary
A brief statement that the project or job is complete, plus a short description of the result(s)
Background
The circumstances affecting the job, such as purpose, terms of reference, schedule, budget, and people involved
Project Highlights
Major achievements, such as work accomplished, problems encountered (plus how they were resolved, and how they affected the project), targets met, and results obtained
Exceptions
Variances from the project plan (if there are any), which may be work that could not be completed or that deviated from the plan; it includes the reason for each exception and describes its effect
Outcome/Action
A closing statement that either comments on the outcome or identifies any follow-up action that must be taken, such as remedying an exception

Figure 4-11 Writing plan for a project completion report.

To: Fred Stokes <fstokes@macroeng.com>
From: Jack Binscarth <jbinscarth@macroeng.com>
Date: 28 October 2010
Subject: Finalizing Cantor Petroleums Project

Summary Statement

I completed the analysis of oil samples for Cantor Petroleums on October 26, nine days later than planned.

Background

The work was done at the refinery, as requested in Cantor Petroleums' purchase order No. 376188 dated September 4, 2010, and was scheduled to start on September 11 and end on October 16. I was assigned to the project under work order No. 2716.

Project Highlights

The work plan called for me to analyse 132 oil samples within the five-week period, but three problems caused me to overrun the schedule and complete four fewer analyses than specified.

Exceptions

The delay was caused by a strike of refinery personnel and a faulty spectrophotometer that had to be sent out for repair and recalibration. The incomplete analyses were caused by four contaminated samples that could not be replaced in less than six weeks.

Outcome

Russ Dienstadt, the refinery manager, agreed to a cost overrun and has corresponded with you separately on this subject. He also agreed that it would be uneconomical for me to return to analyse replacements for the four contaminated samples. When I delivered the 128 analyses to him on October 26, he accepted the project as being complete.

Jack

Figure 4-12 A project completion report.

In both cases the reports can follow the Summary–Background–Facts–Outcome arrangement, as shown in Figure 4-13 on page 68.

Kevin Doherty's building inspection report in Figure 4-14 on page 69 shows how these compartments helped shape a logical, easy-to-follow document:

1. His **Summary** tells the production manager the one thing he most wants to know: can they use the building?
2. The **Background** describes who went where, why, and when.
3. His **Conditions** section (3a) opens with a summarizing general statement (a summary) and then supports it with facts. Because they are not in any particular order, Kevin precedes each condition with a bullet. He presents the **Deficiencies** (3b) as a briefly stated

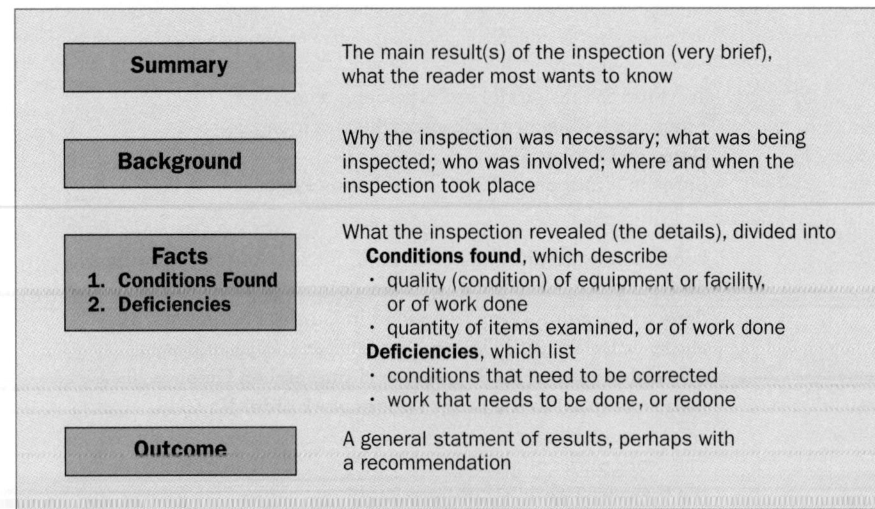

Summary
The main result(s) of the inspection (very brief), what the reader most wants to know
Background
Why the inspection was necessary; what was being inspected; who was involved; where and when the inspection took place
Facts
1. Conditions Found
2. Deficiencies
What the inspection revealed (the details), divided into
Conditions found, which describe
• quality (condition) of equipment or facility, or of work done
• quantity of items examined, or of work done
Deficiencies, which list
• conditions that need to be corrected
• work that needs to be done, or redone
Outcome
A general statment of results, perhaps with a recommendation

Figure 4-13 Writing plan for an inspection report.

It's better to describe conditions and deficiencies in two separate sections

list, which makes it easy to identify what has to be done. He also uses active-voice verbs to demonstrate that the actions must be performed. Because he may need to refer to the deficiencies later, he precedes each with a consecutive number.

4 The recommendation in his **Outcome** supports his summary.

For a short inspection report like this, Kevin presents all the Conditions first and then lists all the Deficiencies. But such an arrangement could become cumbersome for a long report that covers many items. For example, for an inspection at Remick Airlines' workshops, the organization of the Facts section would look like this:

A plan for a short inspection report

A. **Conditions Found:**
   1. Electrical Shop
   2. Avionics Calibration Centre
   3. Flammable Materials Storage
   (etc...)

B. **Deficiencies:**
   1. Electrical Shop
   2. Avionics Calibration Centre
   3. Flammable Materials Storage
   (etc...)

The more departments inspected, the longer the report becomes and the farther apart each department's Conditions and Deficiencies sections grow.

To overcome this difficulty, treat each department as a *separate* inspection and reorganize the report so that for each department the Deficiencies section immediately follows the Conditions section. The organization of the whole report then becomes as shown on page 70.

To: Hugh Smithson <hsmithson@macroeng.com>
From: Kevin Doherty <kdoherty@macroeng.com>
Date: 7 January 2011
Subject: Inspection of Carter Building

1 The Carter Building at the corner of River Avenue and 39th Street will make a suitable storage and assembly centre for the Dennison contract.

2 Christine Lamont and I inspected the Carter Building on January 5 to assess its suitability both for storage and as a work area for 20 assemblers for 15 months. We were accompanied by Ken Wiens of Wilshire Properties.

3 We found the interior of the building to be spacious and to have good facilities, but to be unsightly. Our inspection showed the following:

3a

- There are 460 m^2 of usable floor space (see attached building plan, supplied by Mr Wiens); we need 350 m^2 for the project.
- There are two offices, each 16 m^2, and a large unimpeded space ideal for partitioning into a storage area and four workstations.
- The building is structurally sound and dry, but it is very dirty and smells strongly (the previous tenant was a fertilizer distributor).
- There are numerous power outlets, newly installed with heavy-duty circuits, and the building has excellent overhead lighting.
- Several walls are damaged and many contain obnoxious graffiti.
- There is a new loading ramp on the north side of the building, suitable for semitrailers.
- Washroom facilities are adequate for up to 30 people, but one toilet and two washbasins are broken.

Before we rent the building, the rental agency will have to

3b

1. clean it thoroughly,
2. repair damaged walls, partitions, and toilet facilities, and
3. redecorate the interior.

Ken Wiens said his firm will do this.

4 I recommend we rent the Carter Building from Wilshire Properties, with the provision that the deficiencies listed above be corrected before we move in.

Kevin

Figure 4-14 A short informal inspection report.

A plan for a longer, more detailed inspection report

Summary
Background
Facts:

1. Electrical Shop
    - A. Conditions Found
    - B. Deficiencies
2. Avionics Calibration Centre
    - A. Conditions Found
    - B. Deficiencies
3. Flammable Materials Storage
    - A. Conditions Found
    - B. Deficiencies

(etc...)

Outcome:

Conclusions
Recommendations

Laboratory Reports

Lab reports are written frequently in colleges, less often in industry

There are two kinds of laboratory reports: those written in industry to document laboratory research or tests on materials or equipment, and those written in academic institutions to record laboratory tests performed by students. The former are generally known as *test reports* or *laboratory reports*; those written by students are simply called *lab reports*.

Industrial laboratory reports can describe a wide range of topics, from testing a piece of metal to determine its tensile strength, through analysing a sample of soil (a drill core) to identify its composition, to checking a microwave oven to assess whether it emits radiation. Academic lab reports can also describe many topics, but their purpose is different since they describe tests that are intended to help students learn something or prove a theory.

Laboratory reports generally conform to a standard pattern, although emphasis differs depending on the purpose of the report and how its results will be used. Readers of industrial laboratory or test reports are usually more interested in results than in how a test was carried out. Readers of academic lab reports are usually professors and instructors, who are more likely to be interested in thoroughly documented details, from which they can assess the student's understanding of the subject and what the test proved.

A laboratory report has identifiable compartments, each usually preceded by a heading.

A generic writing plan for a lab report

Compartment	*Heading*	*Contents*
Summary	**Summary**	A very brief statement of the purpose of the tests, the main findings, and what can be interpreted from them. (In short laboratory reports, the Summary can be combined with the next compartment.)
Background	**Objective**	A more detailed description of why the tests were performed, on whose authority they were conducted, and what they were expected to achieve or prove.
		There are four parts here:
Facts	**Equipment Setup**	A description of the test setup, plus a list of equipment and materials used. A drawing of the test hook-up may be inserted here. (If a series of tests is being performed, with a different equipment setup for each test, then a separate equipment description, materials list, and illustration should be inserted immediately before each test description.)
	Test Method	A detailed, step-by-step explanation of the tests. In industrial laboratory reports the depth of explanation depends on the reader's needs: if a reader is nontechnical and likely to be interested only in results, then the test description can be condensed. For lab reports written at a college or university, however, students are expected to provide a thorough description of their method.
	Test Results	Usually a brief statement of the test results or the findings evolving from the tests.
	Analysis (or Interpretation)	A detailed discussion of the results or findings, their implications, and what can be interpreted from them. (The analysis section is particularly important in academic lab reports.)

Compartment	*Heading*	*Contents*
Outcome	**Conclusions**	A brief summing-up, which shows how the test results, findings, and analysis meet the objective(s) established at the start of the report.
Backup	**Attachments**	These are pages of supporting data such as test measurements derived during the tests, or documentation such as specifications, procedures, instructions, and drawings which, if placed in the report narrative, would interrupt reading continuity.

In practice, the writing plan is adapted to suit the industry and the circumstances

The compartments described here are those most likely to be used for an industrial laboratory report, although emphasis and labelling will differ depending on the requirements of the organization and the authority for whom the report is being written.

In a college or university you will often see a slightly different arrangement, with the report being divided into three parts in which the report writer answers the questions listed in Figure 4-15.

Because test laboratories are audited regularly, *every* report they produce must clearly account for every step that is taken in each test. The tests and reports must also comply with professional industry standards such as ISO, GLP (General Lab Practices), and GMP (General Manufacturing Practices). Even at the college/university level your objective should be to consistently achieve a similar standard.

Plan for a Laboratory Report

Introduction

1. What was your **Objective**? Describe what you were trying to achieve.
2. What **Safety Considerations** did you have to take into account when performing the tests?
3. What **Method** did you use? Either describe the test method or refer to the description in a standard operating procedure (SOP).

Test Description

4. What **Materials** did you use? Be very exact: quote *exact* machine(s) and source(s) of materials, so that a reader can replicate exactly what you did.
5. What **Calculations** did you make?
6. What **Information** did you capture? Describe *exactly* what you saw happen, but without offering opinions. You are an objective observer of the work.
7. What **Results** did you obtain? Present factual data, such as graphs, tables, calculations evolving from the test, and comparisons with previous data (again, avoid offering opinions).

Discussion

8. What did the results mean to you? This is your **Analysis**: interpret the results in light of the objectives you established in step 1, and discuss their significance (*now* your opinions can be heard!).

Figure 4-15 Sample plan for a college/university laboratory report.

ASSIGNMENTS

Project 4.1: Damage in the Test Lab

This happened so quickly, you had no time to think or move!

It was 11:25 a.m. and you were talking to Dave, an electrician, who was standing on a stepladder beside the bench on which you were running tests on Torstar Batch 81. Batch 81 was contained in a vat and you were using a Vancourt 2120 calibrator to measure the results.

Dave was replacing a burnt-out fluorescent lamp from over the bench. As he loosened the lamp, he shouted, "Oops! Watch out below!!"

The lamp slipped from his hands, fell on the bench and calibrator, smashed, and bits of glass dropped into the vat. Dave climbed down from the ladder, apologized, examined the meter dial on the calibrator, and showed you that its glass was smashed.

You stopped the test, realizing you'd have to rerun it *and* get a replacement calibrator. You phoned Majestic Electronics, the supplier, who said, "We'll have one for you the day after tomorrow."

To avoid letting the schedule get even further behind, you searched for someone who could work at night to rerun the test. Phil Maybank volunteered to do so. The overtime labour will cost $440.

Write an email to Pat Wyvern, the project manager, to report the incident and the effect on the project schedule. Pat's email address is pwyvern@multind.com.

Project 4.2: An Expensive Insurance Problem

You are an engineering technologist working for Marco Construction Company (MCC) and currently you are inspecting work done by a construction crew at Freedom Lake Narrows. You are driving a leased truck. Here are the lease details:

- The truck is a Nabuchi Major 200.
- It was leased from Cypress Fleet Management (CFM).
- The lease started five months ago, on the 5th of the month.
- The lease cost is $1135 per month.
- Your company declined CFM's insurance coverage, preferring to use its own insurer (ManSask Insurers Ltd).
- On taking out the lease, the MCC purchasing agent initialled the entry on the lease form that says, "Lessee accepts responsibility for full replacement value of any loss." (This is MCC's regular policy for any vehicle lease or rental agreement.)
- CFM listed their purchase value of the truck as $42 500, which is the full replacement value.

Unfortunately, three days ago the truck slid on gravel and rolled down a steep embankment. Fortunately, apart from bruises, no one was badly injured. The truck, however, sustained severe damage.

Today James Weldon of ManSask Insurers examined the truck with you: "It's a write-off," he said and turned to his computer. "The replacement value for a five-month-old Nabuchi Major 200 is $31 300. We will send MCC a cheque for that amount."

MCC now has an expensive problem: there is a difference between the amount your company will receive and the amount your company will have to pay CFM for the loss.

Write an email report to the chief accountant of your company (her name is Fay Reitsma, at f.reitsma@mcc.ca) to inform her of the problem. You think, perhaps, she should negotiate a settlement difference between your company and CFM.

Project 4.3: Theft at Whiteshell Lake

You are the team leader of a four-person inspection crew en route to a remote site 920 km from your office, where construction of a new power generating station is in progress. You are travelling in a company-owned van and after 615 km you and the crew stop for the night at the Towpath Inn, a small motel beside the road that skirts around Whiteshell Lake.

Early the following morning you discover the van has been broken into: the window on the front passenger door has been smashed and the radio and about $8 in loose change (for parking meters) has gone. You check further and find a video camera and videotapes also have gone (from a locked storage box in the back of the van—the lock has been broken off).

You try telephoning your office, but it is too early in the day. The motel has a wi-fi connection so you write an email to your manager, M B Corrigan (mbcorrigan@multind.com), in which you describe what has happened and ask that a replacement video camera be sent to you. Here is some additional information you draw on to write your report:

- You are driving a company panel van, licence number 7AB 38MP; it is a Chevy.
- Your trip was authorized by company Travel Order N-704, dated one week ago.
- The power generating station is being constructed beside the Mooswa River, 27 km north of the small town of Freehampton.
- The video camera is a Nabuchi TX380 Portacam. You rented it from Meadows Electronics at 212 Grassmere Road. Its serial number is 21784B.
- The purpose of your having a video camera is to record construction progress visually. The videotape will be edited and then shown at the Power Authority Directors' Meeting scheduled for the 22nd of next month.
- You telephone the police at Clearwater Village, to report the break-in and theft. They ask you to report in person, which you will do when you leave Whiteshell Lake.
- Ask your manager to ship you the replacement video camera by bus the day after tomorrow. You will meet the bus when it stops in Freehampton.
- Use today's date as the date of your report.

Project 4.4: Reporting Project Progress

You are an engineering technologist on a field assignment installing remote sensing units and associated transmitters on microwave towers at 27 sites that form part of a telemetry communications chain. You are accompanied by engineering technologist Janice Hayden. Usually you are able to complete two sites per day, or 10 per week. You have a Nabuchi Commander van that you drive from site to site.

You started the project two weeks ago and are scheduled to complete it in four days. However, although by the end of the first week you were ahead of schedule, you have since encountered problems that have delayed you.

Here are the details:

- On days 3 and 4 you were able to complete three installations, which put you one whole day ahead of schedule.
- On day 6, however, a major storm accompanied by 50 km/h winds prevented you and Janice from climbing the towers.
- On day 7, the winds were at 30 km/h and you risked climbing the tower at site 11. A sudden, unexpected hailstorm erupted while you were up there and you started to climb down. Janice slipped and fell 4 metres, damaging an ankle. You took her to the hospital in Grange Point, where the injury was X-rayed. Fortunately it was only a sprain. However, the bad weather, the drive into Grange Point, and delays at the hospital cost you a day and a half.
- It's now day 10 and you realize you will not be able to complete the project until two days later than originally scheduled (i.e. one week from today, instead of just three days from today).

You are now in the motel at White River Falls on the evening of day 10. Write a progress report to your manager, Hector Nguyen, which you will email to him. His email is hnguyen@corpmill.ca.

Project 4.5: A Security Problem

You are the maintenance technician at Forrest Distributors, a wholesale distributor of business equipment and furniture, plus some vehicles. The company has a large warehouse and an equally large storage area at the rear of the building for farm machinery, snow blowers, Ski-doos, etc. Because the company experiences a higher-than-average number of break-ins each year, during which goods stored outside are stolen, four years ago video surveillance cameras were installed at eight locations around the property.

These video cameras had a continuous loop of videotape with a 24-hour storage capacity. This meant, following a break-in, having to take a ladder to each of the cameras near where the break-in occurred, and climb up to retrieve the tape. Three months ago, however, management decided to install a centralized survey unit in the security office, into which all data would be fed from the eight cameras and stored digitally. Under this arrangement there was no longer any need to access the cameras and then remove the individual video storage units. Additionally, there would be a continuous 10-day record rather than just a 24-hour one.

Last night there was a break-in and a Ski-doo was stolen. You went to the control unit in the security office, downloaded the storage file onto a memory stick, and then downloaded the file into the office computer. The result, however, was disappointing: there was memory only until nine days ago. After that, the memory unit stopped recording (although the images were still being shown on the monitors in the security office). Here is some salient information:

- Assume the break-in occurred last night, and that today is the 17th of the current month.
- The centralized storage unit is a Vancourt 2010 Security System. It was installed three months ago on the 10th of the month. Its purchase and installation cost was $4250 plus GST. It carries a three-month warranty.
- Vancourt Industries is at 1700 Boundary Road, Vancouver BC, V3Z 2L8. The sales manager there is Jim Winstanley.
- You phoned Jim and he said he will have someone come in to repair the security unit tomorrow (on the 18th).
- The Ski-doo that was stolen is a Highlander 200; it carries a list price of $3600. There was also damage done to the locks on the gate, which will cost $385 to repair.
- Your manager is Karen Korlyshyn, who is manager of office services at Forrest Distributors.

Part 1: Write an email report to your manager. Tell her what has happened, what the cost is, and that the warranty has expired. Also tell her you are writing to Vancourt Industries to claim the repairs to the security system under the warranty (because the system stopped recording just before the warranty expiry date).

Part 2: Write a letter to Vancourt Industries to request that the repair cost for the security unit still be covered under the warranty.

Chapter 5
Longer Reports

Longer Informal and Semiformal Reports
www.csee.umbc.edu/~sherman/Courses/documents/TR_how_to.html
This website gives some excellent advice on writing a technical report, covering how to write the thesis, the components of the technical report, organization, as well as common mistakes to avoid.

In this chapter you will learn how to organize and write

- an investigation or evaluation report,
- a feasibility study,
- a justification (also known as a comparative analysis), and
- a formal report, in either the traditional format or a contemporary format.

Where short reports tend to deal with facts, longer reports often deal with less tangible factors. In a long report you will analyse a situation in depth before drawing a conclusion and, sometimes, making a recommendation. You may be

- investigating a problem or unsatisfactory condition,
- evaluating alternatives to improve a situation,
- determining the suitability of taking a prescribed action, or
- proposing a change in methods or procedures.

In each case you will be expected to write in a fluid narrative style that is both informative and persuasive.

Explore

Writing an Investigation Report

In an investigation report you describe how you performed tests, examined data, or carried out an investigation. You start with known data and then analyse and examine it so the reader can see how you reached the final result and can now make a recommendation. You may write the report as a letter, as an attachment to an email, or as a semiformal document preceded by a title page.

The parts of an investigation report are shown in Figure 5-1, which is an expanded example of the plan for short reports shown in Figure 4-1 on page 51. These parts are identified by the circled number inserted beside the investigation report in Figure 5-2 (see pages 80–82).

❶ For this report, the **Background** is only one sentence, which refers to the email that initiated the investigation. It is short because the reader already knows the circumstances.

2 The **Investigation Details** start here, with a very brief reference to the **Approach.**

3 These are the **Findings.** It also is the start of a comparative analysis (see the section starting on page 82).

4 This is the first of three **Ideas** for resolving the problem.

Comparing each plan, idea, method, or product *only* against the criteria helps a writer be objective

5 These are the **Criteria:** the requirements against which each idea will be measured.

6 The **Analysis** starts here. The table provides a convenient, easy-to-access summary of what each idea will achieve and cost.

7 In the Analysis, each idea is compared to the Criteria. (Note that the ideas are *not* compared one against another.)

8 The **Outcome** starts by drawing a **Conclusion** and continues with a **Recommendation.**

9 The **Attachments** contain drawings, specifications, and detailed cost estimates for each idea.

This expanded writing plan is based on the pyramid seen in earlier chapters

Summary	A brief statement of the situation or problem and what should be done about it	
Background	A more detailed description of the situation or problem and its history	
Investigation Details	The **Facts**, comprising	
	Approach	How the investigation was tackled
	Findings	What the investigation revealed
	Ideas	Different ways the situation can be improved or the problem resolved
	Criteria	Factors that influence the analysis
	Analysis	Evaluation of each idea
Conclusion	The **Outcome**, or result of the investigation; a summing-up	
Recommendation	A positive statement advocating action*	
Attachments	Evidence: detailed facts, figures, and statistics that support the Investigation Details*	

**Included only when appropriate*

Figure 5-1 A writing plan for an investigation report.

KCMO-TV

TO: Dennis Carlisle, Operations Manager
FROM: Phyllis van der Wyck, Engineering Department
DATE: October 21, 2010
SUBJECT: Investigation of High Ambient Sound Level, Satellite Studio Control Room

I have investigated the high ambient sound levels reported in the control room of our satellite studio at 21 Union Road, and have traced them to the building's air-conditioning equipment. The sound level can be reduced to an acceptable level by replacing the blower motor and soundproofing the air-conditioning ducts and blowers. The cost will be $9800. *Summary*

Introduction

1 My investigation was authorized by your email of August 28, 2010, in which you described the audio difficulties your production crews are experiencing when programming from the satellite studio. *Background*

Investigation

2 Tests conducted with a sound level meter at various locations in the control room established that the average ambient sound level is 36.8 dB, with peaks of 38.7 dB near the west wall. This is approximately 7 to 9 dB higher than the sound levels measured in the control room for Studio 1 on Westover Road, where the average ambient sound level is 29.5 dB with peaks of 30.2 dB near the south wall. *Approach*

This two-and-one-half page report benefits from having headings inserted at appropriate places

3 The unusually high sound level is caused by the air-conditioning equipment, which is in an annex adjacent to the west wall of the control room. Air-conditioner rumble and blower fan noise are carried easily into the control room because the short air ducts permit little noise dissipation between the equipment and the work area. The flat hardboard surface of the west wall also acts as a sounding board and bounces the noise back into the room. *Findings*

Solutions

I have considered three methods we could use to reduce the ambient sound level: *Ideas*

Ideas are numbered consecutively for ease of reference

1. Move the air-conditioning equipment to a storage room at the other end of the building, for an estimated 10–12 dB reduction in sound level. This would, however, require major structural alterations that will cost between $22 000 and $26 000.

Figure 5-2 An investigation report with primarily objective development.

Dennis Carlisle – page 2

2. Replace the existing blower fan assembly with a model TL-1 blower manufactured by the Quietaire Corporation of Hamilton, Ontario, and line the ducts with Agrafoam, a new soundproofing product developed by the automobile industry in Germany. Together, these methods would reduce the ambient sound level by about 6.5–7.5 dB. The cost will be $9800.
3. Cover the vinyl floor tiles with Monroe 200 indoor/outdoor carpet, a practice that has proven successful in air-traffic-control centres, and mount carpet on the control room's west wall, for a sound level reduction of about 4.0–4.5 dB. The cost will be $2400.

Analysis

The remedy we select must

5 *Criteria*

- reduce the ambient sound level by at least 7.3 dB, to provide conditions similar to those at the Westover Road control room,
- be implemented quickly (ideally by November 15, when the Holiday Pageant programs will be recorded), and
- cost no more than $10 000, if the modifications are to be completed within the 2010–2011 budget year.

6 As the table shows, none of the three methods singly meets all of the above criteria. Method 2 comes close to doing so. *Analysis*

	Required	***Method 1 Relocation***	***Method 2 Blower/Ducts***	***Method 3 Carpet***
Projected sound level reduction (min)	7.3 dB	10–12 dB	6.5–7.5 dB	4.0–4.5 dB
Time to implement (max)	3 weeks	12 weeks	3 weeks	1.5 weeks
Approximate cost (max)	$10 000	$22–26 000	$9800	$2400

A table simplifies a comparison, making it easier to analyse

- Method 1 will reduce the sound level more than the required minimum but cannot be implemented quickly or within budget.
- Method 2 probably will reduce the sound level to an acceptable level, but only just. It could be implemented quickly and within budget.

Dennis Carlisle – page 3

- Method 3 will reduce the sound level by only one-third of the desired reduction. It could be implemented quickly and within budget.

Conclusion

8 The only method that comes close to meeting our immediate requirements is Method 2. If we were to combine it with Method 3, we could achieve a probable total sound reduction of 8.3–9.8 dB, which would meet the required reduction but would exceed the budget by $2200. (Note that, when combining methods, the total reduction will be *less* than the summation of the two individual sound level reductions.) *Conclusion*

A major recommendation and a minor recommendation

Recommendation

Because Method 2 comes close to the required minimum reduction in sound level, I recommend we replace the blower motor and line the ducts with Agrafoam for a total cost of $9800. However, because actual sound level reductions can differ from those projected, I suggest we retest the sound levels following installation. If a further reduction in sound level proves necessary, then I recommend we install Monroe 200 carpet on the floor and west wall in March 2011 at a total cost of $2400, using $200 from the 2010–2011 budget year and $2200 from the 2011–2012 budget year. *Recommendation*

These modifications will provide the quieter working environment needed by your production crews.

P. Van der Wyck

9 Att: Specifications and cost estimates *Attachments*

Conducting a Comparative Analysis

A comparative analysis is also a justification

Phyllis van der Wyck's evaluation of three sound level methods (see Figure 5-2) is known as a *comparative analysis*. In a comparative analysis you compare different products, plans, ideas, or methods to identify which is the most suitable for a particular situation. It can be written either objectively or subjectively:

- In an *objective* comparative analysis you do not allow your opinions to intrude until the very end of the report, when you make your recommendation (as Phyllis van der Wyck did).
- In a *subjective* comparative analysis you allow your voice to be heard—your opinions to be apparent—much earlier in the report, usually when you analyse the alternatives.

The objective and subjective methods are shown side-by-side in Figure 5-3.

Both objective and subjective development methods provide opportunities to arrange your information for maximum effect

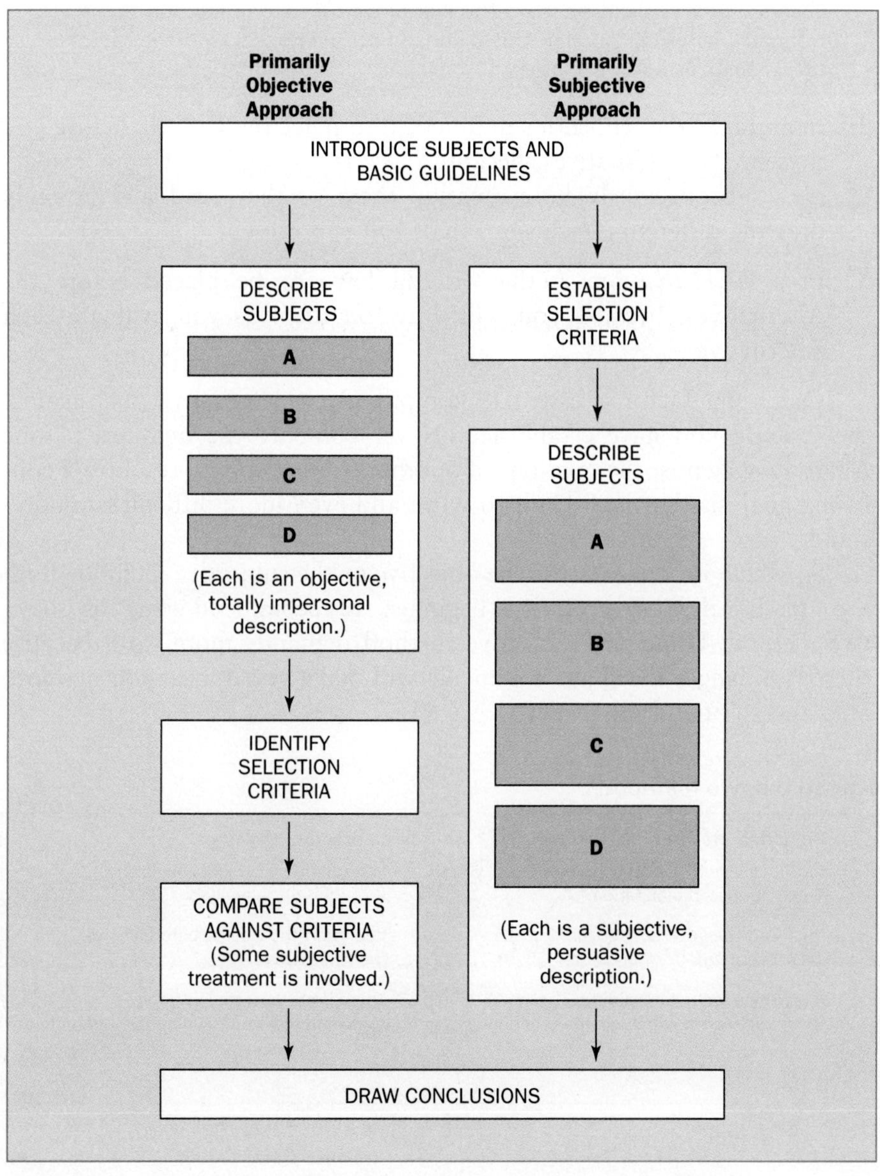

Figure 5-3 Alternative methods for doing a comparative analysis.

Table 5-1 shows the major differences between the objective and subjective methods.

Why do these differences exist?

1. In many reports you write, your role will be simply to present facts and findings. This means being objective and not letting your opinions intrude (it's how Phyllis has written her report in Figure 5-2). Sometimes, however, and particularly if you have been asked for an opinion about what you have observed or discovered, it's acceptable to be subjective, which means inserting opinions as your report evolves. Here is an example:

   My inspection of the Model XP extruder shows that wearing has occurred on a 36 mm section of the drive shaft. This indicates either poor inspection by the manufacturer or that substandard materials have been used. From the nature of the wearing, I suspect the latter.

Present only facts to maintain objectivity

2. In an *objective* report, it's impractical to place the Criteria before you present the Alternatives, because there is a danger that your readers may subconsciously be evaluating them as they read and possibly drawing different conclusions than you will present.

When you offer an opinion, you are immediately subjective

3. In a *subjective* report the Criteria have to be placed before the Alternatives, because you will draw on them as you evaluate each Alternative.

Anticipate your readers' questions

One other factor is essential: compare each Alternative only against the Criteria you have established. Never compare the qualities of one Alternative against the qualities of another—doing so will result in a confusing analysis that is difficult to write and even more difficult to understand.

So which is better: to use the objective or the subjective method? Both are equally valid; however, for a beginner, we recommend using the objective method. Using the subjective method demands more skill, because there is a danger that your comments will make you appear too opinionated and so offend the reader.

Table 5-1 The differences between the two methods.

Difference	Objective Method	Subjective Method
1. Insertion of Opinions	You cannot insert personal opinions until you write your Recommendation.	You can insert personal opinions throughout the analysis.
2. Position of Criteria	You insert the Criteria after you describe the Alternatives.	You insert the Criteria before you describe the Alternatives.
3. Insertion of an Evaluation Compartment	You write a separate Evaluation of the Alternatives after you insert the Criteria.	There is no separate Evaluation compartment. You evaluate the Alternatives in the same paragraphs that you describe them.

Writing an Evaluation Report

Evaluation reports are similar to investigation reports. They often start with an idea or a concept you want to develop, prove, or disprove. First, you establish guidelines to keep your report within prescribed boundaries, and then you research data, conduct tests, and analyse the results to determine whether your idea or concept is valid.

Two titles, but a similar function

The writing plan shown in Figure 5-1 also applies to an evaluation report. Morley Wozniak's evaluation of landfill sites in Figure 5-4 on page 86 and Figure 5-5 on pages 88 to 93 follows this plan.

Morley's report is preceded by a one-page cover letter (Figure 5-4) that *describes and comments on* key implications within the report. Its addressee (Quillicom's town engineer) has the option of distributing it to the town councillors with the report or detaching it and replacing it with a cover letter of his own.

A cover letter can introduce a sensitive issue or confidential information

Recommendation and Feasibility Reports www.io.com/~hcexres/textbook/feas.html This document is one chapter from the online textbook used in Austin Community College's online course, Online Technical Writing (www.io.com/~hcexres/tcm1603/acchtml/acctoc. html). It describes feasibility reports in detail and includes several samples.

The parts of the writing plan shown in Figure 5-1 are identified in Morley's report by circled numbers beside the narrative; they are keyed to the additional comments provided here.

1. Although several factors affect site selection, in his **Summary** Morley focuses primarily on the environmental impact because he believes it is of overriding importance.

2. The **Introduction** provides Background details leading up to the study assigned to H L Winman and Associates, and then to Morley.

3. The **Evaluation Details** start here, with a single paragraph in which Morley outlines his **Approach** (i.e. how he tackled the study). Note that he mentions the three components *in the same sequence* in which he will describe them later in the report.

4. These are Morley's **Findings**—the results of his research. He describes the findings in detail because his readers must fully understand the geology of the area if they are to accept the conclusions he will draw later in his report. He is totally objective here, reporting only facts without letting his opinions intrude.

5. Morley presents the three possible landfill sites as his **Ideas** (even though they were originally presented to him by the client, the Town of Quillicom). In effect he is saying to his readers, "Now that I have described the geology of the land to you, here are three locations within the area for you to choose from." He is still totally objective.

Morley's rationale for organizing and writing his report

H L WINMAN AND ASSOCIATES

May 23, 2011

Robert D Delorme, P.Eng
Town Engineer
Municipal Offices
Quillicom ON P8R 2A2

City, province, and postal code, correctly placed all on one line

Dear Mr Delorme

Our assessment of the three sites selected as potential landfills for the Town of Quillicom shows that each has a disadvantage or limitation. The most serious exists at Lot 18, Subdivision 5N, which is the site preferred by the Town Council. A distinct possibility exists that a landfill located here could contaminate the town's water supply.

The disadvantages of the two other sites affect only cost and convenience:

- Lot 47, Subdivision 6E, will be considerably more expensive to operate.
- Lot 23, Subdivision 3S, will have a much lower capacity.

If the Town Council still prefers to use Lot 18, a drilling program must first be conducted to identify the soil and bedrock structure between the lot and Quillicom. Providing the boreholes show no evidence that contamination will occur, then the site would be a sound choice.

The enclosed report describes our study in detail. I will be glad to discuss it and its implications with you.

Regards

A cover letter accompanying an in-depth report or proposal may be signed by the author for the department manager

for Vincent Hrabi
Branch Manager
H L Winman and Associates
Thunder Bay, ON
enc

Figure 5-4 The cover letter preceding an evaluation report. This letter also is an executive summary.

6 Morley now identifies three general **Criteria** he will use to evaluate the sites. He does not identify specific criteria because they have not been defined.

Proposals
www.io.com/~hcexres/textbook/props.html
Also from Online Technical Writing, this document describes types of proposals, their organization and format, and the common sections in a proposal. Included are several sample proposals and a revision checklist.

7 In his **Analysis**, Morley must clearly establish the factors on which he will base his conclusions. Now he allows some subjectivity to appear in his writing (we can hear his voice behind his words). He is moving down the right side of the plan for a comparative analysis, as shown in Figure 5-3 on page 83.

8 Morley's **Conclusions** identify the main features affecting each site. Note that he simply offers the alternatives without saying or even implying which is preferable. This part of the report, together with the Recommendations, is the Outcome (sometimes referred to as the *terminal summary*).

9 In the **Recommendations** Morley states specifically what he believes the Town Council must do. He must sound definite and convincing, so he starts with "We recommend..." rather than the passive "It is recommended that..."

10 The **Attachment** brings together all the site details in an easy-to-read form, and simultaneously provides readers with evidence to support what Morley says about the landfill sites in the report narrative.

Compare how Phyllis van der Wyck and Morley Wozniak each use the first person (see Phyllis's investigation report in Figure 5-2 on pages 80 to 82). Phyllis uses the informal "I" because she is writing a memo report to another member of the television station where she works. Morley uses the slightly more formal "we" because he knows his report will be distributed to the Quillicom town councillors. (Note, however, that he uses "I" in the personal cover letter to Robert Delorme that accompanies the report.)

We encourage using the first person in letter and report writing

Feasibility Study

Like an evaluation report, a feasibility study starts by introducing an idea or concept, and then develops and analyses the idea to assess whether it is technically or economically feasible. The chief difference lies in the name and application of each document. An evaluation report is generally based on an idea that is originated and evaluated within the same company. A feasibility study is normally prepared at a higher level: the management of company *A* asks company *B* to conduct a feasibility study for it, because company *A*'s staff is not experienced in a specific technical field. For

H L WINMAN AND ASSOCIATES

Evaluation of the Proposed Landfill Sites for the Town of Quillicom, Ontario

Summary

Two of the three locations selected as potential landfill sites for the Town of Quillicom, both southeast of the town, are environmentally safe. There is insufficient data to determine whether the third site, to the north of 1
Quillicom, poses an environmental risk. All three sites are financially viable although one, because of its greater distance from Quillicom, would be more costly to operate.

Introduction

The Background traces the history leading up to the present study

The Town of Quillicom in Northwestern Ontario currently operates a landfill 3.7 km southeast of the town. The landfill was constructed in 1958, and since 1974 2
has also served the mining community of Melody Lake, 2.8 km to the southwest of the landfill. In a report dated February 27, 2010, Quillicom town engineer Robert Delorme identified that the existing landfill was nearing capacity and that a new landfill must be found and operational by April 30, 2012.

Previously, in 2007, the town had identified two sites as potential replacement landfills: Lot 18, Subdivision 5N, 3.4 km north of Quillicom; and Lot 47, Subdivision 6E, 14.6 km to the southeast. The costs to set up and operate both sites were determined, and Lot 18 proved to be more economical ($2000 more to purchase and develop, but $17 000 a year less to operate). It was favoured by the Town Council. However, in a letter to the Council dated November 15, 2008, Mr Delorme expressed his concern that leachate from the site could possibly contaminate the town's source of potable ground water, and recommended that the town first carry out an environmental study.

The town subsequently engaged H L Winman and Associates to examine the sites and determine both their financial viability and their environmental safety. In a letter dated March 15, 2010, Mr Delorme commissioned us to carry out the study, and to include a third potential landfill site at Lot 23, Subdivision 3S, immediately adjacent to the existing landfill, in our assessment.

Figure 5-5 The evaluation report (six pages).

Study Plan

3 We divided our study into three components: (1) an examination of the area geology and its ability to constrain leachate movement; (2) an examination of the physical properties of the proposed landfill sites; and (3) an evaluation of the financial and environmental suitability of the sites.

Area Geology and Hydrogeology

4 Bedrock at Quillicom and in the area of all three proposed landfill sites is chiefly granite and gneiss lying 15 to 30 metres below the surface. A layer of till varying in thickness from 10 to 20 metres covers the bedrock, and is itself covered by 1 to 15 metres of lacustrine silts and clays.

The whole area has experienced repeated glaciation, with the most recent occurring about 20 000 years ago with the advance of the Late Wisconsonian Ice Field. The advancing ice severely scarred this granite and gneiss. When the ice began to retreat 10 000 years later, till was deposited over the region. In addition, meltwater streams below the ice field deposited vast quantities of alluvial material, which today exist as eskers.

The melting ice also created Lake Agassiz and caused silts and clays to be deposited to a depth of up to 30 metres over the entire lake bed. (In the Quillicom area these lacustrine deposits range from 5 to 15 metres deep.) Then, as the lake drained and water levels receded, streams cut into the lacustrine and till deposits. These streams eventually dried up and their channels were filled with windblown silts and sands. Today the channels are known as buried stringers and, if they are water bearing, as stringer aquifers in the weathered bedrock and eskers.

Presenting technical details so they will be understood by all readers takes skill!

The Town of Quillicom obtains its potable water from a stringer aquifer on the surface of the weathered bedrock. Other stringer aquifers are known to exist in the area to the east and south of Quillicom, and likely also exist to the west and north.

The Ontario Water Resources Branch provided us with logs obtained during drillings for ground water wells in the mid-1980s, all to the south and east of Quillicom. We have plotted the locations and types of materials on a topographic map, which shows that

- the bedrock in the area slopes downward, toward the south, from the Town of Quillicom, and
- a major 350-metre wide glacial esker starts 1 km southeast of Quillicom and continues for several kilometres southeast under Highway A806, to beyond the proposed landfill at Lot 47, Subdivision 6E.

As there are very few borehole records for the area north of Quillicom, we could not plot a similar map for that area.

2

The Proposed Landfill Sites

The attributes of the three proposed landfill sites are discussed briefly below and itemized in detail in the attachment. The anticipated life of each site is based on the 2009 population of Quillicom. Similarly, projected operating costs are based on 2009 prices. 5

Lot 23, Subdivision 3S

This narrow, 7.81-hectare strip of land is immediately east of and adjacent to the existing landfill, 3.7 km southeast of Quillicom on Highway A806. As it is the smallest site, it will cost only $9000 to purchase and develop. Its annual operating cost will be $47 000, the same as at the present landfill, and it will have an operational life of 12 to 14 years.

Judicious use of white space makes technical details more readable...

Lot 47, Subdivision 6E

The largest of the three proposed sites at 35.91 hectares, but also the most distant, Lot 47 is a rectangular parcel of land 14.6 km southeast of Quillicom on Highway A806. Its combined purchase and development price will be $20 000, and its annual operating cost will be $64 000. (The high operating cost is caused primarily by the much greater distance the garbage collection vehicles will have to travel.) It will have a lifespan of almost 60 years.

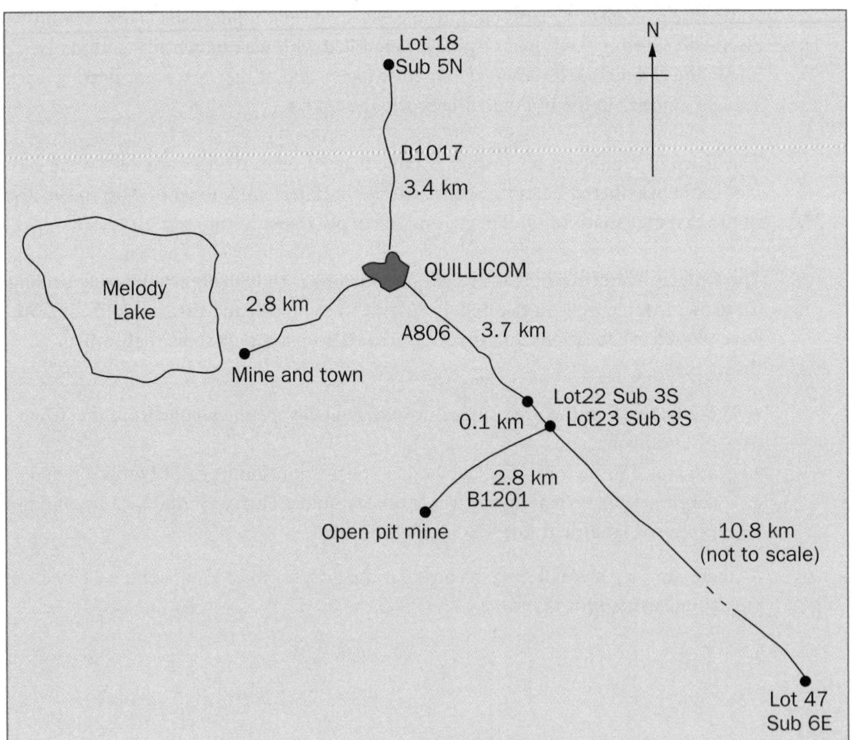

3

Lot 18, Subdivision 5N

A roughly square, 22.75-hectare parcel of land, this lot is 3.4 km directly north of Quillicom on Highway B1017. It will cost $22 000 to purchase and develop, and $47 000 a year to operate (the same as at present). At the current fill rate, it will last for 36 to 40 years.

Site Comparisons

We considered three factors when comparing the three proposed landfill sites: cost, environmental impact, and convenience (see attachment). 6

Cost. We examined cost from two points of view: the immediate expense to purchase and develop the site, and the annual cost to operate it.

- Lot 23, adjacent to the existing landfill, offers the lowest purchase and development cost at $9000, compared with $20 000 and $22 000 for the two alternative sites.
- Lot 23 and Lot 18 (the site north of Quillicom) offer comparable operating costs at $47 000 per year, whereas Lot 47 (14 km southeast of Quillicom) would have the highest annual operating cost of $64 000.

...as does the author's choice not to justify the right margin

However, if the purchase and development costs are spread over 10 years and added to the operating costs, Lots 18 and 23 show a more comparable cost structure:

Site:	Lot 18	Lot 23	Lot 47
Annual Cost:	$49 200	$47 900	$66 000

Environmental Risk. The primary environmental risk is the effect that leachate from the landfill could have on Quillicom's source of potable water. If a landfill lies on a glacial esker, leachate from the landfill will probably contaminate ground water aquifers in the esker. If these aquifers are connected hydraulically to stringer aquifers, the stringer aquifers also probably will become contaminated.

- Lots 23 and 47 (and the existing landfill) lie on a major esker south of Quillicom but offer no environmental risk because the slope of the bedrock in the area is to the south, away from the town. Consequently, even if leachate from the landfill contaminates the ground water, it will flow away from Quillicom and will not contaminate the town's water supply.
- Lot 18, however, is in the uncharted area north of Quillicom, where neither the presence of eskers nor the slope of the bedrock has been determined. Consequently it offers a potential risk that leachate from a landfill located here could contaminate the town's water supply. This will be particularly true if the slope of the bedrock north of Quillicom is the same as south of the town, since then the leachate will flow south, toward Quillicom.

This analysis sets the scene for the conclusions the report author will draw

Convenience. To establish convenience we considered the size of each landfill site (measured as the number of years it can be used before another site must be found) and its proximity to Quillicom.

4

- Lot 47 is the largest site, offering close to 60 years of use, but is four times farther from Quillicom than either of the two other sites.
- Lot 18, to the north, is next largest and can provide between 36 and 40 years of use. It is a comfortable 3.4 km from Quillicom.
- Lot 23, adjacent to the current landfill, is the smallest site and so will have a lifespan of only 12 to 14 years. It also is 3.4 km from Quillicom.

Conclusions

The possibility of leachate contamination of the Town of Quillicom's water supply makes Lot 18, Subdivision 5N, a doubtful choice until sufficient drilling has been done to create a profile of the strata between the lot and Quillicom. 8

The remaining two sites are environmentally sound but have different advantages:

- Lot 47, Subdivision 6E, provides the greatest space but will be costly to operate.
- Lot 23, Subdivision 3S, offers the lowest cost but will have only a limited lifespan.

Remember: conclusions and recommendations must never introduce new information

Recommendations

We recommend that the Town of Quillicom purchase Lot 23, Subdivision 3S, and operate it as a temporary landfill from 2011–2021. We also recommend that the town concurrently conduct a drilling program to the north of Quillicom to determine whether Lot 18, Subdivision 5N, will be an environmentally sound site to use after 2021. 9

Morley Wozniak

Morley Wozniak, P.Eng

5

Attachment

10

Comparison of Proposed Landfill Sites for the Town of Quillicom

Comparison Factor	*Lot 18 Sub 5N*	*Lot 23 Sub 3S*	*Lot 47 Sub 6E*
Distance from Quillicom (driving dist in km)	3.4 N	3.7 SE	14.6 SE
Size (hectares)	22.75	7.81	35.91
Life (years)	36–40	12–14	58–60
Environmental risk (the site's potential for contaminating the Quillicom water supply)	Unknown	None	None
Development costs:			
Purchase price ($)	10 000	2 000	5 000
Construction cost ($)	12 000	7 000	15 000
Ten-year cost ($/yr)	2 200	900	2 000
Operating costs ($/yr)	47 000	47 000	64 000
Combined development and operating costs:			
Year 1, w/o amortization ($)	69 000	56 000	84 000
Per year, w amortization ($)	49 200	47 900	66 000

6

An "open" table (no lines drawn around it) is cleaner for a simple presentation

example, if a national wholesaler engaged solely in the distribution of dry goods were to consider purchasing an executive jet, it would seek advice from a firm of management consultants. The consultants would examine the advantages and disadvantages, and publish their results in a feasibility study that they would issue as either a letter or a formal report.

Writing a Formal Report

Technical Reports
www.io.com/textbook/techreps.html
This document is one chapter from the online textbook used in Austin Community College's online course, Online Technical Writing (www.io.com/~hcexres/textbook/acctoc.html). It describes types of technical reports and their general characteristics and audience, and provides a checklist that can be used for writing technical reports.

A formal report requires more careful and detailed preparation than an informal or semiformal report. Because it most likely will be distributed outside your company, you have to consider the impression the report will convey not only of you but also of the entire company. A well-written, good-looking report can do much to convince prospective clients that you should handle their business, whereas a poorly written, badly presented report can cause clients to question your and your company's capability.

A formal report is made up of several parts, not all of which appear in every report. These parts can be presented in one of two sequences, known as the *traditional arrangement* and the *contemporary arrangement*. In both cases, there are six major and several subsidiary parts, as shown in Table 5-2.

Major Parts

The six major parts form the report's central structure. In the traditional arrangement they are known by the acronym SIDCRA, which is formed from the first letter of each part.

Table 5-2 Traditional arrangement of formal report parts.

Traditional arrangement
Cover or Jacket
Title Page
Summary
Table of Contents
Introduction
Discussion
Conclusions
Recommendations
References or Bibliography
Appendices

Notes:
1. **Major Parts** are in boldface type.
2. A Cover Letter or Executive Summary normally accompanies a formal report.

Summary

The summary is considered by many to be the most important part of a report and the most difficult to write. It has to be informative, yet brief. It has to attract the reader's attention, but must be written in simple, nontechnical terms. It has to be directed to the executive reader, yet be readily understood by almost any reader.

The criteria for a summary are difficult to meet

Normally the summary appears immediately after the title page, where it can be found easily. A summary must be *informative*. In as few words as possible it has to state why the project was carried out and the report was written (the purpose), highlight the most important features of the report, state the main conclusion, and possibly make a recommendation:

Informative Summary

An informative summary answers readers' questions...

> We have tested a specimen of steel to determine whether a job lot owned by Northern Railways could be used as structural members for a short-span bridge to be built at Peele Bay in Yukon. The sample proved to be G40.12 structural steel, which is a good steel for general construction but subject to brittle failure at very low temperatures.
>
> Although the steel could be used for the bridge, we consider there is too narrow a safety margin between the –51C temperature at which failure can occur, and the –47C minimum temperature occasionally recorded at Peele Bay. A safer choice would be G40.8C structural steel, which has a minimum failure temperature of –62C.

Other informative summaries preface the two formal reports that follow (see Figure 5-9 on page 112 and Figure 5-11 on pages 128 to 132) and the semiformal evaluation report in Figure 5-5 (see page 88).

But be careful: you need to avoid writing a *topical* summary. As its name implies, a topical summary simply describes the topics covered in the report without attempting to draw inferences or capture the reader's interest:

Topical Summary

...whereas a topical summary only suggests what can be found within a report

> Construction of the Minnowin Point Generating Station was initiated in 2007, and first power from the 1340 MW plant is scheduled for 2012. A general description of the structures and problems peculiar to the construction of this large development in an arctic climate is presented. The river diversion program, permafrost foundation conditions, and major equipment are described. The latter include the 16 propeller turbines, among the largest yet installed, each rated at 160 000 horsepower.

Because they are less results-oriented, topical summaries are *not* recommended.

Write the summary last, after you have written the remainder of your report. Only then will you be fully aware of the report's highlights, main conclusions, and recommendations, so you can draw on them to form your words. It should have a page to itself, be centred on the page, and be prefaced by the word "Summary." If it is very short, it may be indented equally on both sides to form a roughly square block of information. For examples, see pages 113 and 128.

Introduction

In the introduction you introduce the readers to the purpose and scope of the report, and provide sufficient background information to place them mentally in the picture before they tangle with technical data. A well-written introduction contains exactly the correct amount of detail to lead readers quickly into the major narrative.

The length of an introduction and its depth of detail depend mostly on how well you understand your readers' knowledge of the topic. If you know that the ultimate reader is technically knowledgeable, but at the same time you have to cater to the executive reader who is probably only partly technical, write the introduction (and conclusions and recommendations) in semitechnical language. This permits semitechnical executives to gain a reasonably comprehensive understanding of the report without reading the technical details contained in the discussion.

Knowing your reader influences the depth of detail required

Most introductions contain three parts: **purpose**, **scope**, and **background information**. Frequently the parts overlap, and occasionally one of them may be omitted because there is no reason to include it. Always start the **introduction** on a new page, with the report title at the top of the page. The heading Introduction can be either a centre heading or a side heading, as shown in Figure 5-6.

The **purpose** explains why the project was carried out and the report is being written. You may indicate that the project has been authorized to investigate a problem and recommend a solution, or possibly describe a new concept that you believe should be brought to the reader's attention.

The **scope** defines the parameters of the report. You describe the ground covered by the report and outline the method of investigation you used for the project. If there are limiting factors, you also identify them.

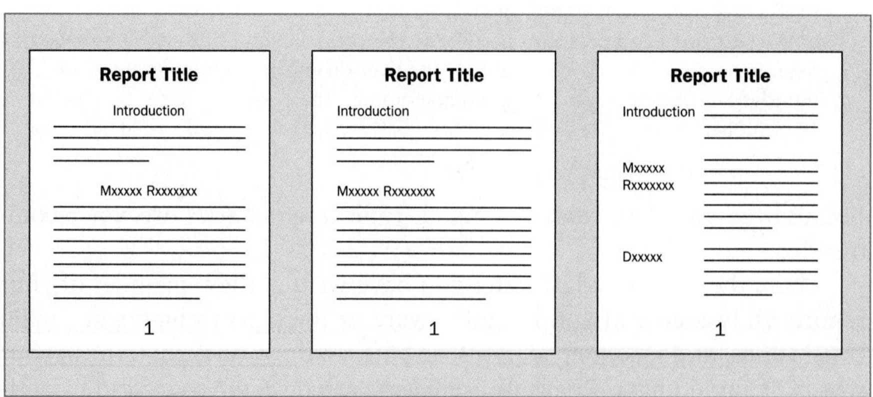

Figure 5-6 Different ways to integrate headings and text.

For example, if 18 methods for improving packaging are investigated in a project but only 4 are discussed in the report, you should explain which factors (such as cost, delivery time, and availability of space) limited the selection. Sometimes the scope may include a short glossary of terms that you need to define before your readers start to read the discussion.

Place a short glossary in the introduction, a longer glossary in an appendix

Background information comprises facts readers must know if they are to fully understand the discussion that follows. You may describe conditions or events that caused the project to be authorized, and details of previous investigations or reports on the same or a closely related subject. In a highly technical report, or when a significant time lapse has occurred between it and previous reports, your background information may also need to provide a theory review and references to other documents.

A good introduction "sets the scene"

The introductions shown here, plus those forming part of the two sample reports later in this chapter, represent the many ways a writer can introduce a topic.

Introduction 1

Background

Northern Railways plans to build a short-span bridge 1 km north of Peele Bay in Yukon and has a job lot of steel the company wants to use for constructing the bridge. In letter NR-70/LM dated March 20, 2010, Mr David L Harkness, Northern Area Manager, requested that H L Winman and Associates test a sample of this steel to determine its properties and to assess its suitability for use as structural members for a bridge in a very low temperature environment. Two Charpy impact tests were performed, one parallel to and the other transverse to the grain of the test specimen, at 10° increments from +22C down to –50C.

Introduction 2

Purpose

H L Winman and Associates was commissioned by Ms Rita M Durand, President and General Manager of Auto Drive-Inns Inc of Toronto, to select a Windsor, Ontario, site for the first of a proposed chain of computerized, automatic drive-in grocery outlets to be built in Canada. Windsor was chosen as the test site because it represents an average community in which to assess customer acceptance of such a service.

Say why you are writing...

...describe what has gone before, and...

Background

Aside from exterior façade and foundation details, Auto Drive-Inns are built to a standard 8.5 by 5.3 metre pattern with an order window at one end of the longer wall and a delivery window at the other end. Auto Drive-Inns carry only a limited selection of groceries, milk, and fruit, but boast 60-second service from the time an order is placed to its delivery at the other end of the building. For this reason, Auto Drive-Inns attract people hurrying home from work, the impulse buyer, and the late-night traveller, rather than the selective buyer. The Drive-Inns depend more on the volume of customers than on the volume of goods sold to each individual.

Scope

...explain factors affecting both the study and the report

The chief consideration in selecting a site must be a location on the homeward-bound side of a main trunk road serving a large residential area. The site must have quick and easy entry onto and exit from this road, even during peak rush-hour traffic. The residential area should be occupied mainly by single persons and younger families in which both parents work. And there should be little competition from walk-in grocery stores.

Discussion

The discussion is the longest part of a report, and so presents all the evidence (facts, arguments, details, data, and results of tests) that readers need to understand the subject. As a report writer, you need to organize this evidence logically and present it imaginatively so that it will hold their interest.

There are three ways you can build the discussion section of a report:

- by **chronological development**—in which you present information in the sequence that the events occurred.
- by **subject development**—in which you arrange information by subjects, grouped in a predetermined order.
- by **concept development**—in which you organize information by concept, presenting it as a series of ideas that imaginatively and coherently reveal how you reasoned your way to a logical conclusion.

Chronological Development

The chronological method is simple to organize and write: you simply arrange your information in the order that events occurred (but at the same time eliminate irrelevant information). This approach is most suitable for laboratory reports showing changes in a specimen, for progress reports showing cumulative effects, or for describing advances made by a project group. It works well when time is a factor, such as when reporting tests carried out over a five-year period on the effects of salt on concrete pavement. Your report would record the extent of erosion at specific intervals and how the erosion increased annually in direct relation to the amount of salt used to melt snow each year.

Chronological development is essentially factual

Subject Development

If the previous investigation had been broadened to include tests on different types of concrete pavements, or if both pure salt and various mixtures of salt and sand had been used, then the emphasis would have shifted to an analysis of erosion on different surfaces or caused by various salt–sand mixtures, rather than a direct description of the cumulative effects of pure salt. For this type of report you would arrange your information in *subject* order.

Subject development sorts information into groups

The subject order could be based on the extent of erosion with different concentrations of salt and sand, starting with a 100% concentration of salt, then continuing with salt–sand ratios of 90–10, 80–20, 70–30, and so on. Alternatively, you could select the different types of pavement as the subjects, arranging them in a specific order and describing the effects of different salt–sand concentrations on each surface.

With the subject method of development, you can often bring in a comparative analysis as described on pages 82–84.

Concept Development

By far the most interesting reports are those using the concept method of development. They need to be organized more carefully than reports using either of the previous methods, but the concept method can help you write creatively and imaginatively.

Concept development has the greatest potential for effectively organizing information

You can apply the concept method to your reports by thinking of each project as a logical but forceful procession of ideas. If you are presenting a concept (an idea, plan, method, or proposal) that readers are likely to accept, then you can use a straightforward four-step approach:

1. Describe your concept in a brief overview statement.
2. Discuss how and why your concept is valid; offer strong arguments in its favour, starting with the most important and working down to the least important.
3. Introduce negative aspects, and discuss how and why each can be overcome or is of limited importance.
4. Close with a restatement of your concept, its validity, and its usefulness.

But if you are presenting a controversial concept, or need to overcome reader bias, then you have to modify your approach by carefully establishing a strong case for your concept *before* you discuss it in detail. This means constantly anticipating your readers' likely reaction to your information.

Ella Watson used this approach in a report she prepared for her friend Paul Dobrin, owner and manager of an Edmonton company making extruded plastic and metal parts. Manufacturing costs had risen steeply over the past two years and Paul's prices had become uncompetitive. Paul thought he should replace some of his older, less efficient equipment, so he asked Ella to evaluate his needs.

Ella quickly realized that if Paul was to avoid going out of business he would have to replace much of his equipment with microprocessor-controlled machines, and do it soon. Because the cost would be high, he would have to lease rather than buy the new equipment.

The concept method leads the reader to the right answer...

In her report, Ella used a carefully reasoned argument to prove to Paul that he needed a lot of new equipment and that the only feasible way he could acquire it would be to lease it. Throughout, Ella wrote objectively but sincerely about her findings, hoping that the logic of her argument would swing Paul around to accepting her recommendation. Here is the step-by-step approach she used:

- She opened with a summary that told Paul that to avoid bankruptcy he would have to invest in a lot of expensive equipment and make extensive changes in his operating methods.
- She produced financial projections to prove her opening statement, and then described the productivity and profitability necessary for Paul to remain in business.
- Ella showed why Paul's equipment and methods were inefficient, introduced the changes Paul would have to make, established why each change was necessary, and demonstrated how each would improve productivity.
- Then she introduced two sets of cost figures: one for making the minimum changes necessary for Paul's business to survive, and the second for more comprehensive changes that would ensure a sound operating basis for the future. She also commented that both would require capital purchases likely to be beyond Paul's financial resources.

...carefully tracing a logical, persuasive, and sometimes intricate path

- Ella outlined alternative financing methods available to Paul, the implications and limitations of each, and the financial effect each would have on Paul's business. (She included leasing but made no attempt to persuade Paul that he would have to lease; she let the figures speak for themselves.)
- Ella concluded by summarizing the main points she had made: that new equipment *must* be acquired; that to buy even the minimum

equipment was beyond the company's financial resources; and that, of the financing methods available, leasing was the most feasible.

- In her recommendation, Ella suggested that Paul make comprehensive changes and lease the new equipment.

Even though the concept method challenges a writer to fashion interesting reports, it is not always the best reporting medium. When a topic and the outcome are clear-cut, there is no need to lead the reader through a lengthy "this is how I thought it out" discussion. Reserve the concept method for topics that are controversial, difficult to understand, or likely to meet reader resistance.

Avoid Clutter

Keep the narrative simple and uncluttered

Whichever method you use, avoid cluttering the discussion with detailed supporting information. Unless tables, graphs, illustrations, photographs, statistics, and test results are essential for reader understanding while the report is being read, banish them to an appendix. But always refer to them in the discussion, like this:

> The test results attached as Appendix C show that aircraft on a bearing of 265°T experienced considerably weaker reception than aircraft on any other bearing. This was attributed to...

Readers *interested only in results* will consider that this statement tells them enough and continue reading the report. Readers interested in *knowing how the results were obtained*—who want to see the overall picture—will turn to Appendix C.

If an illustration or table is essential, try to extract the key points from an appendix and use them to create a miniature illustration or table that you can insert beside or embed into the narrative.

Unless the discussion is very short, divide it into a series of sections that are each preceded by an informative heading. After each heading, start the section with an overview statement to describe what the section is about and suggest what conclusion will be drawn from it. (Overview statements are miniature summaries that direct a reader's attention to the point you want to make.) And then, at the end of each major section, insert a concluding statement that summarizes the results of the discussion within that section. From these section conclusions you can later draw your main conclusions.

Conclusions

There should be no surprises here

Conclusions briefly state the major inferences you have drawn from the discussion. You must base them entirely on previously stated information. *Never* surprise readers by introducing new material or evidence to support your argument. If there is more than one conclusion, state the main conclusion first and follow it with the remaining conclusions in decreasing order of importance. This is shown in the two examples below, which present the same conclusions in both narrative and tabular form.

Narrative Conclusion

If we upgrade to version 4.1 of the *Mosaic* software, we will also have to upgrade our operating system. The one-time cost will be $7600, but we will increase our multimedia production capability by 65%.

Tabular Conclusion

If we upgrade to version 4.1 of the *Mosaic* software, we will

- experience a 65% increase in our multimedia production capability,
- have to upgrade our operating system, and
- incur a one-time cost of $7600.

Because conclusions are *opinions* (based on the evidence presented in the discussion), they must never tell the reader what to do. This task must always be left to the recommendations.

Recommendations

***Now* you can let your voice be heard**

Recommendations appear in a report when the discussion and conclusions indicate that further work needs to be done, or when you have described several ways to resolve a problem or improve a situation and want to identify which is best. Write recommendations in strong, definite terms to convince readers that the course of action you advocate is valid. Use the first person and active verbs, as has been done here:

Strong I recommend that we build a five-station prototype of the Microvar system and test it operationally.

Compare this with the same but much weaker recommendation written in the third person, using passive verbs:

Weak It is recommended that a five-station prototype of the Microvar system be built and tested under operational conditions.

If you feel you cannot use the personal "I," try using the plural "we," to indicate that the recommendations represent the company's viewpoint. For example,

Strong We recommend building a five-station prototype of the Microvar system. We also recommend that you

1. install the prototype in Railton High School,
2. commission a physics teacher experienced in writing programmed instruction manuals to write the first programs, and
3. test the system operationally for three months.

And no surprises here, either!

Because recommendations must be based solidly on the evidence presented in the discussion and conclusions, they must *never* introduce new evidence or new ideas.

Appendices

Place related data not necessary to an immediate understanding of the discussion farther back in the report, in the appendices. The data can vary from a complicated table of electrical test results to a simple photograph of a blown transistor. The appendices are a suitable place for manufacturers' specifications, graphs, analytical data, drawings, sketches, excerpts from other reports or books, cost analyses, and correspondence. There is no limit to what you can place in the appendices, providing that the information is relevant and you refer to it in the discussion.

The appendix is *not* a storage place for information that only *might* be useful

The importance of an appendix has no bearing on its position in the report. Whichever set of data is mentioned first in the discussion becomes Appendix A, the next set becomes Appendix B, and so on. Each appendix is considered a separate document complete in itself and is paginated separately, with its front page labelled 1. An example of an appendix appears at the end of Formal Report 1, in Figure 5-9 on page 125.

Subsidiary Parts

In addition to the six major parts of a formal report, there are several additional parts that perform more routine functions. Although referred to here as "subsidiary," they nevertheless contribute much to a report's effectiveness.

Cover

Almost every major formal report has a cover. It may be made of glossy cardboard printed in multiple colours and bound with a dressy plastic binding, or it may be only a light cover of coloured fibre material stapled on the left side. The cover not only informs readers of the report's main topic but also conveys an image of the company that originated it. This "matching" of subject matter and company image plays an important part in setting the correct tone.

The cover should reflect the company's image

The cover should contain the report title, the name of the originating company and, perhaps, the name of its author. The title should be set in bold letters centred horizontally on the page and separated from any other information.

The choice of title is particularly important. It should be short yet informative, implying that the report has a worthwhile story to tell. Compare the vague title below with the more informative version beneath it.

The report title should capture readers' interest

Original vague title

Radome Leakage

Revised informative title

Porosity of Fibreglass Causes Radome Leakage

Title Page

The title page normally carries four main pieces of information: the report title (the same title that appears on the cover); the name of the person, company, or organization for whom the report has been prepared; the name of the company originating the report (sometimes with the author's name); and the date the report was completed. It may also contain the contract number, a report number, a security classification such as CONFIDENTIAL or SECRET, and a copy number (important reports given only limited distribution are sometimes assigned copy numbers to control and document their issue). All this information must be tastefully arranged on the page, as has been done in the full report in Figure 5-9 on page 112.

Table of Contents

If the T of C seems sparse or disjointed, check that the report narrative has sufficient *descriptive* headings

All but very short reports contain a table of contents (T of C). The T of C not only lists the report's contents, but also tells readers how the report has been arranged.

The pleasing arrangement for a T of C on page 114 uses the single word **Contents** rather than "Table of Contents"; we recommend the shorter title. The contents page also contains a list of appendices, with each identified by its full title. In long reports you may also insert a list of illustrations and their page numbers between the T of C and the list of appendices.

The introductory pages to a report (i.e. the summary and contents pages) are numbered using lower case Roman numerals. All other parts of the report are numbered with Arabic numerals, starting with the **introduction**, which becomes page 1.

Your word-processing software can prepare your T of C for you automatically as you type your report. Be aware, however, that such software may insert a line of dots between each entry and the page number. This is unfortunate, because you will read in many technical writing handbooks that the line of dots should be omitted. The handbook guideline probably will be changed in future years.

References (Endnotes), Bibliography, and Footnotes

Accurate documentation of information sources is essential

A report writer who refers to another document, such as a textbook, journal article, report, or correspondence, or to other persons' data or even a conversation, must identify the source of this information in the report. To avoid cluttering the report narrative with extensive cross-references, the reference details normally are placed in a storage area at the end of the report. This storage area is known as a list of references or a bibliography.

In a **List of References** you type the entries as a sequentially numbered list at the end of the narrative sections of the report (usually immediately ahead of the appendices). Such numbered references are sometimes referred to as *endnotes*. For a short example, see page 124. (Footnotes, which are printed at the foot of the page on which the particular reference appears, are seldom used in contemporary reports.)

In a **Bibliography** you list many of the documents you used to research and conduct your project. You list them in alphabetical order of authors' surnames, and place the list at the end of the report narrative. A bibliography may list many more documents than are referred to in the report.

For the eighth edition of *Technically-Write!* we have moved the section on writing references and bibliographies to become Appendix A: Guidelines for Writing Source References, starting on page 299. We have done this because source-referencing can occur in many types of documents, not just long reports.

Cover Letter

A cover letter introduces a report to its readers. The following cover letter accompanied the report on elevators in Figure 5-11 (see pages 128 to 132).

Dear Mr Merrywell

We enclose our report No. 8-23, "Selecting New Elevators for the Merrywell Building," which has been prepared in response to your letter LDR/71/007 dated April 27, 2010.

If you would like us to submit a design for the enlarged elevator shaft, or to manage the installation project on your behalf, we shall be glad to be of service.

Sincerely

Barry V Kingsley

H L Winman and Associates

A cover letter is often only one or two short paragraphs...

Some cover letters include comments that draw attention to key factors described in the report or that evolve from it, and sometimes summarize or interpret the report's main findings. This is done in the cover letter preceding the "Heating System" report in this chapter (see Figure 5-8 on page 111).

Executive Summary

An executive summary is an analytical summary of the purpose of the report, its main findings and conclusions, and the author's recommendations. Unlike the normal report summary prepared for all readers, the executive summary can present detailed information on aspects of particular concern to senior executives, and often may discuss financial implications. An executive summary can be presented in two ways: externally, as a letter pinned to the outside front of the report; or internally, as an integral part of the report.

...whereas an executive summary usually has two or more paragraphs

If the executive summary is attached to the report like a cover letter,

An integral executive summary rarely contains sensitive or confidential information

the recipient may remove it before circulating the report to other readers. This permits you to make comments that are intended only for that reader's eyes, or to deal with sensitive issues that for political reasons should not be discussed in the body of the report. The executive summary preceding the "Heating System" report serves this purpose (see Figure 5-8 on page 111).

If, however, the executive summary is bound within the report so that it will be read by everyone, its purpose becomes more general and you simply summarize and perhaps comment on the report's major findings. Rather than writing a letter, you type the words **Executive Summary** at the top of the page and then write the summary like a short report.

An executive summary may also precede a major technical proposal, in which a company describes how it can successfully tackle a task at an economical price for the government or another company (see Chapter 6).

The Complete Formal Report

The Main Parts

The same information, but two ways to arrange it

The two reports on the following pages are typical of the quality of writing and presentation that the technical business industry expects of engineering, science, and computer graduates. The first report is presented in the traditional arrangement (see Table 5-3), and the second in the contemporary, "pyramidal" arrangement. In each case the parts of the report remain the same, but their sequence changes. The reports are typed single-spaced with a clear space between paragraphs, which is the style preferred by industry. In comparison, academic institutions tend to prefer double spacing throughout.

Traditional Arrangement of Report Parts

(Conclusions and Recommendations *after* the Discussion)

In the traditional arrangement there is a logical flow of information: the **introduction** leads into the **discussion**, from which you draw **conclusions** and make **recommendations** (the two latter parts are sometimes referred to jointly as the **terminal summary**).

Formal Report 1: Installing a Radiant Energy Heating System for Hartwell Enterprises Ltd

The author of this report (Figure 5-8 on page 111 and Figure 5-9 on page 112) is Karen Woodhouse, an engineer working for H L Winman and Associates. She chose to break with tradition and automatically justify the right margin (make it vertically straight).

Table 5-3 The main parts of the formal report organized in the traditional arrangement.

Cover:	Jacket of report; contains title of report and name of originating company; its quality and use of colour reflect company image.
Title Page:	First page of report; contains title of report, name of addressee or recipient, author's name and company, date, and sometimes a report number.
Summary:	An abridged version of whole report, written in nontechnical terms; *very* short and informative; normally describes salient features of report, draws a main conclusion, and makes a recommendation; always written last, after remainder of report has been written.
Table of Contents:	Shows contents and arrangement of report; includes a list of appendices and, sometimes, a list of illustrations.
Introduction:	Prepares reader for discussion to come, indicates purpose and scope of report, and provides background information so reader can read discussion intelligently.
Discussion:	A narrative that provides all the details, evidence, and data needed by the reader to understand what the author was trying to do, what the author actually did and found out, and what the author thinks should be done next.
Conclusions:	A summary of the major conclusions or milestones reached in the discussion; conclusions are only opinions, so can never advocate action.
Recommendations:	If the discussion and conclusions suggest that specific action needs to be taken, the recommendations state categorically what must be done.
References:	A list of reference documents that were used to complete the project and that the author considers will be useful to the reader; contains sufficient information for the reader to correctly identify and order the documents.
Appendices:	A storage area at the back of the report that contains supporting data (such as charts, tables, photographs, specifications, and test results) that rightly belong in the discussion but, if included with it, would disrupt and clutter the major narrative.

The traditional arrangement provides a continuous narrative

Sometimes the appendices are bulkier than the rest of the report

Comments on the Report Writer's Approach

To understand the circumstances leading up to the report, first read Mark Hesseltine's letter of authorization in Figure 5-7 on page 108. Mark is an architect with No. 5 Design Group who has designed a new building for Hartwell Enterprises Ltd, a specialty manufacturer in Peterborough, Ontario. His client has expressed interest in having radiant energy heating installed in the new building. Because No. 5 Design Group does not have radiant energy expertise in-house, Mark contracts with H L Winman and Associates to evaluate the practicability and cost of installing such a system. The task was assigned to Karen Woodhouse.

Check before you place your hands on the keyboard: the person you are writing to may not be your primary reader

Although Mark would *appear* to be Karen's primary reader, in reality it would be the executives at Hartwell Enterprises. Rather than rewrite Karen's report, Mark would prefer to briefly list its main points in his report, and then include Karen's report as an attachment. Consequently, Karen tailored her approach to suit nontechnical readers and included

The four bulleted items became Karen Woodhouse's project criteria

No. 5 Design Group

240 Victoria Drive – Suite 300
Burlington, Ontario L7R 1R5
Tel: 905 234 1786; Fax: 234 1807
email: mhesseltine@5design.com

November 26, 2010

Vern Rogers, Manager
H L Winman and Associates
970 Birchmount Road
Scarborough ON M1P 3J6

Dear Mr Rogers

As we discussed by telephone earlier today, we are commissioning H L Winman and Associates to prepare a report on the practicability of installing a radiant heating system in the new office and assembly plant we are designing for Hartwell Enterprises Ltd of Peterborough, Ontario. The plant is to be built at the northwest corner of the intersection of Seymour Drive and Graveley Street, with construction starting on April 1, 2011 (see the attached preliminary design).

Our client has indicated interest in radiant heating but needs substantive information before deciding on installing such a system. Consequently, in your report will you please describe

- how radiant heat works and how it differs from traditional heating methods,
- the advantages of installing and using radiant heat,
- the cost to install radiant heat, compared to traditional heating systems, and
- the savings to be accrued by Hartwell Enterprises over, say, a five-year period.

Your contact at Hartwell Enterprises will be operations manager Vincent Correlli. He is aware that you are preparing a study for us and will be ready to answer questions about their operation.

I would appreciate receiving your report by January 10, 2011, because we will be submitting our design to Hartwell Enterprises on January 17. Please call me if you have any questions.

Sincerely

Mark Hesseltine

Mark Hesseltine
Design Associate
No. 5 Design Group

Figure 5-7 Letter authorizing the report in Figures 5-8 and 5-9.

more information than she would have done if she had been writing solely for No. 5 Design Group. **Clearly identifying the reader is an essential first step when writing a comprehensive report.**

Karen also wrote the report *backwards*, which helped her organize her information more effectively. This was her approach:

1. First, she collected data on the three heating systems she would be evaluating, and researched comparative costs with experts in the radiant energy field: Darryl Berkowski in Winnipeg, Manitoba, and Vincent Harding in London, Ontario.
2. Then Karen created a table showing the relative costs of each system (this table became the report's Appendix, on page 125). From this table she also developed smaller tables identifying specific cost factors (these appear in the report's Discussion, on report page 8).
3. Next, she created two sets of illustrations depicting installation and operating costs at one, three, and five years: first a series of bar charts and then a series of graphs. From these she chose the graph in Figure 3 (on report page 9) as the most descriptive and simplest to read.
4. Karen's fourth step was to write the Introduction, to "set the scene." Here, she drew on information in No. 5 Design Group's letter of authorization to establish the background to the report, and its purpose and scope. She knew her primary readers would not have seen the letter.
5. Next, Karen wrote a preliminary outline, which was really an early version of the Table of Contents on page 114. She used this as a loose guide for structuring the report, making changes to it as she wrote.
6. Because her readers would not be knowledgeable about radiant energy heating, she wrote a comprehensive general description, which became the first four pages of the Discussion (see report pages 1 to 4).
7. Next she wrote the comparisons and analyses, using the charts and tables she had prepared earlier.
8. Now Karen wrote the Conclusions. She went back to the Introduction and identified the three questions she had been particularly asked to address, and provided answers to them.
9. She deliberated on whether to write a Recommendation. The authorizing letter did not specifically ask for a recommendation yet she felt that, because she had researched the information and as such was the local expert, she should identify what route she felt Hartwell Enterprises should take.
10. And *last*, Karen wrote the Summary, drawing principally on the Conclusions to compose it.

Writing in reverse order may seem unnatural, yet it results in a better report

Sometimes inserting a recommendation is optional

Remember Karen's "backwards" approach when you have to write your next long report. By documenting all the details *first*, you will find you can organize your ideas much more easily and write more fluidly.

Comments on the Report

Karen's report is in Figure 5-9, on pages 112 to 125, and is preceded by the cover letter in Figure 5-8. The comments below refer to specific parts of the report.

- Karen's cover letter is equivalent to an executive summary because she comments on the report's contents. Because she knows the cover letter will be seen only by Mark Hesseltine, she uses a friendly tone and the first person "I."
- A quick glance at the Contents (report page ii) tells Karen's readers that she has organized her information into a logical, coherent flow, and that there are three main components: background information on radiant energy systems; a plan for installing a radiant energy heating system in the client's building; and a cost projection and analysis.
- In the Introduction (report page 1), the Background is in paragraph 1, the Purpose is in paragraph 2, and the Scope is in the three bulleted points.
- For the Discussion (starting at the bottom of report page 1), Karen has adopted an overall "concept" arrangement of information, but internally it breaks into a subject arrangement when describing the proposed installation and some of the costs.

Writing in the first person means making a decision: "I" or "we"?

- She has written the entire report in the first person plural. "When I am presenting the results of a study I have done personally," she explained, "and I am writing directly to my client, then normally I would use the first person singular: 'I.' But when I am writing on behalf of the company, and simultaneously writing for my client's client, and don't know the client personally, then I use the first person plural: 'We.'"
- The Conclusions, on report pages 9 and 10, are longer than normal because they have to cover all the points the client requested. They show the advantages and disadvantages of radiant energy heating but do *not* advocate what action should be taken. Karen has taken care not to introduce new information into her Conclusions.
- The Recommendation advocates action and does so in strong, definite terms, using "We recommend…" rather than "It is recommended…."
- The Appendix is a *landscape-view* page, and as such has been turned correctly so that the top of the appendix is on the left side of the page (see page 125).

H L WINMAN AND ASSOCIATES

970 Birchmount Road, Scarborough, ON M1P 3J6
email: kwoodhouse@winman.on.ca

January 7, 2011

Mark Hesseltine
Design Associate
No. 5 Design Group
240 Victoria Drive, Suite 300
Burlington ON L7R 1R5

Dear Mark

I am enclosing our report, *Installing a Radiant Energy Heating System for Hartwell Enterprises Ltd*, as requested in your letter of November 26, 2010. The report shows that in the long term radiant energy will be the most economical heating system for Hartwell Enterprises' new building.

To some extent I am concerned that Hartwell Enterprises may hesitate when they see the high front-end cost, particularly in comparison to electric heat. Hence, I have taken care to include a graph which shows clearly that radiant energy heating will be particularly efficient from a cost viewpoint after the fourth year. If the graph on page 9 were to be extended for another five years, the considerably lower operating cost of radiant energy heating would be even more noticeable. You may want to address this factor in your proposal.

Inserting this second paragraph converted Karen's cover letter into an executive summary

Please call me if you need further information on any of the points addressed by the report. I'll be glad to supply it.

Sincerely

Karen Woodhouse

Karen Woodhouse, P.Eng
enc

Figure 5-8 Cover letter/executive summary accompanying the formal report in Figure 5-9.

The appearance of the title page subtly comments on the quality of the information you are presenting

H L WINMAN AND ASSOCIATES

Installing a Radiant Energy Heating System for Hartwell Enterprises Ltd

Prepared for

No. 5 Design Group
Burlington, Ontario

Prepared by

Karen Woodhouse, P.Eng
H L Winman and Associates
Scarborough, Ontario

January 7, 2011

Figure 5-9 Formal Report 1: traditional arrangement (14 pages; full report minus cover page).

Summary

We have evaluated three methods for heating the proposed Hartwell Enterprises Ltd plant designed by No. 5 Design Group for construction in Peterborough, Ontario. Electric heat is the least expensive to install but the most expensive to operate. Gas-fired forced hot air is moderately expensive to install and moderately expensive to operate. Radiant energy heating is the most expensive to install and the least expensive to operate. Long term, however, radiant energy offers the most efficient and cost-effective method.

Installing a radiant energy heating system in a new building means the system can be incorporated into the overall design so that it becomes unobtrusive as well as efficient and cost-effective. It also provides more gentle warming than the other two methods, and the temperature in each area of the building can be controlled separately. The operating cost will be 39% less than for electric heating, and 30% less than for gas-fired hot air heating.

The Summary: the full story in a capsule—difficult to write!

i

The preliminary pages bear Roman page numbers; all other pages carry Arabic numbers

Contents

If more than one appendix, the title changes to "Appendices" and each appendix is identified by a letter: "A," "B," "C," etc.

Appendix

ii

Installing a Radiant Energy Heating System for Hartwell Enterprises Ltd

Introduction

Hartwell Enterprises Ltd assembles and packages modules and specialty products for public and private organizations such as the Department of Defence, NavCan, Multiple Industries Limited, and Northern Paging and Cellular Systems. The company does no original manufacturing itself, confining its role to assembling components supplied by carefully chosen manufacturers. Hartwell Enterprises Ltd has built a solid reputation as a fast, high-quality producer of specialty systems, and the company's business has increased steadily since its inception in 1988. Today, it needs a larger building, but research for suitable accommodation among Peterborough area properties has failed to find a building that can be adapted to the company's special needs.

The Introduction establishes why the project was undertaken and the report has been written

In August 2010, Hartwell Enterprises Ltd commissioned No. 5 Design Group of Burlington, Ontario, to design a building that will meet the company's particular requirements, and to find a site on which to place it. No. 5 Design Group has, in turn, asked H L Winman and Associates to evaluate the efficacy and cost to install a radiant heating system in the new building, rather than a more traditional heating method. Specifically, they asked us to describe

- how radiant heat works and how it differs from traditional heating methods,
- the advantages of and the cost to install a radiant heating system, and
- the savings to be accrued by Hartwell Enterprises Ltd over the first five years.

These requirements were copied almost verbatim from the client's letter of authorization

Radiant Heating vs Traditional Heating

A traditional heating system warms air directly, which we feel on our skin as immediate heat, but its impact is transitory. Turn off the source of the heat, and the space being warmed immediately starts to cool. On a winter's day, for example, a residential furnace pumps hot air into the rooms until a preset temperature is reached, then the thermostat switches off the furnace. The

1

warming effect stops immediately and the air temperature, influenced by cooler windows and walls, begins to drop.

A radiant heating system, rather than warming air directly, radiates heat outwards in all directions until the rays contact another surface. If the surface is cooler than the radiant panel, the surface begins to warm up and the air near to it also warms, but gently, and so our skin feels the warmth as a gentle, comfortable heating. On a cool winter's day, a furnace pumps heat into the radiant panels as hot water or they are heated electrically until a preset room temperature is reached, when the source of the heat is switched off. The warming effect, however, does not stop immediately because the radiant panel continues to radiate residual heat for a considerable time. Consequently, the air in the room cools much more slowly than with hot air heating.

Comparing a complex technical concept to a familiar everyday event helps reader understanding

Compare the difference in heat produced by a gas ring and an electric hotplate. The gas ring provides immediate heat to the surrounding air, but the heat stops immediately when the gas is switched off. The electric hotplate builds up its heat more slowly, but *continues to radiate heat* for 10 to 15 minutes after the electricity is switched off.

A 100% radiant heating system is ideal for locations that are unlikely to be affected by external sources that cause sudden changes in temperature. Yet it still can be effective in areas that are subjected to such changes, such as an aircraft hangar. Lawrence Drake, Executive Director of the Radiant Panel Association, explains that

> Thermal mass in a heated shop or hangar floor responds rapidly to the change of air temperature when a big overhead door is opened. All the heat that has been "trickled" into the slab over time is released quickly to combat the cold air rolling in over the floor. This happens because of the sudden, dramatic increase in temperature difference between the slab and the new air. Once the door is closed the building returns to its normal comfort setting almost immediately.[1]

He adds, however, that under such conditions a combination of radiant energy and a back-up hot air heating system can be even more effective, because occupants of the space immediately feel the heated air.

2

Darryl Berkowski, who installs radiant heating systems in Manitoba and Northwestern Ontario, points out that electric or hot water baseboard heaters may *appear* to produce radiant heat, but in effect they release only a small amount of radiant energy. Primarily, they heat the air.[2]

A statement made in an email message or during a conversation may be documented as a source reference

A particular advantage of radiant heating is that *it can be controlled locally*. In a traditional heating system, hot air is supplied to vents, or hot water to radiators, from a central furnace, the operation of which is controlled by a single thermostat mounted on a wall of only one of the rooms. Thus, the temperature in the other rooms cannot be controlled separately. If, for example, one of the rooms tends to be cooler than the others because it has large windows on a north wall, the heating system is unable to compensate for the variation. Conversely, in a radiant heating system the heat supplied to the radiant panels can be controlled separately in each room. This is true of radiant panels heated either electrically or by hot water.

Radiant Panel Installations

Radiant heating panels may be installed in the wall, ceiling, or floor. Because they heat all objects within their line of sight, floor panels heat the ceiling and walls, wall panels heat the opposite wall, and ceiling panels heat the floor and walls. Similarly, all three heat furniture they can "see" and, of course, the people in the room. The radiant energy is felt as a very gentle, subtle warming, never as a searing blast.

Generally, wall panels tend to be smaller than ceiling panels, and ceiling panels tend to be smaller than floor panels, which often use the whole floor as their radiating surface. Also generally, the smaller the panel the greater the temperature at which it must operate to gain a measurable effect. Consequently, wall panels may be as hot as 65°C, ceiling panels as warm as 40°C, but floor panels rarely exceed 25°C. Lawrence Drake writes that

> A heated floor normally "feels" neutral. Its surface temperature is usually less than our body temperature, although the overall sensation is one of comfort. Only on very cold days when the floor is called on for maximum output will it actually "feel" warm.
>
> Heat coming from a wall radiator can be felt the closer you get to it because its surface is much warmer than your body. Radiant ceiling

Introducing excerpts from an existing document adds credibility to a report

3

panels are also generally warmer than your body so you will feel some warmth on your head and shoulders.[3]

Wall and ceiling panels usually come preassembled and are fixed onto the surface of the wall or ceiling. Floor panels normally are embedded in the floor, as part of the floor construction, and then are covered with a layer of concrete or similar floor material. Consequently the whole floor becomes a single, large radiant panel.

When installed as an integral part of a new installation, either electric elements or water pipes are laid in continuous parallel rows in the floor (see Figure 1). The pipes are made of a strong, durable, light, cross-linked polyethylene (PEX). Connectors are made of noncorroding copper, brass, or plastic.

Although it's possible to install a radiant heating system as a retrofit in an existing building, the ideal arrangement is to design a radiant heating system specifically for a new building. It can then be installed as an integral part of the new structure.

A cutaway illustration like this helps readers visualize the technology

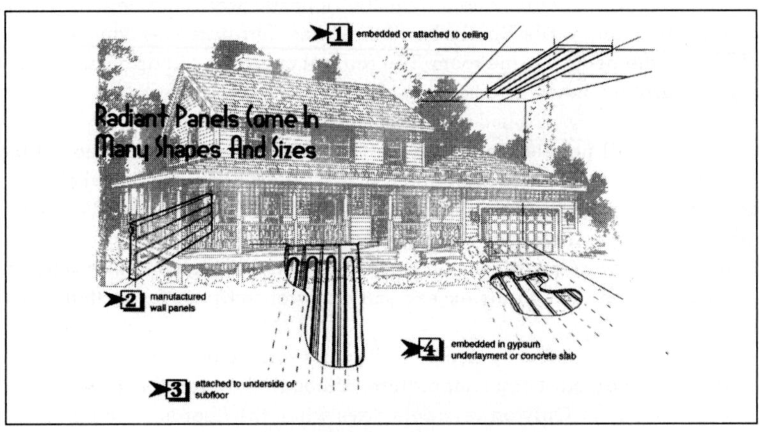

Figure 1. Various types of radiant energy panels
(Illustration courtesy of Radiant Panel Association)

4

Suggested Installation Plan for the Proposed Hartwell Enterprises Building

Hartwell Enterprises' operation is unique, in that it works on a just-in-time method of delivery for the components that are assembled into products. The company's contracts with its suppliers stipulate that components are to be delivered in small lots only a few hours before they are to be assembled. This has two major effects:

Research into a client's business practices can help you focus information accurately

1. Because components are moved rapidly from the delivery semitrailer to the assembly line, and then to the shipping area for packing and storing in a second semitrailer ready for shipping, Hartwell Enterprises requires only a small warehouse area.

2. Because the loading bay doors have to be opened frequently, the loading bay demands special attention from a heating viewpoint.

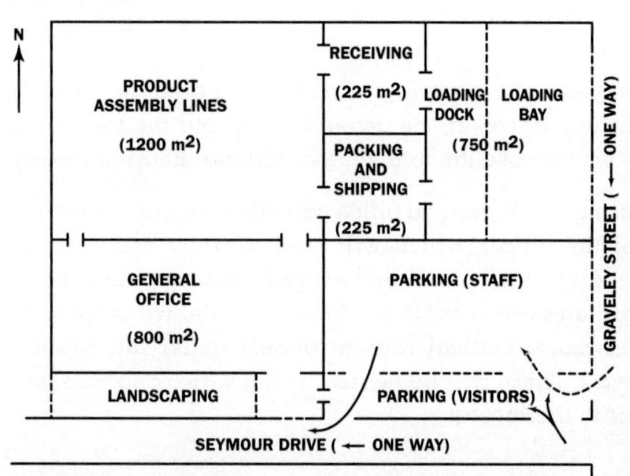

Figure 2. Design of proposed new building for Hartwell Enterprises Ltd

Proposed Heating System

The proposed Hartwell Enterprises building particularly lends itself to heating by radiant energy. The diverse activities in the various parts of the building call for different types and methods of heating. As Figure 2 shows, there will be five main areas of activity, each requiring a different level and form of heating, and each with its own thermostat. The floor in each area will be concrete, but there will be some variations:

The scene has been set: now for the plan!

5

- The general office will have a 0.20 metre thick slab with its upper surface 0.35 metres above grade. It will be covered by Orlando carpet and underlay.

- The product assembly, receiving, and shipping areas will be set on a 0.20 metre thick slab with the floor level at 1.3 metres above grade. There will be basement under these three areas, with a 2.2 metre high ceiling.

- The unloading and loading bays will be at grade level, built on a 0.35 metre reinforced concrete slab.

As the primary source of heat for these areas, we propose installing hot-water pipes embedded in the concrete with a separate circulation system and thermostat for each area. The mechanical room for the hot water boiler and the controls will be set up in the basement. (We are not recommending electrically heated panels, because in Southern Ontario it is on average 20% more expensive to heat the radiant panels by electricity than by natural-gas-fired hot water.[4])

The main paragraphs contain the plan...

The product assembly, receiving, and shipping areas will require no supplementary heating. However, the general office and the loading bays will. For these areas we propose the following additional heating arrangements.

- The ceiling in the general office will slope upward, toward the north (the back of the office), which will tend to draw warm air aloft, into the higher part of the ceiling and away from the south side of the area. To maintain an even warmth on the south side, we propose installing two 1.5×0.8 metre vertical radiant panels under the windows along the south wall. These will be heated by hot water and will be controlled by a separate thermostat.

...while the bulleted subparagraphs introduce variations and exceptions

- The loading bays will cool rapidly in winter when the doors are opened to admit and exit semitrailers. Here we propose installing two overhead hot air heaters, one above each door. They also will be hot-water heaters, and the blowers will be triggered to start up when a door opens and to shut down when a predetermined ambient temperature is reached. (In effect, the radiant energy from the floor panels will restore the temperature quite quickly; the hot air heaters will provide a supplementary, readily noticeable, immediate source of extra heat during extreme cold conditions.)

6

Proposed Cooling System

Although radiant energy panels can provide moderate cooling in the summer, particularly in dry climates, in moist or semimoist conditions they tend to be less efficient.[5] Consequently we propose that all cooling be carried out through a separate system, comprising

- a Hyperion Model 2000 air conditioning unit for cooling the general office, product assembly, and receiving and shipping areas, and
- a Hyperion Model 2720 air conditioning unit for cooling the loading bay.

The two air conditioners will be located in the basement, with the model 2000 at the west end and the model 2720 at the east end. The model 2000 will feed cooled air through ductwork concealed in the ceiling of the office, assembly, and receiving/shipping areas. The model 2720, which will be a fast-response unit designed to recover quickly from rapid changes in temperature, will feed cooled air through ductwork under the roof of the loading bay.

Costs: Radiant vs Traditional Heating

Two cost factors have to be considered when comparing a radiant energy heating system with a traditional heating system: the cost of installation and the cost of operation. The cost of installing and operating air conditioning from May to September also has to be taken into account.

A section-opening paragraph should act like a mini-summary, identifying aspects to be discussed

For this study, we have examined the cost of installing and operating three systems:

1. Radiant energy heating, plus a separate air-conditioning system.
2. All-electric heating, plus a separate air-conditioning system.
3. Forced hot air heating fuelled by natural gas, with integral air conditioning.

Installation Costs

The costs to install these three systems in the proposed Hartwell Enterprises building are listed in Table 1, which at first glance shows that electric heating is the least expensive and radiant energy is the most expensive. However, when air conditioning is included, gas-fired hot air becomes the least expensive.

7

Table 1 lists key cost figures, providing a ready comparison

Table 1. Installation Costs

System	Heating System ($)	Air Conditioning ($)	Total ($)
Radiant energy	47 200	21 600	68 800
All-electric plus air conditioning	26 600	21 600	48 200
Gas-fired hot air with integral air conditioning	38 700	(incl)	38 700

Annual Operating Costs

To calculate potential operating costs, we referred to a 2008 study carried out by Vincent Harding of V Harding Associates, in which he averaged the annual heating costs of 30 industrial buildings in Ontario, Manitoba, and Saskatchewan for the years 2002 to 2007.[6] From these we culled the heating costs for eight light-industry buildings in Southern Ontario, each of a similar size to the proposed 3200 m^2 Hartwell Enterprises Building. Two are heated by electricity, three by gas-fired forced hot air, and three by radiant energy. The results are summarized in Table 2, which shows that radiant energy heating has the lowest annual operating cost and all-electric heating has the highest annual operating cost. A detailed breakdown is shown in the Appendix.

A simple table with key cost figures can be embedded conveniently into the narrative

Table 2. Average Annual Operating Costs

System	Heating Only ($)	With Air Conditioning ($)
Radiant energy	17 300	20 800
All-electric	31 700	35 200
Gas-fired forced hot air	27 600	31 100

Projected Costs over Five Years

In Figure 3, the combined installation and operating costs for both heating and cooling are shown for year one, and then the projected operating costs for heating and cooling are shown cumulatively for years two through five. The graph shows that in the first year the installation and operating cost for electric heating is the least expensive, and radiant energy is the most expensive. However, after one year and five months the positions are reversed, with the cumulative costs of installing and operating radiant energy heating becoming less expensive than electric heating.

Installing and operating a gas-fired forced hot air heating and air-conditioning system remains less expensive than radiant energy for the first three years and two months, after which the cumulative cost of radiant energy heating plus a companion air-conditioning system becomes more economical.

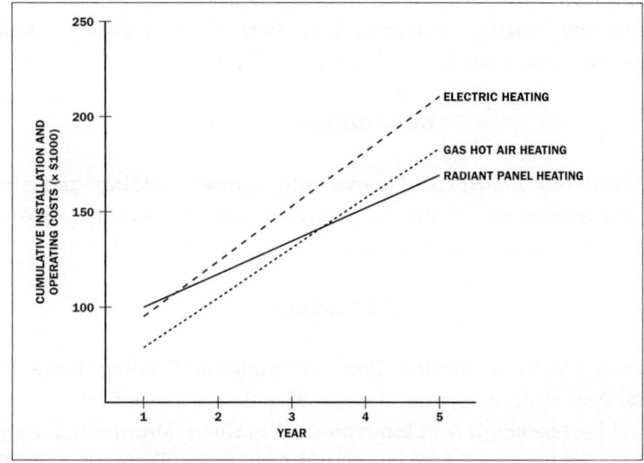

Figure 3. Comparison of installation and operating costs over five years, for radiant energy, hot air, and electric heating systems

Both this graph and the two previous tables are supported by the detailed cost comparison in the Appendix

Conclusions

A radiant energy heating system offers several advantages for the proposed Hartwell Enterprises Ltd office and product assembly plant planned for 1650 Seymour Drive in Peterborough, Ontario:

Conclusions sum up key outcomes but never specifically advocate action

9

- Its operating cost will be 39% less expensive than for electric heating, and 30% less expensive than for gas-fired forced hot air heating.
- It will provide a softer, less obtrusive, and more stable source of warmth than either electric or hot air heating.
- It can be controlled separately for each area of the building.
- It can be designed and installed as an integral part of the new structure and thus be less obtrusive.

The chief disadvantage is that its installation cost will be 77% higher than for an electric heating system, and 22% higher than for a gas-fired forced hot air system.

Conclusions may, however, *imply* the course to be taken

In the long term, however, the combined installation and operating cost of radiant energy heating becomes less than that of electric heating in 17 months, and less than that of forced hot-air heating in 38 months.

Recommendation

Viewing Hartwell Enterprises' move into a new building as a long-term venture, we recommend installing a radiant energy heating system to take advantage of the long-term low operating expenses it will incur.

References

The References section lists all written and spoken information sources

1. Lawrence V Drake, *Radiant Panel Heating and Cooling*. Report: Radiant Panel Association, Hyrum, Utah, 1995, p 3.
2. Darryl Berkowski, D & M Innovators, Winnipeg, Manitoba. Email to Karen Woodhouse, H L Winman and Associates, December 10, 2010.
3. Drake, p 2.
4. Berkowski, p 2.
5. Drake, p 4.
6. Vincent Harding, *Comparison of Costs: Electric, Gas, and Radiant Energy Heating in 30 Industrial Buildings, 2002–2007*. Report: V Harding Associates, London, Ontario, February 23, 2008.

10

Placing a detailed table like this within the report narrative would distract a reader's attention

Appendix

Comparison of Costs: Three Heating/Cooling Systems for Hartwell Enterprises Ltd

Heating/Cooling System	*Installation Cost ($)*	*Annual Operating Cost ($)*	*First Year Costs ($)*	*Cumulative Three-Year Costs ($)*	*Cumulative Five-Year Costs ($)*
Radiant Energy:					
• Heating	47 200	17 300			
• Air-Conditioning	21 600	3 500			
Combined Systems:	***68 800***	***20 800***	***89 600***	***131 200***	***172 800***
Electric Heat:					
• Heating	26 600	31 700			
• Air-Conditioning	21 600	3 500			
Combined Systems:	***48 200***	***35 200***	***83 400***	***153 800***	***224 200***
Gas-Fired Forced Hot Air:					
• Heating	} 38 700	27 600			
• Air-Conditioning		3 500			
Combined Systems:	***38 700***	***31 100***	***68 700***	***130 900***	***193 100***

Pyramidal Arrangement of Report Parts

(Conclusions and Recommendations *before* the Discussion)

A way to address three different levels of reader within a single document

In recent years, more and more report writers have altered the organization of their reports so they more effectively meet their readers' needs. The pyramidal arrangement brings the conclusions and recommendations forward, positioning them immediately after the introduction, so that busy readers do not have to leaf through the report to find the terminal summary (the report's outcome).

The advantages of the pyramidal approach are immediately evident: readers have only to read the initial pages to learn the main points contained in the report, and the writer can help them along by gradually increasing the technical content of the report, catering to semitechnical executive readers up to the end of the recommendations, and to fully technical readers in the discussion and appendix. Although the natural flow of information that occurs in the traditional arrangement is disrupted, Figure 5-10 shows there is now a reader-oriented flow, with the three compartments each containing progressively more technical details.

Segments of a sample report written using the pyramidal approach are shown in Figure 5-11 starting on page 128.

Excerpts from Formal Report 2: Selecting New Elevators for the Merrywell Building

Before reading these excerpts, read the client's letter authorizing H L Winman and Associates to initiate an engineering investigation:

Dear Mr Bailey

The elevators in the Merrywell Building are showing their age. Recently we have experienced frequent breakdowns and, even when the elevators are operating properly, it has become increasingly evident that they do not provide adequate service at the start of work, at noon, and at the end of the working day. I have therefore decided to install a complete range of new elevators, with work starting in mid-August.

Three reports in one, each a complete story in itself

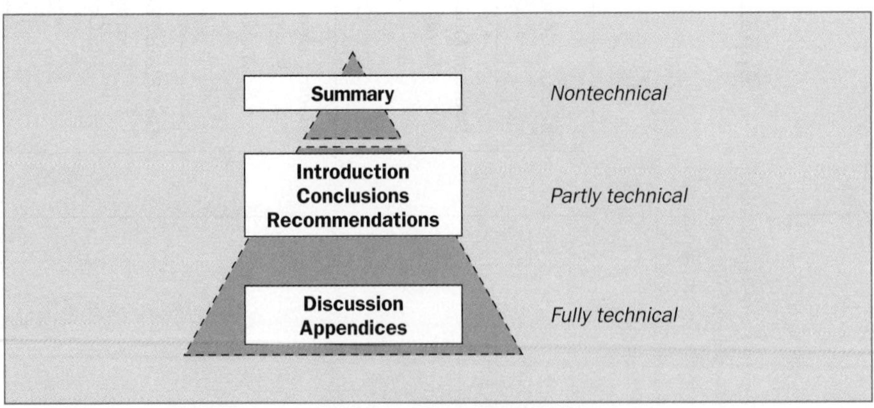

Figure 5-10 The formal report arranged pyramid style.

Before I proceed any further, I am asking you to conduct an engineering investigation for me. Specifically, I want you to evaluate the structural condition of my building, assess the elevator requirements of the building's occupants, investigate the types of elevators available, and recommend the best type or combination of elevators that can be purchased and installed within a proposed budget of $950 000.

The report writer used some of these words in the Introduction on page 129

Please use this letter as your authority to proceed with the investigation. I would appreciate receiving your report by the end of June.

Regards

David P Merrywell, President
Merrywell Enterprises Ltd

By comparing this letter with the conclusions and recommendations, you can assess how thoroughly Barry Kingsley (the report's author) has answered the client's requests.

Comments on the Report

The Summary (page 128) is short and direct because it is written primarily for one reader: the president of Merrywell Enterprises Inc. It encourages him to read the report immediately, and to accept its recommendations, by offering the opportunity to save $60 000.

Although the background information contained in the first two paragraphs of the Introduction (page 129) seems to repeat details the client already knows, Barry recognizes he must satisfy the needs of other readers who may not be fully aware of the situation in the Merrywell Building. He then defines the purpose and scope of the Investigation by stating the client's terms of reference in paragraph 3 of the introduction. (Note that he has copied them almost verbatim from Mr Merrywell's letter.)

A report may be directed to one reader, but also must consider other readers who may see it

The Conclusions present Barry's answers to Mr Merrywell's four requests. Their order is different from that in paragraph 3 of the Introduction because he has chosen to present the main conclusion first (in this case, the best combination of elevators that can be purchased within the stipulated budget), and to follow it with subsidiary conclusions in descending order of importance. Barry is aware that when using the pyramidal report format he must write conclusions that evolve naturally and logically from the introduction, *because his readers have not yet read the discussion.*

Barry uses the first person plural to open his Recommendations because, although he alone is the report's author, he is representing H L Winman and Associates' views to the client.

We have included the first two pages of the Discussion to show that, early in his report, Barry establishes the criteria that will influence how he selects a combination of elevators that will best meet his client's needs. By carefully identifying the five criteria and describing why each is valid, he shows his readers the direction his report will take. (In later sections of his report—not included in the sample pages—he identifies various combinations of elevators that could be installed, and demonstrates which ones meet the criteria, until he finally reaches an optimum configuration.)

A simple, straightforward summary that answers the readers' most immediate question

H L WINMAN AND ASSOCIATES

Summary

The elevators in the 71 year-old Merrywell Building are to be replaced. The new elevators must not only improve the present unsatisfactory elevator service, but must do so within a purchase and installation budget of $950 000.

Of the many types and combinations of elevators considered, the most satisfactory proved to be four 2.45 × 2.15 metre deluxe passenger elevators manufactured by the YoYo Elevator Company, one of which will double as a freight elevator during off-peak traffic times. This combination will provide the fast, efficient service requested by the building's tenants for a total price of $890 000, which will be 6.3% less than the projected budget.

Figure 5-11 Formal Report 2: pyramidal arrangement (5 pages of excerpts from a 16-page report).

Selecting New Elevators for the Merrywell Building

Introduction

When in 1974 Merrywell Enterprises Ltd purchased the Wescon property in Montrose, Alberta, they renamed it "The Merrywell Building" and renovated the entire exterior and part of the interior. The building's two manually operated passenger elevators and a freight elevator were left intact, although it was recognized that eventually they would have to be replaced.

Recently the elevators have been showing their age. There have been frequent breakdowns and passengers have become increasingly dissatisfied with the inadequate service provided at peak traffic hours.

In a letter dated April 27, 2010, to H L Winman and Associates, the president of Merrywell Enterprises Ltd stated his company's intention to purchase new elevators. He authorized us to evaluate the structural condition of the building, to assess the elevator requirements of the building's occupants, to investigate the types of elevators that are available, and to recommend the best type or combination of elevators that can be purchased and installed within the proposed budget of $950 000.

The Introduction, Conclusions, and Recommendations stand alone as a composite section

Conclusions

The best combination of elevators that can be installed in the Merrywell Building will be four deluxe 2.45 × 2.15 metre passenger models, one of which will serve as a dual-purpose passenger/freight elevator. This selection will provide the fast, efficient service desired by the building's tenants and will be able to contend with any foreseeable increase in traffic. Its price at $890 000 will be 6.3% less than the proposed budget.

The primary conclusion comes first, followed by subsidiary conclusions

Installation of special elevators requested by some tenants, such as a full-size freight elevator and a small but speedy executive elevator, would be feasible but costly. A freight elevator would restrict passenger-carrying capability, while an executive elevator would elevate the total price to at least 20% above the proposed budget.

The quality and basic prices of elevators built by the major manufacturers are similar. The YoYo Elevator Company has the most attractive quantity price structure and provides the best maintenance service.

1

The building is structurally sound, although it will require some minor modifications before the new elevators can be installed.

Recommendations

Recommendations should be written in the first person, singular or plural

We recommend that four Model C deluxe 2.45 × 2.15 metre passenger elevators manufactured by the YoYo Elevator Company be installed in the Merrywell Building. We further recommend that one of these elevators be programmed to provide express passenger service to the top four floors during peak traffic hours, and to serve as a freight elevator at other times.

2

Evaluating Building Condition

We have evaluated the condition of the Merrywell Building and find it to be structurally sound. The underpinning done in 1985 by the previous owner was completely successful and there still are no cracks or signs of further settling. Some additional shoring will be required at the head of the elevator shaft immediately above the ninth floor, but this will be routine work that the elevator manufacturer would expect to do in an old building.

The Discussion tells the reader the building is in good shape...

The existing elevator shaft is only 7.5 metres wide by 2.5 metres deep, which is unlikely to be large enough for the new elevators. We have therefore investigated relocating the elevators to a different part of the building, or enlarging the existing shaft. Relocation, though possible, would entail major structural alterations and would be very expensive. Enlarging the elevator shaft could be done economically by removing a staircase that runs up the centre of the building immediately east of the shaft. This staircase is used very little and its removal would not conflict with fire regulations. Removal of the staircase will widen the elevator shaft by 3.35 metres, which will provide sufficient space for the new elevators.

Establishing Tenants' Needs

To establish the elevator requirements of the building's tenants, we asked a senior executive of each company to answer the questionnaire attached as Appendix A. When we had correlated the answers to all the questionnaires, we identified five significant factors that would have to be considered before selecting the new elevators. (There were also several minor exceptions that we did not include in our analysis, either because they were impractical or because they would have been too costly to incorporate.) We considered five major factors:

- Every tenant stated that the new elevators must eliminate the lengthy waits that now occur. We carried out a survey at peak travel times and established that passengers waited for elevators for as much as 70 seconds. Since passengers start becoming impatient after 32 seconds,[1] we estimated that at least three, and probably four, faster passenger elevators would have to be installed to contend with peak-hour traffic.
- Although all tenants occasionally carry light freight up to their offices, only Rad-Art Graphics and Design Consultants Limited considered that a freight elevator would be essential. However, both agreed that a separate

...and then goes on to assess what needs to be done

3

freight elevator would not be necessary if one of the new passenger elevators is large enough to carry their displays. They initially quoted 2.75 metres as the minimum width they would require but later conceded that with other modifications they could reduce the length of their displays to 2.3 metres. All tenants agreed that if a passenger elevator is to double as a freight elevator, they would restrict freight movements to non-peak travel times.

- The three companies occupying the top four floors of the building requested that one elevator be classified as an express elevator serving only the ground floor and floors 6, 7, 8, and 9. Because these companies represent more than 50% of the building's tenants, we considered their request should be entertained.
- Three companies expressed a preference for deluxe elevators. Rothesay Mutual Insurance Company, Design Consultants Limited, and Rad-Art Graphics all stated that they had to create an impression of business solidarity in the eyes of their clients, and felt that deluxe elevators would help convey this image.
- The managements of Rothesay Mutual Insurance Company and Vulcan Oil and Fuel Corporation requested that a small key-operated executive elevator be included in our selection for the sole use of top executives of the building's major tenants. We asked other companies to express their views but received only marginal interest. The consensus seemed to be that an executive elevator would have only limited use and the privilege would too easily be abused. However, we retained the idea for further evaluation, even though we recognized that an executive elevator would prove costly in relation to passenger usage.[2]

Identifying users' needs helps establish clear criteria

We decided that the first two of these factors are requirements that must be implemented, while the latter three are preferences that should be incorporated if at all feasible. The controlling influence would be the budget allocation of $950 000 stipulated by the landlord, Merrywell Enterprises Ltd. In decreasing order of importance, the requirements are

1. Passenger waiting time must be no longer than 32 seconds.
2. At least one elevator must be able to accept freight up to 2.3 metres long.
3. An express elevator should serve the top four floors.
4. The elevators should be deluxe models.
5. A small private elevator should be provided for company executives.

4

(The sample stops here; there were 12 more pages in the original report.)

ASSIGNMENTS

Project 5.1: Correcting a Noise Problem

Assume that today is April 2. This morning you receive a letter from Wendy Partridge, the area manager of Mirabel Realty. (You are the owner/manager of Pro-Active Consultants Limited, which you operate from your home.)

A letter confirming a telephone request

Dear (you)

As I mentioned when I telephoned last week, my staff have been complaining for the past three months that the noise level in our office is too high. They claim it is affecting their work and causing fatigue. I have noticed, too, that staff turnover has been higher lately.

Please look into the problem for me to determine whether their complaints are justified. If they are, will you suggest what can be done to remedy the problem, recommend the most suitable method, and include a cost estimate.

Sincerely

Wendy G Partridge
Area Manager, Mirabel Realty

Part 1

At 4 p.m. on April 3 you visit Mirabel Realty (the office is in room 210, on the second floor of the Fermore Building at 381 Conway Avenue of your city). You notice a background hum, which you consider to be caused by motors in the computers and printers. You are still there when the office staff quits at 4:30. After they go, you notice you can still hear the hum, but at a lower level.

An initial visit shows there may well be a problem

You walk around the office with Wendy and notice that the hum does get significantly louder near the north wall of the office. Then suddenly it dies away. The time is 4:45 p.m.

From Wendy you determine that

- Superior Giftware occupies the office next door (room 208), immediately north of Mirabel Realty.
- Their manager is Saul Ferguson.
- Wendy has talked to him about the noise, but she says he "was pretty hostile" and refused to admit his machines might be the cause.
- The Superior Giftware office quits work at 4:45 p.m. daily.

You arrange to take sound-level measurements on April 10. You want to identify how much of the noise is generated by equipment in the Mirabel Realty office and how much by the company next door.

You consider that a visit to Superior Giftware is essential, since you want to know the sound levels on both sides of the wall between the two companies, from which you will assess the extent of soundproofing to recommend.

Assignment 1: Write to Saul Ferguson and ask for permission to carry out sound-level measurements in his office on April 10.

Part 2

It is now April 10, one week later. You take a Nabuchi Model 1550 Sound-Level Meter with you and return to 381 Conway Avenue. You plan to measure sound levels at various locations in the Mirabel Realty office under four conditions:

- When both businesses are empty.
- When only Superior Giftware is working (4:30–4:45).
- When only Mirabel Realty is working (8:00–8:15).
- When both businesses are working.

You also plan to take readings in Superior Giftware's office.

When you visit Superior Giftware, you notice a packaging and sealing machine only 2.5 metres from the wall separating the two business offices.

You record the measurements you take (see Table 5-4) and compare them to the general ratings for office noise, which you obtain from City of Montrose standard SL2020, dated January 20, 2008. The recommended sound levels for an urban office are:

Quiet office: 30–40 dB
Average office: 40–55 dB
Noisy office: 55–75 dB

You note that the sound level in Mirabel Realty's office increases as you move toward the dividing wall between the two offices (see Figure 5-12 on page 136).

You also notice there seem to be two components of noise in Mirabel Realty's office, some being transmitted through the air and some being transmitted through the structure (from Superior Giftware's machines, through the floor). When you place a hand on the walls or floor, you can feel the vibration. Floors in both offices are tiled.

Assignment 2: Summarize your findings in a brief progress report, which you will email to Wendy Partridge (wpartridge@mirabelrealty.com).

Part 3

It's now April 14 and you are considering possible ways to reduce the sound levels in Mirabel Realty's office:

You have several options, some of which can be used in tandem

1. You could erect a false wall, insulated internally with Corrugon, from floor to ceiling on Mirabel Realty's side of the wall between the two companies.
2. Black cork panels, 18 mm thick, could be glued on Mirabel Realty's side of the wall.
3. You could install carpeting throughout Mirabel Realty's office.

Table 5-4 Average sound levels, second floor, 381 Conway Avenue.

Location	Both Offices Working (dB)	Only Superior Working (dB)	Only Mirabel Working (dB)	No One* Working (dB)
Mirabel Realty				
A	74	73	48	27
B	71	69	51	27
C	66	65	50	27
D	64	61	52	26
E	63	59	51	28
F	59	53	49	26
G	54	49	44	28
Superior Giftware				
H	86	—	—	25
I	83	—	—	26

*Mostly air-conditioner noise.

Note: Measurements made with Nabuchi Model 1550 Sound-Level Meter set to "A" scale.

4. Superior Giftware's machine could be mounted on Vib-o-Rug (insulating rubber that eliminates transmission of vibration from machine to building structure).

You recognize that remedies 1 and 2 are alternatives (they both deal with sound transmitted through the air). Remedies 3 and 4 are also alternatives (they both dampen vibrations and sound carried through the structure). Remedy 3 also quite effectively dampens internal office noise.

You consider the approximate costs:

Remedy 1: $9600
Remedy 2: $1760
Remedy 3: $16 400
Remedy 4: $1050

You consider possible problems that each remedy may present:

Remedy 1. Corrugon is in short supply; delivery time would be a minimum of three months.

The neighbouring packaging machine is the problem, but difficult to remedy at source

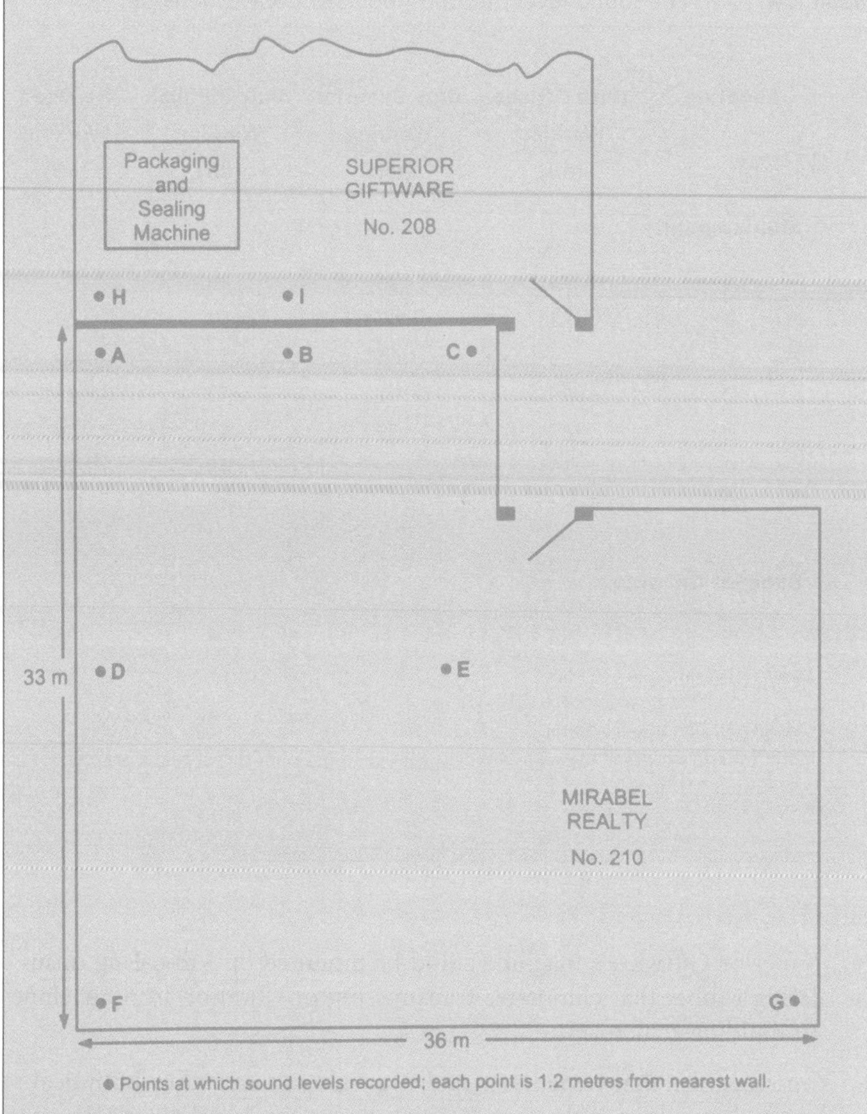

Figure 5-12 Plan of Mirabel Realty's office.

Remedy 2. Cork has an offensive smell; this can be partly corrected by treating the cork with Odoroff.

Remedy 3. The carpet must be dense and have a good quality rubber underlay (included in the approximate cost).

Remedy 4. Depends on cooperation of Superior Giftware's manager.

You calculate the probable sound-level reductions that could be achieved in Mirabel Realty's office:

Remedy 1: 6–10 dB
Remedy 2: 4–7 dB

Remedy 3: 8–12 dB
Remedy 4: 3–5 dB

Assignment 3: Consider which alternative(s) you will recommend to Mirabel Realty, and then write an investigation report describing your findings and suggesting corrective measures. Remember that Wendy Partridge will forward the report to her head office for authorization of the expenditure.

Assignment 4: Also write a brief cover letter to Wendy Partridge in which you very briefly summarize your key findings and corrective measures.

Note: Because Wendy knows little about noise and its effects, you will need to include some explanatory information. (You would also be wise to research and document such information at a library, to establish positive evidence for the statements you make in your report.)

Project 5.2: Resolving a Landfill Problem

You are the assistant engineer for the Town of Quillicom in Northern Ontario. Your boss is Robert D Delorme, P.Eng, who is the town engineer.

Mr Delorme has assigned a landfill project to you: the existing landfill site—at Lot 22, Subdivision 3S—is nearly full and a new site must be found quickly. He hands you a report by H L Winman and Associates and instructs you to read it. (Turn to Figure 5-5, on pages 88 to 93 to read the report.)

Start by researching and reading about what has gone before

Mr Delorme tells you that before the town councillors can make a decision on which site to develop, they will need to know how much it will cost to drill a dozen boreholes north of Quillicom and analyse the results. He asks you to get some price quotations for the work. He also says, privately, that you need to be aware that the councillors have indicated their preference for Lot 18, Subdivision 5N, rather than any other location. Here are some other details:

- Morley Wozniak, at H L Winman and Associates in Thunder Bay, will plot the results of the borehole drilling.
- The positions for the boreholes are to be shown on a map (see Figure 5-5, page 90).
- A list titled "Borehole Specifications for the Area North of Quillicom" contains the exact positions where the drilling must be carried out.
- You are to get at least two (and preferably three) price quotations for the drilling.

From two drilling companies you obtain the following quotations:

Northwest Drillers, Ltd Quillicom, Ontario	$78 520 (GST incl)

M J Peabody and Company Dryden, Ontario	$75 900 (GST extra)

You could not find a third company to give a quotation, but you did talk to Bert Knowles, the assistant superintendent at Melody Lake Mines. He had a suggestion: their open-pit mine is nearly worked out and shortly will close. When it does, the Department of the Environment will insist that Melody Lake Mines cover it with earth and seed it with grass.

An unusual but realistic option for a landfill site

Mr Knowles suggested that Melody Lake Mines will lease the open-pit mine to the Town of Quillicom as a landfill site, for a nominal one dollar a year. There is, however, a condition: the town must spread soil over the compacted garbage—and do it progressively as the site is filled, so there will be no obnoxious smell for the people who live near the mine to contend with—seed it, and plant trees.

You agree: it's something the town would do anyway, before closing a landfill site.

Mr Knowles drives you to the site and you stand on the lip of a shallow, roughly oval excavation varying from about 3 to 18 metres deep. Then you talk to Inga Paullsen, the mine geologist, who calculates the size of the excavation as 24.86 hectares.

You describe the difficulty the Town Council is having in finding a landfill site, mention the three other sites, say the one north of the town could create an environmental problem, and explain you won't know until drilling has been completed there.

A surprising piece of information introduces a new aspect

Inga tells you that drilling has already been done there. When she was a junior at college she worked one summer with an exploration crew that drilled quite a few boreholes north of Quillicom. They were looking for an alternate place to sink a mine shaft, but found no ore deposits north of either Melody Lake or Quillicom. She says the mine does not have the records, only a report from the drilling company.

The drilling company Inga worked for was Mayquill Explorations, but she says it no longer exists. It was owned by Ernie Mays, and when he retired he simply closed down the company. Inga suggests he may still have the records.

Ernie Mays lives at 211 Westerhill Crescent in Quillicom. When you visit him, he tells you that he remembers drilling for Melody Lake Mines and that they sank about 20 boreholes, all north of Quillicom. He could not, however, remember if the bedrock slopes, but he does remember there was evidence of a large sand esker running roughly south–southwest toward Quillicom.

You ask Ernie if he still has the drilling records, but he says he doesn't. He explains that about three years ago Mr Caldicott came to see him and asked for the records. Mr Caldicott now has them.

A second piece of information introduces still another aspect!

Suddenly, everything falls into place. Frank Caldicott is not only general manager of Melody Lake Mines, but also a very influential

Quillicom town councillor. And his youngest sister, Julie, is married to the town engineer—Robert Delorme, your boss.

Now you are ready to write a semiformal report of your findings. (However, you first must decide whether you will include the information you now have about the previous drilling north of Quillicom, and the location of the records.)

Here is some additional data you may need to write your report:

- You are concerned about groundwater contamination problems if the open-pit mine is used as a landfill, so you call Morley Wozniak at H L Winman and Associates in Thunder Bay, who tells you that it will not be a problem because both the lake and the mining community are north of the pit, and the bedrock slopes to the south.
- You calculate that costs to develop the open-pit mine as a landfill will be only $3000, because you can use the buildings and approach roads that are already there.
- The open-pit mine is 4.1 kilometres directly south of Quillicom, but 6.6 kilometres by road (3.8 kilometres southeast along Highway A806, then 2.8 kilometres southwest along Highway B1201).
- The annual operating cost for using the open-pit mine as a landfill will be $49 500, which is $2500 more than the cost for operating the current landfill.
- You obtain a third drilling estimate from Quattro Drilling and Exploration Company in Kenora, which quotes $83 200, HST included.

On a hunch you visit the Land Titles Office in Thunder Bay and look up the surveys for the area north of Quillicom. Against Lot 18, Subdivision 5N, you find the owner listed as *Julie Sarah Caldicott, 207 Northern Drive, Quillicom, Ontario.*

A question of ethics: do you mention the family connection?

Your assignment: Write the report.

Project 5.3: Identifying a Power Plant Problem

You are an independent consultant and operate a business known as Pro-Active Consultants Limited from your home. Four days ago you received a telephone call from Paullette Machon, who is vice-president, operations, of Baldur Agricultural Chemicals (BAC), a company with manufacturing plants across Canada. She assigned you a task: to drive to the BAC plant at Gordontown, where you are to look into a technical problem in the power house. Ms Machon is concerned because power house costs have been rising at Gordontown just at the moment when world fertilizer prices have been decreasing. This is causing BAC to be uncompetitive in both national and international markets.

Ms Machon explained that over the past two years fuel consumption at Gordontown has risen by 18%, numerous breakdowns have occurred that have interfered with production, and there has been a sharp rise in production costs. She has visited the power house repeatedly, but has never found anything that could be attributed to poor operation. In fact, the power house has always been immaculate.

Now Ms Machon wants an independent consultant to take a look, talk to the people in the power house, and try to identify any production problems.

A technical problem affected by the personalities involved

She also hinted that the problem may not only be technical. She explained that the present chief engineer at the BAC power house is Curt Hänness; he is to retire in three months, and she has to decide whether to promote Harry Markham, the existing senior shift engineer, or to bring in a new chief engineer from outside the company. On paper, Markham is ideal for the job. He has worked in the power house for 15 years (he is now 36) and always under Hänness, so his knowledge of the plant and its operations cannot be challenged. Yet the rising costs indicate that all is not as it should be, and Ms Machon wants to be sure that the new chief engineer does not perpetuate the present conditions.

She said she would inform Hänness and Markham that she has engaged you to study the hot water and power generating system in their power house, and that they are to expect you.

You visit the BAC power plant in Gordontown today. During your talks to plant staff and tours of the plant you make the following notes:

These are the "technical" details...

1. Housekeeping excellent—whole place shines (but is this only surface polish for impression of visitors?)
2. Maintenance logs are inadequately kept—need to be done more often. Need more detail. Equipment files not up to date and not properly filed.
3. Boiler cleaning badly neglected. Firm instructions re boiler cleaning need to be issued by head office.
4. Flow meters are of doubtful accuracy. May be overreading. Not serviced for three years. Manufacturer's service department should be contacted (these are Weston meters). Manufacturer needs to be called in to do a complete check and then recalibrate meters.
5. Overreading of meters could give false flow figures—make plant seem to produce more steam than is actually produced.
6. Good housekeeping seems to be achieved by neglecting maintenance. Incorrectly placed emphasis probably caused by frequent visits from company president, who likes to bring in important visitors and impress them. Hänness likes reflected glory (so does Markham).
7. Shift engineers are responsible for maintenance of pumps and vacuum equipment. Not enough time given over to this. They seem to prefer straight replacement of whole units on failure rather than preventive maintenance. Costly method! Obviously more breakdowns: they wait for a failure before taking action. A preventive maintenance plan is needed.

...and these are the "personal" details

8. Markham seems O.K. Genial type; obviously knows his power house. Proud of it! But seems to resist change. Definitely resents suggestions. Does he lack all-round knowledge? Is he limited only to what goes on in his plant? Is he afraid of new ideas because he doesn't understand them? Young staff hinted at this, but were too loyal to say it outright. They felt they were hampered by having to use old techniques that are known to work but are slow. Nothing concrete was said—it is just an impression.
9. Hänness has done a good job training Markham. Made him a carbon copy. Hänness doesn't do much now. Markham runs the show, and has for over a

year. He expects to get the job when Hänness retires. It'll be a real blow to him if he doesn't! BAC might even lose a good company man.

10. Discussed CORLAND 200 digital power panel with staff. Young engineers had read about it in *Plant Maintenance*—eager to have one installed similar to the one at Pinewood Paper Mill. But Hänness and Markham knew nothing about it—didn't seem to be interested. Are they not keeping up to date with technical magazines?

Your assignment: Write two evaluation reports for Ms Machon:

1. The first is to address the technical problems in the power house at Gordontown.
2. The second is to address the personnel difficulties.
   In each case you are to make a recommendation. Here is some additional information you may need:
   - Gordontown is 124 km from your city/town. It has a population of 15 700 and its primary employer is the BAC plant.
   - The BAC office in your city/town is at 1450 Disraeli Crescent.

Project 5.4: Testing Highway Marking Paints

For the past six years the Department of Highways in your province has used "Centrex CL" for marking highway pavement centrelines and lanes. Recent advances in paint technology, however, have brought several new products onto the market, which their manufacturers claim are better than Centrex CL. To meet this challenge, Centrex Inc has developed a new paint ("TL") and has recommended that the Department of Highways use it in place of CL.

In a letter dated March 18 of this year, senior provincial highways engineer Morris Hordern commissioned you to carry out independent tests of the new paints. (You own a home-based consulting company known as Pro-Active Consultants Limited.) You start your project by obtaining samples of white and yellow highway paint from six manufacturers, transferring the samples into unmarked cans and then coding the cans as shown in Table 5-5.

You then place the coding list into a sealed envelope, and lock it away in a safety deposit box at a local bank.

You decide to paint sample stripes on two regularly travelled stretches of highway and to assess the samples in four ways:

1. Spraying characteristics
2. Drying time
3. Visibility after three months
4. Visibility after six months

You assess spraying characteristics as excellent, very good, good, fair, and poor. The ratings are

Very good:	WA, WB, WC, WD, WF, YL, YR
Good:	WE, WG, YM, YN, YO, YQ
Fair:	YP

New technology creates new products for evaluation

Table 5-5 Coding of paint cans.

	Manufacturer	Paint Coding White	Paint Coding Yellow
1.	Centrex Inc, Truro, Nova Scotia Paint type: CL (the "old" paint)	WA	YL
2.	Novell Paint Ltd, Guelph, Ontario Paint type: 909	WB	YM
3.	Hi-Liner Products, Winnipeg, Manitoba Paint type: HILITE	WC	YN
4.	Multiple Industries Corporation, Calgary, Alberta, Paint type: MICC	WD	YO
5.	Wishart Incorporated, Thunder Bay, Ontario, Paint type: ROADMARK 13	WE	YP
6.	Provincial Paint Company, Saskatoon, Saskatchewan, Paint Type: 81-238	WF	YQ
7.	Centrex Inc, Truro, Nova Scotia Paint type: TL (their "new" paint)	WG	YR

Some factors demand personal judgment; others are measurable

You assess drying time in minutes:

WA:16	WC:18	WE:14	WG:19	YM:26	YO:14	YQ:12
WB:33	WD:11	WF:13	YL:13	YN:18	YP:10	YR:15

After three months you assess visibility by day and by night. You use five drivers (you are one) to rate the stripes independently and to place the stripes' visibility on a scale of 1 to 10. You then average the five assessments (night readings are taken with headlights at high beam) and record them in Table 5-6.

After another three months the same drivers again assess stripe visibility, with the results shown in Table 5-7.

You will need to create two comparison tables before writing your report

You consolidate your results into two tables, one for white paint, one for yellow paint, and then

- reject any unacceptable paints (see guidelines below),
- rank acceptable paints in order of suitability,
- identify the best paint(s) to use for highway marking,
- retrieve the paint coding list from the bank deposit box, and
- write your report.

Here are some factors you use to conduct your study and write your report:

- Senior provincial highways engineer Morris Hordern's office address is 416 Inkster Building, 2035 Perimeter Road of your city.
- The paint stripes were painted on two stretches of highway:
  - Highway 14 (concrete surface), 1.7 kilometres north of the intersection with Highway 287.

Table 5-6 Three-month paint check.

Paint	Concrete Pavement		Asphalt Pavement	
Code	Day	Night	Day	Night
WA	8	8	8	9
WB	7	8	7	7
WC	8	9	10	9
WD	9	9	7	8
WE	7	6	7	8
WF	8	9	9	10
WG	7	7	7	8
YL	8	9	9	9
YM	7	7	7	9
YN	7	9	7	8
YO	8	8	7	8
YP	7	8	6	8
YQ	5	6	4	6
YR	9	10	9	9

Table 5-7 Six-month paint check.

Paint	Concrete Pavement		Asphalt Pavement	
Code	Day	Night	Day	Night
WA	6	6	5	7
WB	4	5	5	5
WC	8	8	9	9
WD	6	7	6	8
WE	6	5	6	7
WF	5	7	5	6
WG	6	7	6	7
YL	6	7	7	8
YM	6	7	6	8
YN	6	7	6	7
YO	6	7	6	8
YP	3	4	4	5
YQ	2	3	3	4
YR	8	9	8	9

- Highway 287 (asphalt surface), 1.2 kilometres west of the intersection with Highway 14.

- The paint stripes are applied at night, between midnight and 6 a.m.

- To apply the stripes, you mount a paint stripe applicator on a small garden tractor.
- Paint Manufacturers' Association specification PMA-02-45B states that spraying characteristics for fast-drying highway paint should be at least "Good," and preferably "Very Good." To achieve "Very Good," the paint must flow smoothly and evenly without forming globules or dripping from the nozzle.

These factors help establish acceptability criteria

- You refer to specification ASTM D-711 to establish the maximum acceptable paint drying time, which is 20 minutes.
- Guidelines you give to the drivers assessing paint visibility are shown in Table 5-8. You then average the five assessments.
- You establish minimum acceptable visibility levels for the paints to be
  After three months' traffic wear: 7
  After six months' traffic wear: 6

Note: Calculate real dates for each stage of the study and quote them in your report.

Your assignment: Write the results of your paint evaluation as an investigation report addressed to senior provincial highways engineer Morris Hordern. Your report should not only present the results of your tests, but also analyse them, draw conclusions, and make a recommendation.

Table 5-8 Guidelines for evaluating paint visibility.

	Distance Visible	
Rating	**Day**	**Night**
10	500 m	200 m
8	400 m	160 m
6	300 m	120 m
4	200 m	80 m
2	100 m	40 m

Chapter 6
Technical Proposals

In this chapter you will learn how to

- select the type of proposal to use for a specific situation,
- write an informal local proposal,
- plan and write a semiformal proposal for wider distribution,
- write a student project proposal, and
- use language that gives the reader confidence in you and the project you are proposing.

Technical proposals can be short and informal or long and very formal. They fall into three categories:

1. **Informal Proposal**

   An informal proposal offers an idea and discusses why it should be implemented. Most often it is written as an email and circulated only within an organization. Typical informal proposals might be

   - a plan to introduce a new software-driven electronic calibration system throughout the company,
   - a proposal to research local resources for replacement equipment components, rather than importing them, or
   - a request to attend a conference (a request often is a proposal).

In an informal proposal you can comfortably use the first person "I"

2. **Semiformal Proposal**

   A semiformal proposal also offers an idea and suggests that it be implemented.

   It is sent at management level within an organization or between one organization and another, and can range from a 1-page letter to a 30-page (or longer) document prefaced by a title page and executive summary. It may suggest ways to increase productivity, provide a service, or resolve a problem, or may recommend conducting research. Typical semiformal proposals might

   - propose researching new office space to alleviate crowded conditions in a workplace,
   - offer specialist consulting services to a potential client,
   - suggest amalgamating company departments to provide a more efficient and cost-effective management structure.

Here, "we" is more prevalent

"We" is also common here, to maintain a confident active voice

3. **Formal Proposal**

   A formal proposal is a large, often multiple-volume, document designed to impress to the government or a major organization that the proposing company has the capability to carry out an important, often multi-million-dollar task or project. Such proposals are substantial because they describe in detail what will be done, how it will be done, who will be responsible for specific aspects of the work, and why the proposing company has the potential to complete the project on time, within budget, and to the client's satisfaction.

   Formal proposals are usually prepared in response to a Request for Proposal (RFP) that defines exactly how they are to be organized and what must be covered in the proposal. They are always accompanied by a cover letter or letter of transmittal, which often acts as an executive summary. A formal proposal might

   - suggest to a city that it develop a deep-water holding pond to overcome an overloaded drainage system and flooding following heavy rainfalls,
   - propose to a bank that it hire a consultant to research ways that will improve automatic teller services for customers, or
   - recommend to the Department of Communications that it refurbish its mobile communications units.

Proposals
www.io.com/~hcexres/textbook/props.html
This document is one chapter from the online textbook used in Austin Community College's online course, Online Technical Writing (www.io.com/~hcexres/textbook/acctoc.html). It describes types of proposals, their organization and format, and the common sections in a proposal. Included are several sample proposals and a revision checklist.

In this chapter we will focus on writing informal and short semiformal proposals, which are the types you are most likely to encounter during your first years in industry.

Overall Writing Plan

All proposals, regardless of their length, contain the following parts:

- A **summary** that describes briefly what is being proposed and identifies any significant factors (such as cost).
- **Background** information that outlines the circumstances that have caused the proposal to be prepared.
- Definitive **details** that describe what needs to be done, how it will be done, what the results will be, and why the proposing company is capable of doing the job. This is the body of the proposal.
- An **action statement** that requests approval to go ahead (for an in-house proposal), or make a decision (for a client who will buy the services being offered).
- **Attachments** or **appendices** that contain detailed evidence to support statements made in the body of the proposal (appropriate for most semiformal proposals; not always present in informal proposals).

The overall writing plan is similar to that for semiformal reports

On the following pages we will demonstrate how to use these five writing compartments to suit different proposal configurations.

Short Informal Proposal

Marina Albrecht used the plan in Figure 6-1 to organize the proposal in Figure 6-2 on page 148. It is an in-house proposal because Marina is writing only to her manager, Karen LePage. We have inserted the label for each writing compartment beside the proposal to demonstrate how it was constructed (they were not shown beside the original document).

Marina writes with confidence, and it shows

Longer Informal or Short Semiformal Proposal

Marina has written what is known as a single-solution proposal, a proposal that offers only one way to do something. There are times when you may want to describe alternative solutions, to demonstrate to the reader that you have considered a number of options, one of which you propose should be adopted.

Satisfy your readers' curiosity

For example, suppose the president of your company has instructed you to research local buildings to find a larger office space. You have found three buildings in different parts of the city, each with different advantages, and now you have to write a proposal for the company's executives to review. In your proposal you describe the alternative locations and identify which you consider to be the most advantageous, following the writing plan in Figure 6-3 on page 149.

When writing a proposal that offers alternative solutions, you need to consider five factors that affect how you present your information:

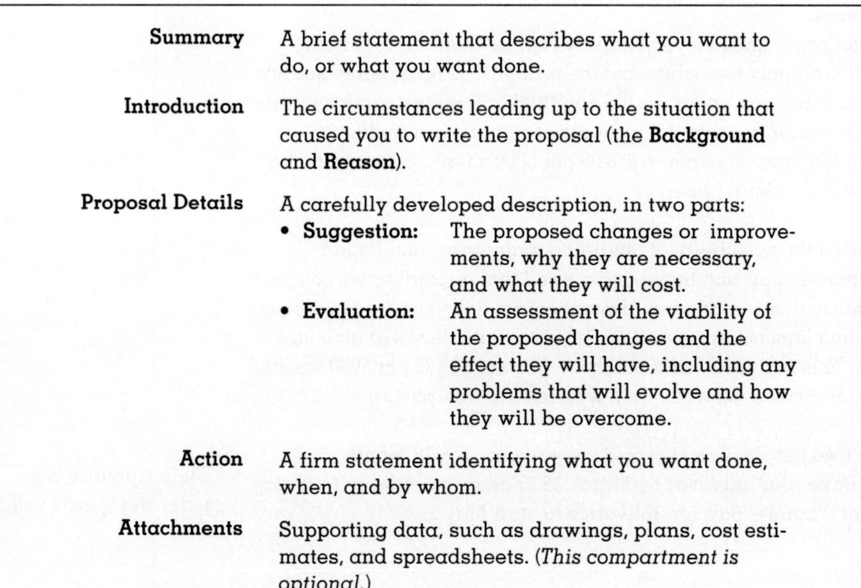

Summary	A brief statement that describes what you want to do, or what you want done.
Introduction	The circumstances leading up to the situation that caused you to write the proposal (the **Background** and **Reason**).
Proposal Details	A carefully developed description, in two parts: • **Suggestion:** The proposed changes or improvements, why they are necessary, and what they will cost. • **Evaluation:** An assessment of the viability of the proposed changes and the effect they will have, including any problems that will evolve and how they will be overcome.
Action	A firm statement identifying what you want done, when, and by whom.
Attachments	Supporting data, such as drawings, plans, cost estimates, and spreadsheets. (*This compartment is optional.*)

Figure 6-1 Writing plan for a short informal proposal.

Explore

Peterborough Environmental Consultants

To: Karen LePage, Office Manager
From: Marina Albrecht, Project Engineer
Date: March 4, 2011
Re: Proposal to Change to Recycled Copy Paper

Summary Statement

When the current supply of regular office copier paper is exhausted, I propose that we change to recycled paper. The cost will be marginally higher, but our company will be seen to be following the advice we give our customers.

Reason/ Background

This is exactly the right moment to make the change. The Canadian public has become increasingly sensitive to the damage being done to the environment by extensive use of paper manufactured from Canada's timber resources. We will not only make a contribution by using recycled paper, but also can use that fact when proposing that other companies do the same. Coincidentally, we will be changing to a Canadian-made product.

Strong, definite statements...

Details: Suggestion

The paper we have used for the past four years is 20 lb Westburn stock, which is imported from Dayton, Ohio, by Manor Industries Inc of Toronto, Ontario. (Our two other offices have similar arrangements with local distributors of imported paper products.) The recycled paper I am proposing is 20 lb Environ stock manufactured by Repap Canada Ltd in Thunder Bay, Ontario.

Details: Evaluation

I bought 1000 sheets of Environ stock and tested them on a trial basis. I found the following:

- The Environ paper fed as well as the Westburn paper and experienced no paper jams.
- The Environ paper appears very slightly coarser than the Westburn paper, and is slightly less white, but the print image is the same quality.
- 1000 sheets of Environ paper are 1.5 mm thicker than the same quantity of Westburn paper, but that does not affect printing or handling.
- The cost of the Environ paper is $76.95 per 5000 sheets, compared with $68.95 for the Westburn paper.

...and the first-person active voice...

I have discussed the possibility of obtaining a discount from Repap Canada in Thunder Bay, and they have agreed that, providing we contract to bulk-purchase all our copy paper from them for one year, for our offices in Winnipeg and Vancouver as well as Peterborough, they will give us a 10% discount. This will result in a purchase price of $69.25 per 5000 sheets, which is only $0.30 more per 5000 than we are currently paying.

Action Statement

I propose that we use Environ recycled copy paper on a 12-month trial basis. May I have your approval by March 25 to place an order with Repap Canada Ltd of Thunder Bay, for deliveries to start May 2, 2011?

...help convince the reader the idea is valid

Figure 6-2 A short informal proposal prepared for an in-house audience.

Summary	A synopsis of the proposal's key points, which identifies the proposal's purpose, main advantages, result, and cost.
Introduction	A description of the situation, condition, or problem that demands attention, and the circumstances leading up to it. This part represents the **Background** and **Reason**.
Proposal Details	The **Details** section is the body of the proposal. It should open with a brief statement that identifies the overall approach. It is then divided into four subcompartments:
Objective	• The **Objective** defines what needs to be achieved to improve the situation or condition, or resolve the problem, and establishes the **Criteria** that must be met.
Proposed Solution	• The **Proposed Solution** offers what the writer considers to be the best way to achieve the objective. It includes a full description of the solution, the expected result or improvement, its advantages, and its cost.
Alternative Solutions	• The **Alternative Solutions** section describes other ways that the objective can be met. Each alternative addresses the same topics as those covered for the proposed solution.
Evaluation	• The **Evaluation** analyses each solution and compares it against the criteria for an optimum solution established in the Objective. The Solutions are compared only against the Criteria, never against each other.
Action	The **Action Statement** recommends what action needs to be taken. It is often titled **Recommendation** and must be written in strong, confident terms.
Attachments	The **Evidence** or **Supporting Data** contains drawings, cost analyses, spreadsheets, etc, that establish the validity of statements made in the body of the proposal.

Figure 6-3 Writing plan for a longer informal proposal or short semiformal proposal.

Avoid saying or implying that this is the best solution...

...let the facts speak for themselves

Show you have anticipated your readers' questions

1. When establishing the criteria you will use to evaluate the different alternatives, you must "prove" any criterion your readers might question. If, in your evaluation of buildings, you write, "We will need a minimum of 700 m^2 of office space immediately, and another 250 m^2 within two years," you will need to determine whether every executive who reads the proposal will be aware of the company's current and upcoming space requirements. If some will not, you will have to explain (i.e. prove) why the figures you quote are valid.
2. When you present your proposal and alternative solutions, take care not to offer opinions. Present only *facts* and do not comment on their advantages or disadvantages (you will do that in the Evaluation

section of your proposal). Nor should you compare one alternative against another: your readers must feel you are being totally objective.

3. When prescribing the second and third alternatives, present the facts about each *in the same sequence* that you presented them for the first solution.

Maintain your objectivity until you make your recommendation

4. When writing the Evaluation, compare each alternative solution *only* against the selection criteria you established earlier in the proposal.

5. When writing the Action Statement: use the active-voice expression "I recommend…" or "We recommend…" rather than the passive-voice expression "It is considered that…" or "It is recommended that…."

When Meridian Engineering Consultants of Thunder Bay decided to provide courses in technical writing for their staff, they inserted a Request for Proposal (RFP) as a display advertisement in *The Globe and Mail* (see Figure 6-4). One of the companies submitting a proposal was Online Writing Trainers Ltd (OWTL) of Winnipeg, Manitoba. The proposal was written by Arlene Tetrault, OWTL's projects manager, and is shown in Figure 6-5 starting on page 152.

Arlene began by listing the advantages of each of the three training methods she would present, and then made in-depth calculations of the cost for each. This showed her that, because the costs were so close, they would not be a governing factor in MEC's choice. She was then able to concentrate on the advantages that each method offered from the MEC learners' point of view.

MEC **Call for Proposals**

Provision of Training Services:
Writing Technical Letters, Email, Reports and Proposals

MEC is soliciting proposals from innovative training consultants to provide courses in technical writing for our 120-person staff, 80% of whom are engineers and engineering technologists working primarily in civil and structural engineering, information technology, and the environmental sciences. The training is to cover letter, email, report and proposal writing, and include methods for sharpening individual writing style.

The training is to start January 17, 2011, and be completed by March 31, 2011. Vendors are to provide three copies of their technical and cost proposal by noon on Wednesday, October 27, 2010, marked RFP 3/014. Late proposals will not be accepted.

Meridian Engineering Consultants Ltd
334 Willows Avenue, Thunder Bay, Ontario, P7B 3X6

Figure 6-4 The Request for Proposal (RFP) that prompted Online Writing Trainers Ltd to prepare the proposal in Figure 6-5.

The design of the proposal, with headings in a narrow column on the left and the text in a wider column on the right, is an effective application of information design principles. Readers can readily see how Arlene has structured her ideas, and can find information easily. The headings also parallel the labels in the writing compartments shown in Figure 6-3. Here are some additional comments on the proposal:

Encourage readers so they *want* to read your words

- The paragraph in the centre of page 1 is Arlene's **Summary**, in which she identifies the preferred training method she recommends and lists its cost. Many people hesitate to state the cost in the Summary, fearing that readers may not continue reading if they feel the cost is too high. We believe it should be there, because it is the first question readers are likely to ask, so they will search for it and may become irritated if they find it has been buried far down in the proposal.
- The first paragraph of the Introduction provides the **Background**, which sets the scene for the information to follow. Arlene draws much of this information from the RFP in Figure 6-4.
- The paragraph at the foot of page 1 provides a quick statement that identifies OWTL's capacity to handle the project. Arlene keeps it short, placing the detailed information in an attachment.
- By listing the **Objectives** (on page 2), Arlene identifies the factors she will use to evaluate the three methods. In Objective 1, she lists the topics that need to be taught. She divides them into two groups to suit the two different groups of employees, which she identifies in Objective 2. She drew Objectives 3, 4, and 5 from MEC's RFP.
- The **Proposed Solution** starts in the centre of page 2 and continues two-thirds of the way down page 3. Arlene presents only *facts*, without commenting on their value at this stage in the proposal.

Maintain your objectivity, almost to the end

- The two **Alternative Solutions** appear on pages 3 and 4. Each is shorter than the Proposed Solution, but the information is presented in the same sequence. Again, Arlene presents only facts.
- In the **Evaluation** of the three methods (page 5), Arlene compares each method against the Objectives she established on page 2. She starts by identifying the objectives met by all three methods, and then continues with comments on the advantages and disadvantages of each method. Here, she allows her (i.e. OWTL's) opinions to appear, for the first time in the whole proposal.
- The **Conclusions** present the outcome of the Evaluation, but Arlene only *suggests* which method MEC should select. Although Figure 6-3 labels this as an **Action Statement**, in which the writer normally makes a strong recommendation that the reader approve the proposal, Arlene chose to move her Action Statement into a cover letter to send with the proposal (see page 157).

Explore

Online Writing Trainers Ltd

Suite 200 – 450 Bridgeview Road
Winnipeg MB R2J 3M4

Proposal to Provide Training Services:
Writing Technical Letters, Email, Reports, and Proposals

Prepared for

Meridian Engineering Consultants Ltd
Thunder Bay, Ontario

In response to

MEC RFP 3/014

Proposal prepared October 26, 2010

Indent the Summary on both sides to catch readers' attention

We have investigated three methods for providing training in letter, email, report, and proposal writing for Meridian Engineering Consultants Ltd. The method we propose is a mix of web-based and traditional classroom-style learning. It will meet the needs of MEC staff who prefer electronic delivery and those who prefer more traditional instruction. The total cost at $51 400 is comparable to solely online or solely classroom instruction.

Introduction

Meridian Engineering Consultants Ltd (MEC) plans to upgrade its technical staff's ability to write effective letters, email, reports, and proposals. Training is to be conducted between January 17 and March 31, 2011, and is to include approximately 96 technical professionals and 24 support staff. MEC published a Request for Proposals (MEC RFP 3/014) in *The Globe and Mail* on October 8, 2010, calling for interested training consultants to submit training and cost proposals for providing the appropriate services.

Highlight company experience only very briefly here; focus on what your company can do for the reader

Online Writing Trainers Ltd (OWTL), of Winnipeg, Manitoba, has been providing onsite courses for engineering and other business organizations in Canada and the US since 1972, and in the UK since 1994 (see Attachment 1 for a detailed company description). To meet the growing demand by both North American and European businesses to access training over the internet, in 2001 we converted our onsite courses for electronic delivery. They are now available online from our corporate website.

1

Figure 6-5 A short semiformal proposal offering alternative solutions.

Objectives

We established the following requirements that must be met:

1. The training is to cover eight main subjects:

   Foundation Topics

   - Getting to the point (identifying and placing key information for immediate access)
   - Organizing the details (developing the remainder of the document)
   - Writing effective email
   - Sharpening language skills

   Advanced Topics

   - Writing business letters and memos
   - Writing short reports
   - Planning and writing formal reports
   - Planning and writing business and technical proposals
2. Technical staff are to receive training on both foundation and advanced topics. Support staff are to receive training only on the foundation topics.
3. The cost for the training must be comparable, whether delivered onsite or online, or in a blended format.
4. The training must be completed within a 2.5 month period, between January 17 and March 31, 2011.
5. The training must accommodate the schedules of technical staff who travel frequently.

Draw on the client's requirements to write the Objectives

Proposed Delivery Method: ***Blended Training***

Our proposal offers a combination of onsite and online courses under a "blended" arrangement, with some portions of the training being taught online and other portions being taught onsite. The costs for implementing blended training will be slightly less than for traditional classroom training.

In the following discussion, we have relabelled the eight topics as four Foundation Courses and four Advanced Courses. See Attachment 2 for course descriptions.

Cover new technology or methods in detail

The **online training** will be held first and will cover the four Foundation Courses, which will be taken by all staff. Because the program is maintained on OWTL's server, participants will not need to download the courses to their individual computers. They will also be able to access the courses from any computer at any location at any time. The system will record their progress and each time participants log on they will be taken immediately to the point where they stopped. There will be an examination at the end of each course, which will be evaluated electronically and the results reported to the participant.

The **onsite training** will cover the four Advanced Courses, which will be presented at spaced intervals, after each person has completed the Foundation Courses online. Support staff will not take the Advanced Courses, because they normally do not write technical correspondence, reports and proposals.

2

Blended Training (continued)

Schedule

The **online segment**, comprising the four Foundation Courses, will be taken over a six-week period, between January 17 and February 25, 2011. The four courses require a total of 6 to 8 hours of study.

Explain how the system will work

The **onsite segment**, comprising the four Advanced Courses, will be covered in a single 8-hour class, with a maximum of 12 participants in each class. To cover the 96 technical professionals, the classes will be held on 8 separate days, 4 between March 7 and 11, and 4 between March 21 and 25. The spread of dates will allow for possible travel absences of engineering staff.

Cost

The cost for providing courses under the blended approach will be $51 400. The cost covers provision of

- 120 individual IDs and passwords for participants to access the 4 Foundation Courses,
- 120 course textbooks
- 8 one-day onsite training sessions, to cover the 4 Advanced Courses, with 12 staff members attending each session,
- 2 instructors for each onsite course,
- evaluation of 2 assignments written by each onsite course participant, and
- instructors' travel and accommodation expenses.

Identify total cost and what it covers in the proposal; put detailed costs in an attachment

Alternative Delivery Method: ***Online Training***

In the online training mode, all 8 courses will be taken electronically. Participants will be able to access the courses from any computer at any location and at a time convenient to themselves. The system will record their progress and each time participants log on they will be taken immediately to the point where they had stopped. There will be an examination at the end of each course.

The 96 technical professionals will register for all 8 courses, which will require approximately 14–16 hours of study. They will also write 4 assignments and submit them electronically to an OWTL instructor, who will return them with feedback.

The 24 support staff will register for the 4 Foundation Courses, which will require approximately 8 hours of study.

All participants will receive a copy of the course textbook, which will become a permanent resource for future reference.

3

Online Training (continued)

Schedule

The courses will be taken between January 17 and March 31, 2011. OWTL will monitor course progress and submit a report to MEC every two weeks. The reports will list those who have started, how far each person has progressed, and those who have completed their courses.

Cost

The cost for providing training online will be $49 220, which will include

- 120 individual IDs and passwords for participants to access the 4 Foundation Courses,
- 120 course textbooks,
- evaluation of 4 assignments submitted by each person completing courses 5 to 8, and
- submission of progress reports at 2-week intervals.

Alternative Delivery Method
Onsite Training

Onsite training is traditional classroom training. We will present 8 two-day workshops for the 96 technical professionals, and 2 one-day workshops for the 24 support staff, with 12 participants attending each workshop. Topics to be covered will include the following:

2-day workshop: All 8 topics
1-day workshop: 4 foundation topics

All participants will receive a copy of the course textbook and approximately 30 pages of additional notes. The workshops will be held on MEC's premises.

Schedule

The workshops will be presented in 4 time frames to accommodate staff absences while on field assignment:

Dates	2-day Workshops	1-day Workshops
January 17–22	2	1
February 1–4	2	–
March 7–11	2	1
March 21–24	2	–

A table summarizes key points and draws readers' attention

Cost

The cost for providing the 10 workshops will be $52 520, which will include

- 2 instructors for each workshop,
- evaluation of 4 assignments completed by participants attending the 2-day workshops,
- 120 course textbooks and course notes,
- instructors' travel and accommodation expenses.

4

Evaluation of Alternative Methods

All 3 of the proposed methods will provide the required depth of training established in the Objectives, can be completed within the required time frame, and will accommodate the schedules of technical staff who travel. The costs also are comparable:

Blended training *(online and onsite)*	$51 400
Solely online training	$49 220
Solely onsite training	$52 520

Identify where cost explanations can be found

The primary differences are in the delivery methods and individual participants' reaction to them. For a detailed cost analysis, see Attachment 3.

Blended Training will meet the needs of both types of course participant: those who prefer electronic instruction and those who prefer the interactive classroom environment. The more basic foundation topics will be taught online. The more intense advanced topics will be presented in person, which will provide participants with personal instruction and the opportunity to ask questions.

The Evaluation permits the writer to air her views

Solely **Online Training** will please participants who prefer privacy and the ability to study on their own time, and at their own pace and location. It will not, however, provide personalized instruction or the interactive environment that some participants prefer.

Solely **Onsite Training** will please participants who prefer to work face-to-face with an instructor and like the interactive environment in which they may ask questions and hear the questions of others. It will not, however, offer much flexibility because participants must attend at a fixed time.

Conclusions

Although all three methods will meet MEC's requirements, we consider that the blended training option will provide the flexibility MEC needs to train both technical and support staff, and will suit employees who often have to travel and work offsite.

Online Writing Trainers Ltd
26 October 2010

5

(Note: the three attachments are not printed here to conserve space in this edition of *Technically-Write!*)

Arlene's cover letter reads as follows:

A cover letter is also known as a transmittal letter or an executive summary

Dear Contracts Manager

I am enclosing our proposal to present courses on writing technical letters, email, reports, and proposals to Meridian Engineering Consultants' staff, in response to MEC RFP 3/014. We recommend that Meridian Engineering Consultants adopt "blended instruction" as the preferred training method, which will be a combination of electronic and in-person delivery of the training. The cost will be $51 400, which is slightly less than for regular classroom-style training. Blended instruction will also meet the needs of staff who prefer electronic delivery and those who prefer personal instruction.

Our corporate website at www.owtl.com provides a detailed description of blended instruction. Please call me at 204.488.1827 if you have further questions.

Sincerely

Arlene Tetrault
Contracts Manager
Online Writing Trainers Ltd

Practise

Student Project Proposal

Many technical students nearing the end of their education have to undertake a technical term project, sometimes working alone but more often working in teams. Although their instructor may assign a project to each team, there are times when the instructor invites each team to identify a technical problem and then write a proposal identifying how the team will tackle it. You can use the writing plan in Figure 6-6 on page 158 to help you.

This practical approach is particularly suited to college writing

The plan shows that you cannot simply decide, without considerable forethought, that "we'll put two computers at different ends of the building and work out whether there is less information loss between them, using fibreoptic cable compared with RS-232 wire cable." That would make a good project, but before writing it up as a proposal you need to work out the amount of cable you will need, how you will get the computers, what software you will be using, how you will measure information loss at different frequencies, how long all this will take you, and so on. Only when you have "done your homework" and have the facts at your fingertips will you be ready to write the proposal.

The Language of Proposal Writing

There can be nothing wishy-washy about the language you use in a proposal. If you have organized your proposal using one of the writing plans shown in this chapter, you will provide a smooth flow of information. Now you must let your language convince your readers that you have a strong case to present.

1. Present Only Essential Information

Before writing, divide all your information into two parts:

Summary	A brief outline of what you plan to do, and what doing it will achieve.
Background	Why the project needs to be tackled. Include historical information concerning the topic and identify the team members.
Proposal Plan	Describe how your project team will carry out the project. Provide the following information:
Details	• Your overall approach or plan. • Who (in your team) will be doing what. • Special equipment or parts you require (attach a list).
Project Schedule	• Identify the dates on which you plan to > complete your research, > finish the design, > complete product construction, and > complete testing and troubleshooting the product.
Reporting Schedule	• Identify the dates when you plan to > submit progress reports, > submit a topic outline for your project report, > submit first draft sections for evaluation, > complete the final project report, and > present your oral report.
Action	Request approval to go ahead with the project.
Evidence	Provide supporting information to validate your plan, plus a list of materials or parts you will need.

This writing plan parallels how project proposals are written in industry

Figure 6-6 Writing plan for a student project proposal.

1. Information the reader *must* have to make a decision (the "need-to-know" details).
2. Information that is of general interest but the reader *does not need* to make a decision (the "nice-to-know" details).

Focus on the need-to-know part by taking a step back and looking at your information from the readers' point of view.

2. Use the Active Voice

The active voice will make you sound firm and definite. Instead of writing,

> The two computers would be connected by means of a metal wire and a fibre-optic cable, whereas alternating from one cable to the other would be accomplished by a Model 1880 switching unit. *(Passive voice: 33 words)*

Write strongly and positively

Write,

> A wire and a fibreoptic cable will connect the two computers, while a Model 1880 switching unit will alternate between them. *(Active voice: 22 words)*

In addition to having 33% fewer words, the active voice makes the second writer sound much more confident and knowledgeable. (For more information on using the active voice, refer to Chapter 11.)

3. Avoid Wishy-Washy Words

Replace weak words like *would, could*, and *should* with a strong word like *will*. In the first example above, about the two cables, the word *would* occurs twice and creates only a "soft" impression (the reader may comment, "Well, I guess that might be okay."). In the second example, the word *would* has been replaced with *will*, creating a much more confident impression (the reader will feel like commenting, "Now that makes sense!")

Avoid LIC expressions

You make a similarly weak impression if you insert inert low-information-content (LIC) expressions into your proposal, such as

...*bring to a conclusion*...	(change to *conclude*)
...*in the direction of*...	(use *toward*)
...*by means of*...	(simply use *by*)

For an extensive list of LIC expressions, refer to Chapter 11, pages 278 and 279.

Another damaging effect occurs if you write vague statements rather than specific information. For example,

...*an adequate supply*...	(write *a three-week supply*)
...*we got some help from*...	(write *two technicians from head office helped us*)
...*many tests were performed*...	(write *we performed 32 tests*)

Note, too, that the suggested changes are all in the active voice.

4. Avoid Giving Opinions

Experienced proposal writers know just when to insert an opinion or a subjective statement. As a beginning proposal writer, you will be much safer if you withhold your opinions until the end of the proposal, when you make your recommendation.

ASSIGNMENTS

Project 6.1: Acquiring Handheld Computers

Assume that you are employed by the local branch of H L Winman and Associates, in a department related to the discipline you are studying—e.g. civil, mechanical, electrical, or computer engineering; biophysics; environmental science; etc. In your work, you and your associates have to travel frequently. Most of you use a laptop computer.

In the coming year's budget, the company has set $30 000 aside to purchase replacement laptops. However, you feel that a handheld device would be more useful. You discuss the idea with your associates and many agree with you. You describe your idea to Tracey Harcourt, your department manager, who likes it and suggests you write a proposal she can take to the next capital budget meeting. She recommends that, in your proposal, you describe

Overcome readers' resistance by anticipating their questions

- why handheld computers would be of value to departmental staff,
- what you can do with a handheld computer, compared to a laptop,
- the advantages of a handheld computer, and
- how many should be purchased.

She also suggests you identify several different handheld computers, evaluate them, and propose that the company buy a specific brand.

Project 6.2: Building a Sunroom

You have friends living in a private home at... (provide the address of a house you know well). Assume that you have had a discussion with these friends, during which you suggested that a sunroom would be a useful addition to their house. They are doubtful, but you are very persuasive until finally they say, "As you seem to be the expert, why don't you get some information for us and *show* us why we should install a sunroom, and what kind of sunroom would be best."

Now you need to take a more detailed look at the house and assess

- where, and off which room, the sunroom should be built,
- what size it should be,
- what zoning requirements apply,
- whether it should be a four-season or three-season sunroom,
- who makes and installs sunrooms, and what they have to offer, and
- what the cost will be.

You decide to write a semiformal proposal for your friends, in which you describe what can be done and recommend the best approach and supplier.

Project 6.3: Installing an Alternative Power Supply

You are a technician employed by H L Winman and Associates and currently you are engaged in a three-month project under contract to a major client: Terrapin Control Systems. The project started seven weeks ago and will run for another eight weeks. The difficulty is that over the past four weeks you have twice experienced power outages that have destroyed the tests for that particular day, which means you are now two days behind schedule and there is no more time available if you are to finish the project by the prescribed completion date. (If there is a delay beyond that date, Terrapin Control Systems will impose a cost penalty of $1000 per day.)

Each day you test two sets of switches, one of which is exposed to extreme heat and the other to extreme cold. At the start of each test the switches are placed in an oven or a freezer chamber, the temperature is increased or decreased to an optimum level, and the switches are made to operate continuously and automatically for 14 hours. To avoid the cost of having a technician present at night, you have installed timers that shut off the chambers at a prescribed time each night. The interruption by power outages means the switches have experienced nonstandard testing and have had to be discarded.

To prevent another power outage from affecting the tests, you realize you must have a backup power supply. Write a proposal for your manager, John Grayson, in which you recommend that the company either buy or lease a backup power supply. You will need to do some research to determine

- what types of power supply are available,
- what strength of power supply will be sufficient (i.e. to do this you may choose your own specifications),
- whether you will require one or two power supplies (one each for the oven and deep-freeze chamber),
- whether it will be more economical to purchase or to lease the power supply, and
- the cost of purchasing versus the cost of leasing.

In your proposal, describe the various power supplies that are available and compare them. Be ready, too, to counter a possible suggestion that it would be less expensive and more efficient to have a technician onsite at night than to buy or lease a backup power supply. Remember that a technician cannot prevent the power outage and so cannot prevent test degradation.

Project 6.4: A Proposal to the Student Council

Write a proposal to the student council (or its equivalent) at your school or college, describing an innovative idea you have that you would like the council to implement. The idea may be one of the following:

1. A plan to set up a two- or three-day skiing trip to one of the ski resorts nearest to your college, to be held during a mid-term or between-term break. Work out the details and use them to answer questions the student council is likely to ask, such as these:
   - When will it happen?
   - How much will it cost?
   - Where is the resort?
   - What lodgings are available, and at what cost?
   - What arrangements will be made to rent a coach, and at what cost?

Answer even more questions than are listed here

- Who will make all the arrangements?
- How will it be marketed?

2. A plan to set up a money-making event that will generate funds for a charity (you choose which one). Identify an event that will be particularly visible and so promote the charity's need for funds. Propose that students taking part in the event obtain sponsors who promise to donate a specified amount if the student they sponsor completes an activity such as a 50 km bicycle ride, a 20-lap swim, a 10 km hike, and so on. Describe why the charity is worth supporting, how the event will be organized, who will do the organizing, and how the event will be publicized, either through the school's internal media or to the general public.

3. A plan to clean up the neighbourhood around the school or college. From time to time there have been complaints from residents living on neighbouring streets that students drop gum and candy wrappers, loose-leaf pages, cigarette packs and butts, and so on, as they walk to and from the local bus stop or their cars. The residents complain that the students' debris makes the neighbourhood shabbier and reduces house values. Suggest that the student council

   - set up cleanup crews who will regularly (once a week?) search the neighbouring streets for rubbish and collect it in large garbage bags, and
   - send out a news release to the local media, to demonstrate that the college's/school's students are very conscious of the image they create and that they want to contribute actively to the neighbourhood's environment.

   Be ready to counter remarks from the student council that the local residents contribute much of the garbage they are complaining about.

Develop your own idea for a project!

If you have a different idea the student council could address, select it as your topic. Whatever topic you select, you will need to research it well if you are to write a confident proposal.

Chapter 7
User Manuals and Instructions

In this chapter you will learn how to

- tailor a user manual to a specific audience,
- develop a writing plan for your user manual,
- create and organize the actions for a task analysis, and
- write a technical instruction that will give the user confidence.

Explore

Most manufacturers provide a user manual with their products, which traditionally has been a printed booklet but today often will be available only electronically from the manufacturer's website. This is particularly true of computer hardware and software. The manual most often contains

1. a brief description of the product,
2. instructions on how to use it, and
3. suggestions for fixing problems that may occur.

It may also provide a set of maintenance instructions containing detailed service and repair procedures, for use by qualified repair specialists. Each publication performs the same task, but for different readers:

- The user manual assumes the reader has only slight technical knowledge.
- The maintenance instructions assume the reader is a technical expert.

User Manual

In this chapter we assume you are writing a user manual for nontechnical readers.

Identify Your Audience

The problem with many user manuals is that they are written by an engineer or a technical person and so may be either too complex or incomplete from the user's viewpoint. To avoid this you need to identify your audience before you start writing and understand the reader's level of knowledge about the product.

The first step in *any* writing situation: know your audience

We often suggest to engineers that they write a brief description of who the user is, so they can refer back to it as they write. This audience analysis often becomes the first section in the user guide, called "Who Should Read This Document."

Develop a Writing Plan

The writing plan for most user manuals has four compartments, as shown in Figure 7-1. The two upper compartments describe the product, while the two lower compartments tell the reader how to use it.

The following pages demonstrate how to use these four compartments. For simplicity, we are assuming the product is basic electronic software.

Describe the Product

The **Summary** briefly describes the product and its main purpose:

> This electronic mail software allows you to communicate with other email users by sending and receiving messages. It allows you to connect to a remote computer, called a server, and access messages people have sent to you. The server will also send messages you write.

The **Product Description** identifies each part and describes its components. For equipment that has several discrete components or parts, the Product Description may be subdivided into two sections: Overview and Detailed Description.

- The **Overview** section simply lists the main components:

  The electronic mail program contains four components:

  - In Tray
  - Out Tray
  - File Cabinet
  - Address Book

List the components in the same sequence you will describe them

Summary	What the product is, and what it does
Product Description	What the product consists of
Operating Instructions	How to use the product
Troubleshooting Techniques	How to remedy a problem

Figure 7-1 Writing plan for a user manual.

- The **Detailed Description** provides more specific information about each component *in the same sequence* that they were presented in the Overview section:

  The In Tray is identified by a square icon with an arrow pointing down. This indicates that messages are directed to you. Any messages that are sent to you are automatically placed in this area. You can view your messages in the In Tray by pointing your mouse on the icon and clicking.

  The Out Tray is identified by a square icon with an arrow pointing up. This indicates that messages are from you to someone else. This is the area where messages you have written are stored until you are ready to send them.

  The File Cabinet is identified by an icon that looks like a traditional two- or three-drawer filing cabinet you might find in an office. This is the area where you can store or file messages that are important or that you want to keep. You can create different folders for different situations and thus create a filing system for your messages.

  The Address Book is identified by an icon that looks like a small book. This is the area where you store the electronic addresses of people to whom you frequently send messages. When you write a message you can select the address of the person or persons you are sending it to directly from the Address Book.

Explore

Clear, simple language helps *all* readers understand

Tell How to Use the Product

Explore

The **Operating Instructions** provide step-by-step instructions for each task the user can perform with the product. One of the major problems with many user manuals is that they are not written from the user's perspective: instead of describing *how* to do something with the product, the manual describes *what* can be done with it. Follow three steps to develop a user manual:

1. Perform a task analysis.
2. Group and label the tasks.
3. Write the steps for each task.

This is similar to the writing process described in Chapter 2 (Figure 2-3 on page 7).

Step 1—Perform a Task Analysis

List everything that users might want *to do* with the product. Focus on the tasks the user *will perform*, not on what the product can do. For example, a task analysis for a simple electronic mailing package might look like this:

Tasks:	*Tasks:*
Sending messages	Adding names to an address book
Receiving messages	Storing messages in folders
Forwarding messages	Creating folders
Addressing messages	Downloading messages
Printing messages	Deleting messages

When writing a task analysis, use verbs that end with "...ing" (*sending, receiving,* etc)

Tasks:
Creating messages
Connecting to the server
Checking spelling
Attaching documents
Installing

Tasks:
Customizing
Calling manufacturer for support
Using the Help system

This list is developed while brainstorming and is not meant to be in any particular order. Later, you can add items; for now, just list the tasks.

Step 2—Group and Label Tasks

Now examine your task list and identify any tasks that are related. For example, "Receiving messages" and "Forwarding messages" are related in the above list, and so are "Creating messages" and "Checking spelling." Now group related tasks by assigning each task in your list with a letter that will identify which group it belongs to. In the list below, each task has been assigned A, B, C, etc.

Identify which tasks seem related

Tasks:	*Groups:*
Sending messages	F
Receiving messages	A
Forwarding messages	A
Addressing messages	B
Printing messages	C
Adding names to an address book	B
Storing messages in folders	A
Creating folders	A
Downloading messages	A
Deleting messages	A
Creating messages	B
Connecting to the server	F/A
Checking spelling	B
Attaching documents	F
Installing	D
Customizing	D
Calling manufacturer for support	E
Using the Help system	E

This becomes the first step toward organizing the information

You can now perform your first organizational step: assign a label to each group. Choose a label that *describes what the user is doing* or trying to accomplish. Use "…ing" words whenever you can because they *indicate an action performed by the user.* Here are labels for the above groups:

A – Handling Incoming Messages
B – Writing Messages

C – Printing Messages
D – Getting Started
E – Getting Additional Help
F – Sending Messages

Your next step is to organize the groups of topics into a logical sequence for the intended audience. User manuals are usually structured in a sequential arrangement, either listing what needs to be done first or introducing easy tasks first. In this example the structure might look like this:

Getting Started *(D)*
- Installing Your Software
- Customizing Your Software

Writing Messages *(B)*
- Creating Messages
- Addressing Messages
- Adding Names to an Address Book

An outline emerges naturally, almost painlessly...

Sending Messages *(F)*
- Sending Messages You Have Written
- Connecting to the Server
- Attaching Documents

Handling Incoming Messages *(A)*
- Connecting to the Server
- Receiving Messages
- Forwarding Messages
- Creating Folders
- Storing Messages in Folders
- Downloading Messages
- Deleting Messages

Printing Messages *(C)*

Getting Additional Help *(E)*
- Using the Help System
- Calling the Manufacturer for Support

You will now have a user-focused, task-oriented structure that describes how to use your product.

Step 3—Write the Steps

✓•–Practise

Now turn each of the identified tasks into an instruction, which together will be the steps the reader needs to take to accomplish the task. Here are two examples from the electronic mail tasks:

...from which a logically flowing instruction can be written

Installing Your Software

1. Unpack the contents of the box and make sure you have
   - this manual,
   - the CD, and
   - the software licence.
2. Turn your computer on and start Windows.
3. Put the CD into your CD drive.
4. When the Install Wizard initiates, follow the directions on the screen.

Connecting to the Server

1. Click on the File menu.
2. Choose the **Connect to Server** command.
3. When a dialogue box appears, enter your ID and password.
4. Click OK.
5. Wait while the system initiates the protocol sequence defined in the **Server Settings** dialog box.
6. When the message **You Are Now Connected** appears on the screen, you have successfully connected to the remote server.

You can now send and receive your electronic mail messages.

Note that each step is short, has a number, and uses verbs in the imperative mood. (For more information on writing instructional steps, see "Give Your Reader Confidence" on page 171.)

Troubleshooting Techniques tell the reader what to do if, despite the reader's having followed the Operating Instructions correctly, the equipment does not work. They also consist of short, numbered steps and use verbs in the imperative mood. For example,

When all else fails, call for help

If the message **Server Connection Failed** appears, follow this procedure:

1. Click on the **Settings** menu.
2. Choose **Server Settings**.
3. Check that your ID, password, and IP address have been correctly identified.
4. Click OK.
5. Try connecting to the server again.
6. If the problem continues, email or call the manufacturer for technical support.

Technical Instruction

Explore

Confusion can exist as to whether the steps the user will follow constitute a *procedure* or an *instruction*. Although the terms often are used interchangeably, there is a difference:

- A **Procedure** describes how things are done:

  Distance is measured with electronic meter DME 297.

- An **Instruction** tells the reader what to do:

  Measure the distance with electronic meter DME 297.

If you hear the term *standard operating procedure* (more often called an SOP), it refers to a company document that establishes *how* the company operates. It does *not* instruct anyone in the company to do anything.

A technical instruction tells somebody to do something. It may be a simple one-sentence statement that defines what has to be done but leaves the time and the method to the reader. Or it may describe step by step exactly what has to be done, and when and how. The latter type of technical instruction will be described here.

An instruction *must* be written from the reader's point of view

The first step is to define your readers and establish their level of technical knowledge and familiarity with your subject. This helps you decide the depth of detail you must provide. If they are familiar with a piece of equipment, you may assume that the simple statement "Open the cover plate" will not pose a problem. But if the equipment is new to them, you may have to broaden the statement to help them first identify and open the cover plate:

> Find the hinged cover plate at the bottom rear of the cabinet. Open it by inserting a Robertson No. 2 screwdriver into the narrow slot just above the hinge and then rotating the screwdriver half a turn counterclockwise.

Start with a Plan

A clearly written instruction contains four main compartments, as shown in Figure 7-2 on page 170. These compartments contain the following information:

- A **Summary Statement** outlines briefly what has to be done:

  The 28 Vancourt Model AL-8 LCD projectors in rooms A4 through A32 are to be bolted to their projection tables...

- The **Purpose** explains why the work is necessary:

  ...to reduce the current high damage rate caused by projectors being accidentally knocked onto the floor.

  (A technician who understands *why* a job is necessary will much more readily follow an instruction.)

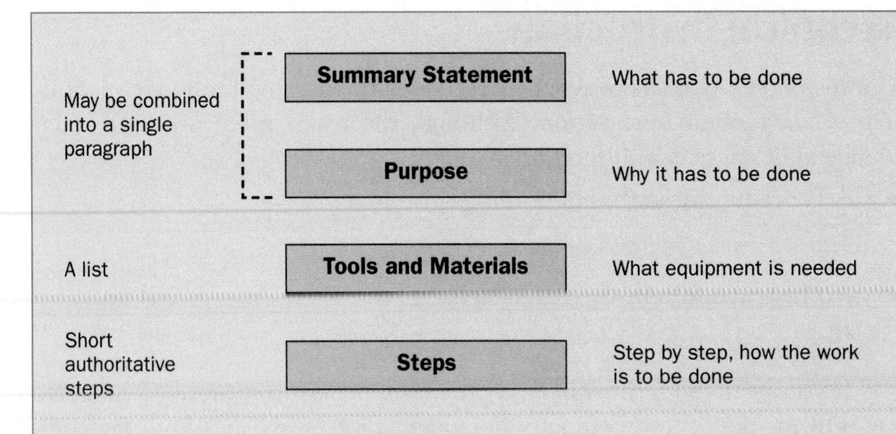

Figure 7-2 Writing plan for an instruction.

Explore

- The **Tools and Materials** identify what is needed to perform the task:

Some manufacturers list the assembly tools on the outside of the shipping carton

To carry out the modification you will require

Modification kit LCD-4, comprising

1 template, LCD-4T

4 bolts, flat head, 50 mm long, 3 mm dia

4 washers, 25 mm dia, with 4 mm dia central hole

A 6 mm drill with a 3.5 mm drill bit

A Phillips No. 2 screwdriver

A slot-head No. 3 screwdriver

A sharp pencil

- The **Steps** tell readers step by step what they must do:

Proceed as follows:

Number the steps: show there is a sequence

1. Disconnect the projector's power cord from the wall socket, then take the projector to a table and turn it on its side.
2. Use a slot-head No. 3 screwdriver to unscrew the four bolts that hold the feet onto the base of the projector. Remove them, but retain them for future use.
3. Place template LCD-4T onto the projection table and position it where the projector is to stand. Using a sharp pencil, mark the table through each of the four holes in the template.
4. Drill four 3.5 mm dia holes through the tabletop at the places marked in step 3.
5. Place the LCD projector on the table with the lens assembly facing the screen. Align the four boltholes identified in step 2 with the four holes drilled in the tabletop.
6. From beneath the table, place a washer under each hole and insert a 50 mm flat-head bolt up through the washer and hole until it engages the corresponding hole in the projector base. Tighten the four bolts in place, using a Phillips No. 2 screwdriver.

Give Your Reader Confidence

Explore

A well-written technical instruction automatically instills confidence in its readers. They feel they have the ability to do the work even though it may be new to them and highly complex. Consider these examples:

Vague	Cut the wire into an appropriate length for each connection and strip a short piece of insulation from each end. Install the wire between the correct terminals and pins.
Clear and Concise	Cut a 0.62 m length of 10-gauge wire and strip 20 mm of insulation from each end. Solder one end of the wire to terminal 7 and the other end to pin 49.

An instruction is not the place for weak, wishy-washy words

The first excerpt is too ambiguous. It only suggests what should be done, it hints where it should instruct, and despite using 29 explanatory words, it fails to define either the length of the wire or the length of insulation to be removed. The second excerpt is assertive and keeps strictly to the point. The verbs *cut*, *strip*, and *solder* make readers feel the writer is confident. Clear commands convince them of the accuracy and validity of the steps.

To sound authoritative, write in the imperative mood. This means beginning each step with a strong verb, so that your instructions are commands:

Ignite the mixture...	*Connect* the green wire...
Mount the transit on its tripod...	*Excavate* 1.4 metres down...
Apply the voltage to...	*Measure* the current at...
Cut a 40 mm wide strip of...	*Insert* the USB cord...

Sometimes, however, the verb may be preceded by an introductory or conditional clause:

Before connecting the meter to the power source, *set* all the switches to "zero."

The following two statements clearly show the difference between an instruction written in the imperative mood and one that is not:

Make each step a command, not a broad statement of intent

A. Disengage the gear, then start the engine. (***Definite: uses strong verbs***)

B. The gear should be disengaged before starting the engine. (***Indefinite: uses weaker verbs***)

Avoid Ambiguity

There is no room for ambiguity in technical instructions. It's most likely that the person following your instructions cannot ask questions, so you must never write anything that could be interpreted more than one way. The following statement is open to misinterpretation:

Align the trace so that it is inclined approximately 30° to the horizontal.

Never leave a statement open to misinterpretation

Each technician will align the trace with a different degree of accuracy, depending on his or her interpretation of "approximately." Replace such vague references with clearly stated tolerances:

Align the trace so that it is inclined 30° (±2°) above the horizontal.

More subtle, but equally open to misinterpretation, is this statement:

Adjust the capstan handle until the rotating head is close to the base.

Here the offending word is "close," and needs to be replaced by a specific distance:

Adjust the capstan handle until the distance between the rotating head and the base is 2.5 mm.

Write specific details; never generalize

Similarly, replace vague references such as "*relatively* high," "*near* the top," and "*an adequate* supply" with clearly stated measurements, tolerances, and quantities.

Avoid weak words such as "should," "could," "would," "might," and "may," because they weaken the authority of an instruction and reduce the reader's confidence in the writer. For example,

Set the meter to the +300 V range. The needle should indicate 120 V (±2 V).

Here "should" implies that the voltage reading is not essential.

The instructions in Figure 7-3 show steps that are clear, concise, and definite. You need not be a specialist in the subject to recognize that they would be easy to follow.

Write Short Steps

You can help technicians who work in tight, crowded conditions by writing short paragraphs, each containing only one main step. If a step is complicated and its paragraph grows too long, divide it into a major step and a series of substeps, numbering the paragraphs and subparagraphs:

Offer short pieces of information

3. List the supporting documents in block J of Form 658. Check that blocks A to G have been completed correctly, then sign the form and distribute copies as follows:
   - 3.1 Attach the supporting documents to Copies 1 and 2 and mail them to the Chief Recording Clerk, Room 217, Civic Centre, Thompson, Manitoba.
   - 3.2 Mail Copy 3 to the Computer Data Centre, using one of the preaddressed envelopes.
   - 3.3 File Copy 4 in the "Hold—Pending Receipt" file.
   - 3.4 When Copy 2 is returned by the Chief Recording Clerk, attach it to Copy 4 and file both in the "Action Complete" file.

Insert Precautions

Insert precautionary comments into instructions whenever you need to warn readers of dangerous conditions, or of damage that may occur if they do not exercise care. There are two recognized notices you can use:

Warning: To alert readers to an element of personal danger (such as unprotected high voltage terminals).

Caution: To tell readers when care is needed to prevent equipment damage.

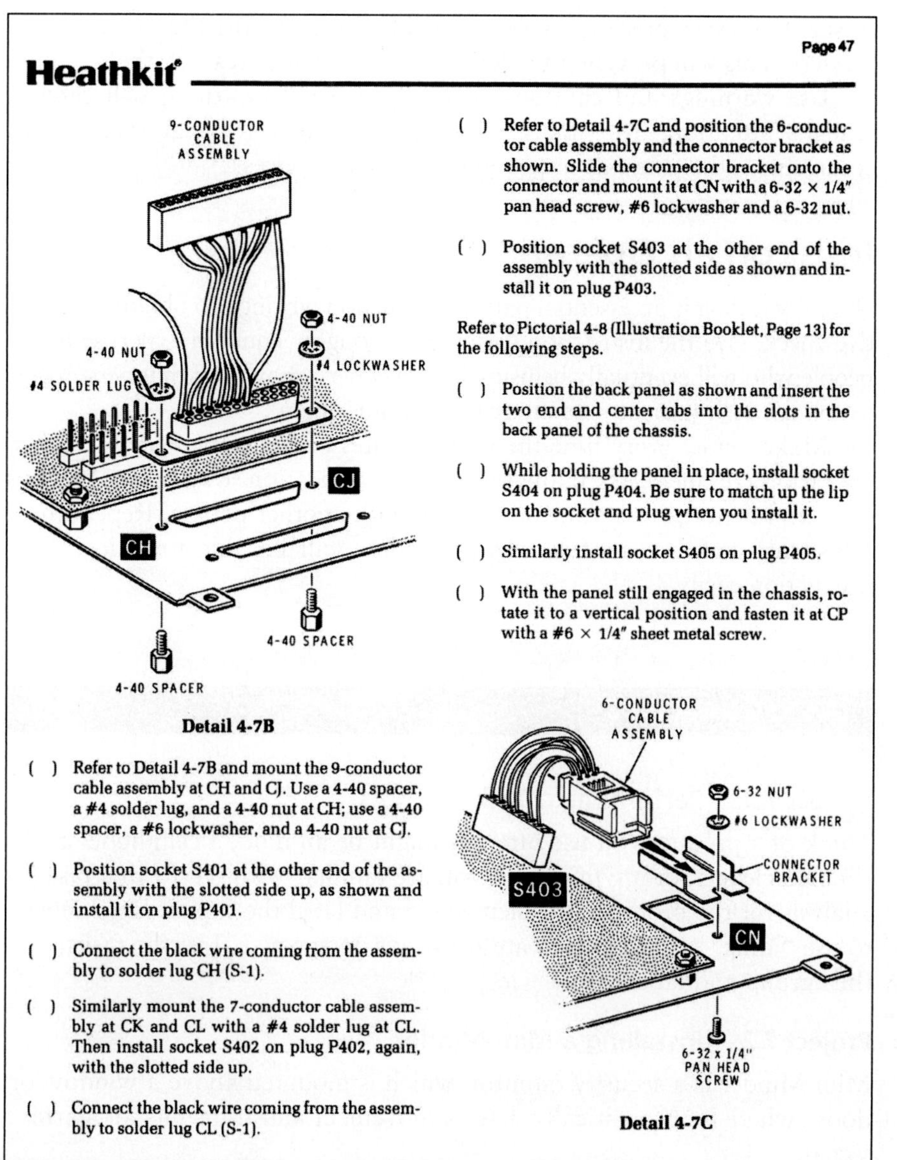

Heathkit® Page 47

Detail 4-7B

( ) Refer to Detail 4-7B and mount the 9-conductor cable assembly at CH and CJ. Use a 4-40 spacer, a #4 solder lug, and a 4-40 nut at CH; use a 4-40 spacer, a #6 lockwasher, and a 4-40 nut at CJ.

( ) Position socket S401 at the other end of the assembly with the slotted side up, as shown and install it on plug P401.

( ) Connect the black wire coming from the assembly to solder lug CH (S-1).

( ) Similarly mount the 7-conductor cable assembly at CK and CL with a #4 solder lug at CL. Then install socket S402 on plug P402, again, with the slotted side up.

( ) Connect the black wire coming from the assembly to solder lug CL (S-1).

( ) Refer to Detail 4-7C and position the 6-conductor cable assembly and the connector bracket as shown. Slide the connector bracket onto the connector and mount it at CN with a 6-32 × 1/4" pan head screw, #6 lockwasher and a 6-32 nut.

( ) Position socket S403 at the other end of the assembly with the slotted side as shown and install it on plug P403.

Refer to Pictorial 4-8 (Illustration Booklet, Page 13) for the following steps.

( ) Position the back panel as shown and insert the two end and center tabs into the slots in the back panel of the chassis.

( ) While holding the panel in place, install socket S404 on plug P404. Be sure to match up the lip on the socket and plug when you install it.

( ) Similarly install socket S405 on plug P405.

( ) With the panel still engaged in the chassis, rotate it to a vertical position and fasten it at CP with a #6 × 1/4" sheet metal screw.

Detail 4-7C

Keep diagrams uncluttered...

...and shown from the reader's point of view

Figure 7-3 Excerpts from an instruction manual. (Courtesy the Heath Company, Mississauga, ON)

Draw attention to a precautionary comment by placing it in a box in the middle of the text, indenting the box from both margins. Precede the cautionary note with the single word WARNING or CAUTION.

Use simple design techniques to create a noticeable warning

WARNING

Disconnect the power source before removing the cover plate.

Usability Testing on Documents
http://jerz.setonhill.edu/design/usability/intro.htm
This document suggests some ways you might conduct tests to measure the usability of your technical documents. It covers the kind of data you should collect, how many test subjects you need, and how you should treat these subjects.

Ensure that every precautionary comment appears *before* the step to which it refers. This will prevent a reader from acting before reading the warning.

Use warnings and cautions sparingly. A single warning will catch a reader's attention. Too many will cause a reader to treat them all as comments rather than as important protective devices.

Insist on an Operational Check

Usability testing is an essential part of instruction writing. To obtain an objective check, give the instruction to someone roughly equal in expertise to the people who will eventually be using it, and observe how well that person performs the task (but do not interrupt or guide them).

Make a note every time the user hesitates or has difficulty; then when the task is complete, ask if any steps need clarification. Rewrite ambiguous steps and then recheck your instruction with another person. Repeat these steps until you are confident your readers will be able to follow your instruction easily.

ASSIGNMENTS

Project 7.1: Performing a Task Analysis

Think of a product you use often. It might be an iPod, a cellphone, a vacuum cleaner, or anything else you are familiar with. Perform a task analysis for the product and then group and label the topics. Remember to use "...ing" words to indicate the user's perspective. List the tasks, then group and label them.

Project 7.2: Installing a Mini-Minder

Mini-Minder is a security monitor, which is mounted above a window or door, where it automatically detects movement and transmits an alarm signal.

The Mini-Minder is shown in Figure 7-4. It is fixed to the wall above the door or window by removing the backplate and screwing the plate to the wall. The unit is then snapped onto the backplate (removing the unit from the backplate also sounds the alarm). The unit is battery-operated.

All materials and hardware are supplied with the Mini-Minder, but the installer will need an electric drill with a 5 mm masonry drill bit, a Robertson No. 2 screwdriver, and a sharp pencil to do the job. The sequence in which the installation should occur is shown by the circled numbers in Figure 7-4.

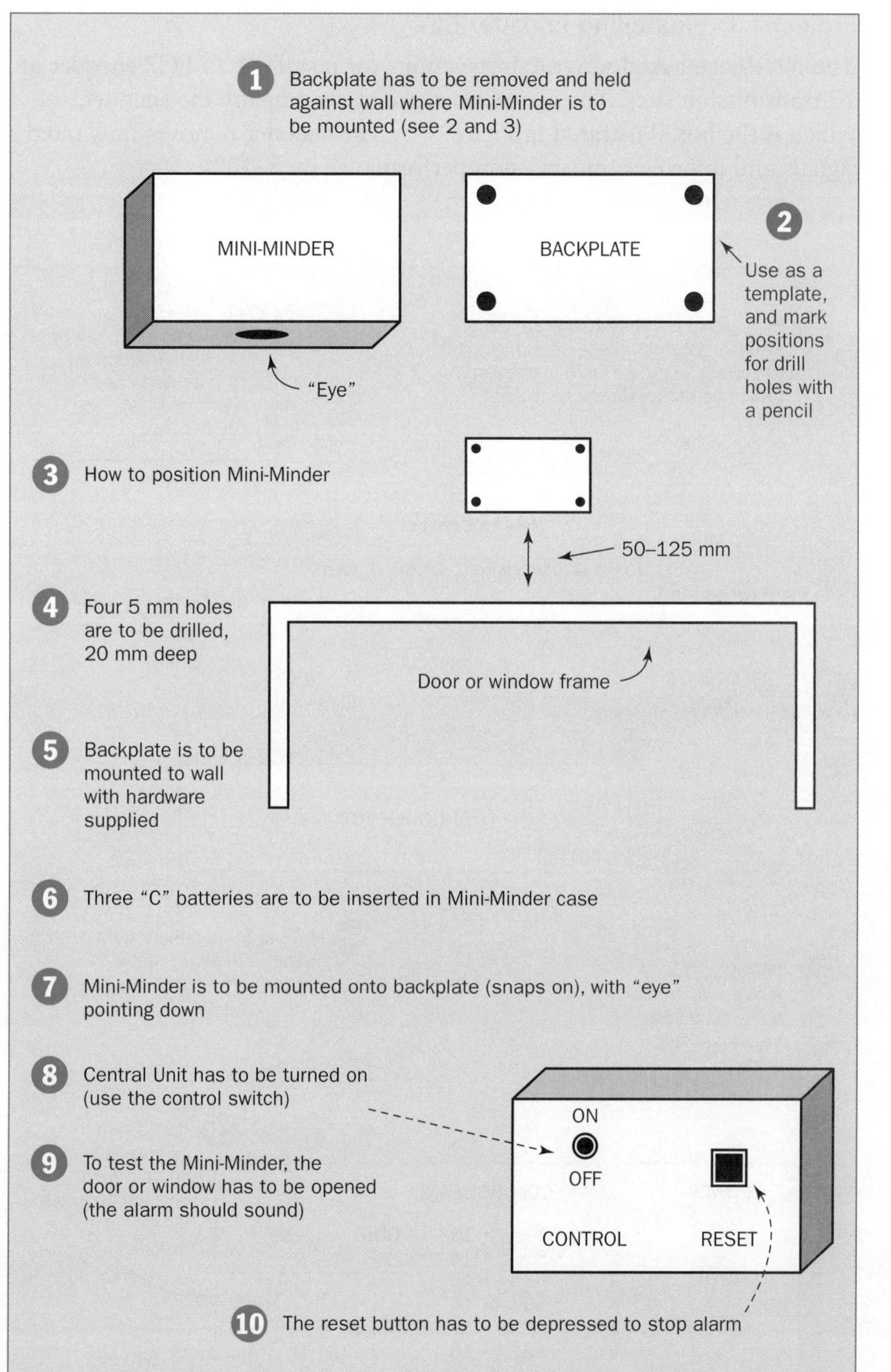

1 Backplate has to be removed and held against wall where Mini-Minder is to be mounted (see 2 and 3)
MINI-MINDER
BACKPLATE
2 Use as a template, and mark positions for drill holes with a pencil
"Eye"
3 How to position Mini-Minder
50–125 mm
4 Four 5 mm holes are to be drilled, 20 mm deep
Door or window frame
5 Backplate is to be mounted to wall with hardware supplied
6 Three "C" batteries are to be inserted in Mini-Minder case
7 Mini-Minder is to be mounted onto backplate (snaps on), with "eye" pointing down
8 Central Unit has to be turned on (use the control switch)
ON
OFF
CONTROL
RESET
9 To test the Mini-Minder, the door or window has to be opened (the alarm should sound)
10 The reset button has to be depressed to stop alarm

Figure 7-4 Installing and testing a Mini-Minder.

A reminder: write in the imperative mood

Project 7.3: Installing Encoder EC7

You will have to extract pertinent points from the illustration

You have been asked to write instructions for installing an EC7 encoder at 17 transmission sites. The instructions are to accompany the encoder, which is the box illustrated in Figure 7-5. The encoder removes unwanted signals and improves transmission performance by 8–10%.

Consider writing in the active voice

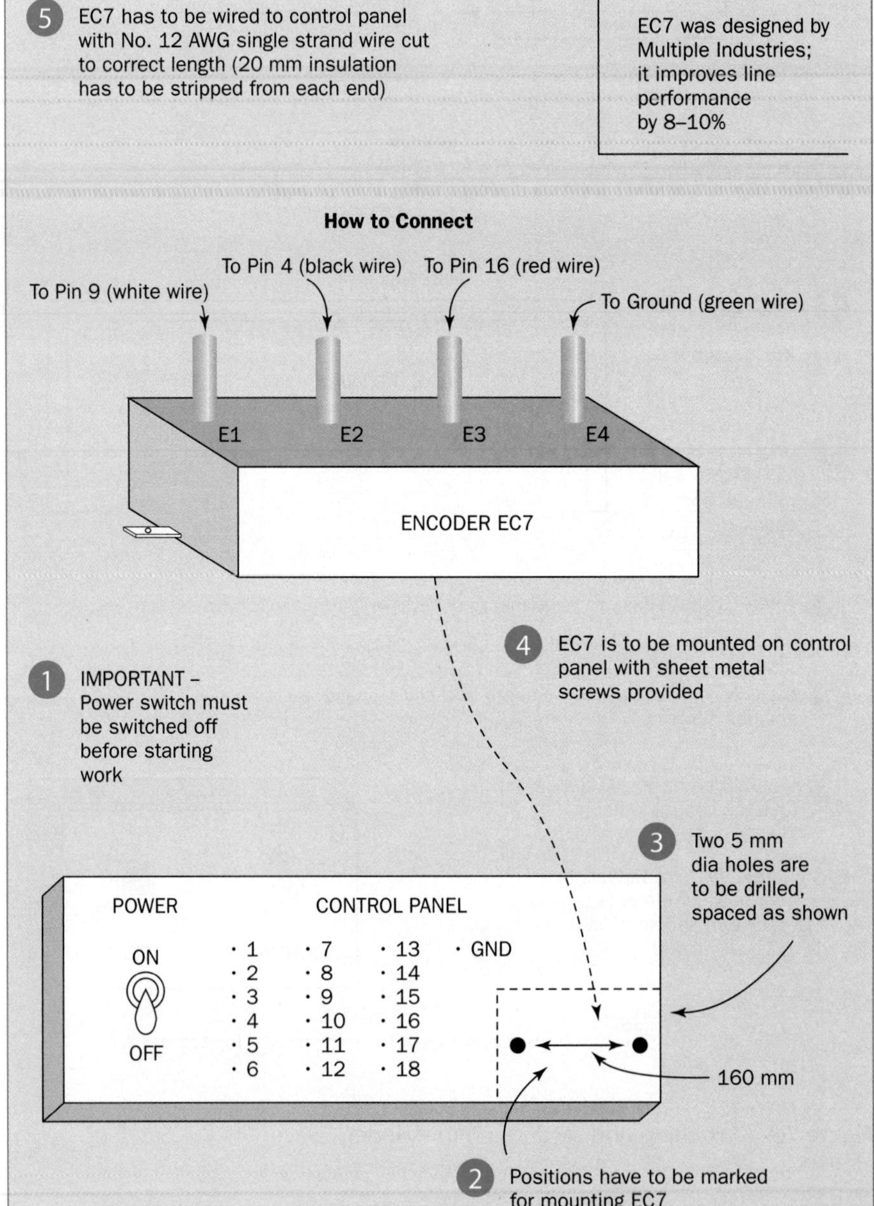

5 EC7 has to be wired to control panel with No. 12 AWG single strand wire cut to correct length (20 mm insulation has to be stripped from each end)
EC7 was designed by Multiple Industries; it improves line performance by 8–10%
How to Connect
To Pin 9 (white wire)
To Pin 4 (black wire)
To Pin 16 (red wire)
To Ground (green wire)
E1
E2
E3
E4
ENCODER EC7
4 EC7 is to be mounted on control panel with sheet metal screws provided
1 IMPORTANT – Power switch must be switched off before starting work
3 Two 5 mm dia holes are to be drilled, spaced as shown
POWER
CONTROL PANEL
ON
OFF
· 1 · 2 · 3 · 4 · 5 · 6
· 7 · 8 · 9 · 10 · 11 · 12
· 13 · 14 · 15 · 16 · 17 · 18
· GND
160 mm
2 Positions have to be marked for mounting EC7

Figure 7-5 Mounting and connecting Encoder EC7.

In your instructions, tell the site technicians to find a suitable location for the encoder at the bottom right of the control panel (see Figure 7-5), drill two holes for mounting the encoder, and connect the encoder with four wires (the connections are shown on the diagram). All materials (such as mounting hardware and wire) are supplied with each encoder, but the technician will need a soldering iron, some Ersin 60/40 resin core solder, a drill with a 5 mm bit, and a Robertson No. 2 screwdriver to carry out the work. The circled numbers on the diagram show the sequence in which the installation is to be carried out.

When the installation is complete, remind the technician to turn on the power to the control panel.

Chapter 8
Illustrating Technical Documents

In this chapter you will learn how to

- create illustrations that effectively support your documentation,
- select which type of illustration is most suitable for depicting different kinds of information,
- identify the difference between *dependent* and *independent variables*, and
- position illustrations for maximum effect.

Because many people are visual learners, technical report writers need to incorporate graphs, charts, tables, designs, and photographs into their documents. The main criterion for preparing an illustration is that it must help explain the narrative adjacent to it; the narrative should not have to explain the illustration.

The suggestions we provide here are intended as an introduction to designing illustrations. More detailed information is available from books and websites devoted solely to the subject.

Primary Guidelines

An illustration must be simple enough for readers to understand the point you are making quickly and easily. Follow these guidelines:

1. Before selecting or designing your illustrations, consider the readers for whom you are writing so you can tailor the illustrations to suit their particular needs.
2. Decide what you want your reader to learn from each illustration.
3. Depict only one point in each illustration, and keep it simple and uncluttered.

Good illustrations attract readers

4. Position each illustration as near as possible to the narrative it supports (see "Positioning the Illustrations" on pages 195 to 196).
5. Label each illustration clearly with a number and a title. The number and title belong *beneath* a figure or chart, and *above* a table. See the samples in this chapter.
6. If necessary, add a caption (that is, comments or remarks) beneath a figure title, to draw attention to significant aspects of the illustration.

7. Refer to every illustration at least once in the report narrative. This helps integrate the text and the visual.
8. Identify the original source of the illustration or image if it is not your original work, and state that permission has been obtained for its use.

Computer-Designed Graphs and Charts

Computer software makes it easy to prepare graphs and charts

Computer software programs will help you create illustrations and graphics. You choose the type of graph or chart you want and then enter the quantities of each function you need to depict. Check, however, that the computer graphic has depicted your information appropriately, because sometimes the graphic can place emphasis incorrectly and so make your chart difficult to understand.

The following sections describe the different types of graphs and charts available. Understanding the benefits of each type will help you decide which is best for your information and audience.

Graphs

Graphs are a simple way to show a change in one function in relation to a change in another. Time is a function used frequently in such comparisons. The other function may be temperature, erosion, wear, speed, strength, or any factors that vary over time.

Assume that you are conducting a study into the cooling rate of different manufactured products, and that you have plotted your results in Table 8-1. Your information will be used by the company's production department to determine how long the product (a manometer case in this example) must cool before assemblers can start working on it with bare hands.

Table 8-1 Cooling rate, manometer case MM-7.

A table provides specific details

Time Elapsed *(min:sec)*	Temperature *(C)*	Time Elapsed *(min:sec)*	Temperature *(C)*
0:30	152.9	5:30	43.9
1:00	123.4	6:00	41.1
1:30	106.7	6:30	38.9
2:00	91.2	7:00	37.2
2:30	77.8	7:30	35.6
3:00	69.5	8:00	34.5
3:30	61.7	8:30	33.4
4:00	55.6	9:00	32.8
4:30	51.5	9:30	31.7
5:00	47.3	10:00	31.1
Ambient temperature 22.8°C		Oven temperature 180°C	

From the table you can see that the temperature of the manometer case drops continuously, is within 8.3C of the ambient temperature after 10 minutes (*ambient* means "surrounding environment"), and is down to the bare-hand temperature after 7 minutes. A closer examination identifies that the temperature drops rapidly at first, then progressively more slowly as time passes. Yet you cannot easily visualize this information just from looking at the table.

Single-Curve Graph

A graph translates the details into an easily understood form

So you convert your data into the graph shown in Figure 8-1. Now it's immediately evident that the temperature drops rapidly at first, then slows down until the rate of change is almost negligible.

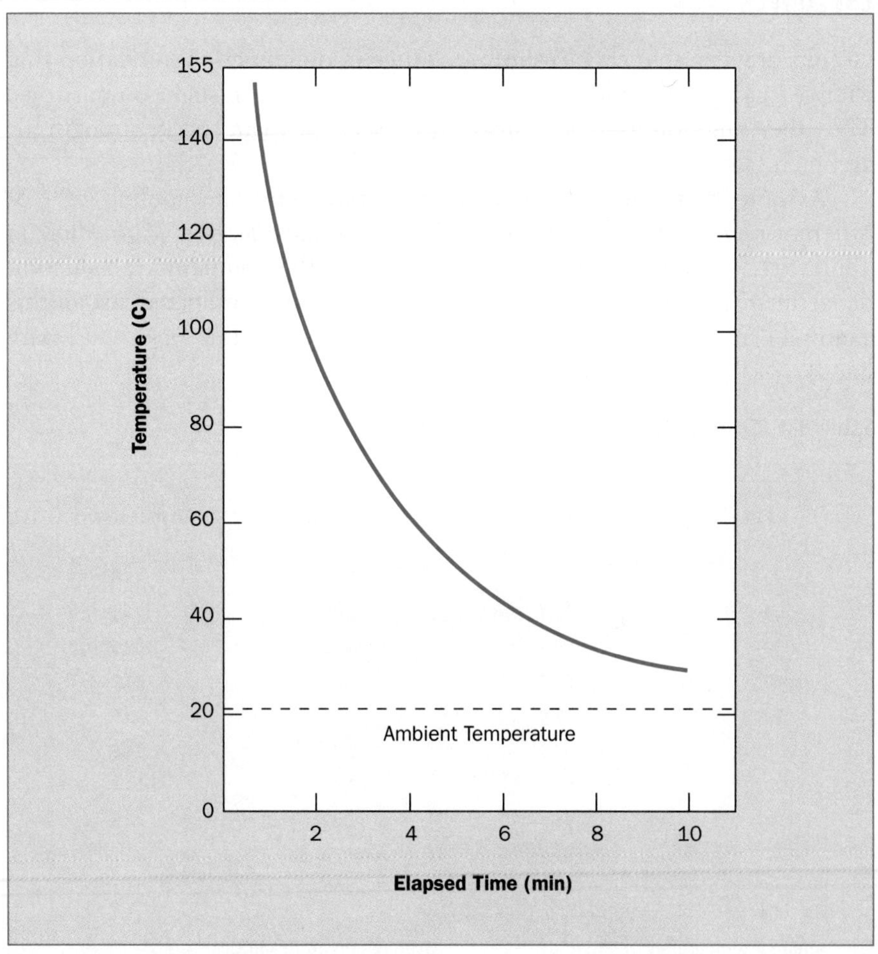

Figure 8-1 Graph with a single curve.

Multiple-Curve Graph

Assume that you extend your study to include comparing temperature readings and cooling rates of two more products: a cover plate and a panel board. This time you decide to simplify the table by showing the temperatures at only one-minute intervals (see Table 8-2).

What can you assess from this table? An obvious conclusion is that after 10 minutes the panel board has cooled down the most, then the manometer case, then the cover plate. You can also see that the initial rate at which the components cooled has varied considerably, but it is difficult to assess whether there were any *changes in the rate of cooling* as time progressed.

So you plot a second graph (Figure 8-2 on page 182), this time with three curves. Now the rapid initial drop in temperature is evident from the initial steepness of the three curves, with each curve flattening out to a slower rate of cooling after two to four minutes. The difference in cooling rates for the three components also is much more obvious. (The lines in Figures 8-1 and 8-2 are commonly referred to as curves, even though in some cases they may be straight lines or a series of short straight lines joining points plotted on the graph.)

Technical Illustration in the 21st Century: A Primer for Today's Professionals
www.ptc.com/WCMS/files/51551/en/2727_TechIllustration_WP_EN.pdf
This document contains a discussion of the purpose of technical illustrations as well as descriptions and samples of product renderings, exploded diagrams, and cutaway views.

Graph Scales

If you plan to present only a general description of temperature trends, the two graphs you have developed will be fine. However, if you also want to discuss exact temperature readings at specific times in your report, then you will need to insert numbers for your readers to refer to.

Both functions may be variable, but only one depends on the other

The two functions to be compared are entered on a horizontal scale (along the bottom) and a vertical scale (along the left side). The scales meet

A multi-factor table can be even more difficult to interpret

Table 8-2 Cooling rates for three components.

Time Elapsed *(minutes)*	Temperature (C) Cover Plate	Panel Board	Manometer Case
0:30	154.5	145.1	152.9
1	136.7	97.3	123.4
2	112.3	67.8	91.2
3	95.1	51.7	69.5
4	82.3	42.3	55.6
5	71.7	36.1	47.3
6	63.9	32.2	41.1
7	55.6	29.5	37.2
8	49.5	27.2	34.5
9	43.4	26.1	32.8
10	38.9	25.0	31.1

A graph can make the same information much more accessible

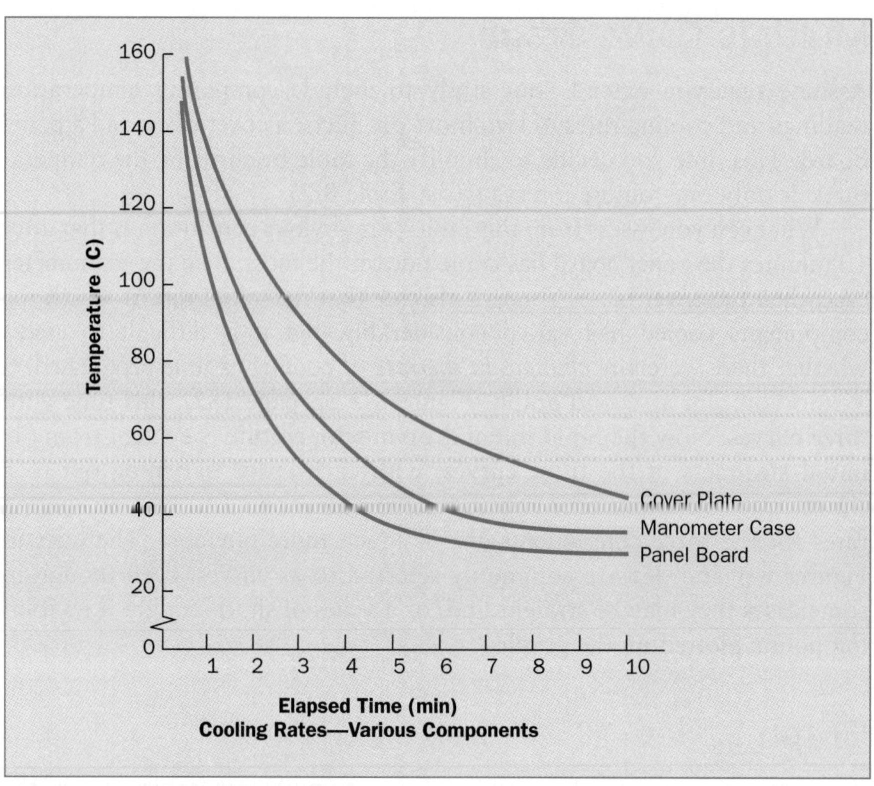

Figure 8-2 Graph with multiple curves.

at the bottom left corner, which normally—but not always—is designated as the zero point for both.

Identify which function depends on the other

These two functions are commonly known as the dependent variables and the independent variables, so named because a change in the dependent variable *depends* on a change in the independent variable. For example, if you want to show how the fuel consumption of a car increases with speed, you would enter speed as the independent variable along the bottom scale, and fuel consumption as the dependent variable along the left side, as in Figure 8-3. (Fuel consumption *depends* on speed; speed does not depend on fuel consumption.) The same applies to the previous temperature measurement graphs: temperature is the dependent variable because it depends on *the time that has elapsed* since the components came out of the oven (which is the independent variable).

When you construct a graph, your first step is to identify which function should form the horizontal scale and which the vertical scale. Table 8-3 lists some typical situations that show that the same function (e.g. temperature) can be an independent variable in one situation and a dependent variable in another. Selection of the independent variable depends on which function can be more easily identified as influencing the other function.

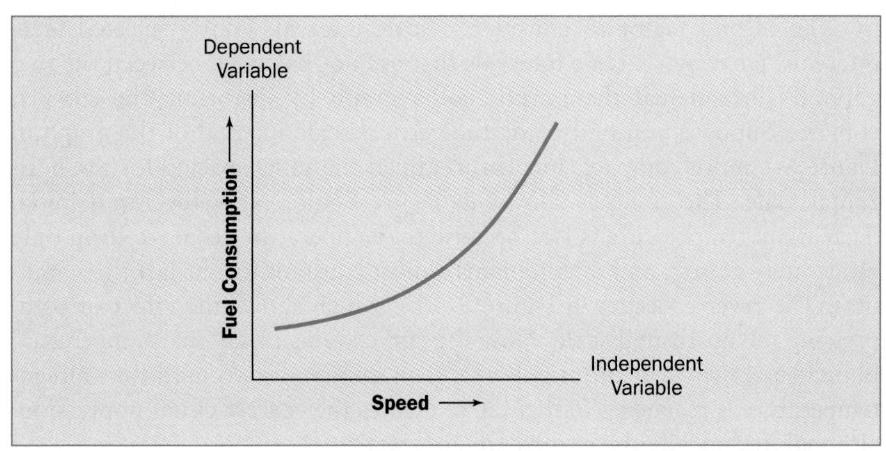

Figure 8-3 The dependent variable depends on the independent variable.

Table 8-3 Identifying dependent and independent variables.

Graph Illustrates	Dependent Variable (vertical scale)	Independent Variable (horizontal scale)
1. How attendance at a ball game varies with temperature	Attendance	Temperature
2. How much a motor's speed affects the noise it produces	Noise	Speed
3. How a change in temperature causes a change in pressure	Pressure	Temperature
4. How much an increase in payload reduces an aircraft's range by limiting the amount of fuel it can carry	Aircraft range (or fuel load)	Payload
5. How much increasing the fuel load of an aircraft to achieve greater range reduces its effective payload	Payload	Fuel load (or aircraft range)

Note: A function can be either dependent or independent, depending on its role in the comparison (see temperature in Examples 1 and 3, and both functions in Examples 4 and 5).

Select scale intervals that will give a *balanced* appearance

The second factor to consider is scale interval. Poorly selected scale intervals, particularly scale intervals that are not balanced between the two variables, can defeat the purpose of a graph by distorting the story it conveys. Suppose you had made the vertical scale interval of the graph in Figure 8-1 more compact, but had retained the same spacing for the horizontal scale. The result is shown in Figure 8-4(a). Now the rapid initial decrease in temperature is lost because the temperature seems to drop only moderately at first, and then remains almost constant for the last three minutes. The reverse occurs in Figure 8-4(b), which shows the effect of compressing the horizontal scale. Now the curve seems to say that temperature plummets downward and it will be only a minute or two until the ambient temperature is reached. Neither curve creates the correct visual impression, although technically the graphs are accurate.

Adjust a scale's starting point to centre the curve(s)

Normally both scales start at zero, which would be the case when the curve is balanced in the graph area. However, if the curve is crowded against the top or the right-hand side, then a zero starting point is unrealistic. In Figure 8-1 the curve occupies the top 75% of the graph area. Since no points will ever be plotted below the ambient temperature (which will hover around 23C), the bottom portion of the vertical scale is unnecessary.

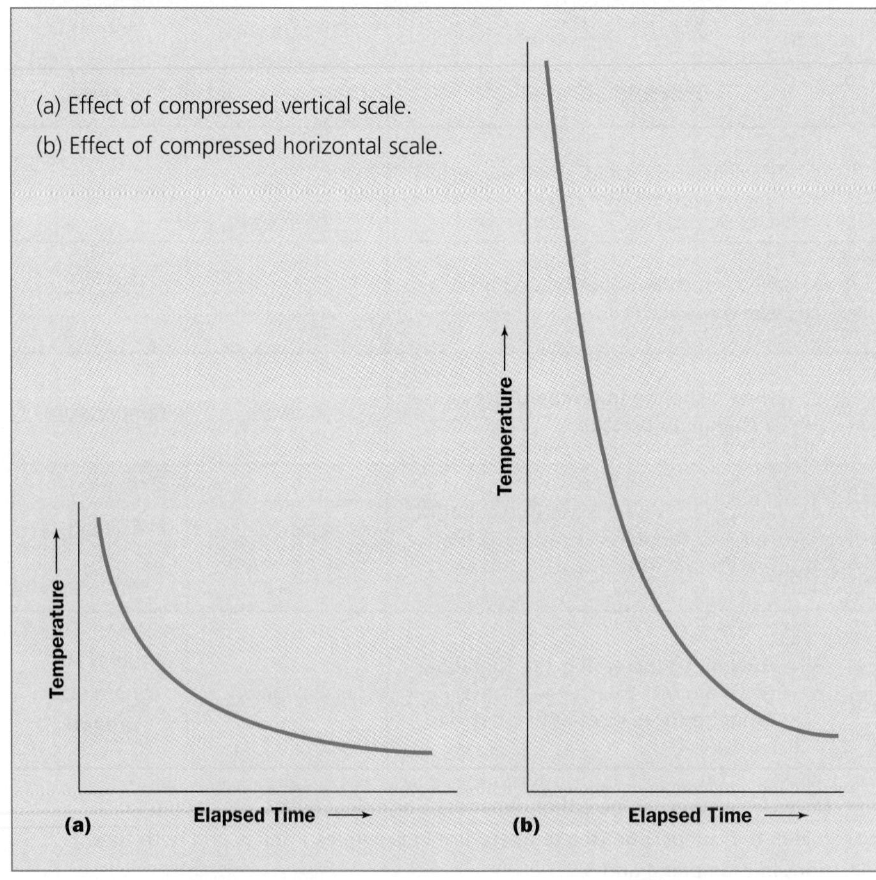

Figure 8-4 Poorly chosen scales can create an inaccurate image.

This can be corrected by starting the vertical scale at a higher value (say 20C, as in Figure 8-5), or by breaking the scale to indicate that some scale values have been omitted (Figures 8-2 and 8-6).

Multiple-curve graphs should have no more than four curves; otherwise they will be difficult to interpret (particularly if the curves cross one another). You can help a reader identify the most important curve by making it heavier than the others (Figure 8-6 on page 186), and can differentiate among curves that cross by creating different line types (Figure 8-7 on page 187). Avoid using coloured lines because many copiers and printers will reproduce all the lines in only one colour (usually black).

Emphasize the most significant curve(s)

Simplicity

Simplicity is important in graph construction. If a graph illustrates only trends or comparisons, and the reader is not expected to extract specific data from it, then you may omit the grid as in Figure 8-5. But if the reader wants to extrapolate quantities, you should include a grid as in Figures 8-6 and 8-7. Note that Figure 8-1 has an *implied* grid that only suggests the grid pattern for the occasional reader who may want to draw in a grid. Note also that you may omit the top and right-hand borders on graphs without grids, as in Figures 8-2 and 8-3.

Omit plot points and ensure that all labels are *horizontal* (the only label that may be entered vertically is the label for the vertical scale function). Insert labels for the curves at the end of the curve whenever possible (Figure 8-2) or, alternatively, above or below the curve (Figures 8-6 and 8–7). Never write a label along the slope of the curve.

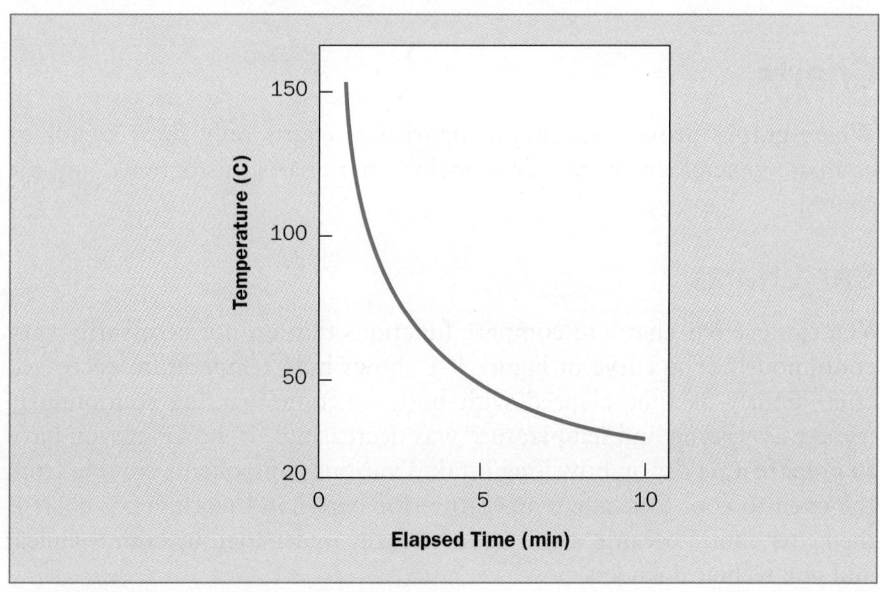

Figure 8-5 A correctly centred curve.

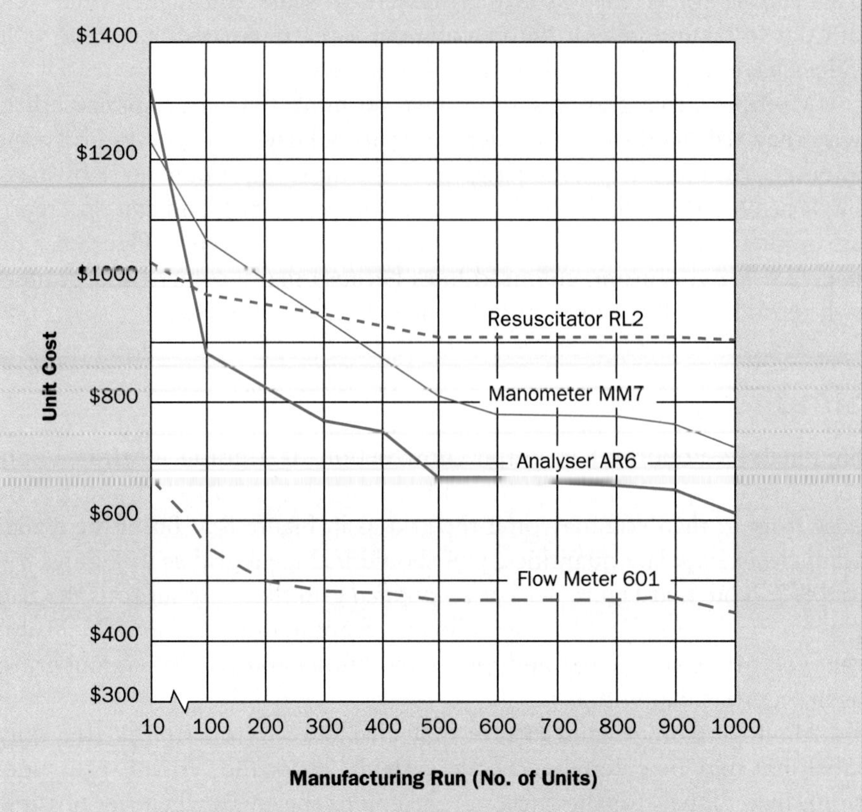

Figure 8-6 Bolder lines draw attention to the most important curve (the one showing maximum benefit from quantity manufacturing). The grid permits readers to draw reasonably accurate data from the graph.

Avoid confusion: limit the number of curves

Charts

Where graphs provide specific comparisons, charts only show trends or compare general quantities. They include bar charts, histograms, and pie charts.

Bar Charts

Illustrating Tech Documents
www.incrediblecharts.com/technical/chart_types.htm
This website shows the different charts that can be created for technical purposes.

You can use bar charts to compare functions that do not necessarily vary continuously. The curve in Figure 8-1 shows how temperature decreased continuously as time elapsed with both functions varying continuously (time was passing and temperature was decreasing). If, however, you have to prepare a report on how long it takes various components coming from the oven to cool to a safe temperature for bare-hand work, a bar chart is the better choice because it will be more easily understood by both technical and non-technical readers.

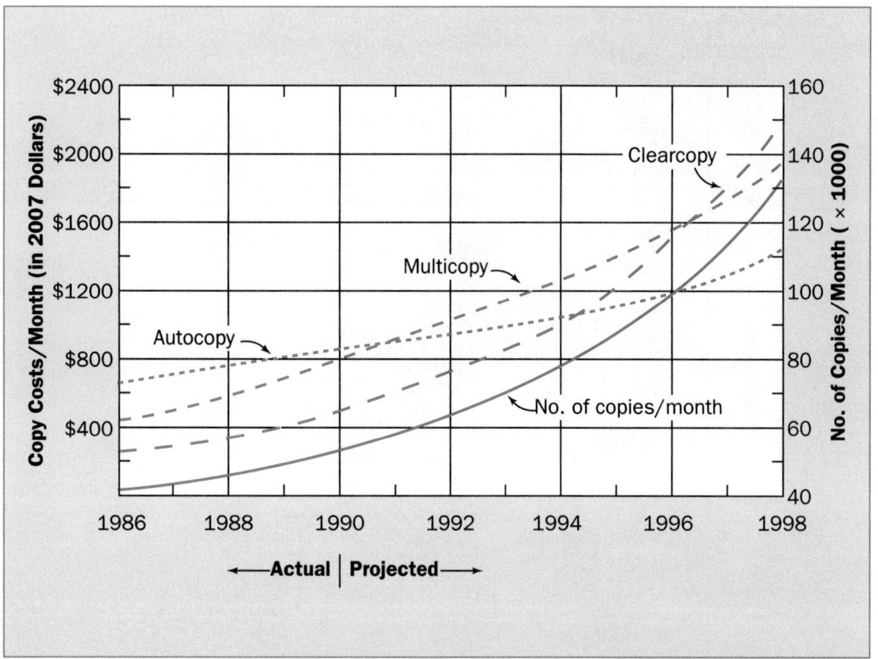

Figure 8-7 Different line types distinguish between curves showing current and projected copying costs for three copiers. Note the two vertical scales, which permit three functions to be shown on one graph.

Avoid writing along the slope of the curve

For this bar chart there is only one continuous variable: elapsed time; the other variable is non-continuous because it represents the products being measured (see Figure 8-8).

Bar charts can be arranged with either vertical or horizontal bars, depending on the type of information they portray; when time is one of the variables, it is usually plotted along the horizontal axis, as in Figure 8-8 on page 188. The bars are normally separated by a space, which can be as wide as each of the bars but more often is less wide.

Some computer software provides only a narrow space between the bars

In a complex bar chart, the bars may be shaded to indicate comparisons within each factor being considered. The vertical bar chart in Figure 8-9 on page 189 uses two shades to describe two factors on the one chart. Individual bars also can be shaded to show proportional content, as has been done in Figure 8-10 on page 189, in which case a legend is inserted beside or below the graph to show readers what each shading represents. Alternatively, each segment may be labelled as in Figure 8-11 on page 190. A 3-D vertical bar graph showing the same information as presented in Figures 8-10 and 8-11 is shown in Figure 8-12 on page 190.

Horizontal bar charts can be used in an unconventional way by arranging the bars on either side of a zero line. This can be done, for example, to compare negative and positive quantities, such as satisfactory and defective products. The chart in Figure 8-13 on page 191 divides products returned for repair into two groups: those that are covered by warranty,

Use horizontal bar charts to depict elapsed time

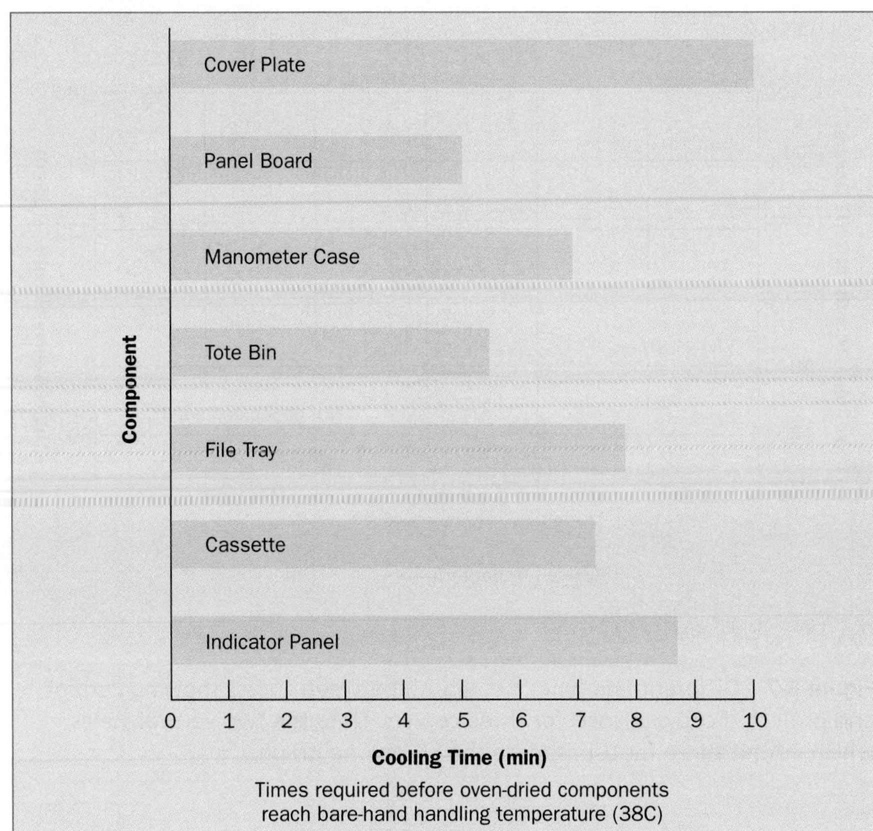

Figure 8-8 Horizontal bar chart with one continuous variable (cooling time).

and those that are not. Each bar represents 100% of the total number of items repaired in a particular product age group and is positioned at about the zero line depending on the percentage of warranty and nonwarranty repairs.

Histograms

Although seen rarely, histograms are useful when there is only limited data

A histogram looks like a bar chart, but functionally it is similar to a graph because it deals with two continuous variables. It is usually plotted like a bar chart because it does not have enough data to plot a continuous curve (see Figure 8-14 on page 191). The major difference between a histogram and a bar chart is that there are no spaces between the bars of a histogram.

Pie Charts

Probably the most widely recognized and readily understood chart

A pie chart shows approximate divisions of a whole unit. The pie chart in Figure 8-15 on page 192 depicts the percentage of work done by Macro Engineering Inc in eight major product or service categories. Figure 8-16 on page 193 is a pie chart showing the stages of product development.

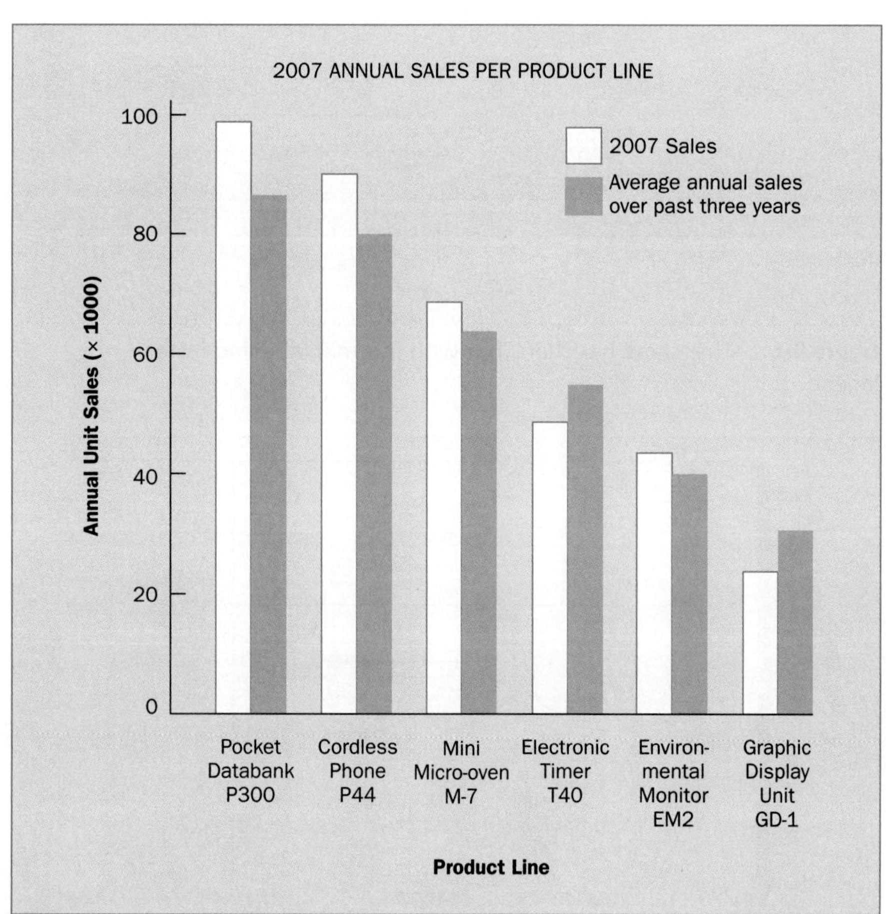

Figure 8-9 A vertical bar chart that lets readers compare current statistics with past statistics, and so determine trends.

Insert a key or legend to help identify the factors

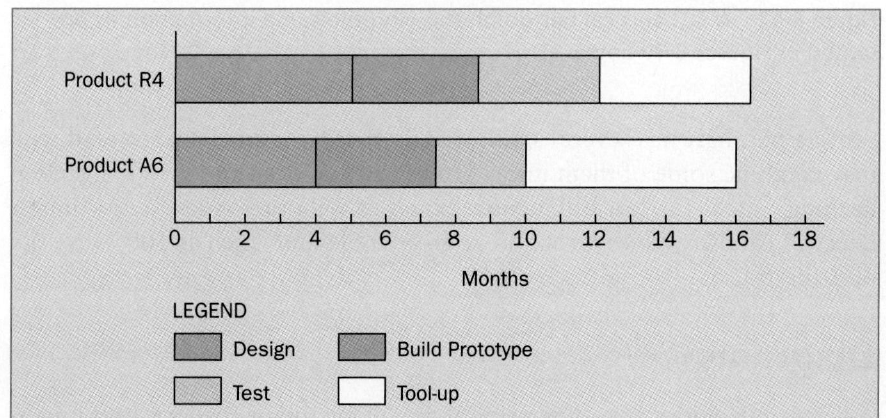

Figure 8-10 The bars in this chart show development times for proposed new products. The legend is included with the chart.

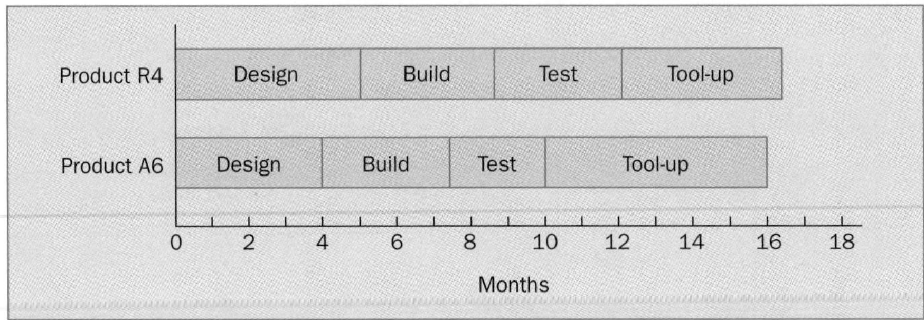

Figure 8-11 The same bar chart, but with internal labelling instead of a legend.

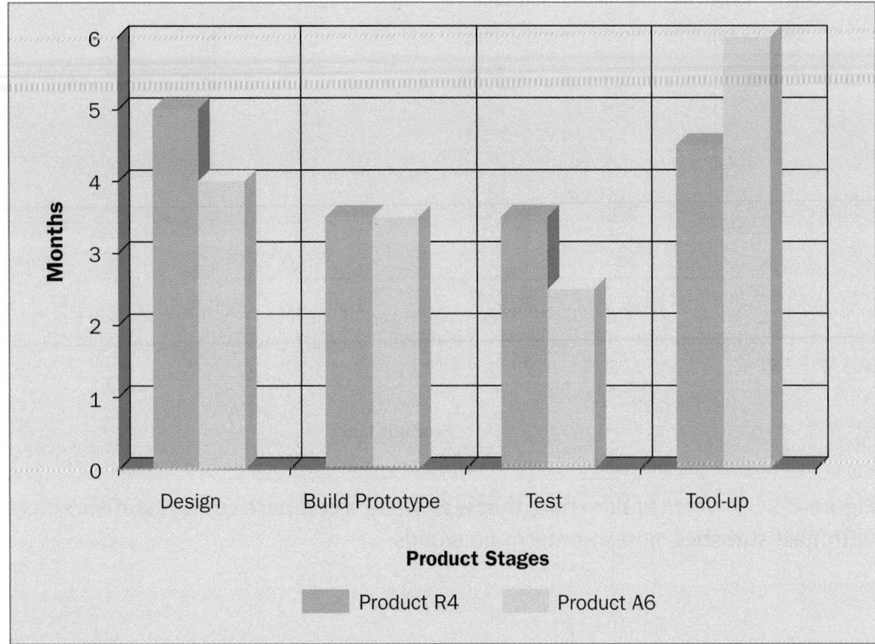

Figure 8-12 A 3-D vertical bar graph showing the same information as presented in Figures 8-10 and 8-11.

If a pie chart has several small wedges that would be hard to read, you may combine some of them into a larger single wedge and give it a general heading, such as "miscellaneous expenses," "other uses," or "minor effects." All the wedges must add up to a whole unit, such as 100%, $1.00, or 1 (unity).

Explore

A diagram must be readily understood; it should rarely need to be explained

Diagrams

A diagram includes any illustration that will help your reader better understand your written words, yet does not fall within the category of graph, chart, or table. It can range from a schematic drawing of a complex circuit to a simple plan of a highway intersection.

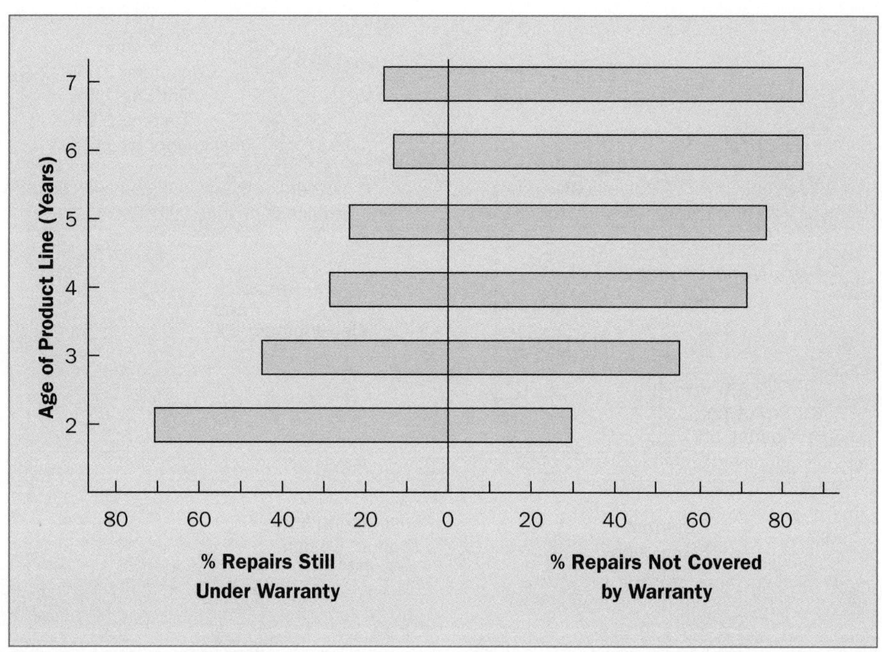

Figure 8-13 A bar chart constructed on both sides of a zero point.

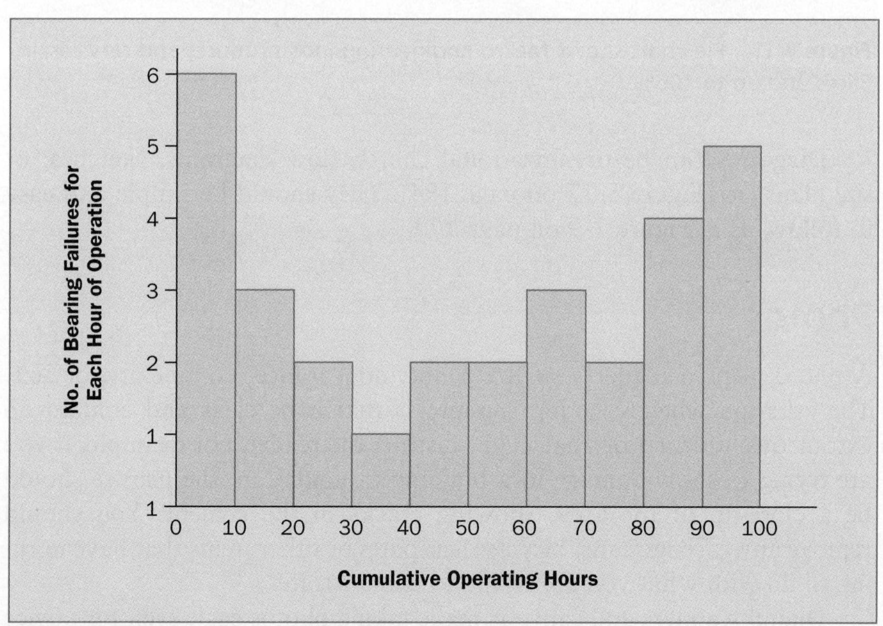

Figure 8-14 This histogram shows the number of bearing failures for every 10 hours of operation. Considerably more data would have been required to construct a curve.

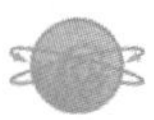

Illustration Samples from NASA's Glenn's Graphics Group
http://grcpublishing.grc.nasa.gov/graphics/samillus.cfm
Several examples of detailed illustrations from NASA's Glenn's Graphics Group are available at this site. A contact address is included for readers who want more information about the preparation of technical illustrations.

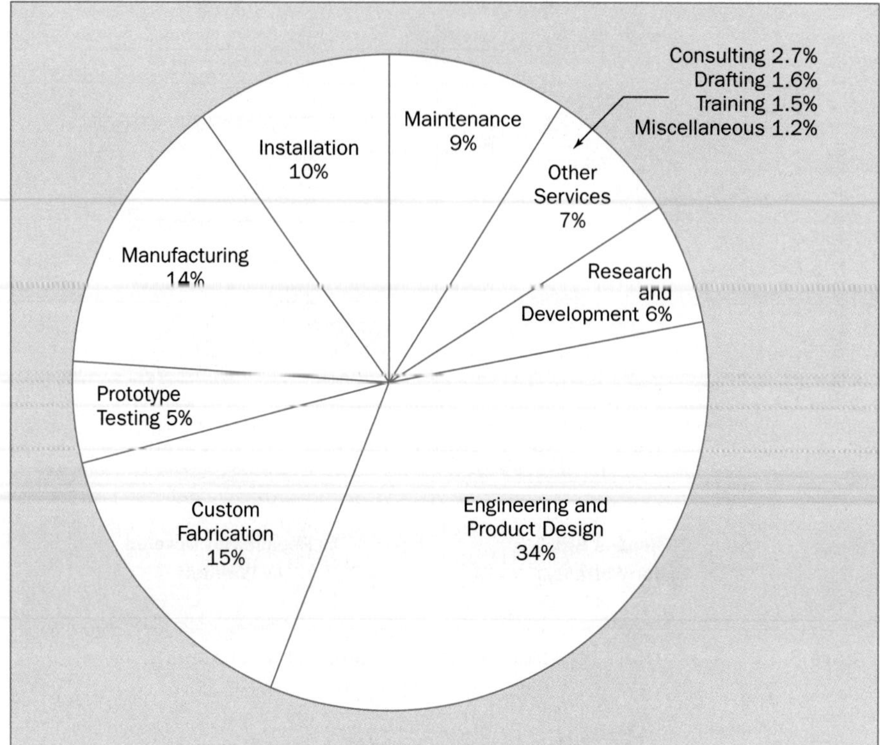

Figure 8-15 Pie chart shows Macro Engineering Inc's products and services. Slices add up to 100%.

Diagrams can be organizational charts, flow diagrams, sketches, or site plans (see Figure 8-17 on page 194). They should be simple and easy to follow, as in Figure 7-3 on page 173.

Photos

A photo helps a reader visualize shape, appearance, complexity, or size. The criterion when selecting a photo is that it be clear and contain no extraneous information that might distract the reader. For example, if you are trying to show damage to a building's foundation, the picture should be a close-up of the area, showing cracks in the cement. You should remove any garbage cans, bicycles, car parts or other items that have nothing to do with what you are trying to demonstrate.

With digital equipment, it's easier to use photos

Digital scanners and cameras make taking photos easy, even for novice photographers, since the image when viewed on a computer screen can be edited electronically. The minimum acceptable quality for a digital image is 130 pixels, which ensures readers will not see the individual dots that form the image. Your output device (normally a printer) should be set for a minimum of 300 dpi (dots per inch). A higher dpi will result in better image quality, so if you are preparing a report for an external client on glossy paper you should consider an even higher dpi.

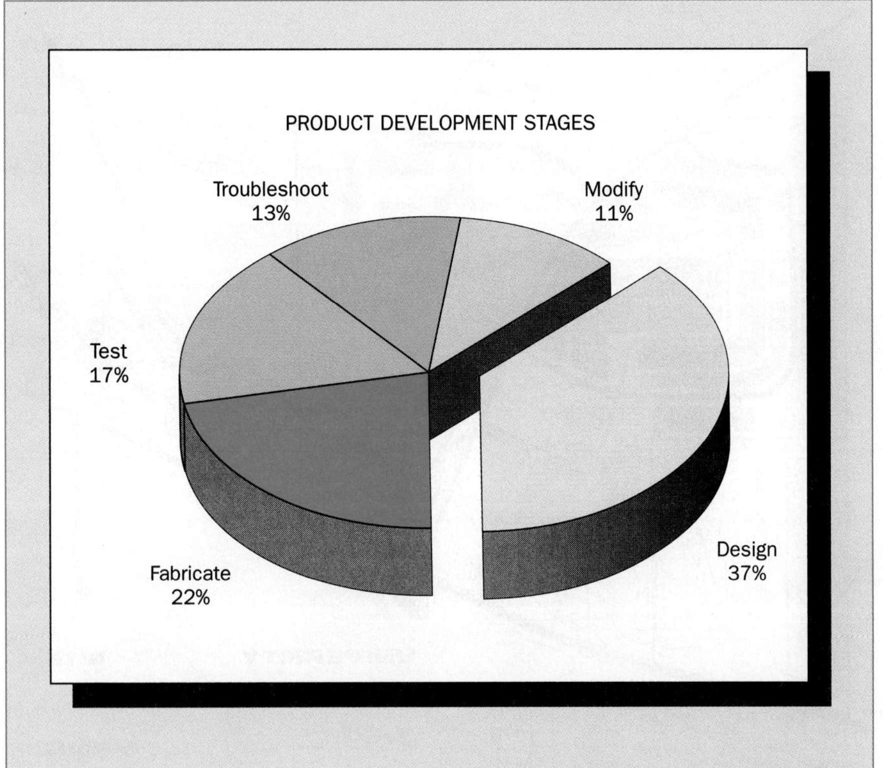

Figure 8-16 An exploded-view pie chart, with one segment emphasized by being pulled partly away.

The pie chart particularly adapts to 3-D presentation

Pay particular attention to the contrast and lighting in a photo. Use image-editing software to manipulate the contrast (the difference in brightness between the light and dark areas of a picture), especially if you know the report will be photocopied, because photocopiers inherently add contrast in the copying process. You will want the image to be of less contrast (a little darker).

Today, many reports are distributed electronically, which means that including images and photographs may increase the file to an unmanageable size. We recommend saving your photos as JPG files (a compressed format for encoding graphic images) to retain their image quality. If, however, you are capturing computer screen images, you'll need to save them as GIF files (graphic interchange format) because the compression of the JPG format deteriorates the screen image.

Digital Clip Art

We now have access to extensive libraries of free (and sometimes ***not*** free) generic graphic images. This simple artwork can add variation to your page design and create reader interest, but make sure the image is professional

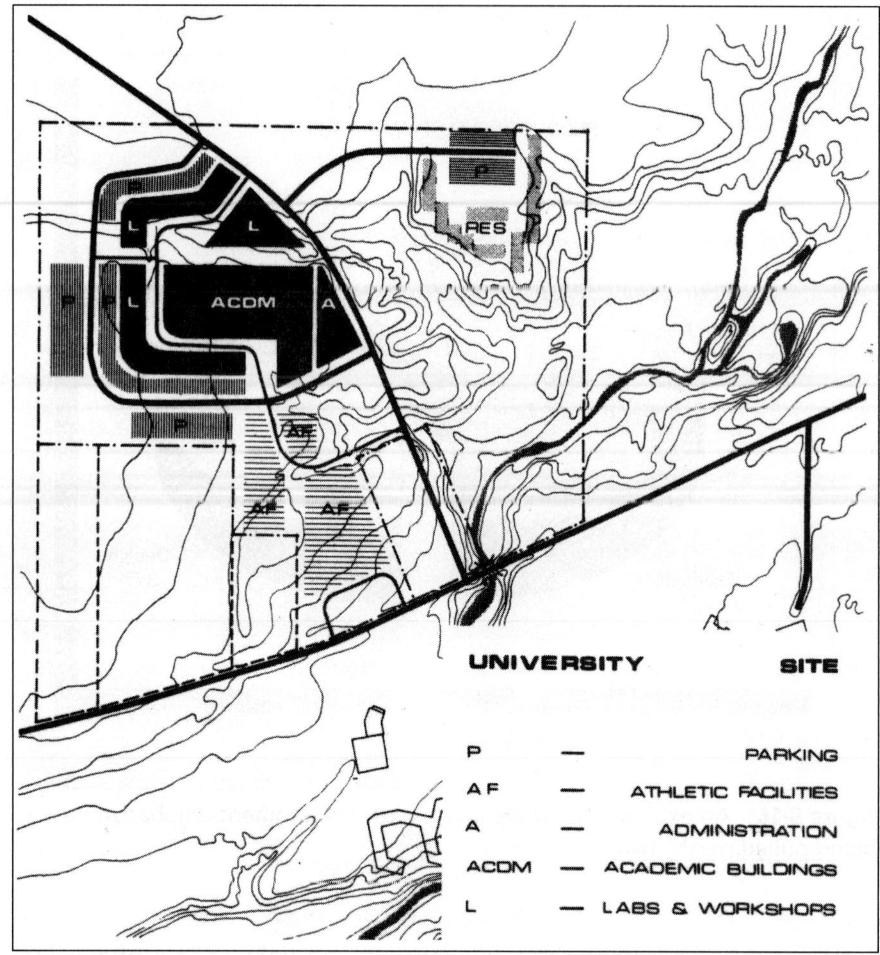

Figure 8-17 A site plan that illustrates where college facilities are to be located. (Courtesy Smith, Carter, Searle—W L Wardrop & Associates Ltd, Winnipeg, Man.)

and relevant to your content. Use these generic images sparingly. Too many basic designs may create an amateur image of you and your content.

Tables

A table may be a collection of technical data, as in Tables 8-1 and 8-2 (pages 179 and 181), or a series of short narrative statements, as in Table 8-3 (page 183). Whether you insert a table into the report narrative or place it in an attachment or appendix depends on three factors:

1. If the table is short (i.e. less than half a page) and readers need to refer to it as they read the report, then include it as part of the report narrative (i.e. in the discussion), preferably on the same page as the text that refers to it.

2. If your readers will be able to understand the discussion without referring to the table as they read the report, but may want to consult the table later, then place the table in an attachment or appendix.
3. If readers need to refer to a table but the data you have will occupy a full page or more, then
   - summarize the table's key points in a short table to be inserted into the report narrative, and
   - place the full table in an attachment or appendix.

Use tables for words as well as numbers

There are four additional guidelines that apply to tables, particularly if the tables contain columns of numerical data:

1. Keep the table simple by limiting it only to data the readers will really need, and create as few columns as possible.
2. Insert units of measurement, such as decibels, volts, kilograms, or seconds, at the head of each column rather than after each column entry (see the "min:sec" and "C" entries at the top of the columns in Table 8-1).
3. Insert a table number and an appropriate title above the table.
4. Draw readers' attention to a table by referring to it in the report narrative and commenting on a specific inference to be drawn from the table. For example,

> The voltage fluctuations were recorded at 10-minute intervals and entered in column 3 of Table 7, which shows that fluctuations were most marked between 8:15 and 11:20 a.m.

Positioning the Illustrations

Explore

Whenever possible, place each illustration on the same page as or facing the narrative it supports. A reader who has to keep flipping pages back and forth between narrative and illustrations will soon tire, and your reasons for including the illustrations will be defeated.

When reports are printed on only one side of the paper, full-page illustrations can be difficult to position. Try to limit the size of illustrations so that they can be placed beside, above, or below the words.

Consider illustrations as an integral part of a document, not just an "add on"

When an illustration is too large to fit on a normal page, or is going to be referred to frequently, consider printing it on a fold-out sheet and inserting it at the back of the report (see Figure 8-18 on page 196). If the illustration is printed only on the extension panels of the foldout, the reader can leave the extension open for continual reference while reading the report. This technique is particularly suitable for circuit diagrams and flow charts.

Position horizontal full-page illustrations sideways on a page so the top of the diagram is at the left-hand side of the page (see Figure 8-19).

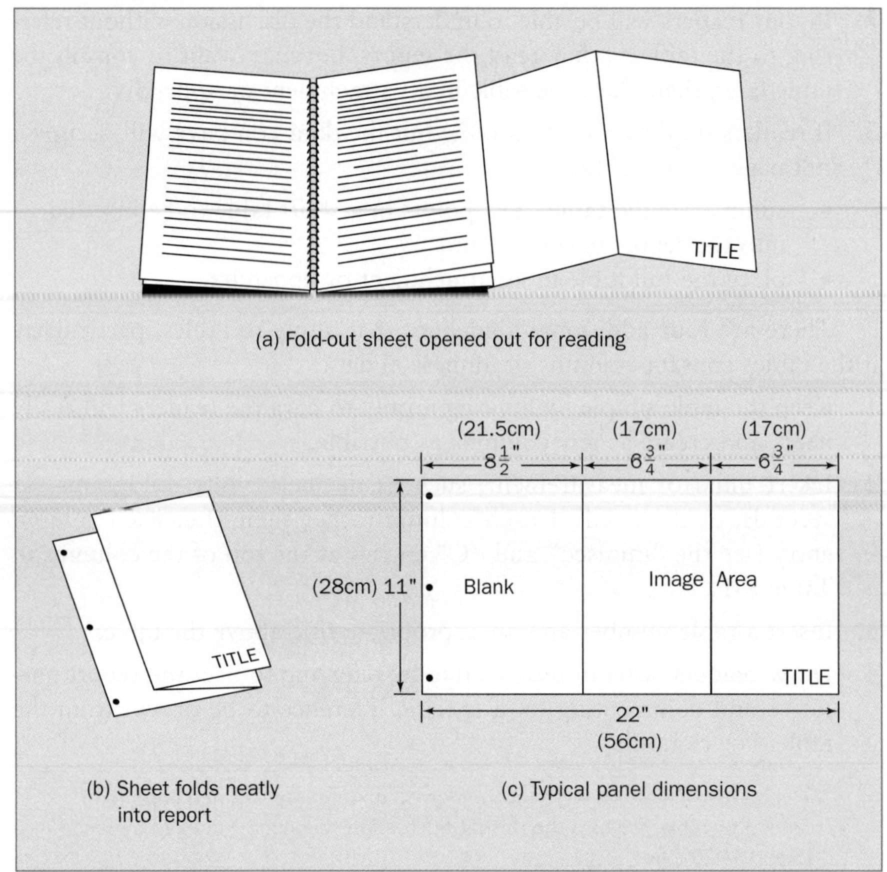

Figure 8-18 Large illustrations can be placed on a fold-out sheet at the back of the report.

You align horizontal or landscaped illustrations this way, even if some words appear to be upside down

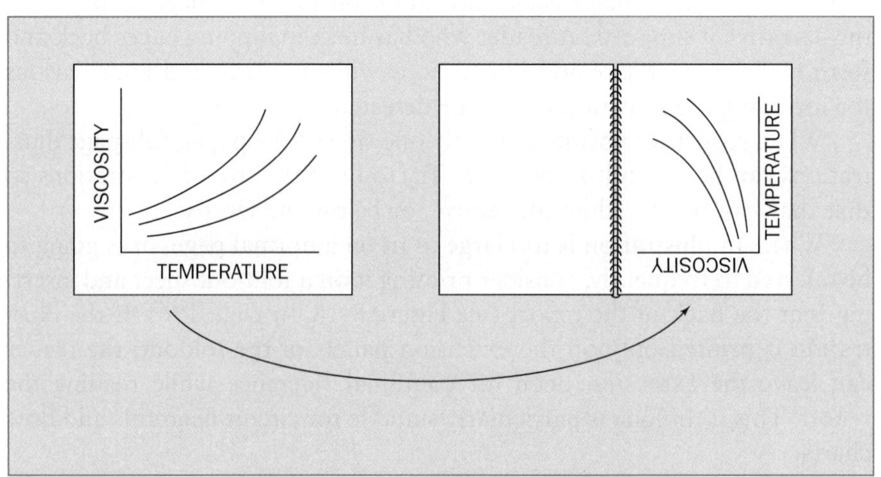

Figure 8-19 Full page horizontal drawings should be positioned so that the top of the diagram is at the left-hand side of the page.

To help your reader refer quickly to illustrations, we suggest you add a list of figures and tables right after your table of contents. Include the figure or table number, its title or caption, and the page number.

ASSIGNMENTS

Project 8.1: Who Buys *4Tell*?

The most successful software your company makes is *4Tell*, a program for forecasting.

Part 1

Make an illustration showing the breakdown of sales for last year, when there were 14 236 sales. The buyers were:

You have to illustrate a consumer survey

Hospitals	1588
Small businesses	1011
Public utilities	2165
Consultants	233
Manufacturers	3176
Architects	217
Newspapers	116
Land surveyors	245
Automobile parts distributors	866
City/town planners	1155
Engineers	1732
Radio and television stations	1299
Miscellaneous	433

Part 2

Now compare last year's sales with those of four years ago, which was the first year your company marketed *4Tell*.

The sales four years ago were

Hospitals	174
Small businesses	1393
Public utilities	1132
Consultants	174
Manufacturers	2351
Automobile parts distributors	958
City/town planners	1306
Engineers	784
Radio and television stations	174
Miscellaneous	261

Part 3

Write an email to the Marketing Manager (David Wolfrom), commenting on any significant changes that the charts show.

Project 8.2: Comparing Electricity Costs

Your company markets heat pumps, and wants to demonstrate to electricity users that a heat pump can significantly reduce their electricity bills. Prepare an illustration based on the following actual monthly bills for four different dwellings last year. The residences are identical five-room homes built at the same time and in the same block on Margusson Avenue. The only differences are that No. 216 and 234 do not have air-conditioning (marked "No AC" in the table), while No. 227 and 248 do (marked "+AC"). No. 234 and 248 each have a heat pump.

Use these figures to create an easy-to-read illustration

Monthly Electricity Bills

	Actual Bills No Heat Pump		Actual Bills With Heat Pump	
	216 No AC	227 +AC	234 No AC	248 +AC
January	$ 48.07	$ 49.23	$ 36.01	$ 37.64
February	45.15	46.01	37.47	34.15
March	43.20	42.86	32.30	31.73
April	41.11	42.20	36.96	38.40
May	38.37	42.15	38.01	38.67
June	35.20	48.16	35.26	42.06
July	33.06	57.19	33.17	38.36
August	32.87	56.80	33.03	39.36
September	34.11	47.10	31.47	39.89
October	38.62	39.20	30.77	30.60
November	41.67	41.10	32.05	30.49
December	43.20	42.89	31.62	31.12

Chapter 9
Technically-Speak!

In this chapter you will learn how to

- plan and present an oral report to a client or management.
- make and use speaking notes effectively,
- develop visual aids for projection during a presentation,
- develop a good platform manner, using body language to good effect, and
- take part in and present information at an office meeting

Although your textbook is titled *Technically-Write!*, we are including a chapter on making oral presentations because technical professionals often have to report their findings orally to a client or explain them to their peers at a business meeting.

Guidelines for communicating at a job interview are covered in Chapter 10.

The Technical Briefing

Your department head approaches your desk and says,

> "We've had a call from the RAFAC Corporation. They're sending in some representatives next Tuesday. I'd like you to give them a rundown on the project you're working on."

Every day engineers and technicians are being called upon to stand up and say a few words about their work. On paper, this sounds straightforward, but to those who have to make the presentation it can be a traumatic experience. Much of their nervousness can be reduced (it can seldom be entirely eliminated, as any experienced speaker will tell you) if they learn a few simple public speaking techniques.

***Many* people fear having to stand up and speak, even more than they fear sky diving**

Establish the Circumstances

Your first step is to establish the circumstances affecting your presentation. Ask the person arranging the event four questions:

1. **Who Will Be in My Audience?**
   To focus your presentation properly and use appropriate terminology, you need to know whether your audience contains technical people who have experience in your field, managers with only a general

It's just like writing a report: first, identify your audience

appreciation of the subject, or laypersons with very little or no technical knowledge.

2. **What Will They Know Already?**
   To avoid boring your listeners by repeating information they already know, or confusing them by omitting essential background details, you need to find out how much they know now about your subject, or will have been told before you address them.

3. **How Long Do You Want Me to Talk?**
   Find out if you are to describe the project in detail or simply touch on the highlights. The answer will directly influence how deeply you cover the topic.

4. **Where Is the Presentation Taking Place?**
   Identify whether you are to make your presentation in your company's conference room or training room, at a client's premises, or at a technical society meeting. Within your own company you can easily identify what audio-visual facilities are available and where your audience will be seated in relation to you. If you will be speaking at an outside location you should ask for a description of the facilities or, even better, be able to view them in advance.

Now you can start making your notes. Jot down the topics you intend to discuss, and arrange them in an interesting, logical order.

Determine Your Audience's Needs

Have you ever sat through a boring, long-winded presentation that seemed to have no direction? We all have.

Have you attended other presentations that seemed to be tailored specifically to your needs? How did the speaker do that?

The problem with an unfocused presentation is that its content is speaker-focused rather than audience-focused. Its speaker describes everything about the topic, rather than focusing on what the audience most wants to know.

List Audience Questions

To make your presentation audience-focused, start by identifying the different types of people who will be there, their level of knowledge and interest in your topic, and what they will do with or how they will use your information. Think of the questions they might ask, and list as many as you can (we suggest at least 15 questions). Here are some examples:

- How will we do this?
- Will it be expensive?

- Who will be responsible for what?
- How long will it take?
- What needs to be done to complete the task?
- What experience do you have in this field?

The answers to these questions will help you identify the areas to address and the audience's concerns before you prepare the content. They will turn your presentation from being speaker-focused:

"This is everything I know about the topic."

To being audience-focused:

"Here are the answers to your questions about the topic."

Organize Your Information

In their book *The Short Road to Great Presentations*,[1] Peter and Cheryl Reimold introduce a formula for structuring a presentation. They call it the Universal Presentation Structure, shown in Figure 9-1.

This Universal Presentation Structure is especially helpful for technical professionals who relate well to formulas.

Introduction:	**1 to 2 minutes**
Body:	**3 to 5 key points**
Conclusion:	**1 minute**

Figure 9-1 The Reimolds' Universal Presentation Structure formula.

Tell Your Story Three Times

This structure, also known as the TELL–TELL–TELL method, will ensure you tell your audience *three times* what you have to tell them, and in *three different ways*:

Tell 1:	Tell your readers what they most need to hear: just the key points. Then outline very briefly the main topics you will cover.
Tell 2:	Now provide all the details, in the same order you mentioned them in *Tell 1*.
Tell 3:	Sum up by very briefly repeating the key points, and possibly offering a recommendation.

Start by telling your audience where you plan to take them...

...and end by telling them where they have been

Capture the Audience's Attention

In your first TELL, the Introduction, you need to accomplish four goals:

1. Establish **Rapport** with your audience
2. Grab the audience's **Attention**
3. State your **Main Message**
4. Outline your **Plan**

Open with a RAMP

The Reimolds define this as your **RAMP** and allow you *only* 1 to 2 minutes. When you start your talk, you have your audience's full attention; don't waste the opportunity by reciting dull information (such as your name, the title of your presentation, or your purpose). Let an opening slide provide that information.

Building **Rapport** is as easy as smiling, connecting with your audience by telling them you are excited to be with them, or greeting them at the door when they come in. This warms them up to you and encourages them to listen to you.

Use an **Attention**-getter that relates to your main message. A joke, an apology, or a thank-you is dull and you risk offending someone. Instead, try a statistic, a photo, or a word of caution. You need to find something that relates to your main message and grabs the audience's attention.

A dull start:	"Today, I want to tell you about the effects of poor quality control when manufacturing electrical products. This happened in the fall of 2009, at our plant in Montreal. The problem began when a supplier failed to monitor production quality adequately..."
An exciting start:	"Have you, in your company, ever built a better mousetrap? A product that significantly outclasses the competition? Well, we did, in the spring of 2009. It was an immediate success and we had to start a second production line to keep up with the demand. But five months later we had a disaster on our hands: warranty returns were reaching an unprecedented 30%!! The reason: poor quality control at one of our suppliers' plants. In the next 20 minutes I will explain to you what we did to reverse that trend, how we established criteria for evaluating suppliers, and what results we expect from our efforts."

Get off to a flying start!

In the RAMP you need to be direct: it's not the time to sound wishy-washy. If you have a plan that can reduce costs by 40%, then say that. If your proposal shows you can alleviate the stormwater issues in a new commercial area, then state that right up front. Your audience will appreciate this and pay more attention to your presentation now that they know what your purpose is and what the topic has to do with them.

Then, as in the second example above, end your Introduction with a **Plan**, which will become a road map for your presentation. It shows your audience that you are organized and what they can expect to hear. We also encourage you to add a slide into your presentation showing your plan.

Using the RAMP in the Introduction is the best way to establish yourself as a confident, interesting speaker.

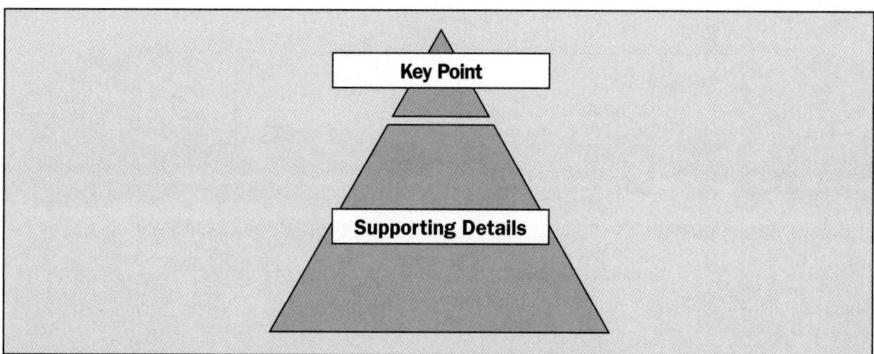

Figure 9-2 Use the pyramid technique to organize each key point.

Select Key Points

In your second TELL, the Body, you identify three to five key points to address, which have evolved from the list of questions you predicted your audience would want you to answer. Even if you have identified 15 or more questions, you will probably be able to discern a pattern among them. This means you can group several questions under one key point. For example, *How much will this cost?*, *Is this expensive?*, and *What is our budget for the project?* can all be addressed under the key point "Cost Factors."

Figure 9-2 shows how to use the pyramid technique to structure each key point. State your key point and follow it with supporting information. Remember that to be convincing you need to provide facts and evidence.

Vary the number of key points you present based on the amount of time you have to speak. If it is just a short 10-minute presentation, stick to only three points. If you have more time, stretch it to five points. But don't be tempted to address more than five points if you are given a longer speaking time. Rather than overloading your listeners with too many points, you can go into greater detail and depth about the five selected points.

Wrap It Up with a Conclusion

The third TELL is your Conclusion. This is your chance to summarize what you have just told your audience. In *The Short Road to Great Presentations*, the Reimolds suggest you say the words *To summarize* or *In conclusion* to pique your audience's attention. (If some of your listeners' attention has drifted in the middle of your presentation, a strong conclusion will help them refocus.) In just one minute, briefly restate your main message and the key points you have made. Don't insert any new details, and never go more than one minute.

Prepare to Speak

Make Speaking Notes

Prepare your speaking notes on cards no smaller than 150 × 100 mm. Write in large, bold letters that you can see at a glance, and use brief headings to

Write in bold letters that can be read from an arm's length away

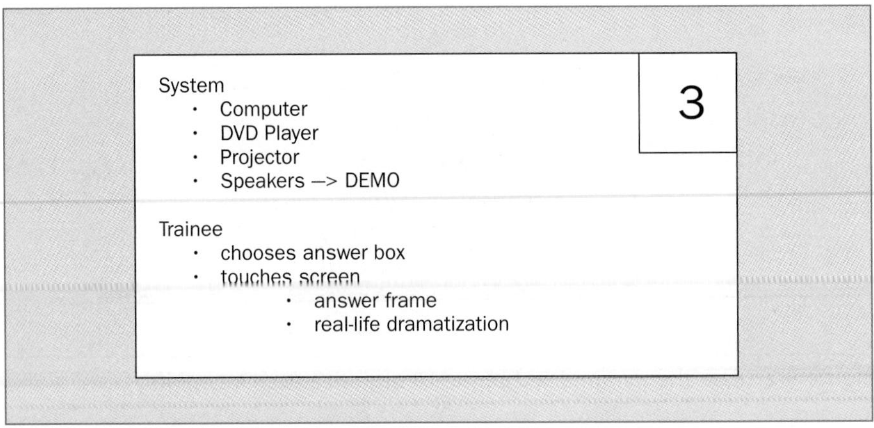

Figure 9-3 Note card for an oral presentation.

develop the information in sufficient detail. A sample note card is shown in Figure 9-3. Avoid using a full sheet of paper for your notes. If you are nervous, your hand may quiver and the paper will shake. You also may be tempted to include far too much information on it and end up reading from the paper.

The amount of information you include will depend on the subject, your familiarity with it, and your previous speaking experience. Your notes should not be so detailed that you cannot quickly pick out points, nor so skimpy that you have to rely too much on your memory.

Explore

Visual Aids in Presentations
http://cte.uwaterloo.ca/teaching-resources/tips/using_visual_aids.html
This document, from the University of Waterloo, contains a summary of the use of visual aids in presentations.

Prepare Visual Aids

Visual aids help clarify and explain your concepts. They are especially important when discussing complex, technical information. Some people are visual learners and need to *see* the information as well as *hear* it. Examples of visual aids are PowerPoint slides, poster boards, physical props, equipment, and hand-drawn diagrams.

Here are some tips for creating effective visuals:

- Strive for simplicity: let each visual make just one point. A visual aid should support your spoken narrative; you should rarely have to explain it.
- Use large, bold letters that will be visible from the back of the room. Use upper- and lowercase letters rather than all capitals.
- Use colour to accentuate key words or parts, but in moderation. Some colours, such as green and blue or red and orange, are difficult to tell apart from a distance.
- Place a short title or heading above or below each slide.

Let each visual provide just one message

To prepare PowerPoint slides, follow these guidelines:

- Select a design that is appealing and provides good contrast between the background colour and the colour of the text.

- Avoid dazzling transitions that tend to take attention away from your message. Choose transitions that make a smooth, effective, but conservative change between items and slides. Maintain continuity by using similar transitions throughout the presentation.
- Create a natural progression from one slide to the next. If you are presenting, say, four bulleted points on a slide, bring in each point one at a time. This prevents losing your audience's attention because they are reading the points ahead of the one you are currently speaking about. As you bring in a new point, show it in dark, bold type, and dim the previous points.
- Print copies of your slides onto 8½ × 11 inch sheets, four or six slides to a page. You can use these as a prompt when presenting the slides, or as a handout for your audience.

Resist the temptation to use fancy transitions!

Explore

Practise

Refer to Chapter 8 for additional suggestions on preparing visual aids such as graphs, charts, and diagrams.

Practise working with your visual aids, first on their own and then as part of the whole presentation. This gives you a chance to check whether you have inserted them in the correct places, and whether the entries in your notes allow you to switch from speech to a visual aid without losing continuity.

Don't overlook the practical aspects of the presentation. If you have equipment to demonstrate, consider the sequence of your presentation and when you want to show the demo. Make sure you are comfortable with the demonstration and have practised your body positioning with any equipment. Avoid walking in front of the display, obstructing it from the audience's view. And to avoid any distractions, keep your demo short and place any visuals or equipment out of sight until you are ready to use them, and immediately after you have used them.

Practise, Practise, Practise

Take a tip from experienced speakers: practise your talk. Run through it several times, working entirely from your prompt cards, until you can speak without hesitating or stumbling over awkward words. If the cards are too hard to follow, or contain too much detail, adjust them. Then ask a colleague to sit through your presentation and give critical comments.

Practise...practise... practise

Modify your notes after each practice reading. Where necessary, insert more information; in other places, delete unneeded words. As you grow familiar with the notes, you will find that your confidence increases and certain sentences and phrases will come to you at the sight of a single word or topic heading; this will help you to maintain continuity.

Time yourself. Aim to speak for slightly less time than allowed; for example, plan to speak for 17 or 18 minutes for a talk scheduled to last 20 minutes. This will give you time to include some previously unanticipated remarks, if you need to at the last minute.

Prepare Handout Notes

During the planning stages, you need to decide whether to provide printed handouts for your listeners. If so, you will also have to decide whether they should be copies of your PowerPoint slides or a specially prepared narrative-style report of the main topics.

There is a trend today for speakers to provide only copies of their slides, which are much simpler to make. However, we recommend you prepare a summary of your presentation which, although it may take longer, will provide your listeners with a useful resource when, in future months, they want to refresh their memories about the topic you presented.

Make Your Presentation

Control Your Nervousness

Prepare well in advance; then relax, knowing you are ready

There are very few people who are not at least a little nervous when the time comes to stand up and speak before an audience. Some nervous tension is perfectly normal and can even help a speaker give a better performance. You will find that, once you start speaking, your nervousness will gradually decrease. A lot depends on the quality of your speaking notes: if you have done a thorough job preparing them, know they are reliable, and have practised using them, you will find that the familiar phrases and sentences form easily. Then you will begin to relax and so speak with even greater confidence, which will help you relax even more.

Here are some additional tips to help calm your nerves:

- Visit the room before you speak. Check the equipment and become comfortable with your surroundings.
- Avoid looking at your notes and rehearsing just minutes before the presentation. It's too late now, and last-minute preparation will only make you more nervous.
- Take a few deep breaths and roll your ankles and shoulders to help you relax any tight muscles.
- If a question arises and you don't know the answer, don't bluff. You can (and should) say you don't know the answer but will follow up on it, ideally by email. And then do so!
- Know that your listeners are there to learn something from you and *you* are the authority. If you have done your research and have prepared well, *it will show*.

Sharpen Your Platform Manner

There are some elementary platform techniques you can use to improve your performance:

- Arrive early and check that the projector, computer, and microphone work. Identify the light switches you will need to control, if you have to dim the lights at any time when presenting.

- Appear businesslike and cheerful.
- Speak from notes. You will lose contact with your audience if you read from a prepared speech.
- Let your enthusiasm *show*. If you present your information with passion, your audience will see that you really enjoy talking about your subject and will listen more attentively.

Be an energetic, enthusiastic speaker

- Vary your voice to create interest: louder, softer, faster, slower.
- Look at your audience. Try to speak to individuals in turn, rather than the group as a whole. Pick out someone in one part of the room and talk to that person for a few moments, then turn to someone in another part of the room. Let each listener feel he or she is being addressed personally.
- Use humour sparingly, and only if it fits naturally into your presentation. Never insert a joke to "warm up" an audience. If you do use humour, make sure your audience is laughing *with* you, not *at* you.
- Speak at a moderate speed. We recommend 120 to 140 words per minute. This will feel a little slower than a normal conversational rate.
- Speak up. If possible try speaking without a microphone, since this gives you much greater freedom of movement and tonal flexibility. If the room is large and you have to use one, try to obtain a lavaliere (travelling) microphone that clips onto your clothing and is wireless.
- Pause occasionally to study your speaker's notes. Never be afraid to stop speaking for a few moments to gather your thoughts and establish that you have covered every major topic.
- Avoid distracting habits that divert audience attention. For example, avoid pacing back and forth, balancing precariously on the edge of the platform, jingling keys or coins in your pocket (put them in a back pocket, out of reach), or playing with objects on the speaker's table.

Watch your body language; make it work for you, not against you

Distribute Your Handouts

When is the best time to give your listeners your handout materials? There are three approaches:

1. If your handouts are simply copies of your slides, then hand them out right at the start of your presentation so listeners can make notes on them while you speak.
2. If you have charts or diagrams you want your listeners to refer to as you speak, hand them out at the appropriate moment during your talk.
3. If your handouts are a detailed narrative-style description of the points you will be making, rather than copies of your slides, and the audience does not need to refer to them as you speak, then we recommend you hand them out toward the end or immediately after your presentation. (If you hand them out at the start, your listeners will tend to leaf

through them to identify "where you are" in your talk, and create a disturbance for their neighbours.)

Reach Out to Your Audience

Although good pre-platform preparation and knowledge of platform techniques can give you confidence, they are not sufficient in themselves to break down the initial barrier between speaker and audience. Successful speakers develop a well-rounded personality they use continuously and unconsciously to establish a sound speaker–audience relationship. When you speak to an audience only once, and then only briefly, probably the most important attributes to develop are enthusiasm and sincerity: enthusiasm about your topic, sincerity in wanting to help your audience learn about it, and a smile!

The time and effort you invest in preparing for a talk will depend on your confidence as a speaker and your familiarity with the subject. No one expects you to give a fully professional briefing at your first attempt, but your listeners (and your employer) will appreciate your efforts when they see that you have prepared your talk carefully and are presenting it in an interesting way.

Taking Part in Meetings

The chair may run the meeting, but the participants control its progress

We all occasionally attend meetings. In industry, you may be asked to sit on a committee set up for a multitude of reasons, from resolving technical problems that are tying up production to organizing the company's annual picnic. The effectiveness of such meetings is controlled entirely by those taking part. Meetings attended by people *aware of their role* as participants can move quickly and achieve good results; those attended by individuals who seize the opportunity to air personal complaints can be dull and can cripple action.

Meetings can be either structured or unstructured, depending on their purpose. A structured meeting follows a predetermined pattern: its chair prepares an agenda that defines the purpose and objectives of the meeting and the topics to be covered. The meeting then proceeds logically from point to point. An unstructured meeting uses a conceptual approach to derive new ideas. Only its purpose is defined, since its participants are expected to introduce suggestions and comments that may generate new concepts (this approach is frequently called "brainstorming"). We will discuss the structured meeting here, because you are much more likely to encounter it in industry.

A meeting is composed of the person who is running the meeting (the chair) and two or more meeting participants, one of whom often is appointed to be secretary for that particular meeting. The secretary makes notes of what happens during the meeting and, after the meeting, writes the *minutes*, or meeting record. Each person's role is discussed here.

The Chair's Role

A good chair controls the direction of a meeting yet leaves ample room for the participants to feel they are making the major contribution to it. The chair must be a good organizer, an effective administrator, and a diplomat (to smooth ruffled feathers if opinions differ widely). Much of the success of a meeting will result from the chair's preparation before the meeting starts and ability to maintain control as it proceeds.

Prepare an Agenda

If you are the chair, no later than two days before the meeting prepare an agenda of topics to be discussed and circulate it to all meeting participants. Your agenda should cover the following points:

- The date, time, place, and purpose of the meeting.
- The topics that will be discussed (numbered, and in the sequence they will be addressed), divided into two groups:

    1. Decision Items
    2. Discussion Items

    This arrangement ensures that participants deal with the most important items early in the meeting.
- The person who is delegated to record the meeting's minutes (the secretary).

Place the most important points at the top of the agenda

A typical agenda is shown in Figure 9-4 on page 210.

Run the Meeting

Your first responsibility is to start the meeting on time: a chairperson with a reputation for being slow in getting meetings started will encourage latecomers. You also need to keep the meeting as short as possible without seeming to "railroad" decisions, and maintain control of the meeting.

Run your meeting roughly according to the rules of parliamentary procedure. Since most in-house meetings are relatively informal, full parliamentary procedure would be too cumbersome. (For more information about these procedures, refer to *Robert's Rules of Order*. You can find this guide in most libraries.) Introduce each topic in turn, invite the person specializing in the topic to present a report, then open the topic for discussion. The discussion offers the greatest challenge for you, since you must

- permit a good debate among the members, yet steer a member who digresses back to the main topic,
- sense when a discussion on a subject has gone on for long enough, then be ready to break in and ask for a decision, and
- know when strong opinions are likely to block resolution of a difficult problem, and assign one person or a small subcommittee to investigate further and present the results at the next meeting.

An effective chair encourages reluctant contributors and dampens overenthusiastic ones

600 Deepdale Drive, Toronto ON M5W 4R9

To: Members, E-Learning Research Committee

The monthly meeting of the E-Learning Research Committee will be held in conference room B at 3:00 p.m. on Friday, September 16, 2011. The agenda will be:

Decision Items:

1. Accelerated completion of the e-learning program for the DPS-2A ultra-narrowbeam system installation. (R Taylor)
2. Purchase of off-the-shelf e-learning software. (W Frayne)
3. Proposals for papers: 2012 International E-Learning Conference and Symposium, Vancouver, BC. (D Thomashewski)

Name **the person who will speak about each particular topic**

Discussion Items:

4. Report on investigation into significance of streaming e-learners according to their ability. (C Bundt)
5. Proposal for beta-testing completed e-learning modules. (R Mohammed)
6. Plans for Annual Research Division banquet. (C Tripp; J Kosty)
7. Other business: (Please send topics to me by 10 a.m. Thursday, September 15.)

This month's meeting secretary: J Kosty.

Daniel H Thomashewski

Daniel K Thomashewski
ELR Committee
September 12, 2011

Figure 9-4 An agenda for a meeting.

Sum Up

Before proceeding from one topic to the next, summarize the outcome of the discussion on the first topic. The outcome may be a general conclusion, a consensus of members' opinions, a decision, or a statement of action defining who is to do what, and when. In this way all members are aware of the outcome, and the secretary knows what to enter into the minutes.

Effective "summing up" helps the secretary identify what should be recorded in the minutes

Also sum up at the end of the meeting, this time reviewing major issues that were discussed and the main results. At the same time, point the way forward by mentioning any important actions to be taken and the time, date, and place of the next meeting (presuming there is to be one).

The best way to learn to be a good chair is to watch others undertake the role. Study those who get a lot of business done without appearing to intrude too much in the decision making. Learn what you should *not* do from those whose meetings tend to wander from topic to topic before a decision is made, allow many "contributors" to speak at the same time, and last far too long.

The Participants' Role

You can contribute most to a meeting by arriving prepared; stating your facts, ideas, and opinions clearly when called on; and keeping quiet much of the time. If you observe the following three basic rules you will help speed up the meeting.

Come Prepared

If a meeting is scheduled to start at 3 p.m., do not wait until 2:30 to gather the information you need. Arriving with a sheaf of papers in your hand and shuffling through them for the first 15 minutes creates a disturbance and causes you (and those around you) to miss much of what is being said. Start gathering information as soon as the agenda arrives, sort your information to identify the specific items you need, then jot down topic headings.

Plan your presentation like a technical briefing

Preparation becomes even more important if you have been researching data on a particular topic and will be expected to present your findings at the meeting. Start by dividing your information into two compartments:

1. Facts your listeners *must* have if they are to fully understand the case you are making and reach a decision (if, for example, you are requesting their approval to take a specific course of action). These become "need-to-know" facts.
2. Details your listeners only *may* be interested in, and do not necessarily need to understand your case or reach a decision. These are "nice-to-know" facts.

Plan to present only the "need-to-know" facts in your presentation, but have the "nice-to-know" facts ready in case one of the listeners asks questions about them.

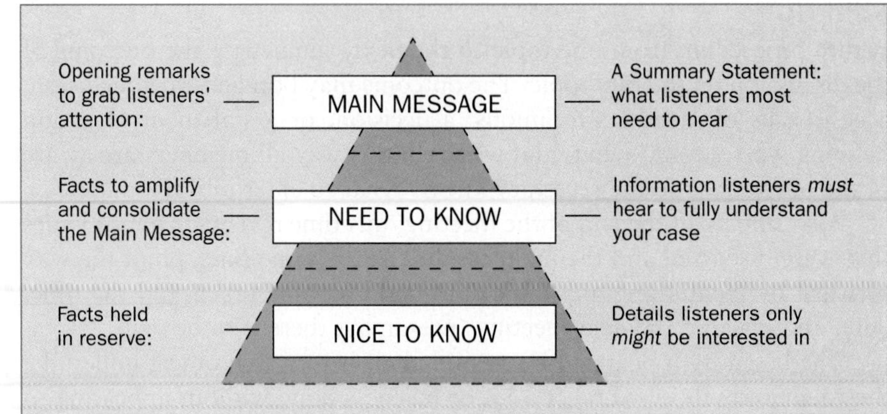

Figure 9-5 Plan for presenting information at a meeting.

Then examine the "need-to-know" facts to identify the one or two pieces of information your listeners will *most* need to hear. This will become your Main Message, or Summary Statement.

Structure your information like a written report or proposal

The three compartments form a pyramid-style speaking plan, as illustrated in Figure 9-5.

Be Brief

In your opening remarks summarize what your listeners most need to hear from you (your Main Message), and then follow immediately with facts and details from the "need-to-know" compartment. If you have statistical data to offer, either project the prepared tables onto a screen or print copies and distribute them when you begin to speak. If you have a lot of information to distribute, print copies ahead of the meeting and ask the chair to distribute them with the agenda, so that everyone can examine your data before coming to the meeting.

Keep your cool; defend your point logically and rationally

At the end of your presentation, invite questions from the meeting participants. For your answers, draw on the data you have prepared for the "nice-to-know" compartment. If some listeners seem to resist your ideas, try to avoid becoming defensive. Say that you can see their point of view, and then explain why your approach is sound or offers a better alternative than the one they may be suggesting. In particular, avoid getting into a personal confrontation with one or more of the meeting participants.

When the chair calls on the members to indicate whether they accept your ideas or will approve your proposal, if they respond negatively be ready to accept their decision gracefully.

Contribute Constructively

Many parts of a meeting require you to be only an interested observer. At these times keep quiet unless you have a relevant question, additional information to contribute, or an educated opinion to offer. Discussion of a topic should be a one-to-one conversation between you and the chair, or sometimes between you and the topic specialist. It should never become a free-for-all with each person arguing a point with his or her neighbour.

When you have a comment to make, raise your hand and look at the chair, then wait for the chair to call on you to present your opinion.

The Secretary's Role

Sometimes an administrative assistant is brought in to record the minutes of a meeting, but more often the chair appoints one of the participants to take minutes. If you happen to be selected, you need to know how to go about it.

Recording minutes does not mean writing down everything that is said. Minutes should be brief, so there is room to mention only the highlights of each topic discussed. Items that must be recorded are

- main conclusions reached,
- decisions made (with, if necessary, the name of those who made them, or the results of a vote),
- what is to be done next, who is to do it, and by when, and
- the exact wording of any policy statements derived during the meeting.

The best way to get this information quickly is to write the agenda topics on a lined sheet of paper, spacing them about two inches apart vertically. In these spaces jot down the highlights in note form, leaving room to write in more information from memory immediately after the meeting.

Write the minutes while the events are still fresh in your mind

The completed minutes should be distributed to everyone present, preferably within 24 hours. They become a permanent record on which the chair can base the agenda for the next meeting, and which participants can use as a reminder of what they are supposed to do. The format shown in Figure 9-6 also provides an "Action" column to draw participants' attention to their particular responsibilities.

600 Deepdale Drive, Toronto ON M5W 4R9

E-Learning Research Committee

Minutes of Meeting

Friday, September 16, 2011, 3:00 p.m.

In Attendance:	C Bundt	R Mohammed
	W Feldman	R Taylor
	W Frayne	D Thomashewski (Chair)
	J Kosty (Secretary)	C Tripp
Regrets:	D Wilton	

Minutes	***Action***
Decision Items:	
1. The e-learning program for the DPS-2A ultra-narrowbeam system is incomplete. Changes had to be made to the storyboard to reflect learning difficulties experienced during usability testing of module 4. The program is now scheduled for completion on October 14.	***R Taylor***
2. The committee approved W Frayne's proposal to purchase three copies of the Telesat software Version 4.3 at a total cost of $2200. The cost will be drawn equally from the E-Learning Research and the Operating budgets.	***W Frayne*** ***R Mohammed***
3. Three papers are to be submitted to the program committee for next year's International E-Learning Conference and Symposium. Deadline for proposals is November 30.	***C Bundt*** ***W Feldman*** ***J Tripp***
Discussion Items:	
4. C Bundt completed Phase 1 of the investigation into streaming e-learners on September 12. She estimates Phase 2 will be complete on October 3.	
6. The Research Division banquet will be held in collaboration with the annual Awards Dinner on March 13, 2012. The banquet committee will establish a joint plan with the Awards Committee.	***C Tripp*** ***J Kosty***

J Kosty

J Kosty, Secretary

Minutes should reflect key outcomes, not describe what everybody said

Figure 9-6 Minutes of a meeting. Note the "Action" column, which draws individuals' attention to their post-meeting responsibilities. (The dotted line indicates a break between two pages and some omitted information.)

ASSIGNMENTS

Speaking situations you are likely to encounter in industry will develop from projects on which you are working. Hence, assignments for this chapter are assumed to grow naturally out of the writing assignments presented in other chapters.

Project 9.1: Speaking Situations Evolving from Other Projects

You have to attend a meeting to present the results of a study or investigation you have carried out, at which you will brief managers or a client on your findings and recommendations. In each of the following instances, which are drawn from projects in Chapters 3, 4, 5, and 6, list in point form the information you would convey

- as your "Main Message," and
- as your "need-to-know" details.

In some projects—mainly in Chapters 3 and 4—you will be able to draw on the details provided in the assignment instructions without first doing the report-writing project itself. In others—primarily in Chapter 5—it will help if you have first completed the study and written the report.

Be ready to present this information orally.

1. **Project 3.4**
   At the next department meeting, Janet Handley asks you not only to describe what happened at Weekaskasing Lake but also to tell the meeting members how Laura Lussier's voluntary help kept the project on schedule.

2. **Project 3.9**
   When the management team for the Multiple Development Industries' construction project meet the following Monday morning, the chair asks you to describe the problem you experienced with the Megablitz 400 drill, how you dealt with it, the financial costs that were incurred, and how you are trying to get the overrun in cost refunded.

3. **Project 4.2**
   Your department manager at Marco Construction Company is Karl Windström. He says the chief accountant mentioned there has been an accounting problem, but has not gone into details. Karl asks you to brief him on what happened.

4. **Project 4.3**
   You drive back to the office to pick up a van to replace the one that was damaged during your drive to the Mooswa River construction site. Your manager—M B Corrigan—telephones and asks you to see

him before you return to Mooswa River. "Please describe the incident to me," he says when you enter his office. "I need the details for when I talk to Meadows Electronics (where you rented the video camera) and the insurance company."

5. **Project 4.5**
   Karen Korlyshyn, your manager, asks you to attend the next management meeting, when there is to be a focus on tightening up company security. She wants you to describe what has been done to improve security of the outside storage area at Forrest Distributors, and how the security system failed to provide evidence of the people making the most recent break-in.

6. **Project 5.1, Part 3**
   When you deliver your sound-level study to Wendy Partridge, you tell her there is a problem at Mirabel Realty and it's going to cost a fair sum to remedy it. She telephones you two days later and says, "Three people from head office will be here next week on a routine visit. I'd appreciate it if you could come in one afternoon to describe your findings to them. You'll do a better job than me, because you know the study better than I do."

7. **Project 5.2**
   Robert Delorme telephones you and asks, "Have you finished the Quillicom landfill study?" You tell him you have, but you have not yet written the report. He responds, "Then I want you to go to the Quillicom Town Council meeting at 7:30 p.m. tonight. The councillors want to hear what recommendations you will be making."

8. **Project 5.3**
   Paullette Machon (vice-president of operations at Baldur Agricultural Chemicals—BAC) telephones to say she will be coming to your office tomorrow and bringing BAC's manager of human resources with her. Rather than wait for your report to reach them, they want you to brief them on your findings about BAC's power house problems, and then they want to discuss the implications with you.

9. **Project 5.4**
   Highways engineer Morris Hordern asks you to brief his highway engineers on the results of your highway paint study.

10. **Project 6.1**
    You have written the proposal for purchasing handheld computers and you handed it to Tracey Harcourt three days ago. Today she emails you with this message: "I want you to present your idea to purchase handheld computers in person at next week's capital

budget meeting. The committee may want to know specifically which model you are recommending and why it is your preferred choice."

11. **Project 6.3**
    The project manager from Terrapin Control Systems flies in to your city a few days after the power outage that caused you to discard the electronic switches. Your manager—John Grayson—asks you to join him and the Terrapin project manager for a 2 p.m. meeting at which you are to describe the cause of the problem and what steps you will be taking to prevent a recurrence. "It's essential we assure him there will be no further work stoppages," Grayson says. "We've been told privately that Terrapin Control Systems is issuing an even bigger contract to us, so we must be sure they understand we have taken positive action to prevent further delays."

12. **Project 6.4**
    When you deliver your proposal to student council president Sharon Gilchrist, she says, "It's a good idea. I'd like you to come to the next meeting and present the proposal in person."

Project 9.2: Informing Technicians of a New Manufacturing Material, Product, or Process

You are to research information on a topic related to your technology and then prepare it for both written and oral presentation. The topic may be a new manufacturing material, product, or process. The written and spoken presentations must

1. introduce the topic,
2. state why it is worth evaluating,
3. describe the material, method, or process,
4. discuss its uniqueness and usefulness, and
5. show how it can be applied in your particular field.

To obtain data for your topic, you will have to research current literature and probably talk to industrial users, manufacturers, and suppliers. Typical examples of topics are a new oil that can be used at very low temperatures, a method for supporting the deck of a bridge during concrete-pouring by building up a base on compacted fill, a new paint for use on concrete surfaces, a new materials-handling system, and a recently developed computer software program. Assume that both your readers and your audience are technicians to whom the topic will be entirely new.

Make an in-depth presentation to unknowledgeable listeners

Part 1
On a sheet of paper write brief notes in point form identifying what you will say under each of the following topic headings:

- Summary Statement
- Purpose (of product, material, or process)
- Details (what it does and why it is unique)
- Conclusions

Part 2
Create your visuals.

Part 3
Deliver your presentation.

REFERENCES

1. Peter and Cheryl Reimold, *The Short Road to Great Presentations: How to Reach Any Audience Through Focused Preparation, Inspired Delivery, and Smart Use of Technology* (IEEE Press and Wiley-Interscience, 2003).

Chapter 10
Communicating with Prospective Employers

In this chapter you will learn how to

- research positions that are open,
- prepare a paper-based or electronic resume and application letter that present your experience and background well,
- complete an *informative* application form,
- prepare for and attend an interview, and
- respond when accepting or declining a job offer.

Watch

When you apply for a job, you have to present yourself as a quality person the potential employer will want to hire. You have to do this personally and in writing. The process starts when you prepare a resume and application letter, then proceeds on to attending an interview or interviews, and ends when you are offered or declined a position.

The job-seeking process comprises five steps, at each of which you have to present a confident and positive image of yourself if you are to proceed to the next step:

The image you convey—on paper or online—has a major impact on a potential employer

Step	Action taken or to be taken	No. of applicants*
1	Initial contact	64
2	Formal application	25
3	Screening interview	9
4	Selection interview	4
5	Offer of employment	1

* The possible number of candidates left at each step.

1. **Initial Contact.** You write an application letter and accompany it with your resume. You can deliver this personally, by regular mail, or electronically.

A resume may be submitted electronically

2. **Formal Application.** You complete an application form so the company can see every applicant documented in the same format.
3. **Screening Interview.** You attend your first interview. Often, this is used by the employer to identify which applicants have sufficient potential to go on to a second interview.

4. **Selection Interview.** If you are a promising candidate, you are asked to attend a second interview at which the manager of the department where you would work also is present.
5. **Offer of Employment.** If you are the selected applicant, you receive a formal offer of employment and respond to confirm you are accepting the offer.

Using the Internet in Your Job Search

The internet offers vast opportunities and possibilities to people seeking employment. It provides an efficient way for employers and potential employees to meet and learn about each other.

You research corporate information online...

You can use the internet to research information about companies, search for job postings, or enter your electronic resume into a database. Both large and small companies are using their websites to advertise employment opportunities and provide information about the company, such as its history, corporate structure, and beliefs and philosophy. This will help you decide whether you want to apply to that organization; later, the information you collect will help prepare you for an interview.

...or announce your availability as a potential employee

You can also use the internet to

- place an advertisement about yourself,
- identify a list of prospective companies that are advertising employment opportunities,
- find commercially run internet services that match people to positions,
- search for job openings on nonprofit bulletin boards, and
- use an internet resume service that specializes in organizing, indexing, and distributing resumes (for guidelines, see the section "Electronic Resume Formats" starting on page 236).

Start by contacting an internet resume specialist

A word of caution: it is just as easy for a potential employer to find information about you from the internet as it is for you to find information about employers. So be careful when writing on the internet: present a confident image of yourself and use language that demonstrates you are a capable communicator. (Remember that employers can just as easily gain a picture of you from the remarks you make on Facebook, on Twitter, or in a blog, and perhaps see you in different light!)

Developing a Personal Data Record

Start a databank: store your history electronically

There are three ways you can go about writing a resume: you can rely solely on your memory; you can dust off and update a previous resume; or you can create a new resume from information you store in a permanent personal data record (PDR). Using a PDR is best, because it provides a much broader information base for you to draw on.

You will find a PDR essential in later years, when one's ability to recall names, addresses, dates, and specific details of earlier employment diminishes. It can also be invaluable if, when calling initially on a potential employer, you are asked to complete an application form on the premises.

If you do not already have a PDR, prepare one. You may find it's a pain to start, but once it exists it's not difficult to update and keep current. You will need to record details in four topic areas:

- Education
- Work Experience
- Extracurricular Activities
- References

Remember, this is not a resume: it's the information you will draw on when planning a new resume. As you progress through your career, you will need to develop a new resume for each potential employer you contact.

Writing in the Job Search
http://owl.english.purdue.edu/handouts/pw/#sub2
The Online Writing Lab at Purdue University has a section devoted to writing job search materials, including applications, resumes, cover letters, acceptance letters, references, and personal statements.

Education

List the schools, colleges, and universities you have attended or are attending, and details about the courses you studied:

- For high school: the name of each school, its address and telephone number, the dates you were there, your graduation date, and (where appropriate) your area of specialization.
- For college and university: courses taken; major studies; and the full name of the certificate, diploma, or degree. Include grades or at least a grade-point average (GPA) for each year.
- The names, locations, and dates of any additional courses or seminars you completed.

Work Experience

For each job you have held in the past—and, if you are currently employed, the job you now hold—list

Be as detailed as possible: don't rely on your memory

- the full name, address, telephone number, and website of the company or organization, and the full name, title, and email address of each supervisor you worked for,
- the dates you started and finished employment and, if you held several positions within the company, the name of the position and the date you were appointed to it,
- your job title, or titles if you held several positions,
- your specific responsibilities and duties for each position, paying particular attention to the supervisory aspects and responsibilities of any job that you carried out without supervision,

- any special skills you learned on the job,
- anything you did that was innovative and probably beyond the basic requirements of the job,
- special awards or words of praise you received, or results you achieved, and
- projects you were involved in, including the type of technology you learned or used.

Extracurricular Activities

List your activities in organizations that were not necessarily part of the jobs you have held or your education, but which show your participation and leadership qualities. These help identify you as a well-rounded, balanced person. For example,

- Membership in a club, society, or group, particularly noting your responsibilities as an active participator or committee member. (For example, member of sports committee or secretary of administrative committee.)
- Participation in community activities such as the Big Brother or Sister Organizations, YMCA or YWCA, 4-H Club, Parent–Teacher Association (PTA), or local community club. In particular, describe any executive or administrative positions you held, with special responsibilities and dates.
- Involvement in a technical society on a local or national level, with particular mention of any conferences you attended or papers you presented or published.
- Participation on a sports team, with special mention of your role as a team leader or coach.
- Involvement in hobby activities—for example, stock car racing or rebuilding, a computer club, or dog breeding.
- Awards you have received for any activities you have been involved in.

Don't overlook your personal attributes and life experience

For each activity, include the dates of your involvement and the name, address, telephone number, and email address of a person who can vouch for your participation. Make sure you indicate whether you were elected to the position or were doing the work voluntarily.

References

List the names of people you feel are best fitted to speak on your behalf. They fall into two groups: those who can vouch for your *capabilities* (as an employee, student, or committee member), and those who can speak for your *character*. Always contact these people first and ask if you may list them as a reference. Then, for each person write down

- full name, professional title (such as Plant Engineer), place of employment, and job position,
- employer's address, telephone number, and website,
- home address, email address, and telephone number, and
- how long you have known them.

Be thorough: you cannot tell in advance who you may want to use as a reference

(If the person has changed jobs, list details of both the previous and current employer.)

For each person you worked with in an extracurricular activity, also list

- the name of the organization you both were involved with, and the referee's position within that organization, and
- whether the person prefers to be contacted at home or at work.

Preparing a Resume

A resume contains key information about you, carefully assembled and presented so that prospective employers will be impressed not only by your qualifications but also by your ability to present yourself effectively. (The correct spelling is "résumé," but common usage has made the accentless "resume" acceptable. Sometimes it's called a *curriculum vitae*, or CV.)

There are no specific rules about the "right" way to prepare a resume. However, there are generally accepted guidelines of what employers expect to see and the type of information they require when evaluating you. You can submit your resume either electronically or on paper, depending on what the employer or job search agency asks for. Ideally, create your resume in both electronic and paper formats. The designs are very different.

Paper Resume Formats

Your resume style must fit your personality...

We present three resume styles that can be submitted on paper. These are

- the traditional resume,
- the focused resume, and
- the functional resume.

Each opens with a summary statement, often called an **Objective** that

1. describes the applicant's strongest qualifications, *from the employer's point of view*, and
2. identifies that the writer is seeking work in a particular field.

The Objective is presented in no more than two or three lines:

Objective
I have four years of experience supervising the installation and testing of wire and fibre optic telephone communication systems, and a recent MSc in electrical engineering with a major in fibre optics. I am now seeking employment where I can apply my knowledge and experience in fibre optics engineering.

...and that of the particular employer you are contacting

An assertive statement like this, right at the top of the resume, immediately draws an employer's attention to your primary experience and education, and also the employment direction you want to pursue. If it does its job well, the employer reads further to learn more about you.

You need to focus this opening statement so that it fits the particular needs of each employer, and then tailor the remainder of your resume to suit.

Explore

Job Star Central
http://jobstar.org/tools/resume/index.php
Job Star Central gives you all the information you need to write your resume, with sample cover letters, resume resources on the web, and samples of different kinds of resumes.

The Traditional Resume

For decades the most widely recognized approach to resume writing has been to divide a job applicant's information into five parts, each preceded by an appropriate heading:

Objective
Education
Experience
Extracurricular Activities
References

The traditional resume is particularly suitable for recent university or college graduates who have limited work experience, or for students who expect to graduate shortly. Alison Witney is a biological sciences undergraduate who has held two previous jobs, totalling three years of full-time employment. Her resume is shown in Figure 10-1. Comments on the resume, plus guidelines you can use to write a resume of your own in the traditional format, are presented here.

A short, concise, directed resume is welcomed by employers!

1. Job applicants with only limited work experience should try to keep their resumes down to one page.
2. Each line of Alison's name, address, telephone number, and email address is centred to give the top of the resume a balanced appearance.
3. There is no need to list all the primary and secondary schools you attended; it is enough to state the name of your high school and the year you graduated. You should then list each college or university you attended, plus the type of course enrolled in, the diploma or degree received, and your year of graduation (or expected graduation). In the example, Allison has included her grade point average (GPA) because it is high. This is optional, but if you do include it be sure to include it for all schools.
4. Experience is usually presented in reverse order, with the most recent work experience appearing first. You should be more

1 **Alison V Witney**
1670 Fulham Boulevard
Truro NS B2N 6C4
2 Tel: (902) 474-6318
email: avwitney@nsonline.net

OBJECTIVE

To work in a position related to Animal Biology or Health Science, where I can use to good advantage both my Diploma in Biological Science and my experience as a veterinary assistant.

EDUCATION AND TRAINING

3
- Will graduate with a Diploma in Biological Science from Amiento Technical College, June, 2011 (GPA to date: 3.7).
- Graduate of Morton Stanley High School, Corisand, Nova Scotia, 2007 (avg: 92.3%)

WORK EXPERIENCE

2009 to date — **Animal Treatment Centre**, Amiento, NS. Veterinary assistant,
4 responsible for reception, grooming, and exercising of animals, assisting veterinarian during operations, changing dressings, administering injections and anaesthetics, and performing administrative duties such as accounting and
5 ordering of supplies. (One year full-time, two years part-time.)

2007 to 2009 — **Remick Airlines**, Fredericton, NB. Accounts clerk in air freight department; coordinating billings, preparing
6 invoices, following up lost shipments, assisting clients, and writing monthly reports. For nine months assisted in payroll preparation.

2001 to date — **Bar None Riding Stables**, Corisand, NS. Part-time employment teaching the care and handling of horses, and basic riding techniques, to young riders. Assisted in grooming, cleaning, feeding, and saddling-up.

7 **ADDITIONAL INFORMATION**

- Winner of two educational awards: Morton Stanley Science Scholarship (2006) and Amiento Technical College Biology Scholarship (2010).
- Active at Truro Recreational Centre since 2001, where I teach swimming and lifesaving
- Interests: horseback riding and jumping, swimming, and water skiing

8 **REFERENCES**

The following people have agreed to supply references on my behalf:

Dr Alex Gavin	Mr Charles Devereaux
Veterinary Surgeon	Owner-Manager
Animal Treatment Centre	Bar None Riding Stables
2230 Wolverine Drive	2881 Westshore Drive
Amiento NS B3R 2G1	Corisand NS B4L 3A2
Tel: 474-1260	Tel: 632-2292
Fax: 474-1355	Fax: 631-3105
email: a.gavin@atlanticvet.net	email: bar.none@nst.ns.ca

An appealing, uncrowded appearance, coupled with good words, will catch an employer's attention

Figure 10-1 A traditional resume or biography of experience.

detailed about recent experience (as Alison is), and about earlier work that is similar to that of the position you are seeking. Quote dates as whole years for long periods of employment, but as month and year for short periods; for example, Jun 2010–Feb 2011.

5 For each employer, state the name of the company or organization first, emphasize it with bold type, and then identify the city and province in which it is located. Then describe the position held (give the job title), and what the work involved. Particularly draw attention to the *responsibilities* of the job rather than merely listing the duties you performed. Use words that create strong images of your confidence, such as

Let the words you use convey a positive impression

coordinated	organized
monitored	implemented
presented	supervised
planned	directed

(Note that Alison uses "responsible for," "administering," "coordinating," and "teaching.")

If you have held several short part-time jobs, describe them together and draw attention to the most important, like this: "Several after-school jobs, primarily as a stock clerk in a small grocery store."

6 The two-column arrangement of dates and work experience is important because it gives a less crowded appearance to the page. If the job descriptions were carried to the left—under the dates—the job details would appear as less visually appealing blocks of information.

An employer wants to see the "whole picture"

7 Information on your hobbies, interests, and participation in sports and community activities tells prospective employers that you recognize your role in society, are not too rigid or too narrow, and adapt well to your environment. Employers reason that such an applicant will make an interesting, active employee who will not only contribute to the company, but also take part in social and sports functions. Outside activities represent a balanced lifestyle and provide outlets for stress.

Explore

8 Try to draw your list of references from a cross-section of people you have worked for, been taught by, or served with on committees, and ensure that their connection to one of your previous jobs or activities is clear. Before including them in your list, check that each is willing to act as a reference. We suggest you always provide references on your resume. Resumes that list "References Available on Request" make the reader take one more step. By providing them in

advance you are making the selection committee's work easier and shorter.

Figure 10-2 presents an alternative way that Alison could prepare the Work Experience part of her resume: by showing the strengths she will bring to the job as a series of bulleted points divided into relevant experience and other experience. The reader can scan this quickly and then obtain details from the now shorter descriptions of her employment history. This is similar to the way Reid Qually offers his key points in the functional resume in Figure 10-4 (pages 233 to 234). You can choose which you feel is most appropriate for the Work Experience section of your resume.

The Focused Resume

Focus your resume to match the employer's primary interest

Job applicants who have more extensive experience to describe do better if they focus an employer's attention on their particular strengths and aims. This means asking yourself what a prospective employer is *most likely to want to know* after reading your opening statement. (Probably it will be something like,

> "What have you done that specifically qualifies you to achieve the objective you have presented?"

or,

> "In what way will you be of particular value to us?"

To answer, focus on your work experience rather than your education, particularly on work that is *relevant to the position* (which means you must first research information about the company).

Specific Experience Working with Animals

- Assisting veterinarian during operations; administering injections and anaesthetics; grooming and exercising
- Horseback riding and jumping; daily care and grooming; teaching

Other Experience

- Training: teaching young people swimming, life saving, horseback riding
- Administration: accounting, invoicing; payroll preparation, general office management, report writing

Employment History

2009 to date	**Animal Treatment Centre**, Amiento, NS. Veterinary assistant to Dr Alex Gavin (1 year full-time, 2 years part-time)
2007 to 2009	**Remick Airlines**, Fredericton, NB. Accounts clerk in air freight department, coordinating shipments and billing (3 years full-time)
2001 to date	**Bar None Riding Stables**, Corisand, NS. Teaching care and handling of horses, and basic riding techniques (10 years part-time)

Figure 10-2 An alternative way to present experience that could replace the Work Experience section of Alison Witney's resume in Figure 10-1.

If your experience is varied, you can take one step further and divide your Work Experience section into two parts, each with a separate heading:

Related Experience
Other Experience

The Related Experience describes positions you have held and work you have done that is similar or leads up to the work done by the potential employer. Ideally, place your work experience immediately after the Objective, so there is a natural flow from one to the other.

Objective (or Aim)
Related Experience
Other Experience
Education
Extracurricular Activities
References

Colin Farrow's two-page resume in Figure 10-3 adopts this sequence. The circled numbers beside the resume refer to the following comments.

1. Colin has sufficient information to warrant preparing a two-page resume, but he should not run over onto a third page. A third page can be used, however, if an applicant has published papers and articles or has obtained patents for new inventions, which can be listed on a separate sheet and identified as an attachment. A separate page can also be used to list references.

2. Colin's objective clearly shows his thrust toward structural engineering and his desire to obtain employment in that field.

Divide your work experience into "directly related" and "less related" compartments

3. The positions described within each Experience section should be listed in reverse order, the most recent experience being described first. The most recent and most relevant experience should be described in greater depth than early or unrelated experience (compare the descriptions of Colin's Northwestern Steel Constructors experience with his Bowlands Stores experience).

4. As in the traditional resume, each employer's name is listed first (in boldface type) and followed by the city and province. The applicant's position or job title is identified next, and then a description of what the job involved. If several positions have been held within the same firm, each is named and its duration stated so that the applicant's progress within the firm is clear. Each position should draw particular attention to the personal responsibilities and supervisory aspects of the job, rather than just listing specific duties.

Colin R Farrow, P.Eng
408 Medwin Street
Brandon MB R7C 0B3
Tel: (204) 548-1612
email: c.farrow@mbonline.com

❶

OBJECTIVE

After four years of comprehensive experience as an engineering technologist installing and testing transmission line towers in Northern Canada, I returned to university where I obtained a B.Sc in Structural Engineering. Now I am seeking employment where I can use my experience and education to research and test tower anchors and grouts in permafrost areas.

❷

Immediately announce your strengths and show how they can be used by the employer

RELATED WORK EXPERIENCE

June 2008 to October 2010	**Fairborne and Warren Associates,** Consulting Engineers, Brandon, Manitoba. Project engineer managing construction of microwave transmission towers and associated structures between Brandon and The Pas, Manitoba, for MTS Allstream. Wrote specifications, coordinated and monitored contractors' work, prepared progress reports, and maintained liaison with client.
June 2000 to August 2004	**Northwestern Steel Constructors Ltd,** Winnipeg, Manitoba. Crew chief, supervising team installing high-voltage transmission line towers between Flin Flon, Manitoba, and Minnowin Point, NWT. After 30 months was assigned to assist project engineers of Ebby, Little and Company, testing concretes and grouts installed in discontinuous permafrost (10 months). For final year, appointed installation coordinator, responsible for scheduling and supervising installation crews. Resigned to attend university.

❸

❹

OTHER WORK EXPERIENCE

January 1995 to February 1999	**Canadian Forces,** Construction and Maintenance Directorate. For first two years, member of crew installing communication systems (buildings and towers) at CF bases between Armstrong, Ontario, and Prince George, BC. For final two years, antenna installation and maintenance technician at CFB Comox, Vancouver Island. Attained rank of corporal.
September 1992 to December 1994	**Bowlands Stores.** Stock clerk in Store No. 26, St. Boniface, Manitoba. (One year part-time while at high school, 1¼ years full-time.)

❺

/2...

Figure 10-3 A focused resume for a job applicant with a varied background.

Colin R Farrow – page 2

EDUCATION

6
- B.Sc in Structural Engineering, University of Manitoba, 2007.
- Diploma in Civil Engineering Technology, Red River College, Winnipeg, Manitoba, June 2000.

If applying to an educational institution, consider placing the Education section ahead of Work Experience

ADDITIONAL ACTIVITIES/INFORMATION

7
- Member, Association of Professional Engineers and Geoscientists of Manitoba (APEGM).
- Member, Certified Technicians and Technologists Association of Manitoba (CTTAM).
- Awarded Orton R Smith Scholarship for proficiency in applied mathematics, Red River College, 1999.
- Courses attended in Canadian Forces:
  - Construction Techniques, 1995.
  - Supervisory Skills Development, 1997.
  - First Aid and Safety Methods (various courses), 1996 to 1998.
- Junior Leader, St Vital YMCA, 1991–1994, teaching swimming and aquatic activities to boys and girls age 9 to 15. Awarded Red Cross Bronze Medallion, 1992. Lifeguard at Grand Beach, Manitoba, summers of 1992 and 1993.

REFERENCES

8 The following people have agreed to provide information regarding my qualifications and work capabilities:

Martin G Warren, M.Sc	Philip G Karlowsky
Projects Coordinator	Contracts Manager
Fairborne and Warren Associates	Northwestern Steel Constructors Ltd
360 Rosser Avenue	3335 Notre Dame Avenue
Brandon, Manitoba R7A 0K2	Winnipeg, Manitoba R3H 2J4
Tel: (204) 544-1687	Tel: (204) 632-1450
Fax: (204) 544-1628	Fax: (204) 632-2177
email: mgw13@aol.com	email: p.karlowsk@norsteel.mb.ca

We recommend including two references, rather than writing "References available on request"

Verbs should be chosen carefully, so they make the position sound as comprehensive and self-directed as possible. If the paragraph grows too long, it can be broken into a list like this:

...appointed crew chief responsible for

- installing interconnection and distribution systems
- hiring, training, and supervising local labour
- ordering and monitoring delivery of parts and materials
- arranging and supervising subcontract work
- preparing progress and job completion reports.

Notice how all the verbs are parallel (they are in the same form).

Economize on space yet appeal to the eye

5 Single-spaced typing should be used as much as possible to keep the resume compact, but use a reasonable amount of white space on each side and between major paragraphs to avoid a crowded effect. Although we normally recommend setting the right margin "ragged right," for Colin's resume a justified right margin does not seem too rigid. See the "Electronic Resume Formats" section starting on page 236 if you are submitting your resume electronically. The guidelines are different.

6 Education can be listed either in chronological or reverse sequence. Identify the city and province of each educational institution attended, the name, and the type of diploma or degree earned.

7 Employers are *interested* in a job applicant's accomplishments and extracurricular activities, particularly those describing community involvement and awards or commendations. This part of a resume can be preceded by a heading such as "Extracurricular Activities."

8 Both people Colin has chosen as references can be cross-referenced to his previous work experience. Telephone numbers and email addresses are important because they are the simplest and fastest way for a potential employer to contact your references.

The Functional Resume

Of the three paper-based resumes discussed here, the functional resume goes furthest in *marketing* a job applicant's attributes. For some employers its approach may seem too assertive or pushy; for others, particularly employers seeking someone for a technical sales position, its approach helps demonstrate that the applicant has strong capabilities.

The functional resume is not for everyone, yet for certain people and jobs its direct approach is ideal

The functional resume is the only one to offer *opinions*: its objective identifies in general terms what you believe you can do to improve the quality of the employer's products or service, and then follows immediately with your key qualifications—the capabilities you believe best demonstrate that you are qualified to do what the Objective proclaims.

To prove your opinions are valid, the third section establishes—with clear facts and figures—what you have done for previous employers or organizations. This results in a revised arrangement of the resume's parts:

Objective
Qualifications
Major Achievements
Employment Experience
Education
Awards/Other Activities
References

The intent of this arrangement is to target the resume not just for a particular employer but also for a particular position. It is especially useful under two circumstances: for job applicants who have experience in marketing and want to be employed in technical sales; and for applicants who have a lean educational background but have proven practical experience that can be of value to a specific employer.

The resume in Figure 10-4 shows how Reid Qually uses the functional method to capture the attention of the marketing manager of a company engaged in selling cellular telephone services. The circled numbers beside his resume relate to the following comments.

Use subtle marketing techniques to promote yourself

❶ Reid has positioned his name in the top right corner of the page because, in a pile of resumes, his name will stand out just where the person's hand is placed to flip through the pages. The line underneath his name helps draw the reader's eye to it. Reid has also saved a few lines by putting his contact address all on one line. If you are going to submit your resume electronically or if you know it will be scanned, the techniques are different. See the "Electronic Resume Formats" section starting on page 236.

❷ Reid has written his Objective with a specific employer in mind. He discovered that King Cell—a West Coast player in the cellular telecommunications field—is planning to expand and hopes to become a major provider of such services across the continent. By echoing the company's philosophy, he is almost certain to catch management's attention.

❸ When the manager at King Cell sees Reid's Objective, he or she is likely to think,

> "You have told me what you want to do, now tell me *why* you think you can do it."

Reid G Qually 

7–2617 East 38th Avenue • Vancouver, BC • V5R 2T9 • Tel: 604-263-4250 • email: qually@interex.net

Reid sets the scene with a commanding, professional approach

Objective 2

To use my proven marketing skills to increase market share for a Canadian company providing cellular telephone services and systems continent-wide.

Qualifications

I have proven capability to 3

- Identify special-interest client groups and develop innovative marketing strategies.
- Create results-oriented proposals and focus them to meet specific client needs.
- Follow through with clients, both before and after a sale.
- Supervise and coordinate the efforts of small groups.
- Establish strong interpersonal relations with clients, management, and sales staff.

Major Achievements

For previous employers and organizations I have

- Devised an innovative lease/purchase marketing plan for first-time customers, resulting in a 34% increase in lease agreements and a 23% increase in follow-on sales over a 12-month period (for Morton Sales and Leasing, in 2007). 4
- Increased sales of Apple iPods by 31% over a nine-month period (for Advent Communications Limited, in 2009–2010).
- Received a company-wide "Salesperson of the Year" award (from Provo Department Stores, in 2004).
- Advised and coordinated Electronic/Computer Technology students who won a nationwide IEEE "Carillon Communication Award" (for Pacific Rim Community College, 2009).

Achievements must be stated strongly and supported with specific details

/2...

Figure 10-4 A functional resume identifies in detail what an applicant feels he or she can do for a particular employer.

Resume of **Reid G Qually** – page 2

Employment Experience

5

June 2009 to the present	**Advent Communications Limited**, Vancouver, BC. Assistant Marketing Manager, responsible for coordinating four representatives selling Apple iPods and other mobile devices to commercial customers.
November 2005 to June 2009	**Morton Sales and Leasing**, New Westminster, BC. Sales representative marketing office furniture and equipment to business accounts and private customers.
July 2002 to October 2005	**Provo Department Stores**, Store No. 17, Calgary, Alberta. Sales representative in Home Electronics Department. Responsible for over-the-counter sales of computers and home entertainment centres.

Education

6

June 2009	Certificate in Commercial and Industrial Sales, Pacific Rim Community College, Vancouver, BC (placed 2nd in course with GPA of 3.84).
2004 to 2008	Various courses in theoretical and applied electronics, at Pacific Rim Community College, Extension Division (partial credit toward electronics technician certificate).

Awards and Other Activities

7

October 2008 and November 2009	Coordinator, IEEE "Papers Night," Pacific Rim Community College, at which students of Electronics and Computer Technology presented term projects.
2006 to present	Associate Member, Institute of Electrical and Electronics Engineers Inc (IEEE).
2005 to present	Member, British Columbia Sales and Advertising Association; currently vice-president.

Information in a functional resume must be easy to find

References

8

Two people will provide immediate references; other names are available.

James B Morton
President, Morton Sales & Leasing
330 Pruden Avenue
New Westminster BC V3J 1J5
Tel: (604) 475-3166
Fax: (604) 475-2807
email: j.morton@bconline.com

Dr Fergus Radji
(Chair, Burnaby Section, IEEE)
Pacific West HV Power Consultants
1920 – 784 Thurlow Street
Vancouver BC V6E 1V9
Tel: (604) 488-1066
Fax: (604) 489-2722
email: radji@pacwest.bc.ca

So Reid immediately offers five reasons, each demonstrating that he can handle the job. Note particularly that

- each is short, so that the reader assimilates the information quickly,
- each starts with a strong "action" verb (i.e. *identify, create, establish*), which creates a strong, definite image, and
- each is an opinion. (Although not recommended for other types of resumes, opinions can be used here because Reid will follow immediately with *evidence* to support his assertions.)

Opinions must be supported by solid evidence

4 Reid's evidence provides *facts*, which demonstrate he has already established a solid track record. He keeps each piece of evidence short and offers definitive details (i.e. percentages, names, and dates) which add credibility to his opinions.

Explore

5 Reid can keep details of his work experience short because he has already identified his major accomplishments. For each job he provides

- start and finish dates (by month),
- employer's name (emphasized, in bold or italic letters),
- employer's location (city and province), and
- his job title and major responsibilities.

An unusual yet conservative appearance can help "sell" you as a strong, imaginative applicant...

To maintain continuity, he lists his employment experience in reverse sequence.

6 Reid has only limited formal education, so he draws attention to his high grade point average (GPA) on returning to school after a long absence.

... but these techniques cannot be applied if you send your resume electronically

7 The "Awards and Other Activities" section provides additional information to support Reid's statements in the Qualifications and Major Achievements sections.

8 Reid has asked several people to act as references but lists only two, partly because they are best able to speak about his qualifications, and partly to keep his resume down to two pages.

Practise

Reid's use of bullets on page 1 and a two-column format with dates on the left on page 2 provide variety in his resume's overall layout yet continuity within each page. The bulleted items on page 1 can be read easily—Reid wants his readers to learn quickly about him—while the facts on page 2 can be examined in more detail.

Electronic Resume Formats

If you submit electronically, be aware of the different requirements

In today's competitive workplace there are more people looking for fewer jobs, which means that Human Resources departments are often flooded with far too many resumes for the jobs they have available. (The Human Resources staff may even hesitate to advertise a position because they fear the overwhelming response they might get!) Instead they tend to maximize their hiring time by using automated computer systems that narrow the search for them. Often, instead of posting a job and seeing who applies, they first go into the databases and see who is out there.

Smart job seekers use every avenue to get their resume "out there"

The paper resume is *not* obsolete: you just have more options. You will still need to carry a resume to the interview. Even a scanned resume that has been key worded and indexed for a computerized retrieval system may end up being viewed or downloaded, once it has been flagged as a possible match. With this in mind, your word choice is critical because it presents an image of you.

There are several variations of an electronic resume and each has its own purpose:

Translating Resumes for the Internet
www.nytimes.com/library/jobmarket/0107sabra.html
This "Careers" article from *The New York Times* gives practical advice about how to design an electronic resume.

If you are sending your resume...	We suggest this format...
As part of an email message	ASCII plain text
To post to a database	ASCII plain text with key word summaries
As an attachment to an email message	A word-processed document in ASCII rich text format (RTF) or converted to PDF
To be scanned into a database	Follow the guidelines listed below

It never hurts to follow up by mailing a paper copy of your resume to an employer.

This section provides only general information on creating e-resumes, because there are many excellent websites that offer detailed tutorials on how to develop and submit a resume electronically.

Plain Text Resumes

Although plain ASCII text is not very appealing to look at, it is the safest way to transfer electronic information and so guarantees your document converts properly. Special formatting, boldface, italic, indents, and bullets, for example, should not be used. Figure 10-5 shows the resume Susan Jenkins emailed to an agency knowing it would be posted to their database.

You can use any word-processing program to create your ASCII plain text document. After you have typed your resume in a normal format, follow these steps to convert it into an electronic document.

1. Change all the text to a non-proportional font, such as Courier 12. This will give you 65 characters per line, which will accommodate most email programs.

```
SUSAN R JENKINS
517-210 Olivia Crescent
London ON N5Z 3E9
Tel: (519) 438-0761    email: s.jenkins@interact.on.ca

KEY WORD SUMMARY
Engineering firm. Computer services. Computer systems design. Computer maintenance. Computer
specialist. Computer integration. Computer engineering. BSc Computer Science. UWO. Manager.
Website design. Consulting. UNIX. C++, C, SQL. HP-UX.

OBJECTIVES
To obtain a position as a computer services consultant/coordinator for a major engineering
firm, so I may use my expertise in computer system maintenance and design.

QUALIFICATIONS SUMMARY
Five years of experience in designing, installing, and troubleshooting computing systems; a
proven track record in identifying problems and developing innovative solutions.

TECHNICAL SKILLS
* PROGRAMMING: C, C++, Visual BASIC, SQL, OSF/Motif, UNIX Shell Script, and JAVA scripting.
* OPERATING SYSTEMS: UNIX, MS Windows, MS DOS, MS Windows NT, Solaris, and HP-UX.
* NETWORKING: TCP/IP, OSI, Microsoft LAN Manager, and Novell Netware.
* APPLICATIONS: Microsoft Office, Microsoft Access, Microsoft Visual C++, Microsoft Project,
Microsoft Publisher, Lotus 123, Lotus Freelance, and others.

PROFESSIONAL EXPERIENCE
Information Technologist
Superior Manufacturing Systems, Cambridge, ON.  May 2009 to Present
* Responsible for upgrading software, configuring new systems and managing computer accounts
and server space for a research and development lab of 138 employees.

Independent Consultant
Jenkins Communication Services, London, ON.  April 2007 to Present
* Part-time business designing and developing websites for small businesses and organizations.

Computer Specialist
Woolland Computer Services, London, ON.  June 2004 to 2007
* One year full-time, after high school graduation; two years part-time while attending
university. Duties included
* direct sales of computers and software
* onsite servicing of computers and training of users
EDUCATION
* BSc in Computer Science, University of Western Ontario, London, ON, 2009: GPA 3.8
Senior Project: Developed a hypertext information system for athletic department.
* East Elms High School, Stratford, ON, 2004: 84.6%
EXTRACURRICULAR ACTIVITIES
Westferry Ski Club, London, ON.  2004 to present
* Received ski instructor certification in 1995, served as club secretary 2005 - present

Theatre for Youth, Stratford, ON.  2002 to 2008
* Actor-in-training for one year, then as electrical/computer technician for five years,
responsible for designing and implementing computer-generated dramatic effects.
SPECIAL AWARDS
* Recipient of Miller Foundation scholarship in Computer Science, UWO, 2008
* Awarded Maitland Trophy for best overall performance, East Elms High School, 2003
REFERENCES
Margaret Ferbrache, Owner/Manager
Woolland Computer Services
313 Oak Street, London ON N2R B6J
519-323-6647  email: ferbrache@woollcom.on.ca
David Singh, Program Director
Theatre for Youth
PO Box 212, Stratford ON N6A 7M3
519-717-6690  email: d.singh@players.net
```

Figure 10-5 Resume saved in ASCII plain text format.

2. Save your resume as "Plain text (*.txt)" (an option listed in your *Save As* dialogue box), then choose "Insert line breaks." This will insert a hard return at the end of each line. If the agency or person you are sending your resume to has requested you use hard returns only at the end of each paragraph, save as plain text but don't choose the option "Insert line breaks." This instructs the software to break the lines whenever it needs and forces a break only where you have entered one.
3. Use a text editor, such as Notepad, to open your new resume. This is what your recipient will see when you email your resume. The text editor will show you any characters that are not ASCII characters, such as bullets or bold. Replace all unsupported characters with an ASCII equivalent. (You can use any character that you can find on a standard keyboard as a replacement.) For example, bullets appear as a question mark when opened in Notepad. They can be replaced with asterisks or hyphens since they are easier to understand than a question mark.
4. Now you can copy and paste this ASCII plain text resume into the body of an email message. Use the same technique to create a short cover letter and paste it into the email message above the resume text.

We suggest that before you send it to the agency or employer, you send it to yourself or a friend to check that it displays properly.

Key Word Summary Resumes

Effective key words are the key to getting noticed!

The resumes that get listed first as the result of a search are the ones that have matched the most key words. So, when developing an electronic resume, you need to think like a Human Resources manager and include as many key words as possible.

A key word is usually a noun, not an action verb. This is a change from how we recommend you write paper resumes, using strong action verbs like *managing*, *implementing*, *installing*. The Human Resources manager will search for words that describe the qualities or skills needed for a particular position, words like *account manager*, *CAD skills*, *member IEEE*. The search often includes other company names, particular tools or technologies, schools, degrees, universities, years experience, and responsibilities.

The key words *Computer Specialist*, *three years experience*, *webpages*, *website design*, and *manager* were used to look for someone to fill a computer services manager position. And the search found Susan's resume. You can see her key word summary in the resume shown in Figure 10-5.

Scanned Resumes

Sometimes an agency or employer will scan a paper resume and convert it to an electronic format. It may then be posted to a database or entered into a resume tracking system. With this in mind, it is imperative that you include key words as described in the previous section. If you know your resume will be scanned by such a service, follow these steps to ensure the scanned result will show up correctly:

- Always send an original resume printed by a laser jet printer (ink jet printers can smear the text). Similarly, photocopied and faxed copies do not scan well.
- Use light-coloured 8½ × 11 inch paper and print on only one side.
- Avoid complex formatting like graphs, shading, italics, boldface, brackets, or horizontal or vertical lines.
- Check that there are no folds or staple marks in the original.

Your resume may appear very bland and generic visually, but it will scan better and be more useful to your potential employer.

Web Portfolios or Resumes

The more global and technical our society becomes the more competitive the job market becomes. Many technical professionals are using the internet to advertise their capabilities. You can do this too, by creating your own web portfolio or resume. This is an HTML version of your resume with a URL to point to it.

Susan Jenkins used a basic menu structure with links to additional information. The first page of her web portfolio is shown in Figure 10-6. Unlike ASCII plain text resumes or scanned resumes, using backgrounds, graphics, and special fonts and characters enhances HTML resumes. But

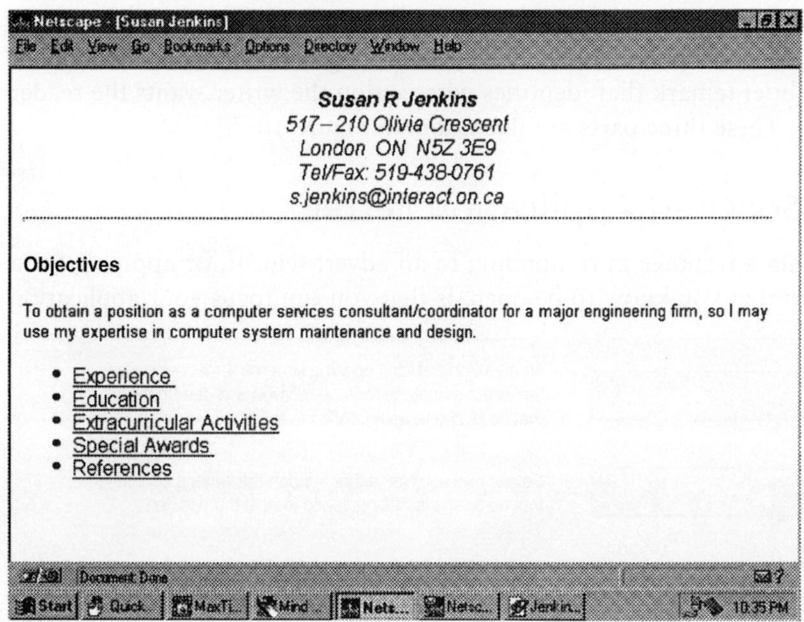

Figure 10-6 An HTML-coded web portfolio.

An employer accessing this homepage clicks on a particular bulleted heading to bring specific details onscreen

be careful: you still want your words to describe you and your capabilities, so don't get carried away designing a complex webpage because the only quality you will demonstrate is your programming skill. Remember, this is still your resume and it needs to sell *you*.

A major difference between electronic resumes posted to a database service and a web portfolio is how people access them. If you create a web portfolio it is your responsibility to attract people to it. When you post your resume to a database, people go there by themselves to search for it.

Most word-processing packages today have tools to help you develop HTML pages. If you need additional help, search the web for a tutorial or find a book on simple HTML coding.

Explore

Writing a Letter of Application

Although some resumes may be delivered personally, the majority are mailed or submitted electronically, both with a covering letter. Because potential employers will probably read the letter first, it must do more than simply introduce the resume. The letter needs to state your purpose for writing (that you are applying for a job) and demonstrate that you have some very useful qualifications that the reader should take the time to consider. It should never simply repeat what your resume says.

Write using a firm yet personable style

An assertive, interesting, and well-planned application letter can encourage employers to place your letter and resume in the pile to interview. Conversely, a dull, unemphatic letter may cause the same employers to drop your application on a pile of "not nows," because its approach and style seem to imply you are a dull, unemphatic person.

A letter of application should adopt the pyramid technique: it should open with a brief summary that defines the purpose of the letter, continue with strong, positive details to support the opening statement, and close with a brief remark that identifies what action the writer wants the reader to take. These three parts are illustrated in Figure 10-7.

Explore

The Solicited Application Letter

The main advantage in responding to an advertisement, or applying for a position that you know to be open, is that you can focus your application

Keep your letter to one page and no more than four paragraphs

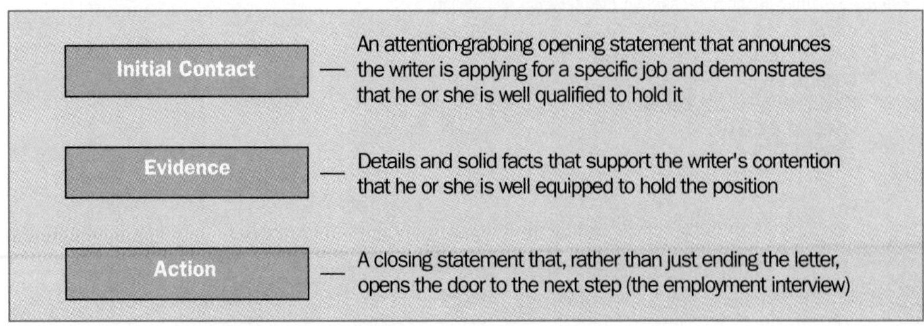

Figure 10-7 Writing plan for a job application letter.

letter on facts that specifically meet the employer's requirements. This has been done by Alison Witney in Figure 10-8 on page 242, which responds to an advertisement in a local newspaper.

The following comments and guidelines relate to the circled numbers beside Alison's letter.

1. Create your own personal letterhead showing your contact information. Include your name, address, telephone number, and email address. Some people have the information all on one line like Reid Qually did with his resume (see Figure 10-4 on page 233) and others centre the information, with each item on a separate line.

2. Whenever possible, personalize an application letter by addressing it by name to the personnel manager or the person named in the advertisement. This gives you an edge over applicants who address theirs impersonally to the "Personnel Manager" or "Chief Engineer." If the job advertisement does not give the person's name, invest in a telephone call to the advertiser and ask the receptionist for the person's name and complete title. (You may have to decide whether to send your letter and resume to someone in the personnel department or to a technical manager who is more likely to be aware of the quality of your qualifications and how you could fit into the organization.)

Never write "Dear Sir or Madam" or "To Whom It May Concern"

3. This is the **Initial Contact**, in which Alison summarizes key points about herself that she believes will most interest her reader and states that she is applying for the advertised position. She creates a purposeful image by stating confidently "I am applying...." This is much better than writing "I wish to apply...," "I would like to apply...," or "I am interested in applying...," all of which create weak, wishy-washy images because they imply she is only interested in rather than purposefully applying for the job. An equally confident opening is, "Please accept my application for...."

4. The **Evidence** section starts here. It should offer facts drawn from the resume and expand on the statements made in the first paragraph. Avoid broad generalizations such as, "I have 13 years of experience in a metrology laboratory," replacing them with shorter descriptions that describe your exact role and responsibilities, and stress the supervisory aspects of each position. The name of a person for whom you worked on a particular project can be usefully inserted here because it adds credibility to the role and responsibilities you are describing.

Draw on key information in your resume to support your opening statement

Alison V Witney 1
1670 Fulham Boulevard
Truro NS B2N 6C4
Tel: (902) 474-6318
email: avwitney@nsonline.net

March 23, 2010

Dr Eugene Cartwright 2
Animal Science Experimental Institute
Mount Ashburn University
Three Hills NB E4K 1A7

Dear Dr Cartwright

I am applying for the position of Research Technician (Animal Sciences) 3
advertised in the March 18, 2010, issue of the *Amiento County Herald*. I have been involved with animals and their care and treatment for many years, and shortly will receive my Diploma in Biological Science.

My interest in animals dates back 12 years, to when I first learned to care
for, groom, and ride horses. I now teach horseback riding in my spare time. 4
For the past three years my employer has been Dr Alex Gavin, veterinary surgeon at the Amiento County Animal Treatment Centre, where I assist in the medical treatment of small animals. It was my interest in horses, plus Dr Gavin's influence, that led to my enrolment in the two-year Biological Sciences course at Amiento Technical College, from which I will graduate
in early June. The attached biographical details provide further information 5
on my education, employment background, and work experience.

I will be visiting your research station from April 21 to 23, as part of my college term research project. May I call on you then, while I am at Three Hills? 6

Regards

7

Alison Witney

Alison V Witney
enc

Figure 10-8 A solicited letter of application prepared by an undergraduate.

5 The **Evidence** section covers the key points an employer is likely to be interested in and draws the reader's attention to the attached resume. If the paragraph grows too long, divide it into two shorter paragraphs (as Colin Farrow has done in Figure 10-9 on page 244).

Explore

6 This paragraph is Alison Witney's **Action Statement**, in which she effectively opens the door to an interview by drawing attention to her upcoming visit to the advertiser's premises. She avoids using dull, routine remarks such as, "I look forward to hearing from you at your earliest convenience" or "I would appreciate an interview in the near future," both of which tend to close rather than open the door to the next step.

7 Contemporary business letters end with a single-word closing such as "Regards" or "Sincerely," rather than the less meaningful "Yours truly."

Practise

The Unsolicited Application Letter

Explore

An unsolicited application letter (see Figure 10-9) has the same three main parts as a solicited letter and looks much the same to the reader. To the writer, however, there is a subtle but important difference: it cannot be focused to fit the requirements of an advertised position. This means you have to make your letter sound both positive and well directed.

Here are some guidelines:

- Make a particular point of addressing your letter to the person, by name and title, who will most likely be interested in you. This may mean selecting a particular department or project head who will immediately recognize your qualifications and how you would fit into the organization, rather than applying to someone in the Human Resources department. Never address an unsolicited letter to a general title such as "General Manager" or "Employment Manager," because if the company does not use such a title and you have not used a personal name, it will likely be the mail clerk who decides who should receive your letter.
- Find out enough information about a firm so you can visualize the type of work it does and how you and your qualifications will fit the company's needs. A Google search can help you here. This will enable you to focus your letter on factors likely to be of most interest to the employer.

Start your research with the company's website

- Try to make your initial contact positive and interesting even though you are not applying for a particular position, as Colin Farrow has done in his unsolicited letter in Figure 10-9.

Explore

The letter's appearance and sans-serif type create a crisp, professional impression

Colin R Farrow, P.Eng
408 Medwin Street
Brandon MB R7C 0B3
Tel: (204) 548-1612
email: c.farrow@mbonline.com

December 15, 2010

Vern A Rogers, P.Eng
Branch Manager
H L Winman and Associates
574 Reston Avenue
Winnipeg MB R3C 4G2

Dear Mr Rogers

As a structural engineer who has specialized in constructing and maintaining transmission line towers and associated buildings for 10 years, and who has particular experience working in permafrost, I am applying for a position with H L Winman and Associates.

My experience evolves from three periods of employment. For four years I installed and maintained communications systems with the Canadian Forces. Subsequently I became a crew chief and installation coordinator with the Northwestern Steel Construction Company, where for four years I was responsible for erecting and testing high-voltage transmission line towers between Flin Flon, Manitoba, and the Northwest Territories. For the past two years I have been a project engineer supervising the construction and installation of microwave towers on MTS Allstream's Brandon–The Pas extension.

The enclosed resume describes my responsibilities in greater detail and my particular involvement in testing structures erected on discontinuous permafrost. I hold a Diploma in Civil Engineering Technology from Red River College in Winnipeg, and a B.Sc in Structural Engineering from the University of Manitoba. I am eager to return to the north and the challenge of building on unstable soil.

I welcome the opportunity to meet you and learn more about your project at Winterton Lake. Because I travel frequently between Brandon and Winnipeg, I will call you when I next expect to be in your city.

Sincerely

Colin R. Farrow

Colin R Farrow
enc

Figure 10-9 An unsolicited letter of application prepared by an experienced engineer.

Completing a Company Application Form

Filling in company application forms (online and on paper) can become a boring and repetitive task, yet any carelessness on an applicant's part can draw a negative reaction from readers. Each company or organization uses its own form which, although it asks for generally the same information, may vary in detail. Consequently the suggestions below apply primarily to the *approach* you should take rather than suggest what you should write:

Jobfind.ca
www.jobfind.ca
Jobfind.ca contains links to more than a thousand Canadian employment-related sites, including job and resume banks, employer sites, and related internet sites.

- Carry your personal data record with you so you can readily search for details (such as dates, telephone numbers, and names of supervisors) when calling on a prospective employer.
- Treat every application form as though it is the *first* one you are completing—write carefully, neatly, and legibly. Never let an untidy application form subconsciously prepare an employer to meet an untidy worker.
- Complete *every* space on the form, entering N/A (not applicable), Not Known, or a short horizontal line in spaces that do not apply to you or for which you genuinely do not have information. This will prevent an employer from thinking that you carelessly (or, worse, intentionally) omitted answering the question.

Take care: every word you write conveys an image of how you approach a task

- Take care that your familiarity with your city and street names does not cause you to abbreviate or omit them. If you write "Wpg" for Winnipeg or omit the "St," "Ave," or "Crescent" from your street name (because you *know* it is a street, avenue, or crescent), you may create the impression that your approach to work is to take short cuts whenever possible.
- Use words that describe the responsibility and supervisory aspects of each job you have held (as you would for a resume) rather than list only the duties you performed.
- Particularly describe extracurricular activities that show your involvement in the community, or activities in which you held a teaching or coaching role.
- Pay particular attention if there is a section on the form that asks you to comment on how your education and past experience have prepared you for the position. Think this through very carefully before you write so that what you say shows a natural progression from past experience to the job you are applying for. If you can, and if they fit naturally, add a few words to demonstrate how the position fits your overall career plan. We agree: this can be a particularly difficult section to write.

The most difficult part to write! You should prepare in advance for such a question

Watch

Attending an Interview

This is the third step in the job application process and might be the first time you meet a prospective employer (or, more often, the employer's representative) face to face.

Prepare for the Interview

Attending an interview can create as much anxiety as speaking before an audience

The key to a good interview is thorough preparation. As soon as you are invited to attend an interview—or, better still, before you are called—start researching facts about the company (or organization, if it is a government establishment). Try to find out background details, such as the number of people the company employs, specific fields in which it is involved, work for which it is particularly well known, its major products and services, locations of branch offices (if any), and the company's involvement in community activities. Such knowledge can be extremely useful during the interview, because it permits you to ask intelligent questions at appropriate places—questions that indicate to the interviewer that you have done your homework.

You also need to prepare for difficult questions an interviewer may ask, like these:

- *Why do you want to join our organization?*
- *How do you think you can contribute to our company?*
- *Why do you want to leave your present employer?*
- *Why did you leave such-and-such company on such-and such date?*
- *What do you expect to be doing in five years? Ten years?*
- *What salary do you expect?*

Lack of preparation will show up in your body language and how you answer questions

If you have not prepared for such questions, and hesitate before answering, an interviewer may interpret your hesitation to mean there are factors you would rather conceal.

An interviewer who asks what salary you expect is partly testing your preparation for the interview and partly assessing how accurately you value yourself. For an undergraduate at a university or college, the question is largely academic: undergraduates compare notes and quickly learn what starting salaries are being offered. Plus the campus career centre can provide guidance. But for a person who recently has been or is currently employed, the question is more difficult.

Decide what salary you think the position can command and also what you feel your experience is worth. Websites that offer career counselling will help you determine a figure. Avoid quoting a salary range, such as "between 42 and 44 thousand dollars," because it indicates unsureness. Quote a definite figure, such as $43 000. If you fear that the salary you are asking is too high, you can add something like "...depending, of course, on the opportunities for advancement and the fringe benefits your company offers."

Be prepared to ask questions during the interview. The interviewer wants to acquire information about you, but you should also learn about the company and the opportunities it can offer. Consider what questions you would like answered, jot them onto a small card, and store the card in a pocket or purse. Then when the interviewer asks, "Now, do you have any questions?" you can pull out the card.

An interview is like a two-way street: traffic should flow in both directions

The quality of your questions will demonstrate how carefully you have thought about the interview.

Create a Good Initial Impression

Remember that you are being evaluated from the moment you step into the interview room. Consequently,

- walk in briskly and cheerfully,
- shake hands firmly (because a limp handshake creates an image of a limp, indefinite applicant),
- repeat the person's name as you are introduced and look him or her directly in the eye, and
- sit when invited to do so, pushing yourself well back in the chair, making yourself comfortable, and avoiding folding your arms across your chest (which psychologically suggests you are resisting questions).

Participate Throughout the Interview

An experienced interviewer will try to ease your nervousness

An interview normally falls into three parts. The first is an exchange of general information during which you may be asked questions on topics you can answer easily, such as a major news item or something from the hobbies and interests section in your resume. This part of the interview normally is short.

The middle part of the interview is much longer: the interviewer will want to hear your opinions and have you demonstrate your knowledge. Although the interviewer will want to control the direction the interview takes, you will be expected to develop your answers and to comment on each topic in sufficient depth to establish that you have real knowledge and experience, backed up by well-thought-out opinions.

The closing portion of the interview also is short. The interviewer will ask if you have any questions and will discuss details about employment with the company. By this stage the interviewer should have a good impression of you, and you should know whether you want to be employed by that company.

Be ready to offer information, but don't monopolize the conversation!

An effective interviewer will pose questions from one discussion point to the next and automatically encourage you to provide comprehensive answers. If, however, you face an inexperienced or unprepared interviewer, you may need to develop your answers in greater depth. For example, if the interviewer asks,

"How long did you work in a mobile calibration lab?"

resist the temptation to say simply,

"Five years."

This means the interviewer has to hurriedly find and ask another question. Instead, inject some detail into your answer:

"For five years. The first three and a half years I was one of four technicians on the North Bay to Sioux Lookout circuit. And then for the next year and a half I was the lab supervisor on the Dana, Saskatchewan, to Prince George, British Columbia, route."

An answer developed in this depth often provides the link for the interviewer to formulate the next question.

Sometimes you will face a single interviewer, while at other times you may face an interview board of several people. In a multiple-interviewer situation,

- direct most of your questions, and your responses to general questions, to the chair (but if an answer is long, occasionally look briefly at and talk momentarily to other board members);
- if a particular board member asks you a specific question, address your response to that person; and
- if a board member has been identified as a specialist in a particular discipline, direct your questions to that board member if they apply to that field.

Be prepared for questions that challenge your thinking or your ethics

In certain interviews—often when applicants are being interviewed for a high-stress position—you may be presented with a stress question. A stress question is designed to place you in a predicament to which there may be two or even more answers or courses of action that could be taken. You are expected to think *briefly* about the situation presented to you and then to select what you believe is the best answer or course of action. Often you will be challenged and expected to defend the position you have taken.

The secret is not to let yourself be rattled and to defend your answer rationally and reasonably even though the questioner's challenging may seem harsh or unreasonable. Remember that the interviewer is probably more interested in seeing how you cope in the stress situation than in hearing you identify the correct answer.

Here are seven additional factors to consider:

- Use your voice to show confidence; make sure everyone can hear you, think out your answers before speaking and, where appropriate, let your enthusiasm *show*.
- Be ready to ask questions, but have a clear idea of what you want to ask before you pose them. The interviewer will recognize a good question and the clarity of thought behind it.

- If you do not know the answer to a question, say you don't know rather than trying to bluff your way through it.
- If you do not understand the question, again don't bluff. Either say you do not understand or, if you think you know what the interviewer is driving at, rephrase the question and ask if you have interpreted it correctly. (Never imply that the interviewer posed the question poorly.)
- Use humour with great care. What to you may seem humorous may not match the interviewer's sense of humour.

Above all, present an image of "the real you"

Finally, try to be yourself. Remember that interviewers want to see the kind of person you really are. If you relax and answer questions comfortably and purposefully, they will gain a good impression of you. If you try too hard to be the kind of person you think the interviewers want you to be, or to give the kind of answers you think they want rather than the answers you really believe in, they may detect it and judge you accordingly.

Accepting a Job Offer

✓ Practise

The telephone rings and the personnel representative you met during your interview tells you that the company is offering you employment at a salary of xxx xxx. You accept the offer! She then says she will confirm the offer in writing. She also may ask you to write a letter confirming your acceptance of the position.

The two letters become, in effect, a contractual agreement: the employer offers you work under certain conditions, which you agree to. The letters can also prevent any misunderstandings from developing, which can occur if arrangements are made only by telephone. Consequently your acceptance letter should

Accept a job offer *in writing*, like sealing a contract

- announce that you are accepting the offer of employment,
- repeat any important details, such as the agreed salary and starting date, and
- thank the employer for selecting you.

The following acceptance letter conforms to this pattern:

Dear Ms Tataryn

I am confirming my telephone acceptance of your May 19 offer of employment as an engineering technologist in the controls department. I understand that I am to join the company on June 15 and that my salary will be $38 000 annually.

Thank you for selecting me for this position. I very much look forward to working for Magnum Electronics.

Sincerely

Also decline a job offer in writing, with a smile

Sometimes an applicant may receive two offers of employment at the same time and have to decline one. The letter declining employment should follow roughly the same pattern:

- decline the offer,
- briefly explain why, and
- thank the employer.

Here is an example:

Dear Mr Genser

I regret that I will be unable to accept your offer of employment. Since my interview with you I have been offered employment elsewhere and have a commitment to the other company. Thank you for considering me for this position.

Regards

Declining a job offer pleasantly and formally in a carefully worded letter like this is insurance for the future: one day you may want to work for that employer!

ASSIGNMENTS

Project 10.1: Preparing a Resume

You are to prepare a resume describing your background, education, work experience, extracurricular activities, and other interests. Do it in three parts.

Part 1
If you do not already have one, prepare a personal data record (PDR).

Part 2
Write down the following information:

- The name of a real employer for whom you would like to work at the end of your course.
- The type of position you would be qualified to hold with that particular employer.
- The type of resume that would be most effective to use.

Part 3
Prepare the resume (assume that you will be graduating from your course in two months). You can decide which format: paper or a particular electronic format.

Create a resume

Project 10.2: Applying for a Locally Advertised Position

From your campus student employment centre or your local newspaper, identify a company currently advertising a position that you could apply for at the end of your course.

Part 1

Write a letter applying for the position (assume that you will be graduating in six weeks). Also assume that you are attaching a resume to your letter. If you are replying to a newspaper advertisement, attach a copy of the advertisement to your letter.

Part 2

Assume that the company you wrote to in Part 1 sends you an application form. Obtain a standard application form from your campus student employment centre and complete it as though it is the advertiser's form. If it is an electronic form, print a copy.

Rehearse applying for a real position

Part 3

Now assume that the company has telephoned and asked you to attend an interview next Tuesday. Prepare five questions you will ask during the interview. After each question explain why the question is important and what answer it might elicit from the interviewer.

Project 10.3: Preparing Different Versions of Your Resume

Assume you have identified a large, multi-location company you want to work for after graduation and have decided to send your information to them even though they are not advertising any open positions. Also assume you have talked to the Human Resources manager who has told you she needs an electronic resume to post in their internal database. She also requested that you send her a paper version.

Part 1

Prepare a paper version of your resume and convert it to a format appropriate for posting to the company's resume database.

Part 2

Besides sending the paper and electronic resumes to the Human Resources manager, you decide also to send the URL of your personal web portfolio. Create a web portfolio that resembles your paper resume but also has professional-looking graphics and additional details about your experience. Remember, this is a reflection of you and it should encourage the visitor to want to hire you.

Project 10.4: Replying to Other Advertisers

This project assumes that you are seeking permanent employment at the end of a technical or engineering-oriented educational program. Reply to any one of the following advertisements, using your present situation and actual background. If it is still early in your studies, assume that it is now two months before your graduation date. In each case enclose a resume and an application letter.

Apply for one of these positions

INTER-MOUNTAIN PAPER COMPANY

We have excellent opportunities for recent graduates or about-to-graduate students to join an expanding manufacturing organization in the pulp and paper industry.

Engineers and Engineering Assistants

Positions are available for mechanical engineers and technologists to assist in the design, installation, and testing of prototype production equipment. Previous experience in a manufacturing plant would be helpful. Innovative ability will be a decided asset.

Electrical Engineering Technologist

This person will assist the Plant Engineer in the maintenance of power distribution systems. Applicants should be graduates of a course in Electrical Instrumentation Technology with good knowledge of automatic controls and machine application. Ability to read blueprints and working drawings is essential.

Electronics Engineer or Technologist

Two positions are open for electronics specialists who will maintain and troubleshoot microprocessor-controlled production equipment.

Computer Specialist

This position will suit either a graduate of a Computer Engineering course or an Electronics Technologist who has specialized in Computer Electronics. Duties will consist of installation, maintenance, and troubleshooting of all computers and networks.

Environment Specialists

Persons selected will test air pollutants and water effluents from our paper mill and production plant, and assess their environmental impact. Applicants should be graduates of a recognized course in the environmental or biological sciences.

Salaries for the above positions will be commensurate with experience and qualifications. Excellent fringe benefit program available. Send application materials to

Manager of Industrial Relations
INTER-MOUNTAIN PAPER COMPANY
Kamloops BC V2D 2R3

(Advertisement in your local newspaper, last week)

H L Winman and Associates
475 Lethbridge Trail
Calgary AB T3M 5G1

Civil Engineers and Technologists

This established firm of consulting engineers needs three Engineers or Technologists to assist in the construction supervision of several grade separation structures to be built over a two-year period. Graduation from a recognized Civil Engineering or Technology course is a prerequisite. Successful applicants will be hired as term employees. Opportunities are excellent for transfer to permanent employment before the project ends.

Apply in writing to

A Rittman, Head
Special Projects Department

(Advertisement on college notice board)

Chapter 11
The Technique of Technical Writing

In this chapter you will learn how, when you write, you can

- set the correct tone,
- establish a comfortable style,
- use language that suits the situation and the reader,
- construct effective paragraphs and sentences,
- choose effective words and use them appropriately,
- abbreviate technical terms correctly,
- use non-gender-specific language, and
- adjust your style and tone to suit non-English-speaking readers.

In this chapter we concentrate on techniques that will help you write quickly and efficiently. We will show you how to create a whole document, structure paragraphs, write individual sentences, use descriptive words, and establish a comfortable writing style. At the end of the chapter you will find several exercises that will test your ability to write well.

We assume you are already proficient in grammar and can recognize and correct basic writing problems. If you need practice, we suggest you refer to a textbook such as *The Brief Penguin Handbook*, second Canadian edition.[1] You can also refer to the Glossary of Technical Usage (in Appendix B, starting on page 309) for information on how to form abbreviations and compound adjectives, spell problem words, and use numerals or spell out numbers in narrative.

The Whole Document

Three factors affect the whole document: the tone you set, the writing style you adopt, and how you arrange the information on the page. Tone is by far the least tangible: a reader is less likely to be aware of the tone you establish than the writing techniques you use and the arrangement of paragraphs and headings.

You need to know your reader if you are to set the right tone

Tone

Whether your writing should be formal or informal depends on the situation and how well you know your reader. Formal reports normally adopt a formal tone, short reports and most business correspondence vary from being moderately formal to semiformal or even informal, while emails generally are very informal.

How tone can vary is evident in the following extracts from three separate documents, all written on the same subject.

1. **Extract from an Email.** John Wood's materials testing laboratory has compression-tested samples of concrete for Karen Woodhouse of the company's civil engineering department. In an email to her, reporting the test results, John writes:

   Informal Tone I have tested the samples of concrete you took from the sixth floor of Tarryton House and none of them meets the 33.25 MPa you specified. The first failed at 28.08 MPa; the second at 26.84 MPa; and the third at 27.95 MPa. Do you want me to send these figures over to the architect, or will you?

2. **Extract from a Letter Report.** Karen conveys this information to the architect in a brief letter report:

   Semiformal Tone Our tests of three samples taken from the sixth floor of Tarryton House show that the concrete at 52 days still was 5.63 MPa below your specification of 33.25 MPa. We doubt whether further curing will increase the strength of this concrete more than another 1.10 MPa. We suggest, however, that you examine the design specifications before embarking on an expensive and time-consuming remedy.

3. **Extract from a Formal Report.** The architect rechecked the design specifications and decided that 28.50 to 29.00 MPa still would not satisfy the design requirements. He then asked Karen to prepare a formal report he could present to the general contractor and the concrete supplier. Karen's report said, in part,

   Formal Tone At the request of the architect we cut three 0.3 x 0.15 metre diameter cores from the sixth floor of Tarryton House 52 days after the floor had been poured. These cores were subjected to a standard compression test with the following results (detailed calculations are attached at Appendix A):

Core No.	*Location*	*Failed at:*
1	0.46 m W of col 18S	28.08 MPa
2	0.84 m N of col 22E	26.84 MPa
3	1.42 m N of col 46E	27.95 Mpa

   The average of 27.62 MPa for the three cores is 5.63 MPa below the design specification of 33.25 MPa. Since further curing will increase the strength of the concrete by no more than 1.10 MPa, we recommend rejecting this concrete pour.

Imagine you are speaking personally to the reader and adjust your tone accordingly

The sequence in which you write longer reports also affects the tone. To set the right tone, try writing *in reverse order*, starting with all the technical details that will appear in the major discussion, and then working forward

Deal with all the details before you start writing

to the brief statements you write in the Summary. The comments on Karen Woodhouse's formal report in Chapter 5 explain how she did this (see pages 107 to 109). They recommend the following writing sequence:

Step 1 Assemble and document all the details and technical data. These will become the appendices to your report.

Step 2 Write the Discussion, or full development. Direct it to the type of technical reader who will use or analyse your report in depth.

Step 3 Write the Introduction, Conclusions, and Recommendations. Keep them brief and direct them to a semitechnical reader or person in a supervisory or management position.

Step 4 Write the Summary. Direct it to a nontechnical reader who has absolutely no knowledge of the project or the contents of your report.

Practise Practise

Style

Style is affected by the complexity of the subject you are describing and the technical level of the reader(s) to whom you are writing. Consequently you need to "tailor" your writing to suit each situation:

Adjust sentence length to suit the subject and the reader's familiarity with it

1. When presenting low-complexity background information, and descriptions of nontechnical or easy-to-understand processes, write in an easygoing style that tells readers they are encountering information that does not require total concentration. Use slightly longer paragraphs and sentences, and insert colourful adjectives and adverbs to enhance the descriptions and make them more interesting.
2. For important or complex data, use short paragraphs and sentences. Present one item of information at a time. Develop it carefully to make sure it will be fully understood before proceeding to the next item. Use simple words. The more punchy style will warn readers that the information demands their full attention.
3. When describing a step-by-step process, start with a narrative-type opening paragraph that introduces the topic and presents any information that the readers should know. Follow it with a series of subparagraphs, each describing a separate step, choosing between two alternative styles:

Style A: Integrated Lead-in Line

Precede subparagraphs with bullets or sequential numbers

In this style the lead-in line becomes part of each subparagraph that follows it, as in this example:

Let each subparagraph

- develop only one item or aspect of the process,
- be short, and
- be parallel in construction (the importance of parallelism is discussed later in this chapter).

Here, the lead-in words (*Let each subparagraph*) do not form a complete sentence and so do not end with a colon. Consequently the bulleted items each start with a lowercase letter and end with a comma (except the last item), because the lead-in words and the bulleted items really make one long, complete sentence.

Style B: Separate Lead-in Line

In this style the lead-in line stands alone, like this:

If you use subparagraphs to present a series of points, follow these guidelines:

1. Indent each subparagraph as a complete unit of information, to show your readers how you are subordinating your ideas.
2. Precede each subparagraph with either a bullet (as in style A) or a sequential number (as in style B).
3. Number the subparagraphs if you want to identify that the information is presented in a prescribed sequence or in decreasing order of importance, or if you want to refer to the subparagraph later in your letter or report. At all other times use bullets.

Here, the lead-in words (*If you use...follow these guidelines:*) create a complete sentence. Consequently the lead-in words end with a colon, and the subparagraphs each start with a capital letter and end with a period. Ideally, leave a 3 pt or 6 pt space between the subparagraphs to make them visually more appealing.

Appearance

If you incorporate *information design* techniques into your writing you can help your readers understand and access information more readily. Information Design can be applied to letters, memos, reports, proposals, instructions, newsletters, and many other documents.

Pick Only One Font

The availability of numerous type styles is not an invitation to mix and match

A font such as Century OldStyle or Helvetica is a set of printing type. Some fonts are called serif (they have a slight finishing stroke—T) and some are called sans serif (they don't have a finishing stroke—**T**). The font you choose will project an image of you, your company, and your document. Statistics show that a serif font such as Times New Roman or Garamond is easier to read because the serifs lead the eye from letter to letter, and so is more suitable for longer documents. This text is printed in a serif type called Sabon; the examples in Figures 11-1 and 11-2 (pages 258 and 260) are in Times New Roman, except for the main heading, which in each case is in Arial.

Although sans-serif fonts like Arial, Helvetica, or **Franklin Gothic** are clean and clear, and portray a neat and modern image, they are not as easy to read. Consequently they are suitable only for short documents and electronic mail.

Main heading (sans-serif)

Guidelines for Integrating Paragraphs and Headings

Set the main centre heading (above) in a larger boldface type than all other headings in the document. You may use a different typeface, such as Arial, for this heading.

Subordinate headings (serif font but also could be sans-serif)

Using Subparagraphs Without Paragraph Numbers

If you use a subsidiary centre heading, as done immediately above, it's acceptable to set it in a sans-serif font (but probably simpler to type if you keep it in the same font as the body text).

Side Headings

For headings, vary font size and use boldface type rather than underlining the words

A side heading introduces a new section of text. Set it, and the paragraphs that follow, flush against the left margin. In technical writing, the first line normally is not indented.

Inserting Subparagraph Headings and Subparagraphs

Indent subparagraph headings, and the paragraphs that follow, about 1 cm from the original left margin. Type each subparagraph as a solid indented block, so your readers can see how you have subordinated your ideas.

Creating Secondary Subparagraphs

If further subparagraphing is necessary, indent each heading and the text that follows it a further 1 cm to the right.

Building a Heading into a Paragraph. If you use a paragraph heading, continue writing the text immediately after the heading. Usually, this type of heading is followed by only one paragraph of text.

Figure 11-1 Guidelines for integrating paragraphs and headings.

Select character size to suit font style and readers' visual acuity

For example, Daniel Thomashewski chose a sans-serif font to type the agenda for the E-Learning Research Committee meeting in Figure 9-4 on page 210. Morley Wozniak, however, used a serif font for his report evaluating proposed landfill sites in Figure 5-5 on pages 88 to 93.

We recommend using 11 pt or 12 pt type for serif fonts, and 10 pt for sans-serif fonts.

Insert Headings as Signposts

In longer documents, you can help your reader by inserting headings. Each heading must be short yet informative, summarizing clearly what is covered in the paragraphs that follow. Here are some guidelines:

Make your headings *contribute* to the overall appearance

- Use upper- and lowercase letters rather than all capital letters.
- Use boldface type rather than underlining the headings.
- Keep headings in the same font as the main text.
- Use larger point sizes for the principal headings, and progressively smaller point size for each level of subsidiary heading.

Figure 11-1 illustrates how this can be done.

Insert Paragraph Numbers

In some documents—particularly specifications, technical instructions, and military reports—the paragraphs and subparagraphs are numbered. A simple paragraph numbering system starts at 1 and continues consecutively to the end of the document. More complex systems combine numbers, decimals, and letters to allow for subparagraphing, as shown in Figure 11-2. (Note that Roman numerals are *not* used.)

Justify Only on the Left

Word processors make it easy to justify both the left and right margins, which permits you to create lines of exactly the same length, as in this paragraph. Yet research has shown that it is better to justify only the left margin and leave the right margin "ragged" for business reports (as has been done in Figures 11-1 and 11-2). Otherwise, your computer will generate spaces between words and characters to force the right margin to be straight, which can create uneven spacing between words from line to line.

Sometimes a writer may use a justified right margin to create a particular impression for a report, as Karen Woodhouse has done in her formal report on radiant heating in Figure 5-9 (see pages 112 to 125).

Use Two Columns

Many people hesitate to change the standard settings that come with word-processing programs, which normally provide a single 155 mm (6 in.) typing line, yet sometimes it can be advantageous to create two columns, one for headings and one for the text. Figure 11-3 on page 261 compares (a) normal headings and paragraphs with (b) two columns containing the headings on the left and the text on the right. The latter takes more space, but it makes its information much more accessible. We suggest a 45 mm (1.75 in.) column for the headings and a 110 mm (4.25 in.) column for the text.

Let careful use of white space focus readers' attention

Guidelines for Combining Headings and Paragraph Numbers

If your main centre heading runs into two lines, always ensure the second line is shorter than the first (it's visually more appealing).

1. Side Headings

You may use one brief unnumbered paragraph immediately following a side heading, without giving it a number.

1.1 You can also use the brief introductory paragraph (above) to introduce a series of points, each in a numbered paragraph.

1.2 When there is more than one paragraph, assign each a consecutive number (1.1, 1.2, etc), as has been done here. Indent the paragraph number so that it is flush with the start of the heading above it.

1.3 **Subparagraph Headings and Subparagraphing**

Limit the use of paragraph numbers to only one decimal point (as shown above). If you have subparagraphs, assign each a lowercase letter:

a. This will be the first subparagraph.

b. This will be the second subparagraph.

c. You can also subdivide a subparagraph into a series of very short points, using a number enclosed within brackets before each:

(1) Here is a secondary subparagraph.

(2) Limit each secondary subparagraph to only one sentence.

Figure 11-2 Guidelines for integrating a paragraph-numbering system.

Use Subparagraphs to Present Ideas

We recommend using bulleted lists to break up text and make it visually more appealing. Morley Wozniak's use of white space in his report evaluating proposed landfill sites (see Figure 5-5 on pages 88 to 93), and particularly the "chunks" of information on its fourth page, provide an effective example. Here is an excerpt from another report that is not effective:

> I have analysed our present capabilities and estimate that we can increase our commercial business from $20 000 to $30 000 per month. But to meet this objective we will have to shift the emphasis from purely local customers to clients in major

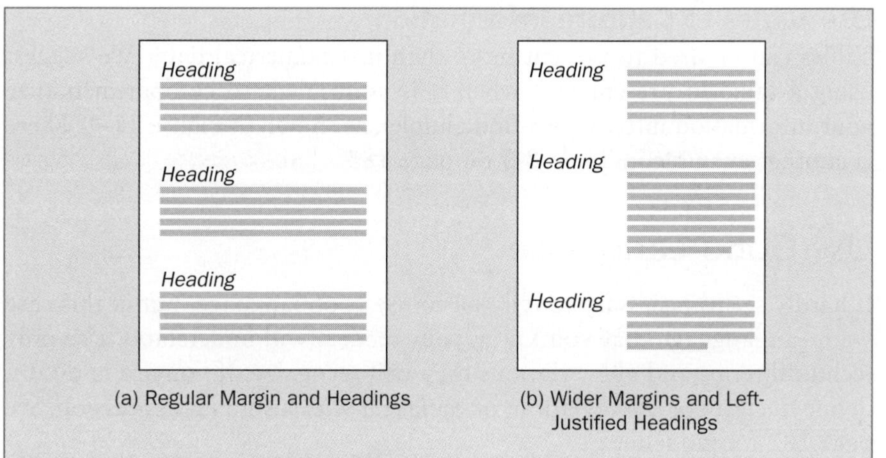

Figure 11-3 Using (a) standard margins and (b) columns to provide a wide left margin for inserting headings.

Shaping your information can encourage readers to keep reading

L-O-N-G paragraphs build reader resistance

> centres. To increase business from local customers alone will require extensive sales effort for only a small increase in revenue, whereas a similar sales effort in a major centre will attract a 30% to 40% increase in revenue. We will also have to increase our staff and manufacturing facilities. The cost of additional personnel and new equipment will in turn have to be offset by an even larger increase in business. Properly administered, such a program should result in an ever-increasing workload. And, third, we will have to create a separate department for handling commercial business. If we remove the department from the existing production organization it will carry a lower overhead, which will result in products that are more competitively priced.

If this writer had broken up the second long sentence by inserting *take three steps* and a colon after *steps*, and then made a numbered list of the actions to be taken, the information would have been much easier to read and understand.

Short paragraphs build reader acceptance

> I have analysed our present capabilities and estimate that we can increase our commercial business from $20 000 to $30 000 per month. But to meet this objective we will have to take three steps:
>
> 1. Shift the emphasis from purely local customers to clients in major centres. To increase business from local customers alone will require extensive sales effort for only a small increase in revenue, whereas a similar sales effort in a major centre will attract a 30% to 40% increase in revenue.
> 2. Increase our staff and manufacturing facilities. The cost of additional personnel and new equipment will in turn have to be offset by an even larger increase in business. Properly administered, such a program should result in an ever-increasing workload.
> 3. Create a separate department for handling commercial business. If we remove the department from the existing production organization it will carry a lower overhead, which will result in products that are more competitively priced.

Use Tables to Capture Information

Tables can be used to present more than just numerical data. We suggest using a table to present text when it is convenient to compartmentalize your information into easy-to-find chunks, as shown in Figure 11-4. There is another example in Table 8-3 on page 183.

Use Good Language

It hardly seems necessary to tell you to use good language, but in this case we mean language that you know your readers will understand. Use only technical terms and abbreviations they will recognize. If you are in doubt, define the term or abbreviation, or replace it with a simpler expression. See page 282 for guidelines.

Paragraphs

The role of the paragraph is complex. It has to stand alone but normally is not expected to. It has to contribute to the whole document, yet it must not be obtrusive (except when called on to emphasize a specific point). And it has to convey only one idea, although made up of several sentences each containing a separate thought.

Good paragraph writing depends on three elements:

Unity
Coherence
Development

A table can create distinct compartments of information

Instructions for Completing Travel Expense Forms

Expense	*Guidelines*	*Receipts Required*
Air Travel	• Book with Haynes Travel Services • Charge to Account A78641	• Haynes's invoice • Ticket stub
Accommodation	• Request corporate rate (quote file 2120) • Pay with company VISA card	• Hotel/motel receipt
Meals	• Per diem rate is $35	• Receipt not required unless meal cost is over $25 (excluding tip)

Figure 11-4 Using a table to present written information.

These elements cannot stand alone. All three must be present if a paragraph is to be useful to its reader.

Unity Within the Paragraph

To have unity, each paragraph must be built around a central idea. This idea is expressed in a topic sentence—often the first sentence—and developed in supporting sentences. This is like the pyramid technique, with the topic sentence taking the place of the summary and the supporting sentences representing the full development (see Figure 11-5).

Although the topic sentence does not always have to be the first sentence in a paragraph, for technical writing we recommend you place it there.

The following paragraph has the topic sentence right up front. It has strong unity because its topic is clearly expressed and the supporting sentences develop it fully.

> Content reuse means writing content once and reusing it many times. Traditional documents are written in files that consist of sections. Reusable content is written as objects or elements, not documents. Documents are therefore made up of content objects that can be mixed and matched to meet specific information needs. For example, a product description (paragraph) could be used in a brochure, on the web, in a parts catalogue, in product support documentation, or even on the product.

Coherence in the Paragraph

To be coherent, a paragraph must be assembled into a solid, logical, well-organized block of information. A coherent paragraph is abundantly clear: its readers can easily follow the line of reasoning and have no problem progressing from one thought to the next. However, simply summarizing a paragraph in the topic sentence, and then following it with a series of supporting sentences, does not necessarily make a coherent paragraph. The sentences

Good sequencing and effective transitions help create coherent paragraphs

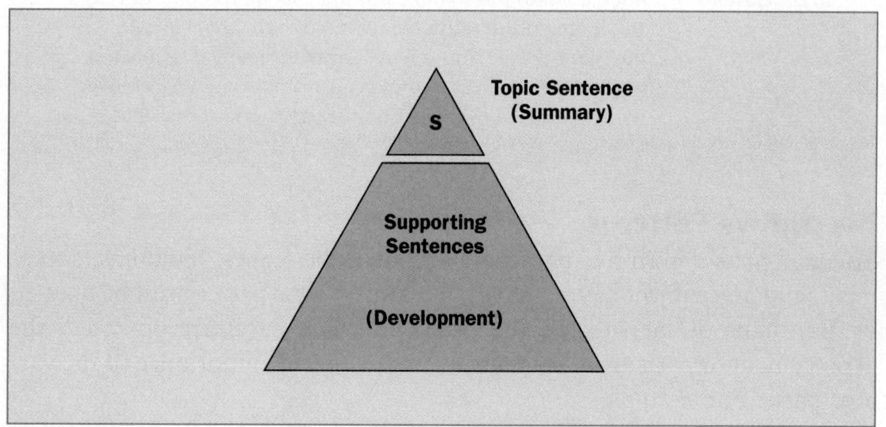

Figure 11-5 Pyramid technique applied to the paragraph.

Every supporting sentence must amplify or evolve from the topic sentence

must be arranged in an identifiable order, following a pattern that helps the reader to understand what is being said.

Sequential Patterns

You can write narrative-type paragraphs to describe a sequence of steps or events. The past–present–future pattern of a progress report or occurrence report, such as Bob Walton's incident report in Figure 4-3 (see page 54), is a typical example. The pattern should be clearly evident, as in two of the following three paragraphs:

A coherent paragraph (in chronological order)

The accident occurred when Dennis Friesen was checking in at the Remick Airlines counter. He placed the company's Nabuchi 300 digital camera on the counter while he completed flight boarding procedure. When the passenger ahead of him lifted a carry-on bag from the counter, its shoulder strap tangled with the camera's carrying strap and pulled the camera to the floor. Dennis examined the camera and discovered a 40 mm crack across its back. Remick Airlines' representative Kathy Trane took details of the incident and will be calling you to discuss compensation.

Two treatments of the same information

A much less coherent paragraph (containing the same information but not presented in an identifiable pattern)

The accident occurred when Dennis Friesen was checking in at the Remick Airlines counter. Kathy Trane, a Remick Airlines representative, took details of the incident and will be calling you to discuss compensation. The damaged camera received a 40 mm crack across the back. When the passenger ahead of Dennis removed a carry-on bag from the counter, its shoulder strap tangled with the carrying strap of the company's Nabuchi 300 digital camera and pulled it to the floor. Dennis had placed the camera on the counter while he completed flight boarding procedure.

A coherent paragraph (tracing events from evidence to conclusion)

We noticed a mild shimmy at speeds above 80 km/h about 10 days after the new tires had been installed. A visual check of all four wheels revealed no obvious defects, so we rotated the four wheels to different positions on the vehicle. This did not eliminate the shimmy but did change its point of origin. To pin down the cause we replaced each wheel in turn with the spare wheel, and found that the shimmy disappeared when the spare was in the left front position. We removed the wheel from that position, tested it, and found that it had been incorrectly balanced.

Descriptive Patterns

You can write descriptive paragraphs to describe scenes, buildings, equipment, and any subject having physical features. This pattern can be defined by the shape of the subject, the order in which parts are operated, the arrangement of parts from smallest to largest, or the importance of the various parts. For example,

Excerpt from paragraph (features in order of importance)	The most important control on the bomb aimer's panel is the firing button, which when not in use is held in the black retaining clip at the bottom left-hand corner. Next in importance is the fusing switch at the top right of the panel; when in the "OFF" position it prevents the bombs from being dropped live. Two safety switches, one immediately above the firing button retaining clip and the other to the right of the bank of selector switches, prevent the firing button from being withdrawn from its clip unless both are in the "LIVE" (up) position.	**The topic sentence sets the scene**

Continuity

A fully coherent paragraph must also have smooth transitions between its sentences. Smooth transitions make your readers feel comfortable, because there is a logical flow from one sentence to the next. You can achieve this by using linking words and by referring back to what has already been said. In the example just quoted, there is a natural flow from "The most important..." in the first sentence to "Next in importance..." in the second. The third sentence then refers back to the firing button and so relates the newly introduced safety switches to the previous information.

The transitions are equally good in the first paragraph describing damage to a digital camera: each sentence develops a point from one of the previous sentences. This is not true of the second camera-damage paragraph, in which each new sentence introduces a new subject with hardly any reference to what has already been said.

Paragraph Development

You want to say enough, but not ramble on, and on, and on...

To achieve good paragraph development, you need to identify your reader clearly before you write. Only then can you look at each paragraph from the reader's point of view, and so see whether your supporting sentences adequately evolve from and amplify the topic.

The supporting sentences must contain the right amount of information, never too little or too much. Too little results in fragmented paragraphs that offer snippets of information that arouse readers' interest but do not satisfy their curiosity. Too much information can lead to long, repetitious paragraphs that annoy readers. Compare the following paragraphs, all describing the result of exploration crews' first venture with machinery across the Peel Plateau in the Yukon, intended for a reader who is interested in the problems of working in northern Canada, but who has never seen what the terrain is like.

Inadequate development	Trails left by tractors look like long narrow scars cut in the plateau. Many of them have been there for years. All have been caused by permafrost melting. They will stay like this until the vegetation grows in again.	**Each paragraph has a good topic sentence...**
Adequate development	To the visitor viewing this far northern terrain from the air, the trails left by tractors clearing undergrowth for roads	

across the plateau look like long, narrow scars. Even those that have been there for as long as 28 years are still clearly defined. All have been caused by melting of the permafrost, which started when the surface moss and vegetation were removed and will continue until the vegetation grows in again—perhaps in another 30 years.

...but the development is erratic

Over-development

To conservationists, whose main interest is the protection of the environment, viewing this far northern terrain from the air is a heartrending sight. To them, the trails left by tractors clearing undergrowth for roads across the plateau look like long, narrow scars. The tractors were making way for the first roads to be built by man over an area that until now had been trodden only by Inuit indigenous to the area, and the occasional trapper. Some of these trappers had journeyed from Quebec to seek new sources of revenue for their trade. But now, in the very short time span of 28 years, man has defiled the terrain. With his machines he has cut and gouged his way, thoughtlessly creating havoc that will be visible to those that follow for many decades. The indigenous people who preceded him for centuries had trodden carefully on the permafrost, leaving no trace of their presence. The new trails, even those that have been there for 28 years, are visible almost as though they had been cut yesterday. And all were caused by melting of the permafrost...

The above paragraphs shift from one extreme to the other:

- The first paragraph leaves the reader with questions: What were the tractors doing? For how many years? How soon will the vegetation grow in again?
- The second paragraph develops the topic sentence in just enough detail; it explains why the tractors left semipermanent scars and predicts how long they will remain.
- The third paragraph, although interesting, is filled with irrelevant information (e.g. where the trappers came from) and repetitive statements that detract from the main theme. It might be suitable for a novel but not for a technical report.

Correct Length

We recommend that, for a 6 in. (152 mm) typing line, you try to limit paragraph length to no more than 8 printed lines. But also keep these points in mind:

If your work will be printed in narrow, newspaper-like columns, write shorter paragraphs

- You can adjust paragraph length to suit the complexity of the topic and the technical level of the reader. Generally, complex topics demand short paragraphs containing small portions of information, while general topics can be covered in longer paragraphs.

- Variety in paragraph length has a lively visual effect. Conversely, if you write a series of equal-length paragraphs you may create an impression of dullness.
- If you write too many short paragraphs close together, your readers may feel you are providing them with incomplete snippets of information. Conversely, if you write a succession of very long paragraphs, your readers may feel they are facing "heavy going."
- Readers attach importance to a paragraph that is clearly longer or shorter than those surrounding it.

Sentences

Although sentences normally form an integral part of a larger unit—the paragraph—they still must be able to stand alone. Three elements apply to their construction:

Unity
Coherence
Emphasis

Unity and coherence perform a function in the sentence similar to their role in a well-written paragraph.

Unity Within the Sentence

A unified sentence presents and develops a single thought. It can be a simple statement:

> We completed the installation on May 28.

Or it can be more complex, containing a primary clause plus one or more subsidiary clauses that enlarge on the primary clause:

> We completed the installation on May 28, which comprised assembling a template for each unit and then bolting down and aligning the components.

Compare these two sentences:

A unified sentence that expresses one main thought	The Amron Building will make an ideal manufacturing plant because of its convenient location, single-level floor, good access roads, and low rent.
A complicated sentence that tries to express two thoughts	The copier should never have been placed in the general office, where those using it interrupt the work being done by the administrative staff, who have been consistently over-worked since the beginning of the year.

Every subordinate clause must either develop or actively support what has been said in the primary clause.

The first sentence has unity because everything it says relates to only one topic: that the Amron Building will make a good manufacturing plant. The second sentence does not have unity because readers cannot tell whether they are supposed to be agreeing that the copier should have been placed elsewhere, or sympathizing that the administrative staff have been overworked.

Coherence Within the Sentence

Coherent sentences are continuously clear, even though they may have numerous subordinate clauses. This requires arranging the clauses in logical sequence, linking them through direct or indirect reference to the primary clause, and writing them in the same grammatical form. Parallelism, discussed at the end of this chapter, plays an important role here.

The unified sentence describing the Amron Building (on the previous page, 267) has good coherence because its purpose is continuously clear and each of its subordinate clauses links comfortably back to the lead-in statement (through the phrase, "because of its…"). The clauses are written in parallel form (i.e. they have the same grammatical pattern), which is the best way to carry the reader smoothly from point to point.

Read examples of good writing in technical journals and magazines (e.g. *Scientific American*; *IEEE Spectrum*)

The first sentence below lacks coherence because there is no logic to the arrangement or form of the subordinate clauses. Compare it with the second sentence, which despite its greater length is still coherent because it continuously develops the thought of "late" and "damaged" expressed in the primary clause.

An incoherent sentence	The Amron Building will make an ideal manufacturing plant because of its convenient location, which also should have good access roads, the advantage of its one-level floor, and it commands a low rent. **(34 incoherent words)**
A coherent sentence	Many of the 61 samples shipped in December either arrived late or were damaged in transit, even though they were shipped one week earlier than usual to avoid the holiday mail tie-up, and were packed in polyurethane as an extra precaution against rough handling. **(45 coherent words)**

Emphasis Within the Sentence

Properly placed emphasis helps readers identify a sentence's important parts. You can attach importance to the whole sentence, to a clause or phrase, or even to a single word.

Emphasis on the Whole Sentence

Too many sentences all the same length imply the information is dull!

You should aim for variety in sentence length, although there may be times when you will need to adjust the length of a particular sentence to give it greater emphasis. Readers will attach importance to a short sentence placed among several longer sentences, or to a long sentence among predominantly short ones. They will also detect a sense of urgency in a series of short sentences that carry them quickly from point to point. This technique is used effectively by storytellers:

The prisoner huddled against the wall, alone in the dark. He listed intently. He could hear the guards, stomping and muttering. Cursing the cold, probably.

In technical writing you will have little occasion to write sentences like these, except perhaps to impart urgency to a warning of a potentially dangerous situation:

Dangerously high voltages are present on exposed terminals. Before opening the doors,

1. set the master control switch to "OFF," and
2. hang the red "NO" flag on the operator's panel.

Never cheat the interlocks.

Neither should you err in the opposite direction and write overly long sentences that are confusing. Adjust sentence length to suit the complexity of the topic and the technical level of the reader. If your sentences tend to exceed 22 words, they are probably too long.

Similarity of shape can signify that all parts of a sentence are of equal importance. Clauses separated by a coordinate conjunction (mainly *and*, *or*, *but*, and sometimes a comma) tell a reader that they have equal emphasis. The following sentences are "balanced" in this way:

Keep sentence parts parallel, particularly the verbs

Eight test instruments were used for the rehabilitation project *and* were supplied free of charge by the Dere Instrument Company.

The gas pipeline will be 420 km shorter than the oil pipeline *but* will have to cross much more difficult terrain.

The upper knob adjusts the instrument in the vertical plane, *and* the lower knob adjusts it in the horizontal plane.

Emphasis on Part of a Sentence

Coordination means giving equal weight to all parts of a sentence; subordination means emphasizing a specific part and deemphasizing all other parts. It is effected by placing the most important information in the primary clause and placing less important information in subordinate clauses. In each of the following sentences, the main thought is italicized to identify the primary clause:

When the technician momentarily released his grip, *the control slipped out of reach.*

The bridge over the underpass was built on a compacted gravel base, partly to save time, partly to save money, and partly because materials were available on-site.

He lost control of the vehicle when the wasp stung him.

When the wasp stung him, *he lost control of the vehicle*.

Emphasis on Specific Words

Where we place individual words in a sentence has a direct bearing on their emphasis. Readers automatically tend to place emphasis on the first and last words in a sentence. If we place unimportant words in either of these impact-bearing positions, they can rob a sentence of its emphasis:

Let a noun have the last word!

Emphasis misplaced	Such matters as equipment calibration will be handled by the standards laboratory however.
Emphasis restored	Equipment calibration, however, will be handled by the standards laboratory.
Emphasis misplaced	Change the oil every six days at least.
Emphasis restored	Change the oil at least every six days.

The verbs you use can have a powerful influence on emphasis. Strong verbs attract the reader's attention; weak verbs will tend to divert it. Verbs in the active voice are strong because they tell *who did what.* Verbs in the passive voice are weak because they merely pass along information; they describe *what was done by whom.* The sentences in Figure 11-6 are written using both the active and the passive voice; the active-voice versions are consistently shorter and more direct.

There are occasions when you will choose to use the passive voice, because you are reporting an event without knowing who took the action, or prefer not to name a person. For instance, you may prefer to write,

The strain gauge should have been read at 10-minute intervals.

rather than,

Kevin McCaughan should have read the strain gauge at 10-minute intervals.

The passive voice lacks emphasis

The active voice implies action

Passive Voice	*Active Voice*
Elapsed time is indicated by a pointer.	A pointer indicates elapsed time.
The project was completed by the installation crew on May 2.	The installation crew completed the project on May 2.
It is suggested that meter readings be recorded once every hour.	I suggest you record meter readings once every hour.
The samples were passed to quality control for inspection, and then to the shipping department, where they were packed in polyurethane.	Quality control inspected the samples and then the shipping department packed them in polyurethane.

Figure 11-6 Comparison of the passive and the active voice.

Completeness

Every day we see examples of incomplete sentences—on television, in magazines, and especially in advertising. Media writers use them to create a crisp, intentionally choppy effect:

SHEER COMFORT!

8200 metres high. Wide seats, just like your living room.
Tempting snacks. Complimentary refreshments.
Only on Remick Airlines. Our Business Class. Try us!

But if we do the same in our business letters and reports, our sentences are likely to be read with raised eyebrows.

Avoid Writing Sentence Fragments

It's easy to form a sentence fragment. Normally you correct it later, when you are checking what you have written, but sometimes your familiarity with the information may cause you not to notice it. Consider these two pieces of information:

- The meeting achieved its objective. Even though three members were absent.
- The staff were allowed to leave at 3 p.m. Seeing the air conditioning had failed.

All right for a first rough draft...

The first sentence in each of these examples is complete (it has a subject–verb–object construction), but the two second sentences are incomplete because each depends on information in the first sentence.

A useful way to check whether or not a sentence is complete is to read it aloud entirely on its own. If it contains a complete thought it will be understood just as it stands. For example, *The meeting achieved its objective* is a complete thought because you do not need additional information to understand it. *The staff were allowed to leave at 3 p.m.* is also complete. But you cannot say the same when you read these aloud:

- Even though three members were absent.
- Seeing the air conditioning had failed.

In most cases a sentence fragment can be corrected by removing the period that separates it from the sentence it depends on, inserting a comma in place of the period, and adding a conjunction or connecting word such as *and, but, which, who,* or *because*:

- The meeting achieved its objective, even though three members were absent.
- The staff were allowed to leave at 3 p.m. *because* the air conditioning had failed. ("*Seeing*" has been changed to "*because*.")

...but it should be corrected by the second draft

Here are two others:

- Staff will have to bring bag lunches or go out for lunch from October 6 to 10. While the lunchroom is being renovated. (*Change the period to a comma.)*

- All 20-year employees are to be presented with long-service awards. Including three who retired earlier in the year. At the company's annual banquet. *(Change both periods to commas.)*

In particular, check sentences that start with a word that ends in "…ing" (e.g. referr*ing*, answer*ing*, be*ing*) or an expression that ends in "to" (e.g. with reference *to*):

- With reference to your letter of June 6. We have considered your request and will be sending you a cheque. *(Change the period to a comma.)*
- Referring to the problem of vandalism to employees' automobiles in the parking lot. We will be hiring a security guard to patrol the area from 8 a.m. to 6 p.m., Monday through Friday. *(Although the period could be changed to a comma, a better sentence could be formed by reconstructing the fragment.)*

This sentence starts much better:

- To resolve the problem of vandalism to employees' automobiles in the parking lot, we will be hiring…

Avoid Forming Run-on Sentences

A similar sentence error occurs if you link two separate thoughts in a single sentence, joining them with only a comma or even no punctuation. For example,

Your reader will know what you are saying, but will feel uncomfortable reading your words

- Ms Solvason has been selected for the word-processing seminar on March 11, she is eager to attend.

This awkward construction is known as a run-on sentence. It can be corrected by

- replacing the comma with a period, to form two complete sentences:

  …on March 11. She is eager to attend.

- or retaining the comma and following it with *which* or *and:*

  …on March 11, which she is…
  …on March 11, and she is…

A run-on sentence with no punctuation is even more noticeable:

The customer said he never received an invoice I made up a new one.

Either a period, or a comma and a linking word, must be inserted between the words *invoice* and *I*:

…an invoice. I made up…
…an invoice, so I made up…

Position End Punctuation Correctly

There are particular rules for inserting punctuation after quotation marks and closing brackets:

- If a sentence ends with a quotation mark, place the period *inside* the quotation mark:

"That's the information we need," the chief engineer remarked.
"Now we can start the project." ↑
↑

(The above example also shows that when a comma ends an introductory statement, it is also placed *inside* the closing quotation mark.)

These are North American rules; they differ in Great Britain

- If a sentence ends with a closing bracket, place the period *outside* the bracket if the words within the bracket do not form a complete sentence:

  Sound levels measured in the laboratory exceeded the tolerance specification (as shown in Table 2).
  ↑

- However, if the opening bracket is preceded by a period, and the words within the bracket create a complete sentence, then place the period *inside* the bracket:

  Sound levels measured in the laboratory exceeded the tolerance specification. (They were above 82 dBA for more than two hours per day.)
  ↑

Words

The right words in the right place at the right moment can greatly influence your readers. A heavy, ponderous word will slow them down; an overused expression will make them doubt your sincerity; a complex word they do not recognize will annoy them; and a weak or vague word will make them think of you as indefinite. But the right word—short, clear, specific, and necessary—will help them understand your message quickly and easily.

The key word here is "specific"

Words That Tell a Story

Words should convey images. We have many strong, descriptive words in our individual vocabularies, but often we don't use them because the same old routine words spring easily to mind. We write "put" when we would do better to write "position," "insert," "drop," "slide," or any one of the numerous descriptive verbs that better describe the action, as shown in Figure 11-7 on page 274. One descriptive word that defines size, shape, colour, smell, texture, or taste is much more valuable than a dozen words that only generalize.

You can use an analogy to describe an unfamiliar technical item in a way that a nontechnical reader will understand.

A resistor is a piece of ceramic-covered carbon about the size of a cribbage peg, with a 50 mm length of wire protruding from each end.

Specific words tell the reader that you are a definite, purposeful individual. Vague generalities make you sound as though you are not sure:

It is considered that a fair percentage of the samples received from one of our suppliers during the preceding months contained a contaminant.

Whenever possible, insert specific words rather than generalizations

Vague Words	*Descriptive Words*
While the crew was in Thunder Bay they *got* some spare parts.	*Replace "got" with* bought purchased borrowed requisitioned
I have *contacted* the site.	Replace "*contacted*" with telephoned visited written to emailed faxed text-messaged
The Ardmore project will *take a long time*.	Replace "*take a long time*" with last four months require 300 work hours employ two installers for three weeks

Figure 11-7 Replacing nondescriptive words with descriptive words.

This sentence would give a reader four opportunities to wonder whether you really know much about the topic:

1. "It is considered"	Who has voiced this opinion?
2. "a fair percentage"	How many?
3. "one of our suppliers"	Who? One in how many?
4. "contained a contaminant"	What contaminant? In how strong a concentration?

All these generalizations can be avoided in a shorter, more specific sentence:

> We estimate that 60% of the samples received from RamSort Chemicals in June were contaminated with 0.5% to 0.8% mercuric chloride.

Combining Words into Compound Terms

The trend is to compound multiword expressions into a single word

One of the biggest problems for technical writers is knowing whether multiword expressions should be compounded fully, joined by hyphens, or allowed to stand as two or more separate words. For example, should you write

> cross check, cross-check, or crosscheck?
>
> counter clockwise, counter-clockwise, or counterclockwise?
>
> change over, change-over, or changeover?

The tendency today is to compound a multiword expression into a single term. But this bare statement cannot be applied as a general rule because there are too many variations, some of which appear in the Glossary (Appendix B, starting on page 309).

Most multiword expressions are compound adjectives. When two words combine to form an adjective they are either joined by a hyphen or compounded to form one word. They are usually joined by a hyphen if they are formed from an adjective-noun expression:

Adjective + Noun	*As a Compound Adjective*
heavy water	heavy-water production
four channels	four-channel receiver
high frequency	high-frequency oscillator

But when one of the combining words is a verb, they often combine into a one-word adjective. Under these conditions they will normally also compound into a single-word noun:

Two Words	**As a Noun**	**As an Adjective**
lock out	lockout	lockout voltage
shake down	shakedown	shakedown test
cross over	crossover	crossover network

Three or more words that combine to form an adjective in most cases are joined by hyphens. For example, *lock test pulse* becomes *lock-test-pulse generator*. Occasionally, however, they are compounded into a single term, as in *counterelectromotive force*. Specific examples are listed in the Glossary.

Refer to the Glossary for the more common multi-word expressions

However, these guidelines cannot be regarded as firm rules because they do not always apply. Useful guides for doubtful combinations are contained in many dictionaries, and in *The Brief Penguin Handbook* referenced earlier.

Spelling "Canadian Style"

English-speaking Canadians have inherited a spelling problem. Should we continue to spell words such as "theatre" and "labour" as they are traditionally spelled in Britain? Or should we spell them "theater" and "labor," as they are spelled by our neighbours (or *neighbors*) in the United States?

Unfortunately, there are no clearcut guidelines for the correct spelling of such words in Canada, which means that each of us must decide individually whether we want to spell according to contemporary British usage, or align ourselves with the standards current in the United States.

Do you write "metre" or "meter"?; "harbor" or "harbour"?

If almost all of your business correspondence is with people and organizations in Canada, and if your reports are seldom read in the US, then you can safely adopt the British spellings. But if you correspond frequently with people in the US, and write reports that will be read on both sides of the border, then you probably should use US spelling as your standard.

You need a good dictionary to guide you. We recommend

- *The Canadian Oxford Dictionary*,[2] if you prefer a style close to the traditional British style, and
- *Webster's New Collegiate Dictionary*,[3] if you choose US style.

These dictionaries show both the preferred and the alternative spellings of words that can be spelled more than one way. For example, the *Canadian Oxford* dictionary lists

theatre, *theater (the asterisk means "chiefly US")

whereas the *Webster's* dictionary lists

theater or theatre.

The first word in each case is the preferred spelling for the country in which the dictionary has been published, and the second spelling is an alternative, much less common, spelling for that country. (Few people in Britain would write *program*, and even fewer Americans would write *programme.*)

A third choice is *Funk & Wagnalls Canadian College Dictionary*,[4] which tends to lean toward US spelling style.

We use the *CP Stylebook* as our style guide

We have chosen to use a widely respected Canadian guideline as our authority for most spellings, both throughout previous chapters and in the Glossary. This is *The Canadian Press Stylebook*[5] and its companion booklet *Caps and Spelling*.[6]

Two features of the *Stylebook* are its preference for the "re" spelling for words such as "centre" and "theatre," and the "...our" spelling for words such as "honour" and "favour." This is reflected throughout Appendix B's "Glossary of Technical Usage" in this book and is reinforced on page 7 of CP's *Caps and Spelling*:

> The *Canadian Oxford Dictionary* is the authority for Canadian Press spelling...(so) CP style is *our*, not *or*, for *labour*, *honour* and other such words of more than one syllable in which the "u" is not pronounced.

Where there is a spelling choice, the Glossary in Appendix B describes the alternatives and then identifies which spelling we recommend for use in Canada, like this:

favo(u)r *favour* pref in Br and rec in Can.; *favor* pref in US
(pref = preferred; rec = recommended; Can. = Canada)

Note that the emphasis is on the word "recommend": we only *recommend* which spelling we believe to be preferable; the ultimate choice is yours, but you need to be consistent.

Long Versus Short Words

Avoid using an 89-cent word when an equally suitable 25-cent word is available

Big words create a barrier between writer and reader. There are many long scientific words that we have to use in technical writing; we should surround them with short words whenever possible so our writing will not become ponderous.

Low-Information-Content Expressions

Words and expressions of low information content (LIC) contribute little to a sentence. Remove them and the sentence says just as much! Consider this paragraph:

Vague and Wordy	Pursuant to the client's original suggestion, Mr Richards is of the opinion that the structure planned for the client would be most suitable for erection on the site until recently occupied by the old established costume manufacturer known as Garrick Garments. In accordance with the client's anticipated approval of this site, Mr Richards has taken great pains to design a multi-level building that will use the property to an optimum extent.

"Waffle" describes such cumbersome writing. By eliminating unnecessary expressions (such as *pursuant to*; *of the opinion that*; *for erection on*; *in accordance with*; *to an optimum extent*), we can cut the original 71 words to a much more effective 40 words:

Clear and Direct	Mr Richards believes the building planned for the client should be erected on the site previously occupied by Garrick Garments. He has assumed the client will approve this site, and has designed a multi-level building that fully develops the property.

Low-information-content words are untidy lodgers

Table 11-1 on page 278 contains some of the words and phrases you should delete from your writing. For example, in the following sentences the LIC words have been italicized; they should be either deleted or replaced, as indicated by the notes in brackets.

- Flow is controlled by *means of* No. 3 valve. **(delete *means of*) Or:** No. 3 valve controls the flow. **(active voice)**
- Adjust the control *as necessary* to obtain maximum deflection. **(delete *as necessary*)**
- Tests were run for *a period of* three weeks. **(delete *a period of*)**
- By Wednesday we had a backlog of 632 units, *and for this reason* we adopted a two-shift operation. **(replace *and for this reason* with *so*)**

Clichés and wordy expressions are similar to LIC words and phrases. If you refer to yourself as "the writer," start and end letters with overworked phrases such as, "We are in acknowledgment of…" and "…please feel free to call me," or use semilegal jargon such as "the aforementioned discussion," you will be known as a wordy writer. Further examples are listed in Table 11-2 on page 279.

Some Fine Points

Keeping Points Parallel

Good parallelism has a subtle, mostly hidden effect on readers

Parallelism in writing means "similarity of shape." Good parallelism makes readers feel comfortable: even in long or complex technical sentences they never lose their way.

Table 11-1 Examples of low-information-content (LIC) words and phrases.

The LIC words and phrases in this partial list are followed by an expression in brackets (to illustrate a better way to write the phrase) or by an (X), which means that it should be dropped entirely.

actually (X)	in colour, in length, in number, in size (X)
a majority of (most)	in connection with (about)
a number of (many; several)	in fact, in point of fact (X)
as a means of (for; to)	in order to (to)
as a result (so)	in such a manner as to (to)
as necessary (X)	in terms of (in; for)
at present (X)	in the course of (during)
at the rate of (at)	in the direction of (toward)
at the same time as (while)	in the event that (if)
at this time (X)	in the form of (as)
bring to a conclusion (conclude)	in the light of (X)
by means of (by)	in the neighbourhood of; in the vicinity of (about; approximately; near)
by use of (by)	involves the use of (employs; uses)
communicate with (talk to; telephone; write to)	involves the necessity of (demands; requires)
connected together (connected)	is a person who (X)
contact (talk to; telephone; write to)	is designed to be (is)
due to the fact that (because)	it can be seen that (thus; so)
during the course of, during the time that (while)	it is considered desirable (I; we want to)
end result (result)	it will be necessary to (I; you; we must)
exhibit a tendency (tend)	of considerable magnitude (large)
for a period of (for)	on account of (because)
for the purpose of (for; to)	previous to, prior to (before)
for this reason (because)	subsequent to (after)
in all probability (probably)	with the aid of (with; assisted by)
in an area where (where)	with the result that (so, therefore)
in an effort to (to)	
in close proximity to (close to; near)	

Note: Many of these phrases start and end with words such as *as, at, by, for, in, is, it, of, to,* and *with*. This knowledge can help you identify LIC words and phrases in your writing.

This is only a partial list; there are many more LIC expressions

The Grammatical Aspects

If you keep your verb forms similar throughout a sentence in which all parts are of equal importance (i.e. in which the sentence has coordination, or is balanced), you will have taken a major step toward preserving parallelism. For example, if you write "unable to predict" in the early part of a sentence, you should write "able to convince" rather than "successful in convincing" later in the sentence:

Table 11-2 Typical clichés and wordy expressions.

all things being equal	in the foreseeable future
a matter of concern	in the long run
and/or	in the matter of
as a matter of fact	last but not least
as per	many and diverse
attached hereto	needless to say
at this point in time	please feel free to
enclosed herewith	pursuant to your request
for your information (as an introductory phrase)	regarding the matter of
	this will acknowledge
if and when	we are pleased to advise
in our opinion	we wish to state
in reference to	with reference to
in short supply	you are hereby advised

Readers feel uncomfortable when parallelism is violated

Parallelism violated Mr Johnson was *unable to predict* the job completion date, but was *successful in convincing* management that the job was under control.

Parallelism restored (A) Mr Johnson was *unable to predict* the job completion date, but was *able to convince* management that the job was under control.

Parallelism restored (B) (more direct alternative) Mr Johnson *predicted* no completion date, but *convinced* management that the job was under control.

Here are two other examples:

Parallelism violated Pete Hansk likes surveying airports and to study new construction techniques.

Parallelism restored Pete Hansk likes to survey airports and study new construction techniques.

or

Pete Hansk likes surveying airports and studying new construction techniques.

Parallelism violated Following graduation, you will be able to find employment in environmental resources management or in developing research tools.

Parallelism restored Following graduation, you will be able to find employment in environmental resources management or in research tools development.

or

Following graduation, you will be able to find employment managing environmental resources or developing research tools.

Parallelism is particularly important when you are joining sentence parts with the coordinating conjunctions *and*, *or*, and *but* (as in the examples above), with a comma, or with correlatives such as

either...or
neither...nor

Be particularly careful when using the expression *not only...but also*

Each part of a correlative must be followed by an expression in the same grammatical form. That is, if *either* is followed by a verb, then *or* must also be followed by the same form of verb:

Parallelism violated	You may either repair the test set or it may be replaced under the warranty agreement.
Parallelism restored	You may either *repair* the test set or *replace* it under the warranty agreement.

Application to Technical Writing

When building sentences that have a series of clauses, you can help your reader see the connection between the different parts by writing them in the same shape throughout the sentence. Continuity is lost in the following sentence because it lacks parallelism:

Parallelism violated	We inadvertently omitted listing the 7 lathes in room B101, 5 milling machines in room B117, and from the next room, B118, we also forgot to include 16 shapers.

You can restore the clarity by rewriting the sentence so that its parts all have a similar shape:

Maintain similarity of shape within each sentence...

Parallelism restored	We omitted listing 7 lathes in room B101, 5 milling machines in room B117, and 16 shapers in room B118.

Within the paragraph, parallelism has to be applied more carefully, because if it is too obvious the similarity in construction can be dull and repetitive. The verbs are often the key: keep them generally in the same mood and they will help bind the paragraph into one cohesive unit. This paragraph has good parallelism:

...and within each paragraph

The effects of sound are difficult to measure. What to some people is simply background noise, to others may be ear-shattering, peace-destroying drumming. The roar of a jet engine, the squeal of tires, the clatter of machinery, the hiss of air conditioning, the chatter of children, and even the repetitive squeak of an unoiled door hinge can seriously affect many people and create a distinct feeling of uneasiness.

Similarity of shape is most obvious in the third sentence, with its rhythmic use of "sound" words:

roar of a jet engine	*hiss* of air conditioning
squeal of tires	*chatter* of children
clatter of machinery	*squeak* of an unoiled door hinge

Here we have words that paint strong images. They not only have the same grammatical form but also are bound together by their relation to the same sense: hearing.

Even if the subject has a less noticeable impact, you should still try to use parallelism to carry your reader smoothly through your description, as in this description of a surveyor's transit:

> Two sets of clamps and tangent screws are used to adjust the levelling head. The upper clamp fastens the upper and lower plates together, while the upper tangent screw permits a small differential movement between them. The lower clamp fastens the lower plate to the socket, while the lower tangent screw turns the plate through a small angle. When the upper and lower plates are clamped together they can be moved freely as a unit; but when both the upper and lower clamps are tightened the plates cannot be moved in any plane.

Very technical, yet the rhythm binds the parts together

Application to Subparagraphing

Subparagraphing is used frequently in technical writing to separate events or steps, describe an operation or procedure, or list parts or components. Subparagraphing always demands good parallelism, which is *not* present in the following example:

> Three tests were conducted to isolate the fault:
> 1. A matrix was imposed upon the video screen to provide greater clarity.
> 2. Voltage was measured between terminals 4 and 9 to check for line losses.
> 3. To provide additional monitoring, a continuity tester was connected to the unit.

The third subparagraph is not parallel with the first two. To be parallel it should first say what was done and then explain why:

It's when writing point form that parallelism becomes particularly important

> 3. A continuity tester was connected to the unit to provide additional monitoring.

An alternative is to use active verbs together with parallelism to build a strong, emphatic description:

> To isolate the fault we
> 1. *imposed* a matrix upon ...
> 2. *measured* voltage between...
> 3. *connected* a continuity tester to ...

A running lead-in line and imperative-mood verbs create a convincing effect

To change from the first person to the third person, only the lead-in sentence has to be rewritten:

> In tests conducted to isolate the fault, the laboratory
> 1. *imposed...*
> 2. *measured...*
> 3. *connected...*

See pages 256 to 257 for more information on inserting bullets and paragraph numbers.

Abbreviating Technical and Nontechnical Terms

You may abbreviate any term you like, and in any form you like, provided you indicate clearly to the reader how you intend to abbreviate it. The first time you use the term, write it out in full and then follow it with its abbreviation enclosed within brackets. For example,

> In technical narrative, spell out single-digit numbers (sdn). However, when inserting an sdn into a series of single- and multiple-digit numbers, write it in numeral form.

These guidelines are recognized worldwide

When forming abbreviations, observe these three basic rules:

1. **Use lowercase letters,** unless the abbreviation is formed from a person's name:

centimetre	cm
kilogram	kg
approximately	approx
decibel	dB (the *B* represents *Bell* [Alexander Graham Bell])

2. **Omit all periods,** unless the abbreviation forms another word:

horsepower	hp
cubic centimetre	cm^3
cathode-ray tube	crt
metre	m
pascal	Pa
number	no. (also often abbreviated as *No.*)

3. **Write plural abbreviations in the same form as the singular abbreviation:**

28 metres	28 m
7.2 pascals	7.2 Pa
11 kilograms	11 kg
3 hours	3 h *or* hr
42 pounds	42 lb

There are, however, exceptions which, through continued use, have been generally accepted as the correct form. For example,

for example *(exempli gratia)*	e.g.	*(There is a slowly growing trend to write these as eg and ie)*
that is *(id est)*	i.e.	
morning *(ante meridiem)*	a.m.	
afternoon *(post meridiem)*	p.m.	
inside diameter	ID	

The Glossary of Technical Usage offers a comprehensive list of standard abbreviations and some technical abbreviations. For specific technical terms, refer to a list of abbreviations compiled by a technical society in your discipline.

Writing Numbers in Narrative

The conventions that dictate whether a number should be written out or expressed as numerals differ between ordinary writing and technical writing. In technical writing you are much more likely to express numbers in numeral form.

The rules listed below are intended mainly as a guide. They will apply most of the time, but there will be occasions when you will have to make a decision between two rules that conflict. Your decision should then be based on three criteria:

- which method will be most readable,
- which method will be simplest to type,
- which method you used previously, under similar circumstances.

Good judgment and a desire to be consistent will help you select the best method each time.

Numerals are more common than spelled-out numbers in most technical narrative

The basic rule for writing numbers in technical narrative is

- spell out single-digit numbers (one to nine inclusive), and
- use numerals for multiple-digit numbers (10 and above).

However, there are exceptions to this rule, as shown in Table 11-3.

Table 11-3 Guidelines for writing numbers in narrative.

Guideline	*Example (where applicable)*
Always use numerals for the following:	
• Specific technical information, such as test results, dimensions, tolerances, temperatures, statistics, and quotations from tabular data.	
• Any number that precedes a unit of measurement.	3 mm; 7 kg; 121.5 MHz
• A series of both large and small numbers in one passage.	On May 28 we tested 7 transmitters, 49 receivers, and 38 power supplies.
• Section, chapter, page, figure (illustration), and table numbers.	Chapter 7; Figure 4; page 219
• Numbers that contain fractions or decimals.	$7^1/_2$; 3.25
• Percentages.	3% gain; 5% GST
• Years, dates, and times.	At 3 p.m. on January 9, 2008; 08:17; 20 Feb 08
• Sums of money.	$2000; $28.50; 27 cents or $0.27
• A person's age.	Nearly 8 years old
Always spell out the number for the following:	
• Round numbers that stand alone.	about five hundred; approximately forty thousand
• Fractions that stand alone.	Repairs were made in less than three-quarters of an hour.
• Numbers that start a sentence. *(Or, better, revise the sentence so the number is not at the beginning.)*	

There are also five additional general rules:

- Spell out one of the numbers when two numbers are written consecutively and are not separated by punctuation: 36 fifty-watt amplifiers or thirty-six 50-watt amplifiers. (Generally, spell out whichever number will result in the simplest or shortest expression.)

Always place a "0" in front of an open decimal

- Insert a zero before the decimal point of numbers less than one: 0.75; 0.0037.
- Use decimals rather than fractions (they are easier to type), except when writing numbers that are customarily written as fractions: $^3/_4$ in. plywood.
- Insert spaces in large numbers containing five or more digits: 1 275 000; 27 291; 4056. (Insert a space in four-digit numbers only when they appear as part of a column of numbers.) We recommend using spaces rather than commas, because in many European countries the comma is used to represent a decimal point.
- Write numbers that denote position in a sequence as 1st, 2nd, 3rd, 4th...31st...42nd...103rd...124th...

When writing and abbreviating numerical prefixes such as "giga" and "kilo," follow the guidelines in Table 11-4.

Writing Metric Units and Symbols (SI)

The Glossary of Technical Usage includes terms and symbols prescribed by the International System of Units (SI). The trend toward worldwide adoption of metric units of measurement means that for some time both the imperial inch/pound system and the metric (SI) system will be in use. The terms and symbols introduced here are those you are most likely to encounter.

This guideline is also recognized worldwide

Table 11-4 Numerical prefixes and abbreviations.

Multiple/ Submultiple	Prefix	Symbol	Multiple/ Submultiple	Prefix	Symbol
10^{24}	yotta	Y	10^{-1}	deci	d
10^{21}	zetta	Z	10^{-2}	centi	c
10^{18}	exa	E	10^{-3}	milli	m
10^{15}	peta	P	10^{-6}	micro	µ
10^{12}	tera	T	10^{-9}	nano	n
10^{9}	giga	G	10^{-12}	pico	p
10^{6}	mega	M	10^{-15}	femto	f
10^{3}	kilo	k	10^{-18}	atto	a
10^{2}	hecto	h	10^{-21}	zepto	z
10	deca	da	10^{-24}	yocta	y

The acronym "SI" represents the name "Système International d'Unités." Both the acronym and the name were adopted for universal usage in 1960 by the eleventh Conférence Générale des Poids et Mesures (CGPM), which is the international authority on metrication. Since then, many of the metric terms the conference established have become part of our language. *Hertz*, the unit of frequency measurement, which replaced *cycles per second* in 1960, is a typical example, as are the following:

	non-SI	*SI*
Temperature:	degrees Fahrenheit	degrees Celsius
Length:	miles, yards, feet, inches	kilometres, metres, millimetres
Weight:	tons, pounds, ounces	tonnes, kilograms, grams, milligrams
Liquid volume:	gallons, quarts	kilolitres, litres

The "...re" spelling is correct for *litre* and *metre*, although only the "...er" spelling is recognized in the US

There are nine general guidelines for writing SI symbols, which must be written, typed, or printed as listed below:

1. In upright type, even if the surrounding type slopes or is in italic letters.
2. In lowercase letters, except when the name of the unit is derived from a person's name (e.g. the symbol F for *farad* is derived from *Faraday*). In some cases a symbol has two letters, in which case only the first letter of the symbol is capitalized (e.g. Wb for *weber*).
3. With a space between the last numeral and the first letter of the symbol: **355 V, 27 km** (*not* 355V, 27km).
4. With no space between the letters forming the symbol: **3.6 kg, 150 mm, 960 kHz.**
5. With no "s" added to a plural: **1 g, 236 kg.**
6. With no period after the symbol, unless it forms the last word in a sentence.
7. With a solidus (oblique stroke: /) to represent the word *per*: **m/s** (metres per second). There can be only one solidus in each expression.
8. With a dot at midletter height (·) to represent that symbols are multiplied: **lm·s** (lumen second).
9. Always as a symbol when a number is used with the SI unit (e.g."the tank holds 400 L"), but spelled out when no number is used with the unit (e.g "capacity is measured in litres" [*not* "capacity is measured in L"]).

The abbreviation for *litre* is L, because in some fonts a lower case letter l looks like the numeral 1

Writing Non-Gender-Specific Language

History has provided us with a scenario in which men were the warriors and hunters, and subsequently the breadwinners, and women were the homebodies who cooked meals and reared children and catered to their men's needs. Today, all that has changed and it is universally recognized in developed countries that women and men are equal and can mostly have equal occupations and equal roles. Consequently, we now see men as administrative assistants, nurses, and child care workers, and women as airline pilots, engineers, truck drivers, and backhoe operators.

Unfortunately, our language has not kept pace and we still see some people who write like this:

Awareness is the key to writing non-gender-specific language

> A secretary will be brought in to record the minutes of the client/contractor project meeting. *She* will be responsible for making travel arrangements for all meeting participants.
>
> After much deliberation, the committee decided to hire an engineer to look into the problem. *He* will evaluate the extent of erosion that occurred when the river overflowed its banks.

Neither of these writers knew whether the secretary and the engineer were going to be male or female, yet *they automatically assumed* that the secretary would be a woman and the engineer would be a man.

It's our job to eradicate presumptuous gender-specific references from our writing:

Interestingly, these examples are shorter than the originals

> A secretary will be brought in to record the minutes of the client/contractor project meeting, and to make travel arrangements for all meeting participants.
>
> After much deliberation, the committee decided to hire an engineer to evaluate the extent of erosion that occurred when the river overflowed its banks.

Eliminate Masculine Pronouns

When describing engineers, scientists, architects, managers, supervisors, technical people, and even accountants and lawyers, historically our language has abounded with masculine pronouns. Here is an excerpt from a company's operating procedures:

> **17.3 Senior Systems Engineer.** *His* primary role is to plan, schedule, manage, and coordinate the activities of the engineers within the Systems Engineering Department. *He* also is responsible for preparing budgets and maintaining fiscal control of operations performed by the department, and for maintaining liaison with and reporting progress to clients.

There are several ways you can remove the male pronouns:

1. Repeat the job title, and abbreviate it:

> **17.3 Senior Systems Engineer (SSE).** The SSE's primary role is to plan, schedule, manage, and coordinate the activities of the engineers within the Systems Engineering Department. The SSE also is responsible for preparing budgets and maintaining fiscal control of operations performed by the department, and for maintaining liaison with and reporting progress to clients.

2. Use a bulleted list:

This is probably the clearest and most comfortable revision

> **17.3 Senior Systems Engineer.** The Senior Systems Engineer is responsible for
>
> - planning, scheduling, managing, and coordinating the activities of the engineers within the Systems Engineering Department;
> - preparing budgets and maintaining fiscal control of operations performed by the department; and
> - maintaining liaison with and reporting progress to clients.

3. Create a table:

17.3 Senior Systems Engineer

Primary Responsibility	Secondary Responsibilities
To plan, schedule, manage, and coordinate the activities of the engineers within the Systems Engineering Department.	To prepare budgets and maintain fiscal control of operations performed by the department. To maintain liaison with and report progress to clients.

This revision employs good information design principles

4. Replace the male pronoun with "you" and "your":

17.3 Senior Systems Engineer. *Your* primary role is to plan, schedule, manage, and coordinate the activities of the engineers within the Systems Engineering Department. *You* also are responsible for preparing budgets and maintaining fiscal control of operations performed by the department, and for maintaining liaison with and reporting progress to clients.

(Note: If you use "you" in one part of a document, be consistent and use it throughout the document. Avoid bouncing back and forth between "you" and "he" or "she.")

5. Change singular pronouns to plural pronouns:

17.3 Senior Systems Engineers. *Their* primary role is to plan, schedule, manage, and coordinate the activities of the engineers within the Systems Engineering Department. *They* also are responsible for preparing budgets and maintaining fiscal control of operations performed by the department, and for maintaining liaison with and reporting progress to clients.

Suggestions 4 and 5 are less comfortable revisions

(Note: This method can be used only when the description lends itself to using plural nouns and pronouns; i.e. there must be more than one Senior Systems Engineer.)

We do not recommend using the expressions "he or she," "he/she," or "s/he."

Replace Gender-Specific Nouns

Each province in Canada has its Workers' Compensation Board, an organization that provides financial help to employees who are injured at work. Yet, not many years ago, all Workers' Compensation Boards in Canada were known as *Workmen's* Compensation Boards. The previous title seemed to imply that the board provided help *only* to male workers, which was not true. Similarly, until about 20 years ago, flight attendants on airlines were known as stewardesses, implying that the job was held only by females. Again, particularly today, this is plainly inaccurate.

Many other job titles are gender-specific and predominantly male-oriented. Table 11-5 on page 288 shows some that have been replaced in recent years.

Table 11-5 Preferred names for gender-specific titles.

If you are tempted to write:	Consider replacing it with:
actor; actress	actor (for both sexes)
chairman	chair; chairperson
cowboy	cattle rancher
fireman	firefighter
foreman	supervisor
man-hours	work-hours or staff hours
Miss or Mrs	Ms (always!)
newsman	reporter
policeman; policewoman	police officer
postman	letter (*or* mail) carrier
repairman	service technician
salesman	sales representative
spokesman	spokesperson
workman	worker; employee
waiter; waitress	server (or "waiter" for both sexes)

Be Consistent When Referring to Men and Women

Be particularly careful when addressing letters and writing the salutation

Men throughout recent history have been given the courtesy title *Mr* before their names. Until 20 years ago, women had two courtesy titles, to denote whether they were married or single: *Mrs* and *Miss*. Today, a woman's marital status is *never* implied in her title: always address a woman as *Ms*.

Writing for an International Audience

In a growing global economy, we have to be aware of and adapt to cultural differences

People in many European and Asian countries are much more formal in their correspondence than we tend to be in North America. Where a Manitoban writing to Paul Villeneuve in Quebec would write *Dear Paul* quite early in an exchange of letters, an Italian or Norwegian (for example) would continue to write *Dear Mr Villeneuve* for much longer.

Adapt the pyramid to suit the reader's culture

This formality extends to how you use the letter-writing pyramid described in Chapter 3, particularly for countries in Eastern Europe and Asia. Rather than discard the pyramid, you will need to insert two additional writing compartments, one at the beginning and one at the end, as shown in Figure 11-8. The opening compartment often will contain a greeting and polite remarks about the reader's family, and their health and happiness. The closing compartment will also contain polite remarks, perhaps wishing the reader continuing good health and prosperity in the months and years ahead.

Avoid jargon: choose words that will be understood by both writer and reader

When you write in English to readers who normally speak another language—German, French, Italian, Spanish, Malay, or Chinese, for

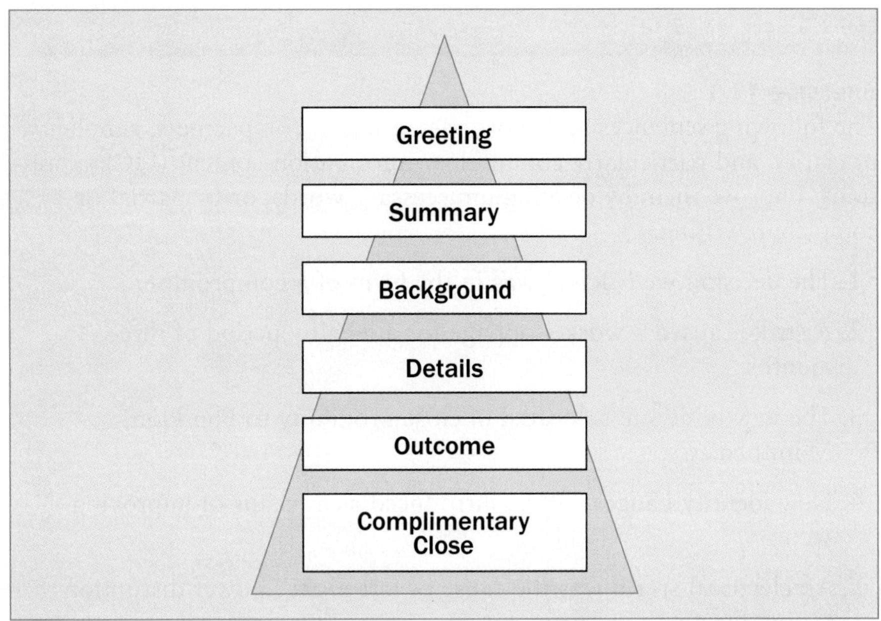

Figure 11-8 "Adapted" pyramid for a letter to an Eastern European or Asian reader.

example—you have to choose words that will be clearly understood. This also holds true for different cultures who speak the same language. Here are some guidelines to follow:

- Avoid long, complex sentences.
- Avoid long, complex words. If you have a choice between two or more words or expressions that have roughly the same meaning, choose the simpler one. For example, write "pay" rather than "salary" or "remuneration."
- Use the same word to describe the same action or product consistently throughout your letter. Decide, for example, whether you will refer to money in the bank as *funds, currency, deposits, capital,* or *money*.
- Always use a word in the same sense. You would confuse a foreign-language reader if you were to write, "It would not be *appropriate* to transfer funds from Account A to Account B" (meaning it would not be suitable to do it), and then in another sentence write, "We had insufficient capital to *appropriate* Company A" (meaning to take over Company A, or buy it out).

Two sources for more information about writing to and observing the communication culture of different countries can be obtained through the Society for Technical Communication (STC), which has a Special Interest Group concentrating on global communication (www.stc.org), and from a book by Nancy L Hoft titled *International Technical Communication.*[7]

ASSIGNMENTS

Exercise 11.1

The following sentences and short passages lack compactness, simplicity, or clarity, and particularly contain low-information-content (LIC) expressions. Improve them by deleting unnecessary words, or by partial or complete rewriting.

1. The decision we reached was in the form of a compromise.
2. A strike caused a work stoppage for a lengthy period of three months.
3. The new mine site is located in close proximity to Flin Flon, Manitoba.
4. New identity badges will be introduced as a means of improving security.
5. An electrical storm was the cause of last night's power disruption lasting for a period of two hours.
6. Before making any attempt to close the valve, be sure as a first step to check that the master control is in the up (OFF) position.
7. The end result of rotating the control clockwise will be in the form of an increase in flow.
8. There will be little or no advantage at this point in time in carrying out any further tests.

Simple ideas confused by wordy, rambling sentences

9. Check for porosity with the use of a Vancourt 300 calibrator at intervals of not greater than, at the very most, 48 hours apart.
10. In the interest of achieving better customer satisfaction, it is our recommendation that the company consider the possibility of purchasing the Nabuchi 220 reliability software.
11. There was a 15% drop in the level of customer complaints in the month of February, following the introduction of the Midway training program.
12. For your information, the Mayerling report on the permafrost study conducted in the region of Lac La Biche will be readily available in the company library with effect from October 24.
13. It is a point of considerable concern to us, that since 2005 there is evidence of higher levels of toxicity in the waters of Lake Winnipeg.
14. The road traffic study to be conducted on the bypass around the region of the town of Corrigan will last for a period of two weeks starting on or about May 16.

15. During the time of the spring audit, the auditors identified an accounting error in the amount of $130 000.
16. It is entirely within the realm of possibility that the Prometheus Project may be divided between two contractors.
17. In an effort to increase reliability of our products, the Quality Assurance Department will conduct random checks during the stage of module assembly.
18. The final phase of testing planned for October will bring the installation project to a conclusion.
19. For the balance of the current year, it is expected that the company will be in the process of hiring seven additional technicians.
20. When a contractor is inspecting underwater bridge structures, it is a Labour Department specification that the contractor is required to provide a minimum of two or more divers who will be connected together by a cable of no more than 3 metres in length.

Exercise 11.2

The following sentences offer choices between words that sound similar or are frequently misused. Select the correct word in each case.

These word choices offer unexpected surprises!

1. The technician reported that the flywheel became (stationary/stationery) 127 seconds after power was cut off.
2. (Preventive/Preventative) maintenance has to be performed on the engine after 800 hours of (continual/continuous) nonstop operation.
3. In his welcoming speech to staff, the newly appointed director (implied/inferred) there would be no layoffs for at least 18 months.
4. The proposed change will be difficult to (affect/effect) because over 80% of the employees will be (affected/effected).
5. On reception, signals are separated into two (discreet/discrete) channels.
6. No (farther/further) payments have been made to the outstanding account.
7. Because the storm has cut off power to site 17, you will be unable to (elicit/illicit) a response from the site for 48 hours.
8. The inspection team (is/are) experiencing difficulty and will be unable to complete (its/it's/their) investigation of the equipment until May 17.
9. The (amount/number) of installations we will be able to undertake in 2012 will decrease by 27% from the 2011 total, because we will have 24 (fewer/less) staff to carry out the work.
10. It is essential to carry out (a disinterested/an uninterested) personal evaluation when considering an employee for promotion.

11. From the technician's report, telephoned to me on June 10, it (appears/seems) unlikely the project will be completed on schedule.
12. No work will be done on the project between December 23 (and/to) January 3.
13. Over 70% of the repairs will be carried out by December 31; the (balance/remainder) will be completed in the following year.
14. Although the data (has/have) been evaluated, (its/it's) unlikely the results will be available before October 12.

Some words are so similar it can be difficult to choose between them

15. Before taking any measurements, check that the pointer on the rotating ring has been (oriented/orientated) to point at exactly 216°.
16. When the transformer blew out, we had to choose an (alternate/alternative) power source from our neighbouring provinces.
17. The agenda (was/were) too detailed to handle in a single meeting.
18. Forty-eight hours after the concrete was poured on the second floor of the new parking structure, we took seven drill cores to ensure the pour was (free from/free of) flaws.
19. The number of hirings in 2010 showed a 20% increase compared (to/with) the hirings in 2009.
20. Our (principal/principle) reasons for including this exercise in the eighth edition of *Technically-Write!* (is/are) to draw your attention to the Glossary of Technical Usage at the end of the book.

Exercise 11.3

Rewrite the following sentences to make them more emphatic (in many cases, change them from the passive to the active voice). Create a "doer" if one is not identified.

1. The specifications for the Carlton project were circulated by Mary Warboys on April 20.
2. The August 15 meeting was interrupted at 3:10 p.m. by a fire alarm.
3. The supply of natural gas was cut off for a period of 18 hours by a fracture in the pipeline near Snow Lake.
4. In the interest of public safety, it is recommended by the Workplace Health and Safety Committee that hard hats be worn by all visitors to the site.
5. The design proposal written by Muriel Boyd was edited by Samantha Wiens and printed by David Nguyen.
6. Because the storm was instrumental in cutting off power to site 17, our inspection was not completed on schedule.

7. Entrance to the lab on the night of April 7 was effected by a thief using a duplicate set of keys.
8. On a recommendation by the Chief of Quality Assurance, the seven Meteor calibrators used by our lab technicians have been replaced by two Vancourt model 370 multi-function calibrators.
9. The pH level in the city's three swimming pools has been reduced by 3.5%, in order to meet the requirements stipulated by the health inspector in her August 12 report.
10. It is company policy that a cellphone must be carried by all drivers travelling outside the city limits during winter months.
11. Before departure, it is a further requirement that it is the responsibility of the driver to ensure the cellphone's battery is in a fully charged condition.
12. Before the drugs could be shipped, a release certificate had to be signed by the health inspector that they were in conformance with the requirements of specification A1637/2.
13. Over $80 000 in damage was sustained by equipment in the laboratory, when a fire was caused by an overloaded electrical power circuit.
14. It is of some concern to me that on two occasions a scheduling problem has been experienced by the production department with the result that a complaint has been filed by the client.

A passive-voice sentence is longer than an active-voice sentence

15. It is essential that the chlorine and pH levels of the campus swimming pool be tested on a daily basis and, if an imbalance occurs, for corrective action to be taken immediately by the resident technician.
16. The tendency, as exhibited by some drivers, to consistently make a fast getaway when a stoplight turns from red to green, has been shown by a prominent consumer analysis to be the major cause of high fuel consumption.

Exercise 11.4

Improve the parallelism in the following sentences.

1. Finding someone to keystroke the report on Friday evening was easy, but it was difficult to find a clerk willing to print, collate, and bind it on Saturday morning.
2. Kevin Sales will be transferred to the Thompson office for a period of six weeks to 9 months.
3. A survey of staff showed that 35% prefer the blue logo design, 27% prefer the gold, but retention of the existing design is favoured by 33%. The remaining 5% indicated they had no preference.

4. There is severe vibration at flywheel speeds between 3200 and 3800 rpm but, surprisingly, above 4500 rpm the vibration disappears completely.

5. It will take 12 days to carry out the survey, which we can accept, but it is not acceptable that it will take a further 18 days to process the results.

Keep the ideas—like trains—on parallel tracks

6. The new software has not only reduced project downtime but also errors in transferring data to the mainframe computer have been eliminated.

7. Version 5.5 of the *Find-It* software not only corrects the printer interface problems we have experienced, but it also has the advantage of coming in at a low price.

8. Inspection of your furnace showed
   - a crack in the heat exchanger,
   - rust on the blower motor,
   - the clamps on the fresh-air inlet pipe are loose, and
   - a clogged filter and bellows assembly.

9. We recorded sound levels on the east side of the lab at 68.6 dB, but they decreased to only 47.5 dB on the west side of the room.

10. Wendy Rogers will coordinate the project, the administrative responsibilities will be undertaken by Fiona Gerrard, and a study of the proposed documentation process will be initiated by Colin Levinworth.

Exercise 11.5

Improve the punctuation in the following sentences.

1. Minutes of the meeting were recorded by Dave Johannson. In the absence of Janet Daniels.

2. We apologize for the delay in submitting our report, a copy is attached.

3. Your claim for travel expenses incurred from 28 October to 5 November has been reduced by $38.76, see the attached list.

4. I am in receipt of your letter of Nov 17 you'll be glad to hear the damage to your equipment will be repaired at no cost to you.

5. We propose building a 24 inch culvert from the east end of the parking lot at Richmond Mall, the whole lot slopes down toward the east end. A drop in grade of 0.89 metre overall.

6. We measured sound levels in the new lab, they were 1.45 dB higher at the north end of the room; compared to the south end.

7. All office thermostats are to be turned down to 16C at the end of work each day. To reduce overnight heating costs.

8. We are transferring your account to the Sarnia, Ontario, branch. As requested in your email of December 13.

9. Please schedule a meeting for 2 p.m. on May 22, this confirms my telephone call of May 3 and all staff engaged in the Romulus project if on site are to attend with no exceptions, please send me a list of those who are scheduled to be off site on that date by May 18.

10. Repairs to the heating system will cost $1735.00, $335 more than we had estimated in our proposal of January 20. Corrosion in the pipes above the shipping area was the main problem, also rust in the furnace blower unit.

Exercise 11.6

Correct any quantities, abbreviations, or numbers that are presented incorrectly in the following sentences. Also correct improperly spelled words or improperly used punctuation.

1. The distance between the two measurement points is exactly .2576 metres.

2. With affect from February 1st, radio station DMLZ's radio frequencies will be moving from 101.37 khz to 103.6 khz on the A.M. band and from 98.7 MHZ to 95.7 MHZ on the F.M. band.

3. We will be flying to Abbotsford, B.C., on the evening of 07/06/08, arriving at 09.17, and returning on the 14th of the next month (Jly), departing at 10.32 am.

4. Each bottle contains one-and-one-half litres (1.5 l) of triple-filtered water, which it is essential that at all times should be kept above freezing point (either 32C or zero F).

5. Please prepare a checque for two hundred and eighty-seven dollars and fifty cents payable to Multiple Industries Inc, cross-reference it to there purchase order 2,817, and send it by Express Post.

6. The high sound level's of 69 db and 72 db (decibels) measured at two points beside the west wall are caused by a packaging machine in the ajoining room, situated only 1.2 metres from the dividing wall that seperates the two rooms.

7. 34 tanks were filled during the week ending May twenty-first, which was thirteen percent more than were filled during the week ending May 14th.

8. For further information, turn to paragraph two on page seven.

9. To connect the 2 sites will mean stringing a decimal five five millimetre cable between the poles for approximately three kms.

10. We estimate the cost to repair your company's delivery van will be three thousand, four hundred and sixty dollars ($3,460).

11. Thirteen model six-four-six transmitters bearing thirteen consecutive serial Nos. between 11728 and 11730 have been shipped to Site Seven.
12. We will need to instal a three km long, twentyfour inch Diameter pipe to handle the runoff from the new developement site beside Highway 276, three point 6 Kilometres west of the city.

Exercise 11.7

Select the correctly spelled words among the options offered below.

1. The (computer/computor) is supplied with a built-in 99-year (calendar/calender).
2. A (coarse/course)-grained (aggregate/agreggate) is used as a base before pouring the concrete.
3. Profits in the (forth/fourth) quarter increased by (forty/fourty) percent.
4. The (affluent/effluent) produced by the paper mill is (enviromentally/environmentaly/environmentally) sound.
5. The preface to a book or report is sometimes called a (forward/foreward/foreword).
6. The (cite/site) is (inaccessable/inaccessible) except by helicopter.
7. Version 6.0 of *4Tell for Windows 05* (supercedes, supersedes) version 5.5.
8. The tests show that the materials have (similar/similiar) properties.
9. To a young business owner seeking a cash flow loan, the (colatteral/collatteral/collateral) demanded by the bank may seem (exhorbitant/exorbitant).

Well? How good are you at spelling?

10. When Multiple Industries bought all the outstanding shares of Torrance Electronics, the latter company became a (wholely/wholly)-owned subsidiary.
11. It's better to edit your own writing on (hard copy/hardcopy) rather than (online/on line).
12. Silica gel is a drying agent, or (desiccant/dessiccant/dessicant), that is packed with electronic equipment before shipment.
13. Software designers who have (entepreneurial/entrepeneurial/entrepreneurial) drive do not (necessarily/neccessarily) have good management expertise.
14. After (lengthy/lengthly) deliberation, the executive committee admitted that Ken Wynne's innovative design was indeed (ingenious/ingenuous).
15. After we have (accumulated/accummulated) all the results from product tests, we will (prescribe/proscribe) definitive purchase specifications.

16. An (auxiliary/auxilliary) heater cuts in when temperature drops below 3°C.

17. The (eigth/eighth) test demonstrated that the process is (feasable/ feasible).

18. The incandescent lamps have been replaced with (flourescent/ fluorescent/fluourescent) lamps.

19. The sales manager was (embarassed/embarrassed/embarrased) that customers were being (harassed/harrassed/harrased) by overly zealous sales staff.

20. Well? How many words did you (mispell/misspell)?

All these words are in the Glossary in Appendix B

Exercise 11.8

Improve the following passages so they contain no gender-specific language and (where appropriate) are better conveyors of information:

1. Memo to all lab technicians:

   The Department of Defence has informed us that a D.O.D. inspector will visit our calibration lab on May 17. He will be evaluating our equipment and calibration hierarchy to determine whether our lab meets MIL-STD-202 specifications. Please extend him every courtesy and your co-operation.

2. To: Andy Rittman:

   Please inform each field technician that from April 1 he will be covered by company-sponsored travel insurance arranged through ManSask Assurance Corporation. They won't have to pay for it, but belonging to the scheme won't be automatic, they have to apply for it. I suggest you write a personal memo to each technician and enclose a copy of the enclosed application form and explanatory brochure. In each case be sure to remind him to apply by March 25, otherwise he'll have to wait until May 1 for his coverage to start.

3. To all staff:

   Construction will start shortly in room B101, which is to become a child day-care centre that will accommodate 20 children ages 1 to 5. If you have preschoolers and would like to take advantage of this service, have your wife call Rick Davis in Personnel and ask for form CCC01.

   Additionally, we will be hiring three experienced child-care workers to man the facility. If you or your spouse knows of someone who might be suitable, ask her (the child-care worker) to telephone Rick for an application form.

Correcting gender-specific terms can be more subtle than is immediately evident

4. From a company notice board:

> **Holiday Cheer Is About to Start!**
>
> Are you planning to attend the Holiday Party? Tell your most significant other it will be at O'Halloran's on December 15 and to expect a royal feast!
>
> Line up a babysitter today and tell her to expect to stay late...!
>
> Call Dave Michaelson at extension 207 if you want to announce your intentions or to reserve a table, or if you want more information.

REFERENCES

1. Lester Faigley, Roger Graves and Heather Graves, *The Brief Penguin Handbook*, 2nd Canadian ed (Toronto: Pearson Education Canada, 2010).
2. *The Canadian Oxford Dictionary*, 2nd ed, Katherine Barber, ed (Don Mills, Ontario: Oxford University Press), 2004.
3. *Webster's New Collegiate Dictionary*, 9th ed (Springfield, Massachusetts: G & C Merriam Company, 1989).
4. *Funk & Wagnalls Canadian College Dictionary* (Markham, Ontario: Fitzhenry & Whiteside, 1986).
5. *The Canadian Press Stylebook*, 12th ed (Toronto: The Canadian Press, 2002).
6. *Caps and Spelling*, 17th ed (Toronto: The Canadian Press, 2005).
7. Nancy L Hoft, *International Technical Communication: How to Export Information About High Technology* (New York: John Wiley & Sons, Inc, 1995).

Appendix A
Guidelines for Writing Source References

Source references can be written many ways. The most common are the styles recommended by the Modern Language Association (MLA)[1] and the American Psychological Association (APA),[2] although there are many others. The style we show here most closely parallels the MLA approach, but with some differences that suit the technical documentation field. If you are writing in industry, the suggested approach will work well for you. If you are writing in an academic situation or for a technical journal, you should enquire which style your professors or the journal editor prefers.

Bibliography Styles Handbook
www.english.uiuc.edu/cws/wworkshop/bibliography.html
The Bibliography Styles Handbook, one section of the University of Illinois's Writers' Workshop, provides information about the bibliographic styles of the American Psychological Association (APA) and the Modern Language Association (MLA), and about the old MLA style.

Until the mid-1990s, most source referencing was to printed documents. Today, however, you will often be gaining information from an electronic resource, which may be by email or searching on the web. Because internet sources may only be transitory, whenever possible you will need to quote more source information.

In appearance, reference and bibliography entries differ:

- In a list of references the entries are listed in the order in which you refer to them in your report, and each is preceded by a number: 1, 2, 3, etc.
- In a bibliography the entries are listed in alphabetical order of the author's surname (family name), or the first-named author if there is more than one author, regardless of the sequence in which you refer to the source in your report. (If there is no author name, use the first word of the document title, to determine its sequence in the list.) Bibliography entries are not numbered. See Figure A-1 on page 307.

Preparing a List of References

References should contain specific information, arranged in this sequence:

(a) Author's name or authors' names (in natural order: first name and/or initials, and then surname)
(b) Title of document (article, book, paper, report)
(c) Identification details, such as

For a book: city and province, state, or country of publication, publisher's name, and year of publication.

For a magazine or journal article: name of magazine or journal; volume and issue number; date of issue.

For a report: report number; name and location of issuing organization; date of issue.

Each reference source must be recorded exactly as it appears on the original document

For email: name and email address of sender; name and address of recipient; the date sent.

For a text message: name and cellphone number of sender; name and cellphone number of recipient; the date sent.

For correspondence: name and location of issuing organization; name and location of receiving organization; the letter's date.

For a conversation or speech: name and location of speaker's organization; name, identification, and location of listener; the date.

For an excerpt from a webpage: the name of the author/designer (if known); the title of the page or source; the name of the organization that owns the site; the latest update; the date the information was accessed; and the URL.

(d) The page number (if applicable) on which the referenced item appears or starts.

Referencing a Book

If you are referring to information in a book authored by only one person, the entry in your list of references should contain:

(a) Author's name
(b) Title of book (set in italic type)
(c) City of publication, publisher's name, and year of publication (all within one set of parentheses)
(d) Page number (the first page of the referenced pages)

If it is your first reference, and you are referring to an item on page 174 of the book, your entry would look like this:

Each reference entry is given a sequential number

1. Laurinda K Wicherly, *Fibreoptic Modes of Communication* (Toronto, Ontario: The Moderate Press Inc, 2009), p 174.

If a book has two authors, both are named:

2. David B Shaver and John D Williams, *Management Techniques for a Research Environment* (Edmonton, Alberta: Witney Publications, 2010), p 215.

But if there are three or more authors, only the first-named author is listed and the remaining names are replaced by "and others":

3. Donald R Kavanagh and others,... *(etc).*

If a book is a second or subsequent edition (as this book is), the edition number is entered immediately after the book title:

4. Ron Blicq and Lisa Moretto, *Technically-Write!* Canadian 8th ed (Toronto, Ontario: Pearson Prentice Hall, 2012).

Some books contain sections written by several authors, each of whom is named within the book, with the whole book edited by another person. If your reference is to the whole book, identify it by the editor's name:

5. Donna R Linwood, ed, *Seven Ways to Make Better Technical Presentations* (Vancouver, BC: Bonus Books Ltd, 2011).

But if your reference is to a particular section of the book, identify it by the specific author, enclose the section title in quotation marks, set the book title in italics, then name the editor:

6. Kevin G Wilson, "Preparation: The Key to a Good Talk," *Seven Ways to Make Better Technical Presentations*, ed Donna R Linwood (Vancouver, BC: Bonus Books Ltd, 2010), p 71.

External document titles are listed in italic type; internal section titles are listed within quotation marks

(In examples 5 and 6, "ed" means "editor" or "edited by.")

Referencing a Magazine or Journal Article

Similarly, if you are referring to an article in a magazine or journal, list these details:

(a) Author's (authors') name(s)
(b) Title of article (always in quotation marks)
(c) Title of journal or magazine (set in italics)
(d) Volume and issue numbers (shown as two numbers separated by a colon)
(e) Journal or magazine issue date
(f) Page on which article or excerpt starts (optional entry)

If an article is your seventh reference, it would look like this:

7. Lilita Rodman, "You-attitude: A Linguistic Perspective," in *Technostyle*, 17:2, Winter 2002, p 55.

If a magazine article does not show an author's name, then the entry starts with the title of the article:

8. "Selling to the EEC: Challenge of the New Millennium," in *Technical Marketing*, 11:5, May 2007, p 113.

Referencing a Report

To refer to a report written by yourself or another person, list this information:

Reports, memos, and email messages can be listed as reference sources...

(a) Author's (authors') name(s) if the author is identified on the report
(b) Title of report, in italics
(c) Report number, or other identification (if any)
(d) Name and location (city, plus province or state) of organization issuing report
(e) Report date
(f) Page number (if a specific part of the report is being referenced)

Here is an example:

9. Derek A Lloyd, *Effective Communication and Its Importance in Management Consulting*. Report No. 61, Smyrna Development Corporation, Montreal, Quebec, February 18, 2010.

Referencing an Email, Letter, or Memo

For an email message, the entry should look like this:

10. Christine Lamont (c.lamont@macroeng.com), "Replacing Vancourt Meters." Email to Wayne Kominsky (kominsky@7designgrp.net), 31 October 2011.

For a letter or memo, the email references are replaced by company name and location, the title often is omitted, and the word "email" is replaced by "letter" or "memo"):

11. Christine Lamont, Macro Engineering Inc, Toronto, Ontario. Letter to Wayne Kominsky, No. 7 Design Group, Winnipeg, Manitoba, 31 October 2011.

Referencing a Conversation or Speech

For a conversation or speech follow these examples:

...as can talks and telephone or face-to-face conversations

12. David R Phillips, Lakeside Power and Light Company, Thunder Bay, Ontario, in conversation with Anna King, H L Winman and Associates, Calgary, Alberta, January 7, 2011.

13. Francis R Cairns, Elwood Martens and Associates, Fredericton, New Brunswick, speaking to the 8th Potash Producers' Conference, Regina, Saskatchewan, September 16, 2010.

Referencing an Excerpt from a Webpage

If information is available only on a webpage, and is *not* printed elsewhere, list

(a) Author's (authors') name(s) (if an author is identified)
(b) Title of the specific piece of information (enclosed within quotation marks)
(c) The title of the page or source (in italics)
(d) The name of the institute or organization that owns the webpage
(e) The date the information was entered, or the latest update, using day (numeral), month (first three letters, spelled out), year (numeral)
(f) The date the information was accessed
(g) The web identification (the URL, within angle brackets)

For example,

14. Göran Nordlund, "Documentation for Medical Equipment – a Real Cross-Cultural Challenge," in *Forum 2003 Preliminary Programme*, 19 Nov 2002, retrieved 2 Mar 2003 **<http://www.intecom.org/Forum 2003 Preliminary Programme>**

However, if the information has also been published in print form, the entry should refer to the original document *and* the website. List

(a) The full printed identification (for a book, article, technical paper, etc)
(b) The date the information was entered on the website (day, month, year)
(c) The URL identification (within angle brackets)

Here is an example:

> 15. "Keeping Track of Your Performance," in *RGI News*, No. 13, Winter 2001–2002, 18 Mar 2002, retrieved 16 Jul 2003 **<http://www.rgilearning.com/newsletters>**

If you need to insert a digital object identifier (DOI) as part of your source reference, insert it at the end of the reference. (A DOI is a multiple-digit system developed by international publishers to provide simple and direct cross-referencing of journal articles.) The DOI appears at the end of the entry and is preceded by the letters *doi* (lowercased). For example,

> Kevin Wilholden, "Techniques for Retrieving Deleted Documents," in *Canadian IT News*, 13:07, doi 10.1687/8976-2140.3.871.

When a DOI is used, the URL (and sometimes other details) can be omitted, since the DOI on its own will take the reader directly to the source.

For further information, we recommend you refer to pages 189 to 192 and 198–199 of the APA manual referenced at the end of Appendix A.

Referencing Information from a Newsgroup, Blog, Facebook Comment, or Twitter

Although it is possible to refer to a blog, Facebook, or Twitter comment, it is unlikely you will need to do so for a reference entry in a technical report. However, if it should happen, we suggest using a simplified version of a reference to a web entry, like this:

(a) Originator's real name (if known) or screen name
(b) The date of the comment
(c) The letters "Re:" followed by a short statement that identifies the message content, such as

> Re: Parallel research into water purity

(d) The type of message, stated in brackets, such as (blog message); (Mailing list message); (Facebook message); (Twitter message)
(e) The words: Retrieved from http://xxxxxxx

Referencing an Excerpt from an Online Book

The entry should contain this information:

(a) Author's (authors') names
(b) Title of chapter (in quotation marks)
(c) Title of book (in italics)
(d) Book identification (city of publication, publisher, copyright date), if available
(e) Date of electronic publication, or latest update
(f) Name of the organization responsible for the website
(g) Date the information was accessed
(h) URL identification

Here is an example:

16. Marvin LeTouche, "Maintaining Quality Levels," *Quality Control in the Mining Industry*. Chicago: Bronzeline Publishers, 2006. 15 Oct 2006; Mainstream Mining Inc; retrieved 8 Jan 2007 **<http://www.mainstream.ca/qc>**

Referencing an Excerpt from an Online Magazine Article

The following information should be recorded:

(a) Author's (authors') names (if author is identified)
(b) Title of article (in quotation marks)
(c) Title of magazine or journal (in italics)
(d) Issue number plus year of publication (in brackets)
(e) Page number
(f) Date accessed
(g) URL identification

For example,

17. Margery Leduc, "Are Handheld Computers Taking Over from Laptops?" *Computers Unlimited*, 8.3 (2006), retrieved 23 Oct 2006 **<http://www.bearskincollege/lib/online.html>**

Referencing Information in an Online Database

The information to be recorded is as follows:

(a) Author's (authors') names (if identified)
(b) Title of information (in quotation marks)
(c) Name of database (in italics)
(d) Name of organization owning site (if available)
(e) Date accessed
(f) URL identification

Here is a typical example:

18. "Radiant Heat in Tomorrow's Homes," *Heating Industry Standards Institute*. Heating Industry Institute, retrieved 10 May 2003 **<http://www.heating.standards.com/market/2455/616.html>**

For a text message:

(a) Sender's name
(b) Sender's cell or handheld device telephone number
(c) Recipient's name
(d) Recipient's cell or handheld device telephone number
(e) The date

For example,

19. Wilson Korminsky, 204-381-4770; text message to Renée LaPorte, 316-427-1137; 13 May 2011.

Additional Factors to Consider

Remember that when a magazine article, technical paper, or report is published as one of several documents bound into a volume, then it is listed within quotation marks (only the title of the volume is set in italics). But if the article, technical paper, or report is published as a *separate* document, the quotation marks are omitted and the title of the article, paper, or report is set in italic type, as in entry No. 9.

Every entry in a list of references must have a corresponding reference to it in the body of your report. At an appropriate place in the narrative you should insert a superscript (raised) number to identify the particular reference. It should look like this:

> Earlier tests[3] showed that speeds higher than 2680 rpm were impractical.
> *(Alternatively, the raised 3 could go here.)*

Numbering each entry simplifies cross-referencing between the text and the list of references

If you refer to the same document several times, your list of references needs to show full details for that document only the first time you refer to it. Subsequent references can be shown in a shortened form containing only the author's name (or authors' names) and the page number. For example, if the first reference you make is to an item on page 48 of the particular book described below, the entry in the list of references would be

> 1. Wayne D Barrett, *Management in a Technical Domain* (Halifax, Nova Scotia: Martin-Baisley Books, 2011), p 48.

Now suppose that your second and third sources are other documents, but for your fourth source you again refer to *Management in a Technical Domain*, this time quoting from page 159. Now you need list only the author's surname and the new page number.

> 4. Barrett, p 159.

Do the same for each future reference to the same document, simply changing the page number each time. (Note that the Latin terms *ibid.* and *op. cit.* are no longer used.) You can even make repeated references to several different documents by the same author by simply inserting the year of publication for the particular document between the author's name and the page number:

> 9. Barrett, 2011, p 159.

Preparing a Bibliography

A bibliography lists not only the documents to which you make direct reference, but also many other documents that deal with the topic. The major differences between a list of references and a bibliography are as follows:

- Bibliography entries are *not* numbered 1, 2, 3, etc.
- The name of the *first-named* author for each entry is reversed, so that the author's surname becomes the first word in the entry. (If there is a second-named author, that name is *not* reversed.)

In a bibliography, authors' surnames are used for easy cross-referencing

- The *first* line of each bibliography entry is extended about 12 mm to the left of all other lines (see Figure A-1).
- The entries are arranged in alphabetical sequence of first-named authors.
- Punctuation of individual entries is significantly different, with each entry being divided into three compartments separated by periods: (1) author identification (name, etc); (2) title of book or specific article; and (3) publishing details. (Positions of periods are shown in Figure A-1.)
- Page numbers are usually omitted, since generally the bibliography refers to the whole document. (Reference to a specific page is made within the narrative of the report.)

Most bibliography entries contain three distinct groups of information

Figure A-1 shows how to list bibliography entries from various sources. The entries for this bibliography have been created from some of the "reference" entries listed earlier. The number to the right of each entry is cross-referenced to the explanatory list below:

1. Book by one author
2. Book by two authors, seventh edition
3. Conference speech
4. Web source
5. Email
6. Report
7. Conversation
8. Journal/magazine article
9. Magazine article, with no author identification
10. Book by two authors
11. Section of book with section written by one author and whole book edited by another

Because a bibliography is not numbered, you cannot cross-refer directly to it simply by inserting a superscript number in the report narrative, as can be done with a list of references. The most common method is to insert a parenthetical reference in the narrative that includes the author's name (or authors' names) and the page number:

The text states author's name and relevant page number

> Although the tests conducted in the Northwest Territories (Faversham, p 261) showed only moderate decomposition...

Bibliography

1 Barrett, Wayne D. *Management in a Technical Domain*. Halifax, Nova Scotia: Martin-Baisley Books, 2011.

2 Blicq, Ron, and Lisa Moretto. *Technically-Write!*, Canadian 8th ed. Toronto, Ontario: Pearson Prentice Hall, 2012.

3 Cairns, Frances R, Elwood Martens and Associates, Fredericton, New Brunswick. Speaker at the 8th Potash Producers' Conference, Regina, Saskatchewan, September 16, 2010.

4 "Keeping Track of Your Performance." *RGI News*, No. 13, Winter 2001–2002. 23 June 2002. Retrieved 30 November 2003 <http://www.rgilearning.com/newsletters>

5 Lamont, Christine, Macro Engineering Inc, Toronto, Ontario. Email to Wayne Kominsky, No. 7 Design Group, Winnipeg, Manitoba, 31 October, 2011.

6 Lloyd, Derek A. *Effective Communication and Its Importance in Management Consulting*. Report No. 61, Smyrna Development Corporation, Montreal, Quebec, February 18, 2010.

7 Phillips, David R, Lakeside Power and Light Company, Thunder Bay, Ontario. Conversation with Anna King, H L Winman and Associates, Calgary, Alberta, January 7, 2011.

8 Rodman, Lilita. "You-attitude: A Linguistic Perspective." *Technostyle*, 17:2, Winter 2002.

9 "Selling to the EEC: Challenge of the New Millennium." *Technical Marketing*, 11:5, May 2007.

10 Shaver, David B, and John D Williams. *Management Techniques for a Research Environment*. Edmonton, Alberta: Witney Publications, 2010.

11 Wilson, Kevin G. "Preparation: The Key to a Good Talk." *Seven Ways to Make Better Technical Presentations*, ed Donna R Linwood. Vancouver, BC: Bonus Books Ltd, 2010.

Extending the first line of each entry to the left helps readers find specific source references

Figure A-1 A typical bibliography.

The full descriptive listing for Faversham's book or report would be carried in the bibliography.

If several publications by the same author are listed in the bibliography, then the date of the particular publication is included as a parenthetical reference to identify which document is being mentioned:

> The most significant tests were those conducted 22 km south of Old Crow, in the Yukon (Crosby, 2006, p 17), which showed that...

References

1. *MLA Handbook for Writers of Research Papers*, Seventh Edition (New York: The Modern Language Association of America, 2009).
2. *Publication Manual of the American Psychological Association*, Sixth Edition (Washington, DC: American Psychological Association, 2010).

Appendix B
Glossary of Technical Usage

A standard glossary of usage contains rules for combining words into compound terms, for forming abbreviations, for capitalizing, and for spelling unusual or difficult words. The glossary in *Technically-Write!* also offers suggestions for handling many of the technical terms peculiar to industry. Hence, it is oriented toward the technical rather than the literary writer.

The entries in the glossary are arranged alphabetically. Among them are words that are likely to be misused or misspelled, such as

- words that are similar and frequently confused with one another, such as *imply* and *infer*, *diplex* and *duplex*, *principal* and *principle*,
- common minor errors of grammar, such as *comprised of* (should be *comprises*), *most unique* (*unique* should not be compared), *liaise* (an unnatural verb formed from *liaison*), and
- words that are particularly prone to misspelling, such as *desiccant, oriented,* and *immitance*, and words for which there may be more than one "correct" spelling, (e.g. *program* or *programme*; *center* or *centre*).

Where two spellings of a word are in general use (e.g. *symposiums* and *symposia*), the glossary lists both and states which is preferred.

Definitions have been included when they will help you select the correct word for a given purpose, or to differentiate between similar words having different meanings. These definitions are intentionally brief and are intended only as a guide; for more comprehensive definitions, consult one of the authoritative dictionaries we recommend in Chapter 11 (pages 275 to 276).

All entries in the glossary are in lower case letters. Capital letters are used where capitals are recommended for a specific word, phrase, or abbreviation. Similarly, periods have been eliminated except where they form part of a specific entry. For example, the abbreviation for "inch" is *in.*, and the period that follows it is inserted intentionally to distinguish it from the word "in."

Finally, think of the glossary as a guide rather than a collection of hard and fast rules. Our language is continually changing, so that what was fashionable yesterday may seem pedantic today and a cliché tomorrow. We expect that in some cases your views will differ from ours. Where they do, we hope that the comments and suggestions we offer will help you to choose the right expression, word, abbreviation, or symbol, and that you will be able to do so both consistently and logically.

Occasionally you will see an abbreviation or spelling that does not conform exactly to the guidelines spelled out in Chapter 11. These anomalies are caused when an expression has been commonly accepted in the discipline in which the expression is used. The periods after B.Sc. are an example.

For further information on how to form compound terms, see pages 274 to 275.

A further reference is available on the web, provided by the International Organization for Standardization (commonly abbreviated to **ISO**), in ICS Fields 01.120 and 01.140.

The Glossary

General abbreviations used throughout the glossary:

abbr	abbreviate(d); abbreviation	n	noun
adj	adjective	pl	plural
Br	Britain; British	pref	prefer; preferred; preference
Can.	Canada; Canadian	rec	recommend(ed)
CP	Canadian Press	SI	International System of Units
def	definition	US	United States
lc	lower case	v	verb

A

a; an use *an* before words that begin with a silent *h* or a vowel; use *a* when the *h* is sounded or if the vowel is sounded as *w* or *y*; *an hour* but *a hotel, an onion* but *a European*

aberration

above- as a prefix, *above-* combines erratically: *aboveboard, above-cited, aboveground*

above-mentioned avoid using this expression in technical writing

abrasion

abscess

abscissa

absence

absolute abbr: **abs**

absorb(ent); adsorb(ent) *absorb* means to swallow up completely (as a sponge absorbs moisture); *adsorb* means to hold on the surface, as if by adhesion

abut; abutted; abutting; abutment

ac abbr for alternating current

accelerate; accelerator; accelerometer

accept; except *accept* means to receive (normally willingly), as in *he accepted the company's offer of employment*; *except* generally means exclude: *the night crew completed all the repairs except rewiring of the control panel*

access; accessed; accessible

accessory; accessories abbr: **accy**

accidental(ly)

accommodate; accommodation

account abbr: **acct**

accumulate; accumulator

acetaminophen

achieve means to conclude successfully, usually after considerable effort; avoid using *achieve* when the intended meaning is simply to reach or to get

acknowledg(e)ment *acknowledgment* pref in US, rec in Can.; *acknowledgement* pref in Br

acquiesce def: agree to

acquire; acquisition

across not *accross*

actually omit this word: it is seldom necessary in technical writing

actuator

adapt; adept; adopt *adapt* means to adjust to; *adept* means clever, proficient; *adopt* means to acquire and use

adapter; adaptor *adapter* pref

adaptation pref spelling; *adaption* also used in US but less common

addendum pl: *addenda*

adhere to never use *adhere by*

ad hoc def: set up for one occasion

adjective (compound) two or more words that combine to form an adjective are either joined by a hyphen or compounded into a single word; see pp 274–275; abbr: **adj**

adsorb(ent) see **absorb**

advanced power manager abbr: **apm** (pref) or **APM**

advantageous

adverse; averse *adverse* means unsatisfactory or unsuitable, as in *driving speed was adversely affected by the 20 cm of snow on the highway*; *averse* means in opposition to, as in *the staff were averse to working overtime* (they did not want to)

advice; advise use *advice* as a noun and *advise* as a verb: *the engineer's advice was sound; the technician had to advise the driver to take an alternative route*; spell: **adviser, advisable**

ae; e *ae* is pref in Br and common in Can., as in *aesthetic* and *anaemic*; *e* is pref in US and rec in Can., as in *esthetic* and *anemic*

aerate

aerial see **antenna**

aero- a prefix meaning *of the air*; it combines to form one word: *aerodynamics, aeronautical*; in some instances it has been replaced by *air: airplane, aircraft*

aesthetic; esthetic *esthetic* pref; see **ae**

affect; effect *affect* is used only as a verb, never as a noun; it means to produce an effect upon or to influence (*the potential difference affects the transit time*); *effect* can be used either as a verb or as a noun; as a verb it means to cause or to accomplish (*to effect a change*); as a noun it means the consequences or result of an occurrence (as in *the detrimental effect upon the environment*), or it refers to property, such as *personal effects*

aforementioned; aforesaid avoid using these ambiguous expressions

after- as a prefix, usually combines to form one word: *afteracceleration, afterburner, afterglow, afterheat, afterimage*; but *after-hours*

agenda although plural, *agenda* is generally treated as singular; *the agenda is complete*; pl *agendas* also is acceptable

aggravate the correct definition of *aggravate* is to increase or intensify (worsen) a situation; try not to use it when the meaning is *annoy* or *irritate*

aggregate

aging; ageing *aging* pref in US, rec in Can.; *ageing* pref in Br

agree to; agree with to be correct, you should *agree to* a suggestion or proposal, but *agree with* another person

air- as a prefix, normally combines to form one word: *airborne, airfield, airflow, airlift, airmail*; exceptions: *air-condition(ed) (er) (ing), air-cool(ed) (ing), air strike*

air horsepower abbr: **ahp**

airline; air line an *airline* provides aviation services; an *air line* is a line or pipe that carries air

algae

algorithm

alkali; alkaline pl: *alkalis* (pref) or *alkalies*

allot(ted)

all ready; already *all ready* means that all (everyone or everything) is ready: *already* means by this time: *the samples are all ready to be tested; the samples have already been tested*

all right def: everything is satisfactory; never use *alright*

all together; altogether *all together* means all collectively, as a group; *altogether* means completely, entirely: *the samples have been gathered all together, ready for testing; the samples are altogether useless*

allude; elude *allude* means refer to; *elude* means avoid

almost never contract *almost* to *most*; it is correct to write *most of the software has been tested*, but wrong to write *the software is most ready*

alphanumeric def: in alphabetical, then numerical, sequence

alternate; alternative *alternate(ly)* means by turn and turn about: *the inspector alternated between the two construction sites*; *alternative(ly)* offers a choice between two or more things: *the alternative is to find a replacement speaker, change the meeting into a workshop, or cancel the event*

alternating current abbr: **ac**

alternator

altitude abbr: **alt**

AM abbr for audio modulation

a.m. def: before noon (*ante meridiem*)

amateur

ambience; ambient abbr: **amb**

ambiguous; ambiguity

American standard code for information exchange abbr: **ASCII**

American Wire Gauge abbr: **AWG**

among; between use *among* when referring to three or more items; use *between* when referring to only two; avoid using *amongst*

amount; number use *amount* to refer to a general quantity: *the amount of time taken as sick leave has decreased*; use *number* to refer to items that can be counted: *the number of applicants to be interviewed was reduced to six*

ampere(s) abbr: **A** (pref) or **amp**; other abbr: **kA, mA, µA, nA, pA, A/m** (amperes per minute)

ampere-hour(s) abbr: **Ah** (pref) or **amp-hr** (more common)

amplitude modulation abbr: **AM**

an see **a**

anaemic; anemic *anemic* pref; see **ae**

anaesthetic; anesthetic *anesthetic* pref; see **ae**

analog(ue) *analog* pref in US; *analogue* pref in Br, rec in Can. (except in electronics and computers, as in *an analog cellphone*)

analogous; analogy

analyse; analyze *analyse* pref in Br, rec in Can.; *analyze* pref in US; also: **analyser; analysing**

analysis pl: **analyses**

anesthetic; anesthesia see **ae**

AND-gate

and/or avoid using this term; in most cases it can be replaced by one word

anemia; anemic see **ae**

angle def: an angular unit of measurement; an *angel* has wings

ångström abbr: **Å**

anion def: negative ion

anneal; annealed; annealing

annihilate; annihilated; annihilation

anomaly pl: *anomalies*

anonymous

ANSI abbr for American National Standards Institute

antarctic see **arctic**

ante- a prefix that means before; combines to form one word: *antecedent, anteroom*

ante meridiem def: before noon; abbr: **a.m.**; can also be written as *antemeridian*

antenna the proper plural in the technical sense is *antennas*; use *antennae* for zoology; *antenna* has generally replaced the obsolescent *aerial*

anti- a prefix meaning opposite or contradictory to; generally combines to form one word: *antiaircraft, antiastigmatism, anticapacitance, anticoincidence, antisymmetric*; if combining word starts with i or is a proper noun, insert a hyphen: *anti-icing, anti-American*

antimeridian def: the opposite of meridian (of longitude); e.g. the antimeridian of 96°30′W is 83°30′E

anybody; any body *anybody* means any person; *any body* means any object: *anybody can attend; discard the batch if you find any body containing foreign matter*

anyone; any one *anyone* means any person; *any one* means any single item: *you may take anyone with you; you may take any one of the samples*

anyway; any way *anyway* means in any case or in any event; *any way* means in any manner: *the results may not be as good as you expect, but we want to keep them anyway; the work may be done in any way you wish*

apm abbr for advanced power manager

apparatus; apparatuses

apparent; apparently

appear(s); seem(s) use *appears* to describe a condition that can be seen: *the equipment appears to be new*; use *seems* to describe a condition that cannot be seen: *the temperature seems to be low*

appendix def: the part of a report that contains supporting data; pl: *appendices* (pref in Br and Can.) or *appendixes* (pref in US)

applets def: JAVA computer programs

approximate(ly) abbr: **approx**; but *about* is a better word

aquarium(s)

arbitrary

arc; arced; arcing

archeology; archeologist; archeological

Archie

architect; architecture

arctic capitalize when referring to a specific area: *beyond the Arctic Circle*; otherwise use lc letters: *in the arctic*; never omit the first *c*

area the SI unit for area is the *hectare* (abbr: **ha**)

areal def: having area

around def: on all sides, surrounding, encircling

arrester, arrestor *arrester* pref

article

artifact

artwork

as avoid using when the intended meaning is *since* or *because*; to write *he could not open his desk as he left his keys at home* is incorrect (replace *as* with *because*)

ASCII abbr for American standard code for information exchange

as per avoid using this hackneyed expression, except in specifications

asphalt *asfalt* also used in US, but less pref

assembly; assemblies abbr: **assy**

assure means to state with confidence that something has been or will be made certain; it is sometimes confused with *ensure* and *insure*, which it does not replace; see **ensure**

asthma; asthmatic

as well as avoid using when the meaning is *and*

asymmetric; asymmetrical

asynchronous

atmosphere abbr: **atm**

atomic weight abbr: **at. wt**

attenuator

atto def: 10^{-18}; abbr: **a**

audible; audibility

audio frequency abbr: **af** (pref) or **a-f**

audiovisual

audit; auditor

auger; augur an *auger* is a tool; *augur* means to sense something

aural def: that which is heard; avoid confusing with *oral*, which means that which is spoken

author; writer avoid referring to yourself as *the author* or *the writer*; use *I, me,* or *my*

authoritative

authorize; authorise *authorize* pref

auto- a prefix meaning self; combines to form one word: *autoalarm, autoconduction, autogyro, autoionization, autoloading, automation, automaton, autotransformer, autoworker*

automatic frequency control abbr: **afc** (pref) or **AFC**

automatic volume control abbr: **avc** (pref) or **AVC**

auxiliary abbr: **aux**; pl: **auxiliaries**

average see **mean**

averse def: reluctant; see **adverse**

avocation def: an interest or hobby; avoid confusing with *vocation*

ax; axe *axe* pref in Br, rec in Can.; *ax* pref in US; pl: *axes*

axis the plural also is *axes*

azimuth abbr: **az**

B

bachelor of science abbr: B.Sc. (BS in US)

bacillus pl: **bacilli**

back- as a prefix in n form normally combines into one word: *backboard, backdate(d), backlog, backup*; but *back burner* (two words)

bacterium pl: **bacteria**

balance; remainder use *balance* to describe a state of equilibrium (as in *discontinuous permafrost is frozen soil delicately balanced between the frozen and unfrozen state*), or as an accounting term; use *remainder* when the meaning is the rest of: *the remainder of the shipment will be delivered next week*

balk(ed)/baulk(ed) *balk* pref in US; *baulk* pref in Br, rec in Can.

ball bearing

bandwidth

bare; bear *bare* means barren or exposed; *bear* means to withstand or to carry (or a wild animal)

barometer abbr: **bar.**

barrel, barrel(l)ed, barrel(l)ing *ll* pref in Br, rec in Can., single *l* pref in US; the abbr of *barrel(s)* is **bbl**

barretter

barring def: preventing, excepting

bases this is the plural of both *base* and *basis*

basically

basic input/output system abbr: **bios** (pref) or **BIOS**

baud; baud rate

baulk see **balk**

because; for use *because* when the clause it introduces identifies the cause of a result: *he could not open his desk because he left his keys at home*; use *for* when the clause introduces something less tangible: *he failed to complete the project on schedule, for reasons he preferred not to divulge*

becquerel def: a unit of activity of radionuclides (SI); abbr: **Bq**; other abbr: **PBq, TBq, GBq, kBq**

behavior/behaviour *behaviour* pref in Br and rec for Can.; *behavior* pref in US

benefit; benefit(t)ed; benefit(t)ing single *t* pref

beside; besides *beside* means alongside, at the side of; *besides* means as well as

between see **among**

bi- a prefix meaning two or twice; combines to form one word: *biangular, bicultural, bidirectional, bifilar, bilateral, bilingual, bimetallic, bizonal*

biannual(ly); biennial(ly) *biannual(ly)* means twice a year; *biennial(ly)* means every two years

bias; biased; biases; biasing

billion def: 10^9 (Can. and US); 10^{12} (Br)

billion electron volts although the pref abbr is **GEV**, *beV* and *bev* are more commonly used

Bill of Materials abbr: **BOM**

bimonthly def: every two months

binary

binaural

bioelectronics

bionics def: application of biological techniques to electronic design

bios basic input/ouput system: a program that starts the computer and manages data flow between the operating system and the hard disk, video adapter, keyboard, mouse, printer, etc

bird's-eye (view)

bit; kilobit abbr: **b; kb** (pref) or **kbit**

Bitnet

bits per second abbr: **bps**

biweekly def: every two weeks

blow- as a prefix, combines to form one word as a noun: *blowhole, blowoff, blowout*

blueprint

blur; blurred; blurring; blurry

board feet abbr: **fbm** (derived from *foot board measure*)

boiling point abbr: **bp**

boldface (type)

bookkeeper

boot *to boot* means the operating system is being loaded into the computer; also *reboot*

borderline

bps bits per second

brakedrum; brake lining; brakeshoe

brake horsepower; brake horsepower-hour abbr: **bhp, bhp-hr**

brand-new

break- when used as a prefix to form a compound noun or adj, *break* combines into one word: *breakaway, breakdown, breakup*; in the verb form it retains its single-word identity: *it was time to break up the meeting*

bridging

Brinell hardness number abbr: **Bhn**

British thermal unit abbr: **BTU**

B.Sc. abbr for Bachelor of Science

budget; budgeted; budgeting

build- compounds as one word in n or adj form, as in *corrosive buildup*; use two words in v form, as in *to build up our resources, we have...*

buoy; buoyant

burned; burnt *burned* pref in Can. and US; *burnt* pref in Br

bur(r) *burr* pref

buses; bused; busing; bus bar

business; businesslike; businessperson avoid using *businessman* or *businesswoman* unless referring to a specific male or female person

by- as a prefix, *by-* normally combines to form one word: *bylaw, byline, bypass, byproduct*

byte abbr: **kbyte** and **Mbyte** (pref), or **kB** and **MB**

B2B abbr for business-to-business (or **e-biz**); the exchange of products, services or information between businesses

B2G abbr for business-to-government; permits businesses and government agencies to use central websites to exchange information and do business with each other

C

cache memory

calendar; calender; colander a *calendar* is the arrangement of the days in a year; *calender* is the finish on paper or cloth; a *colander* is a sieve

calibre; caliber *calibre* pref in Br and rec in Can.; *caliber* pref in US

calk/caulk *caulk, caulked, caulking* pref in Br, rec for Can.; *calk* pref in US

cal(l)iper *caliper* pref

calorie abbr: **cal**

calorimeter; colourimeter a *calorimeter* measures quantity of heat; a *colourimeter* measures colour

cancel(l)ed; cancel(l)ing *ll* pref in Br, rec in Can.; single *l* pref in US; **cancel** always has single *l*; **cancellation** always has *ll*

candela def: unit of luminous intensity (replaces *candle*); abbr: **cd**; recommended abbr for candela per square foot and square metre are **cd/ft²** and **cd/m²**

candlepower; candlehour(s) abbr: **cp, c-hr**

candoluminescence

cannot one word pref; avoid using *can't* in technical writing

canvas; canvass *canvas* is a coarse cloth used for tents; *canvass* means to solicit

capacitor

capacity for never use *capacity to* or *capacity of*

capillary

capital letters abbr: **caps.**

car- as a prefix normally combines to form one word: *carload, carlot, carpool, carwash*

carburet(t)or *carburetor* pref; a third, seldom used spelling is *carburetter*; also: **carburetion**

carcino- as a prefix combines to form one word

cartilage

case- as a prefix normally combines to form one word: *casebook, caseharden, casework(er)*; exceptions: *case history, case study*

cassette

caster; castor use *caster* when the meaning is to swivel freely, and *castor* when referring to castor oil, etc

catalog(ue) *catalogue(d)* and *cataloguing* pref in Can. and Br; *catalog(ed)* and *cataloging* pref in US

catalyst; catalytic

cathode-ray tube abbr: **crt** (pref) or **CRT** (commonly used)

cation def: positive ion

caulk pref spelling; also see **calk**

CD-ROM

-ceed; -cede; -sede only one word ends in *-sede*: *supersede*; only three words end in *-ceed*: *exceed, proceed, succeed*; all others end in *-cede*: e.g. *precede, concede*

cellphone abbr: **cell**; called *mobile* in Br

Celsius abbr: **C**; see **temperature**

cement; concrete *cement* is the powder used to make concrete; *concrete* is the hard, finished product

central processing unit abbr: **cpu** (pref) or **CPU**

centre; center *centre, centred, centring, central* pref in Br, rec in Can.; *center, centered, centering, central* pref in US

centreline abbr: ℄(pref) or CL

centre-to-centre abbr: c-c

centi- def: 10^{-2}; as a prefix combines to form one word: *centiampere, centigram*; abbr: **c**; other abbr:

centigram	**cg**
centilitre	**cL**
centimetre	**cm**
centimetre-gram-second	**cgs**
centimetres per second	**cm/s**
square centimetre	**cm^2**

centigrade abbr: **C**; in SI, *centigrade* has been replaced by *Celsius*; see **temperature**

centri- a prefix meaning centre; combines to form one word: *centrifugal, centripetal*

cga colour/graphics adapter

chair avoid using *chairman* or *chairwoman*

chamfer

changeable; changeover (n and adj); **change over** (v)

channel(l)ed; channel(l)ing *ll* pref in Br, rec in Can.; single *l* pref in US

chargeable

chassis both singular and plural are spelled the same

chat room a website, part of a website, or an online service in which users with a common interest can communicate in real time (see **real time**)

check- as a prefix combines to form one word: *checklist, checkoff, checkpoint* and *checkup* are one word as n or adj, but two words in v form

checksum def: a term used in computer technology

cheque in US, spelled *check*

chisel(l)ed; chisel(l)ing *ll* pref in Br, rec in Can., single *l* pref in US

chlorophyll

chrominance

chromosome

chunk; chunking

cipher in Br also spelled *cypher*

circuit abbr: **cct**; also: **circuitous; circuit breaker**

cite def: to quote; see **site**

cleanup (n and adj); **clean up** (v)

climate avoid confusing *climate* with *weather*: *climate* is the average type of weather, determined over a number of years, experienced at a particular place; *weather* is the state of the atmospheric conditions at a specific place at a specific time

clockwise (turn) abbr: **CW**

cmc computer-mediated communication

cmos complementary metal-oxide conductor

co- as a prefix, *co-* generally means jointly or together; it usually combines to form one word: *coexist, coequal, cooperate, coordinate, coplanar* (*co-worker* is an exception); it is also used as the abbr for *complement of* (an arc or angle) as in *codeclination* and *colatitude*

coalesce; coalescent

coarse; course *coarse* means rough in texture or of poor quality; *course* implies movement or passage of time; *a coarse granular material; the technical writing course*

coaxial abbr: **coax.**

Cobol def: common business-oriented language

coefficient abbr: **coef**

coerce; coercion

collaborate; collaborator avoid writing *collaborate together* (delete *together*)

collapsible

collateral

collide use *collide* to describe two moving objects that bang or crash into one another; use *drove into* or *bumped into* if one object is stationary

cologarithm abbr: **colog**

colon when a colon is inserted in the middle of a sentence to introduce an example or short statement, the first word following the colon is not capitalized; see guidelines on pp 256–257 for inserting a colon at, or omitting it from, the end of a sentence that introduces a list or subparagraphs; a hyphen should not be inserted after a colon

colo(u)r *color* pref in US; *colour* pref in Br, rec in Can.

colour/graphics adapter abbr: **cga** (pref) or **CGA**

colourimeter see **calorimeter**

column abbr: **col.**

combustible

comma a comma normally need not be used immediately before *and, but,* and *or*, but may be inserted if to do so will increase understanding or avoid ambiguity

commence in technical writing, replace *commence* with the more direct *begin* or *start*

commit; commitment; committed; committing

committee

communicate it is vague to write *I communicated the results to the client*; use a clearer verb: *I emailed/faxed/wrote/telephoned/text-messaged*

compare; comparable; comparison; comparative use *compared to* when suggesting a general likeness; use *compared with* when making a definite comparison

compatible; compatibility

complement; compliment *complement* means the balance required to make up a full quantity or a complete set; to *compliment* means to praise; *in a right angle, the complement of 60° is 30°; Mr Perchanski complimented Janet Rudman for writing a good report*

complementary metal-oxide conductor abbr: **cmos** (pref) or **CMOS**

composed of; comprising; consists of all three terms mean "made up of" (specific items); if any one of these terms is followed by a list of items, it implies that the list is complete; if the list is not complete, the term should be replaced by *includes* or *including*

compound terms two or more words that combine to form a compound term are joined by a hyphen or are written as one word, depending on accepted usage and whether they form a verb, noun, or adjective; the trend is toward one-word compounds (see pp 274–275)

comprise; comprised; comprising to write *comprised of* is incorrect, because the verb comprise includes the preposition *of*

computer-mediated communication abbr: **cmc** (pref) or **CMC**

concrete the hard, rock-like substance used to make roads, bridges and buildings; avoid confusing with *cement*

concur; concurred; concurrent; concurring

condenser

conductor

config.sys a text file containing DOS commands that tells the operating system how the computer is set up

conform use *conform to* when the meaning is to abide by; use *conform with* when the meaning is to agree with

connection; connexion *connection* pref in Can. and US; *connexion* is alternative spelling in Br

conscience; conscientious

conscious

consensus means a general agreement of opinion; hence to write *consensus of opinion* is incorrect; e.g. write: *the consensus was that a further series of tests would be necessary*

consistent with never *consistent of*

consists of; consisting of see **composed of**

contact *contact* should not be used as a verb when *email, write, visit, speak, fax,* or *telephone* better describes the action taken

continual; continuous *continual(ly)* means happens frequently but not all the time: *the generator is continually being overloaded* (is frequently overloaded); *continuous(ly)* means goes on and on without stopping: *the noise level is continuously at or above 80 dB* (it never drops below 80 dB)

continue(d) abbr: **cont**

continuous wave abbr: **cw**

contra- as a prefix normally combines into a single word

contrast when used as a verb, *contrast* is followed by *with*; when used as a noun, it may be followed by either *to* or *with* (*with* pref)

control; controlled; controlling; controller

convenor

conversant with never *conversant of*

converter; convertible

conveyor

cooperate or **co-operate**

coordinate; coordinator

copyright not *copywrite*

corollary

correlate

correspond *to correspond to* suggests a resemblance; *to correspond with* means to communicate in writing

corroborate

corrode; corridible; corrosive

cosecant abbr: **csc** (pref) or **cosec**

cosine abbr: **cos**

cotangent abbr: **cot**

coulomb def: a quantity of electricity, electric charge (SI); abbr: **C**; other abbr: **kC, mC, μC, nC, pC, C/m²**

counter- a prefix meaning opposite or reciprocal; combines to form one word: *counteract, counterbalance, counterflow, counterweight*

counterclockwise (turn) abbr: **CCW**

counterelectromotive force abbr: **cemf**; also known as *back emf*

counts per minute abbr: **cpm**

course see **coarse**

cpu; CPU central processing unit; see **microprocessor**

criteria; criterion the singular is *criterion*, the plural is *criteria*: e.g. *one criterion; seven criteria*

criticism; criticize; critique

cross- as a prefix combines erratically: *cross-border, cross-check, cross-examine, crosshatch, crosstalk, cross-purpose, cross section*

cross-refer(ence) abbr: **x-ref**

crt abbr for cathode-ray tube

cryogenic

cryptic

crystal abbr: **xtal**

crystalline; crystallize

cubic abbr: **cu** or ³; other abbr:

cubic centimetre(s)	**cm³** (pref); **cc**
cubic decimetre(s)	**dm³**
cubic foot (feet)	**ft³** (pref); **cu ft**
cubic feet per minute	**cfm** (pref); **ft³/min**
cubic feet per second	**cfs** (pref); **ft³/sec**
cubic inch(es)	**in.³** (pref); **cu in.**
cubic metre(s)	**m³**
cubic millimetre(s)	**mm³**
cubic yard(s)	**yd³** (pref); **cu yd**

curb; kerb *curb* pref in Can. and US; *kerb* pref in Br

curie abbr: **Ci**; other abbr: **mCi, μCi**; in SI the *curie* is replaced by the *becquerel* (**Bq**)

current; currant *current* refers to a flow (of water, electricity); a *currant* is a dried fruit

curriculum pl: *curriculums* (pref) or *curricula*

cursor

cw continuous wave

cyberspace

cycles per minute abbr: **cpm**

cycles per second abbr: **cps**; although occasionally used, this term has been replaced by *hertz*

cylinder; cylindrical abbr: **cyl**

D

daraf def: the unit of elastance

data def: gathered facts; although *data* is plural (derived from the singular *datum*, which is rarely used), it is more acceptable to use it as a singular noun: *when all the data has been received, the analysis will begin*

database

dateline

date(s) avoid vague statements such as "last month" and "next year" because they soon become indefinite; write a specific date, using day (in numerals), month (spelled out), and year (in numerals): *January 27, 2008,* or *27 January 2008* (the latter form has no punctuation); to abbreviate, reduce month to first three letters and year to last two digits: *Jan 27, 08* or *27 Jan 08*; "th" is unnecessary after the "27"

day- as a prefix, generally combines to form one word: *daybook, daylight, daytime, daywork*

days days of the week are capitalized: *Monday, Tuesday*

dc direct current

de- a prefix that generally combines to form one word: *deaccentuate, deactivate, decentralize, decode, decompress, deemphasize, deenergize, derate, destagger*; exceptions are *de-ionize* and *de-ice*

dead- as a prefix combines erratically: *deadbeat, dead centre, dead end, deadline, deadweight, deadwood*

debug; debugged; debugging

decelerate def: to slow down; never use *deaccelerate*

decibel abbr: **dB**; the abbr for decibel referred to 1 mW is **dBm**

decimals for values less than unity (one), place a zero before the decimal point: *0.17, 0.0017*

decimate def: to reduce by one-tenth; can also mean to destroy much of

decimetre abbr: **dm**

declination abbr: **dec**

deductible

defective; deficient *defective* means unserviceable or damaged (generally lacking in quality); *deficient* means lacking in quantity (it is derived from *deficit*), and in the military sense incomplete: *a short circuit resulted in a defective transmitter; the installation was completed on schedule except for a deficient rotary coupler that will not be delivered until June 10*

defence; defense *defence* pref in Can. and Br; *defense* pref in US; **defensive** always has an *s*

defer; deferred; deferring; deferrable; deference

definite; definitive *definite* means exact, precise; *definitive* means conclusive, fully evolved; e.g. *a definite price* is a firm price; *a definitive statement* concerns a topic that has been thoroughly considered and evaluated

defuse; diffuse *defuse* means to ease tension; *diffuse* means scattered

degree(s) abbr: **deg** (pref in narrative) or ° (following numerals); see **temperature**

demarcation

demi- a little-used prefix meaning half (generally replaced by *semi-*); combines to form one word: *demivolt*

demonstrate; demonstrator; demonstrable not *demonstratable*

depend; dependence; dependent (adj); **dependant** (n); **dependable**

deprecate; depreciate *deprecate* means to disapprove of; *depreciate* means to reduce the value of: *the use of "as per" in technical writing is deprecated; the vehicle's value depreciated by 50% the first year and 20% the second year*

depth

desiccant, desiccate(d)

desirable

desktop

desktop publishing abbr: **dtp** (pref) or **DTP**

desktop video conference abbr: **dtv** (pref) or **DTV**

deter; deterred; deterrence; deterrent; deterring

deteriorate

develop not *develope*

device; devise the noun is *device*, the verb is *devise*: *a unique device; he devised a new software program*

dext(e)rous *dexterous* pref

diagnose; diagnosis pl: *diagnoses*

diagram(m)ed; diagram(m)ing *mm* pref in Can. and Br; single *m* pref in US; **diagram** always has a single *m*; **diagrammatically** always has *mm*

dial(l)ed; dial(l)ing *ll* pref in Br, rec in Can.; single *l* pref in US

dialog(ue) *dialogue* pref

dialysis

diameter abbr: **dia**

diaphragm

diazo

didn't never use this contraction in technical writing; use *did not*

die; dye; dying *die* means to end life; *dye* means a change of colour

dielectric

diesel; diesel-electric

dietitian

differ use *differ from* to demonstrate a difference; use *differ with* to describe a difference of opinion

different *different from* is preferred; *different to* is sometimes used; *different than* should never be used

diffraction

diffusion; diffusible

digital library a collection of documents organized electronically

dilemma means to be faced with a choice between two unhappy alternatives; should not be used as a synonym for *difficulty*

diplex; duplex *diplex operation* means the simultaneous transmissions of two signals using a single feature, e.g. an antenna; *duplex operation* means that both ends can transmit and receive simultaneously

direct current abbr: **dc**

directly def: immediately; do not use when the meaning is *as soon as*

disassemble; dissemble *disassemble* means to take apart; *dissemble* means to conceal facts or put on a false appearance

disassociate see **dissociate**

disc; disk *disc* pref in Br, rec in Can. (except in computer technology, where *disk* is more common); *disk* pref in US

discernible

discolo(u)r *discolour* pref in UK, rec in Can.; *discolor* pref in US

discreet; discrete *discreet* means prudent or discerning: *his answer was discreet*; *discrete* means individually distinctive and separate: *discrete channels*; **discretion** is formed from *discreet*, not from *discrete*

disinterested; uninterested *disinterested* means unbiased, impartial; *uninterested* means not interested

disk cache

disk operating system abbr: **DOS**

dispatch; despatch *dispatch* pref

dispel; dispelled

disseminate

dissimilar

dissipate

dissociate; disassociate *dissociate* pref

distil(l) *distil* pref in Can. and Br; *distill* pref in US; **distillate, distillation, distilled** and **distiller** always have *ll*

distribute; distributor

don't; doesn't such contractions should not appear in technical writing

donut; doughnut for electronics/nucleonics, use *donut*

doppler capitalize only when referring to the Doppler principle

DOS disk operating system

double- as a prefix combines erratically: *double-barrelled, doublecheck, doublecross, double-duty, double entry, doublefaced, doubletalk*

down- as a prefix combines into one word: *downgrade, downrange, downtime, downwind*

dozen abbr: **doz**

drafting; draftsperson avoid writing *draftsman* or *draftswoman*

drawing(s) abbr: **dwg**

drier; dryer the adjective is always *drier*; the pref noun is *dryer* in Can. and US, and *drier* in Br: *this material is drier; place the others back in the dryer*

drop; droppable; dropped; dropping

dtp desktop publishing

dtv desktop video conferencing

due to an overused expression; *because of* pref

duo- a prefix meaning two; combines to form one word: *duocone, duodiode, duophase*

duplex see **diplex**

duplicator

dye; dying also see *die*

dynamic data exchange an operating system function which allows information to be shared between programs

dysfunction not *disfunction*

E

each abbr: **ea**

east capitalize only if *east* is part of the name of a specific location: *East Africa*; otherwise use lc letters: *the east coast of Canada*; abbr: **E**; the abbr for *east-west* (control, movement) is **E-W**; *eastbound* and *eastward* are written as one word

e-Bay

e-biz abbr for business conducted electronically

eccentric; eccentricity

echo; echoes

ecommerce electronic commerce, or EC; the buying or selling of goods and services on the internet; also called **e-business**

economic; economical use *economical* to describe economy (of funds, effort, time); use *economic* when writing about economics: *an economical operation* (it did not cost much); *an economic disaster* (it will have a major effect on the economy)

EDI Electronic Data Interchange; a standard format for exchanging business data

effect see **affect**

efficacy; efficiency *efficacy* means effectiveness, ability to do a job; *efficiency* is a measurement of capability, the ratio of work done to energy expended: *we hired a consultant to assess the efficacy of our training methods; the power house is to have a high-efficiency boiler*

e.g. def: *for example*; avoid confusing with **i.e.**; no comma is necessary after **e.g.**; may also be abbr **eg**

ega enhanced graphics adapter; abbr also **EGA**

eighth

electric(al) if in doubt, use *electric*; generally, *electric* means produces or carries electricity, whereas *electrical* means related to the generation or carrying of electricity; abbr: **elec**

electro- a prefix generally meaning pertaining to electricity; it normally combines to form one word: *electroacoustic, electroanalysis, electrodeposition, electromechanical, electroplate*; if the combining word starts with *o*, insert a hyphen: *electro-optics, electro-osmosis*

e-learning

electromagnetic units abbr: **emu**

electromotive force abbr: **emf**

electronic(s) use *electronic* as an adjective, *electronics* as a noun: *electronic countermeasures; your career in electronics*

electronic mail abbr: **email**

electron volt(s) abbr: **eV** (pref) or **ev**

electrostatic units abbr: **esu**

elicit; illicit *elicit* means to obtain or identify; *illicit* means illegal

eligible; illegible *eligible* means "meets the required conditions"; also: *eligibility*; *illegible* means unreadable

ellipse; ellipsis pl: *ellipses*

email

embarrass; embarrassed; embarrassing; embarrassment

embed; embedded

embryo; embryos

emf abbr for electromotive force

emigrate; immigrate *emigrate* means to go away from; *immigrate* means to come into

emit; emitter; emittance; emission; emissivity

emu abbr for electromagnetic units

emulate; emulation

enamel(l)ed; enamel(l)ing *ll* pref in Br, rec in Can.; single *l* pref in US

encase; incase *encase* pref

encipher

enclose; inclose *enclose* pref; *inclose* is used mainly as a legal term

endeavo(u)r *endeavour* pref in Br, rec for Can.; *endeavor* pref in US

enforce not *inforce*

engineer; engineered; engineering

enhanced graphics adapter abbr: **ega** (pref) or **EGA**

enquire; inquire *enquire* pref

enrol; enroll both are correct, but *enrol* pref; universal usage prefers *ll* for **enrolled** and **enrolling,** but a single *l* for **enrolment**

en route def: on the road, on the way; never use *on route*

ensure; insure; assure use *ensure* when the meaning is to make certain of: *the new meter will ensure accurate calibration*; use *insure* when the meaning is to protect against financial loss: *we insured all our drivers*; use *assure* when the meaning is to state with confidence that something has been or will be made certain: *he assured the meeting that production would increase by 8%*

entrepreneur; entrepreneurial

entrust; intrust *entrust* pref

envelop; envelope *envelop* is a verb that means to surround or cover completely; *envelope* is a noun that means a wrapper or a covering

environment; environmental; environmentally

EPROM def: abbr for erasable programmable read-only memory; can also be abbr as **eprom**

equal; equal(l)ed; equal(l)ing *equal, equality, equalize* always have single *l*; *equaled, equaling* pref in US, rec in Can.; *equalled, equalling* pref in Br; *equalize* can be spelled *equalise* in Br

equi- a prefix that means equality; combines to form one word: *equiphase, equipotential, equisignal*

equilibrium; equilibriums

equip; equipped; equipping; equipment

equivalent abbr: **equiv**

erase; erasable

errata although *errata* is plural (from the singular *erratum*, which is seldom used), it can be used as a singular or plural noun: both *the errata are ready* and *the errata is complete* are acceptable

erratic

erroneous

escalator

esker

especially; specially *specially* pref when it refers to an adjective, as in: *a specially trained crew*; *especially* should introduce a phrase, as in: *they were well trained, especially the computer technicians*

esthetic see **ae**

esu abbr for electrostatic unit

et al. def: and others; now rarely used

et cetera def: and so forth, and so on; abbr: **etc**; use with care in technical writing: *etc* can create an impression of vagueness or unsureness: *the transmitters, etc, were tested* sounds much less definite than *the transmitter, modulator, and power supply were tested* (or, if to restate all the equipment is too repetitious, *the transmitting equipment was tested*)

euro European currency; abbr: EUR

everybody; every body *everybody* means every person, or all the persons; *every body* means every single body: *everybody was present; every body was examined for gun-powder scars*

everyone; every one *everyone* means every person, or all the persons; *every one* means every single item: *everyone is insured; every one of the samples had to be tested in a saline solution*

exa def: 10^{18}; abbr: **E**

exaggerate

exceed

excel; excelled; excellent; excelling

except def: to exclude; see **accept**

exhaust

exhibit; exhibitor

exorbitant

expedite; expediter (pref) or **expeditor**

explicit; implicit *explicit* means clearly stated, exact; *implicit* means implied (the meaning has to be inferred from the words): *the supervisor gave explicit instructions* (they were clear); *that the manager was angry was implicit in the words he used*

extemporaneous

extracurricular

extranet a private network that uses the internet to securely share part of a business's information with users outside an organization

extraordinary

extremely high frequency abbr: **ehf**

eye- as a prefix, normally combines into one word: *eyeball, eyesight, eyewitness*; also: **eyed**

F

face- as a prefix normally combines to form one word: *facedown, facelift, faceplate*; exceptions: *face-saver, face-saving*

Fahrenheit abbr: **F**; see **temperature**

fail-safe

fallout one word as n; two words as v

familiarize; familiarization

farad def: a unit of electric capacitance; abbr: **F**; other abbr: **μF, nF, pF**

farfetched; far-out; far-reaching; farseeing; farsighted

farther; further *farther* means greater distance: *he travelled farther than the other salespeople*; *further* means a continuation of (as an adjective) or to advance (as a verb): *the promotion was a further step in her career plan*, and *to further his education, he took a part-time course in industrial drafting*

fasten; fastener

faultfinder; faultfinding

favo(u)r *favour* pref in Br and rec in Can.; *favor* pref in US; also *favourite* in Br and Can.

feasible; feasibility

February

feet; foot abbr: **ft**; other abbr:

foot board measure (board feet)	**fbm**
feet per minute	**fpm**
feet per second	**fps**
foot-candle(s)	**fc** (pref); **ft-c**
foot-pound(s)	**fp** (pref); **ft-lb**
foot-pound-second (system)	**fps** system

femto def: 10^{-15}; abbr: **f**; other abbr:

femtoampere(s)	**fA**
femtovolt(s)	**fV**

ferri- a prefix meaning contains iron in the ferric state; combines to form one word: *ferricyanide, ferrimagnetic*

ferro- a prefix meaning contains iron in the ferrous state; combines to form one word: *ferroelectric, ferromagnetic, ferrometer*

ferrule; ferule a *ferrule* is a metal cap or lid; a *ferule* is a ruler

fewer; less use *fewer* to refer to items that can be counted: *fewer technicians than we predicted have been assigned to the project*; use *less* to refer to general quantities: *there was less water than predicted*

fibre; fiber; fibrous *fibre, fibreglass, fibreoptic* pref in Br, rec in Can.; *fiber, fiberglass, fiberoptic* pref in US; *Fiberglas* is a US trade name

field- as a prefix normally does not combine into a single word or hyphenated form: *field glasses, field test, field trip*; but: *fieldwork(er)*

figure numbers in text, spell out the word *Figure* in full, or abbr it to **Fig.**: *the circuit diagram in Figure 26* and *for details, see Fig. 7*; use the abbreviated form beneath the illustration; always use numerals for the figure number

file transfer protocol abbr: **ftp** (pref) or **FTP**

final; finally; finalize

fire- as a prefix combines erratically: *firearm, fire alarm, firebreak, fire drill,* *fire escape, fire extinguisher, firefighter, firepower, fireproof, fire sale, fire wall*

firmware

first to write *the first two…* (or three, etc) is better than to write *the two first…*; never use *firstly*; as a prefix, *first-* combines erratically: *first-class, firsthand, first-rate*

fix in technical usage, *fix* means to firm up or establish as a permanent fact; avoid using it when the meaning is to repair

flameout; flameproof

flammable def: easily ignited; see **inflammable**

flatcar

flavo(u)r *flavour* pref in Br, rec in Can.; *flavor* pref in US

flexible

flight- usually combines to form two words: *flight control, flight deck, flight plan*

flip-flop

floe floating ice

flotation this is the correct spelling for describing an item that floats: *flotation gear*

flowchart

fluid abbr: **fl**; the abbr for fluid ounces is **fl oz**

fluorescence; fluorescent

fluorine; fluoridation; fluorite; fluorocarbon; fluoroscope

flyer not *flier*

FM abbr for frequency modulation

focus; focused; focusing; focuses pl: *focuses* (pref in Can. and US) or *foci* (pref in Br)

followup one word as n or adj; two words as v: **follow up**

foot- as a prefix normally combines into one word: *footbridge, footcandle, foothold, footnote, footwork*; also see **feet**

for see **because**

forceful; forcible use *forceful* to describe a person's character; use *forcible* to describe physical force

fore- def: that which goes before; as a prefix normally combines into one word: *foreclose, forefront, foreground, foreknowledge, foremost, foresee, forestall, forethought, forewarn*

forecast this spelling is correct for present and past tense

forego; forgo *forego* means to go before; *forgo* means to go without

foreman avoid using in a general sense, except when referring to a person specifically, as in *John Hayward, the foreman*; never use *forewoman* (a better word is *supervisor*)

foresee; foreseeable

forestall

foreword; forward a *foreword* is a preface or preamble to a book; *forward* means onward: *the scope is defined in the foreword to the book; he requested that we move forward*

for example abbr: **e.g.** (pref) or **eg**

former; first use *former* to refer to the first of only two things; use *first* if there are more than two

formula pl: *formulas* (pref in Can. and US) or *formulae* (pref in Br)

Fortran def: formula translation

forty def: 40; it is not spelled *fourty*

fourth def: 4th; it is not spelled *forth*

fractions when writing fractions that are less than unity, spell them out in descriptive narrative: *by the end of the heat run, nine-tenths of the installation had been completed*; for technical details use decimals rather than fractions, as in *a flat case 0.75 m wide by 0.060 m deep*, except when a quantity is normally stated as a fraction (such as *3/8 in. plywood*)

free- as a prefix normally combines into one word: *freehand, freehold, freestanding, freeway, freewheel*

free from use *free from* rather than *free of*: *he is free from prejudice*

free on board abbr: **fob** (pref), **f.o.b.** (commonly used), or **FOB**

frequency abbr: **freq**

frequency modulation abbr: **FM**

ftp file transfer protocol

fulfil(l) *fulfil, fulfilment* pref in Br, rec in Can.; *fulfill, fulfillment* pref in US; fulfilled and fulfilling always have *ll*

fungus pl: *fungi*

funnel(l)ed; funnel(l)ing single *l* pref

further see **farther**

fuse as a verb, means join together or weld; as a noun, means a circuit protection device or (in Br) a detonation initiation device

fuselage

fuze def: a detonation initiation device

G

gadget; gadgetry

gage US alternative spelling of *gauge*

gallon gallons differ between US (3.785 dm^3) and Br (4.546 dm^3); abbr: **gal**; other abbr:

gallons per day	**gpd**
gallons per hour	**gph**
gallons per minute	**gpm**
gallons per second	**gps**

gang; ganged; ganging

gas; gases; gassed; gassing; gaseous; gassy

gauge *gauging* does not retain the *e*

gearbox; gearshift

geiger (counter)

gelatin(e) *gelatin* pref

genealogy; genealogist

geo- a prefix meaning of the earth; combines to form one word; *geocentric, geodesic, geomagnetic, geophysics*

giga def: 10^9, abbr: **G**; other abbr:

gigabecquerel(s)	GBq
gigahertz	GHz
gigajoule(s)	GJ
gigaohm(s)	GΩ; Gohm
gigapascal(s)	GPa
gigavolt(s)	GV

gimbal

glue; glueing; gluey

glycerin(e) *glycerine* pref in Br, rec in Can.; *glycerin* pref in US

gnd abbr for *ground*

Gopher def: an internet search tool

government capitalize when referring to a specific government either directly or by implication; use lc if the meaning is government generally: *the Canadian Government; the Government specifications; no government would sanction such restrictions*

gram abbr: **g**; abbr for **gram-calorie** is **g-cal**

grammar; grammatical(ly)

grateful not *greatful*

gray def: absorbed dose of ionizing radiation (SI); abbr: **Gy**; other abbr: **mGy, µGy**; in SI, the *gray* replaces the *rad*

Greenwich mean time abbr: **GMT**

grey; gray def: a colour; *grey* pref in Br, rec in Can.; *gray* pref in US

grill(e) when the meaning is a loudspeaker covering or a grating, *grille* pref; when referring to cooking, use *grill*

ground (electrical) abbr: **gnd**; *groundcrew; ground floor*

GST abbr for goods and services tax (Canada)

guage wrongly spelled; the correct spelling is *gauge*

guarantee never *guaranty*; also *guarantor*

guesstimate

GUI a graphical (rather than textual) user interface to a computer; pronounced *goo-ee*

guideline

gyroscope abbr: **gyro**

H

half; halved; halves; halving as a prefix, *half* combines erratically; some common compounds are *half-hourly, half-life, half-monthly, halftone, halfwave*; for others, consult your dictionary

hand- as a prefix normally combines to form one word: *handbill, handbook, handful, handfuls, handhold, handmade, handpicked, handset, handshake*

hangar; hanger a *hangar* is a large building for housing aircraft; a *hanger* is a supporting bracket

harass; harassed; harassment

harbo(u)r *harbour* pref in Br, rec in Can.; *harbor* pref in US

hard- as a prefix normally combines into one word: *hardbound, hardhanded, hardhat, hardware*; exceptions: *hard-earned, hard-hitting*

haversine abbr: **hav**

H-beam

head- as a prefix normally combines into one word: *headfirst, headquarters, headset, headstart, headway*

heat- as a prefix, *heat* combines erratically; some typical compounds are: *heatresistant, heat-run, heatsink, heat-treat, heat wave*; for others, consult your dictionary

heavy-duty

hectare def: a large unit of area, used in surveying and agriculture; in SI, *hectare* replaces *acre*; abbr: **ha**

height (not *heighth*) abbr: **ht**; also: *heighten, heightfinder, heightfinding*

helix pl: *helixes* (pref) or *helices*

hemi- a prefix meaning half; combines to form one word: *hemisphere, hemitropic*

hemophilia; hemorrhage see **ae**

henry def: a unit of inductance; abbr: **H**; other abbr: **mH, µH, nH, pH**

here- whenever possible avoid using *here-* words that sound like legal terms, such as *hereby, herein, hereinafter, hereof*; they make a writer sound pompous; as a prefix, *here-* combines to form one word

hertz def: a unit of frequency measurement (similar to *cycles per second*, which it replaces); abbr: **Hz**; other abbr: **THz, GHz, MHz, kHz**

heterodyne

heterogeneous; homogeneous *heterogeneous* means of the opposite kind; *homogeneous* means of the same kind

hexadecimal

high- as a prefix either combines into one word or the two words are joined by a hyphen: *highhanded, highlight;* as compound adj: *high-frequency, high-power, high-priced, high-speed*

high frequency abbr: **hf** (pref) or **HF**

high-pressure (as an adjective) abbr: **h-p**

high voltage abbr: **hv** (pref) or **HV**

hinge; hinged; hinging

homogeneous see **heterogenous**

hono(u)r *honour* pref in Br, rec in Can.; *honor* pref in US

horizontal abbr: **hor**

horsepower abbr: **hp**; the abbr for horse-power-hour is **hp-hr**

hotkey

hovercraft

hour(s) abbr: **hr** or **h** (SI)

HTML hypertext markup language

http Hypertext Transfer Protocol; rules for exchanging files on the world wide web

humo(u)r *humour* pref in Br, rec in Can.; *humor* pref in US; but **humorous** and **humorist** each have only one *u*

hundred abbr: **C**

hundredweight def: 112 lb; abbr: **cwt**

hybrid

hydro- a prefix meaning *of water*; combines to form one word: *hydroacoustic, hydroelectric, hydromagnetic, hydrometer*

hyper- a prefix meaning *over*; combines to form one word: *hyperacidity, hypercritical*

hyperbola the plural is *hyperbolas* (pref) or *hyperbolae*

hyperbole def: an exaggerated statement

hyperbolic cosine, sine, tangent abbr: **cosh, sinh, tanh**

hyperlink

hypertext information organized into related chunks or units; the web is a massive set of hypertext information

hypertext markup language abbr: **html** (pref) or **HTML**

hyphen in compound terms you may omit hyphens unlesss they need to be inserted to avoid ambiguity or to conform to accepted usage; e.g. *preemptive* is preferred without a hyphen, but *photo-offset* and *re-cover* (when the meaning is *to cover again*) both require one; refer to individual entries in this glossary

hypothesis pl: *hypotheses*

I

I-beam

ibid. def: Latin abbr for *ibidem*, meaning in the same place; used in footnoting, but becoming obsolete

icon

ID card

i.e. def: *that is*; avoid confusing with **e.g.**; no comma is necessary after *i.e.*; may also be abbr **ie**

ignition abbr: **ign**

ill- as a prefix combines into a hyphenated expression: *ill-advised, ill-defined, ill-timed*

illegible def: not readable; also see *eligible*

im- see **in-**

imbalance this term should be restricted for use in accounting and medical terminology; use *unbalance* in other technical fields

immalleable

immaterial

immeasurable

immigrate see **emigrate**

immittance

immovable

impasse

impel; impelled; impelling; impeller

imperceptible

impermeable

impinge; impinging

imply; infer speakers and writers can *imply* something; listeners and readers *infer* from what they hear or read: *in his closing remarks, Mr Smith implied that further studies were in order; the technician inferred from the report that no further changes were necessary*

impracticable; impractical *impracticable* means not feasible; *impractical* means not practical; a less-preferred alternative for impractical is *unpractical*

in; into *in* is a passive word; *into* implies action; *ride in the car; step into the car*

in-; im-; un- all three prefixes mean not; all combine to form one word: *ineligible, impossible, unintelligible*; if you are not sure whether you should use *in-, im-,* or *un-*, use *not*

inaccessible

inaccuracy

inadmissible

inadvertent

inadvisable; unadvisable *inadvisable* pref

inasmuch as a better word is *since*

inaudible

incalculable not *incalculatable*

incandescence; incandescent

incase *encase* pref

inch(es) abbr: **in.**; other abbr:
inches per second **ips**
inch-pound(s) **in.-lb**

inclose see **enclose**

includes; including abbr: **incl**; when followed by a list of items, *includes* implies that the list is not complete; if the list is complete, use *comprises* or *consists of*

incomparable

incompatible

incur; incurred; incurring

index pl: *indexes* pref, except in mathematics (where *indices* is common)

indicated horsepower abbr: **ihp**; the abbr for indicated horsepower-hour is **ihp-hr**

indifferent to never use *indifferent of*

indiscreet; indiscrete *indiscreet* means imprudent; *indiscrete* means not divided into separate parts

indispensable

indorse *endorse* pref

industrywide

ineligible

inequitable

inessential; unessential both are correct; *unessential* pref

inexhaustible

inexplicable

infallible

infer; inferred; inferring; inference also see **imply**

infinitesimal

inflammable def: easily ignited (derived from *inflame*); *flammable* is a better word: it prevents readers from mistakenly thinking the *in* of *inflammable* means *not*

inflexible

infrared

infrastructure

ingenious; ingenuous *ingenious* means clever, innovative; *ingenuous* means innocent, naive; *ingenuity* is a noun derived from ingenious

in-house

inoculate

inoperable not *inoperatable*

input/output abbr: **I/O**

inquire; enquire *enquire* pref in Br, rec in Can.; *inquire* pref in US; also: *enquiry*

insanitary; unsanitary both are correct; *insanitary* pref

inseparable

inside diameter abbr: **ID**

in situ def: in the normal position

instal(l) *install, installed, installer, installing, installation* pref; but *instalment* pref in Br, rec in Can.; *installment* pref in US

instantaneous

instil; instilled

instrument

insure the pref def is to protect against financial loss; can also mean make certain of (particularly in US); see **ensure**

integer

integral; integrate; integrator

intelligence quotient abbr: **IQ**

intelligible

inter- a prefix meaning among or between; normally combines to form one word: *interact, intercarrier, interdependence, interdigital, interface, intermodulation, interoffice*

intermediate-pressure (as an adjective) abbr: **i-p**

intermittent

internal abbr: **int**

internet a worldwide computer network of networks that allows users at one computer to access information from another computer

internet relay chart abbr: **irc** or **IRC** (pref)

interrupt

into see **in**

intra- a prefix meaning within; normally combines to form one word: *intranet, intranuclear*; if combining word starts with *a*, insert a hyphen: *intra-atomic*

intranet an organization's private internet network, used to share company information and computing resources among employees

intrust *entrust* pref

I/O input/output

IQ

irc internet relay chat

irrational

irregardless never use this expression; use *regardless*

irrelevant frequently misspelled as *irrevelant*

irreparable also see repairable

irreversible

irritate also see *aggravate*

ISO International Organization for Standardization

iso- a prefix meaning the same, of equal size; normally combines to form one word: *isoelectronic, isometric, isotropic*; if combining word starts with o, insert a hyphen: *iso-octane*

its; it's *its* means belonging to; *it's* is an abbr for it is: *the transmitter and its modulator; if the fault is not in the remote equipment, then it's most likely in master control*; in technical writing *it's* should seldom be used: replace with *it is*

J

jackhammer

jobholder; jobseeker; job lot

joule def: a unit of energy, work, or quantity of heat (SI); abbr: **J**; other abbr: **TJ, GJ, MJ, kJ, mJ, J/m³, J/K** (joule(s) per kelvin), **J/kg, J/mol** (joule(s) per mole)

journey; journeys

judg(e)ment *judgment* pref in US and Can.; *judgement* pref in Br

judicial; judicious *judicial* means related to the law; *judicious* means sensible, discerning

K

kelvin def: the SI unit for thermodynamic temperature; abbr: **K**

kerb Br equivalent of *curb* (road edge)

key- as a prefix normally combines to form one word: *keyboard, keypunch, keying, keynote, keystroke*; but *key word*

kilo def: 10^3, abbr: **k**; other abbr:

kiloampere(s)	**kA**
kilobecquerel(s)	**kBq**
kilobyte(s)	**kbyte** (pref) or **kb**
kilocalorie(s)	**kcal**
kilocoulomb(s)	**kC**
kilogram(s) (see **kilogram**)	**kg**
kilohertz	**kHz**
kilohm(s)	**kΩ**; kohm
kilojoule(s)	**kJ**
kilolitre(s)	**kL**
kilometre(s)	**km**
kilometres per hour	**km/h**
kilomole(s)	**kmol**
kilonewton(s)	**kN**
kilopascal(s)	**kPa**
kilosecond(s)	**ks** (pref); **ksec**
kilosiemens	**kS**
kilovolt(s)	**kV**
kilovolt-ampere(s)	**kVA**
kilovolt-ampere(s) reactive	**kVAr**
kilowatt(s)	**kW**
kilowatthour(s)	**kWh** (pref); **kw-hr**

avoid writing *kilo* in text as an abbr for *kilogram* or *kilometre*

kilogram def: the SI unit for mass; abbr: **kg**; other typical abbr: **Mg, g, mg, µg**; also:

kilogram-calorie(s)	**kg-cal**
kilogram(s) per metre	**kg/m**
kilogram(s) per square metre	**kg/m²**
kilogram(s) per cubic metre	**kg/m³**
kilogram metre(s) per second	**kg·m/s**

knockout as noun or adjective, one word

knot abbr: **kn**

know-how (n); **know how** (v)

knowledge; knowledgeable

L

label(l)ed; label(l)ing single *l* pref

laboratory abbr: **lab**

labo(u)r *labour* pref in Br, rec in Can.; *labor* pref in US; also: *laboursaving*

lacquer

lambert abbr: L; use the abbr L with care: it is also the SI abbr for *litre*

lampholder

laptop (computer)

large scale integration abbr: **LSI**

laser def: light amplification by stimulated emission of radiation

last; latest; latter *last* means final; *latest* means most recent; *latter* refers to the second of only two things (if more than two, use *last*); it is better to write *the last two* (or *three*, etc) than *the two last*

lath; lathe *a lath* is a strip of wood; a *lathe* is a machine

latitude abbr: **lat** or ∅

lay- as a prefix generally combines to form one word (as noun or adj): *layoff, layout, layover*

LCD liquid crystal display

lead; led as a n, *lead* is a metal; as a v, *lead* means to show the way, as a leader would; the past of the v is *led*: *a lead-filled pipe; he was asked to lead the project team; he led the project team*

learned; learnt *learned* pref

LED light emitting diode

leeway

left-hand(ed) abbr: **LH**

length the SI unit of length is the *metre*, expressed in multiples and submultiples of *kilometres* (**km**), *metres* (**m**), and *millimetres* (**mm**)

lengthy not *lengthly*

less see **fewer**

letter- as a prefix combines erratically: *letterhead, letter-perfect, letter writer*

letter of intent; letter of transmittal pl: *letters of intent, letters of transmittal*

level(l)ed; level(l)er; level(l)ing *ll* pref in Br, rec in Can.; single *l* pref in US

liable to means under obligation to; avoid using as a synonym for *apt to* or *likely to*

liaison liaison is a noun; it is sometimes used uncomfortably as a verb: *to liaise*

libel(l)ed; libel(l)ing *ll* pref in Br, rec in Can.; single *l* pref in US

library

licence; license in Can. and Br, the noun is *licence* and the verb is *license*; in US, *license* is pref for both noun and verb

life- as a prefix combines erratically: *lifebelt, lifeboat, life cycle, lifeless, lifelong, life-size, lifespan, lifetime*

light- as a prefix *light-* generally combines to form one word: *lightface* (type), *lightweight*; but *light-year*; the past tense is *lighted*, but *lit* is common in Can. and Br

light emitting diode abbr: **LED**

lightening; lightning *lightening* means to make lighter; *lightning* is an atmospheric discharge of electricity

likable not *likeable*

linear abbr: **lin**; the abbr for lineal foot is **lin ft**

lines of communication not *line of communications*

liquefy; liquefiers; liquefaction

liquid abbr: **liq**

liquid crystal display abbr: **LCD**

listserv

litre; liter the SI spelling is **litre** (pref in Can. and Br), but in US *liter* is more common; abbr: **L**; other abbr: **kL, mL, µL**; the abbr for *litre(s) per day/hour/minute/second* are **L/d, L/h, L/m, L/s**

lock- as a prefix combines into a single word: *locknut, lockout* (n), *locksmith, lockstep, lockup, lockwasher;* but two words as a v: *lock out*; *lock up*

locus pl: *loci*

logarithm abbr: (common) **log**; (natural) **ln**

logbook

logistic(s) use *logistic* as an adj, *logistics* as a n: *logistic control; the logistics of the move*

long- as a prefix normally combines into a single word or is hyphenated: *long-distance, longhand, longplaying, long-range, long-term, long-winded*; but *long shot*

longitude abbr: **long.** or λ

loophole

looseleaf

loran abbr for long-range air navigation system

lose; loose *lose* is a verb that refers to a loss; *loose* is an adjective or a noun that means free or not secured: *three loose nuts caused us to lose a wheel*

louvre; louver *louvre* pref in Can. and Br; *louver* pref in US

low frequency abbr: **lf** (pref) or **LF**

low-pressure (as an adjective) abbr: **l-p**

LSI large scale integration

lubricate; lubrication abbr: **lub**

lumbar; lumber *lumbar* is the lower back; *lumber* is wood

lumen def: a unit of luminous flux (SI); abbr: **lm**; other abbr:

lumen-hour(s)	**lm-h** (pref); **lm-hr**
lumens per square foot	**lm/ft²**
lumens per square metre	**lm/m²**
lumens per watt	**lm/W**
lumen-second(s)	**lm·s**
microlumen(s)	**µlm**
millilumen(s)	**mlm**

luminance; luminescence; luminosity; luminous

lux def: a unit of illuminance (SI); abbr: **lx**; other abbr: **klx**

M

Mach

macro- a prefix meaning very large; combines to form one word: *macroscopic; macroview*

magneto pl: *magnetos*; as a prefix normally combines to form one word: *magnetoelectronics, magnetohydrodynamics, magnetostriction*; if combining word starts with *o* or *io*, insert a hyphen: *magneto-optics, magneto-ionization*

magneton; magnetron a *magneton* is a unit of magnetic moment; a *magnetron* is an electronic device controlled by an external magnetic field

maintain; maintained; maintenance

majority use *majority* mainly to refer to a number, as in a *majority of 27*; avoid using it as a synonym for many or most; e.g. do not write *the majority of technicians* when the intended meaning is *most*

make- as a prefix normally combines to form one word as a n or adj: *makeshift, makeover, makeup*; as a v, use two words: *make over, make up*

malfunction

malleable

manage; managed; manageable; managing

manoeuvre; maneuver *manoeuvre, manoeuvred, manoeuvring* pref in Br, rec in Can.; *maneuver, maneuvered, maneuvering* pref in US

manufacturer abbr: **mfr**

marketplace

marshal; marshal(l)ed; marshal(l)er; marshal(l)ing *ll* pref in Br, rec in Can.; single *l* pref in US

mass see **kilogram**

Master of Science abbr: **M.Sc.**

mat; matt a *mat* is a covering; *matt* is a dull finish

material; materiel *material* is the substance or goods out of which an item is made; when used in the plural, it describes items of a like kind, such as *writing materials*; *materiel* are all the equipment and supplies necessary to support a project or undertaking (a term commonly used in military operational support)

matrix *matrixes* pref in US, rec in Can.; *matrices* pref in Br

maximum pl: *maximums* (pref) or *maxima*; abbr: **max**; like *minimize, maximize* can be used as a verb

maybe; may be *maybe* means "perhaps": *maybe there is a second supplier*; the verb form *may be* means "perhaps it will be" or "possibly there is": e.g. *there may be a second supplier*

mda monochrome display adapter; also **MDA**

meagre not *meager*

mean; median the *mean* is the average of a number of quantities; the *median* is the midpoint of a sequence of numbers; e.g. in the sequence of five numbers 1, 2, 3, 7, 8, the mean is 4.2 and the median is 3

mean effective pressure abbr: **mep**

mean sea level abbr: **msl** (pref) or **MSL**

mediocre

medium when *medium* is used to mean substances, liquids, materials, or communication or advertising, the pref plural is *media*; in all other senses the pref plural is *mediums*

mega def: 10^6, abbr: **M**; other abbr:

megabyte(s)	**Mbyte** (pref) or **Mb**
megacoulomb(s)	**MC**
Megaelectronvolt(s)	**MeV**
megahertz	**MHz**
megajoule(s)	**MJ**
meganewton(s)	**MN**
megohm(s)	**MΩ;** **Mohm**
megapascal(s)	**MPa**
megavolt(s)	**MV**
megawatt(s)	**MW**

memorandum pl: *memorandums* (pref in US, rec in Can.) or *memoranda* (pref in Br); abbr: **memo** (singular); the pl is **memos**

memory the electronic holding place for instructions and data that a computer's microprocessor can reach quickly

merit; merited; meriting

metal(l)ed; metal(l)ing *ll* pref in Br, rec in Can.; single *l* pref in US; **metallic** and **metallurgy** always have *ll*

meteorology; metrology *meteorology* pertains to the weather; *metrology* pertains to weights, measures, and calibration

meter def: a measuring instrument (n) or to measure out (v)

metre; meter def: metric unit of length; the SI spelling is *metre* (pref in Can. and Br), but in US *meter* is more common; abbr: **m**; other typical abbr:

square metre(s)	$\mathbf{m^2}$
cubic metre(s)	$\mathbf{m^3}$
metres per second	**m/s**
newton-metre(s)	**N·m**
newtons per square metre	$\mathbf{N/m^2}$
kilogram(s) per cubic metre	$\mathbf{kg/m^3}$

metrication

micro def: 10^{-6}; abbr: **μ** (pref) or **u**; other abbr:

microampere(s)	**μA**
microcoulomb(s)	**μC**
microfarad(s)	**μF**
microgram(s)	**μg**
microgray(s)	**μGy**
microhenry(s)	**μH**
microhm(s)	**μΩ; μohm**
microlumen(s)	**μlm**
micromho(s)	**μmho**
micrometre(s)	**μm**
micromole(s)	**μmol**
micronewton(s)	**μN**
micropascal(s)	**μPa**
microsecond(s)	**μs** (pref); **μsec**
microsiemens	**μS**
microtesla(s)	**μT**
microvolt(s)	**μV**
microwatt(s)	**μW**

micro- as a prefix meaning very small, normally combines to form one word: *microammeter, microcomputer, micrometre, microprocessor, microswitch, microview, microwave*; but *micro-organism*

microchip a logic chip; often called an integrated circuit in computer circuitry

microphone abbr: **MIC** (pref) or **mike**

microprocessor a computer processor on a microchip; the "engine" that runs a computer; previously called the **CPU**

Microsoft disk operating system abbr: **MS-DOS**

mid- a prefix that means in the middle of; generally combines into one word: *midday, midpoint, midweek*; if used with a proper noun, insert a hyphen: *mid-Atlantic*

mile the word mile is generally understood to mean a statute mile of 5280 ft (1609 m), so the statement *I drove 326 miles* implies statute miles; when referring to the *nautical mile* (6080 ft; 1853 m), always identify it as such: *the flight distance was 4210 nautical miles* (or *4210 nmi*); abbr:

statute mile(s)	**mi**
nautical mile(s)	**nmi** (pref) or **n.m.**
miles per gallon	**mpg**
miles per hour	**mph**

mileage; milage *mileage* pref

milli def: 10^{-3}; abbr: **m**; other abbr:

milliampere(s)	**mA**
millicoulomb(s)	**mC**
millicurie(s)	**mCi**
millifarad(s)	**mF**
milligram(s)	**mg**
milligray(s)	**mGy**
millihenry(s)	**mH**
millijoule(s)	**mJ**
millikelvin(s)	**mK**
millilitre(s)	**mL**
millilumen(s)	**mlm**
millimetre(s)	**mm**
millimho(s)	**mmho**
millimole(s)	**mmol**
millinewton(s)	**mN**
milliohm(s)	**mΩ; mohm**
millipascal(s)	**mPa**
milliroentgen(s)	**mR**
millisecond(s)	**ms** (pref); **msec**
millisiemens	**mS**
millitesla(s)	**mT**
millivolt(s)	**mV**
milliwatt(s)	**mW**
milliweber(s)	**mWb**

milli- as a prefix, combines to form one word: *milliammeter, milligram, millimicron*

millibar def: a unit of pressure (= 100 Pa); abbr: **mbar**

mini- as a prefix combines to form one word: *minicomputer, minireport*

miniature; miniaturization

minimum pl: *minimums* (pref) or *minima*; abbr: **min**; also **minimize**

minority use mainly to refer to a number, as in *a minority by 2*; avoid using it as a synonym for several or a few; to write *a minority of the technicians* is incorrect when the intended meaning is *a few technicians*

minuscule not *miniscule*; def: very small

minute abbr:

time	**min**
angular measure	**′**

mis- a prefix meaning wrong(ly) or bad(ly); combines to form one word: *misalign, misfired, mismatched, misshapen*

miscellaneous

miscible

misspelled; misspelt *misspelled* pref (note double *s*)

mitre; miter *mitre* pref in Br, rec in Can.; *miter* pref in US

mnemonic

model(l)ed; model(l)er; model(l)ing *ll* pref in Br, rec in Can.: single *l* pref in US

mole def: the SI unit for amount of substance; abbr: **mol**; other abbr: **kmol, mmol, μmol, mol/m^3**

momentary; momentarily both mean *for a moment*, not *in a moment*

money- as a prefix normally combines to form one word: *moneymaking*

monitor

mono- a prefix meaning one or single; combines to form one word: *monopulse, monorail, monoscope*

monochrome display adapter abbr: **mda** (pref) or **MDA**

months the months of the year are always capitalized: *January, February,* etc; if abbr, use only the first three letters: *Jan, Feb,* etc; the abbr for *month* is **mo**

mortice; mortise *mortise* pref

mosaic

most never use as a short form for *almost*; to say *most everyone is here* is incorrect

motherboard

mo(u)ld *mould* pref in Br, rec in Can.; *mold* pref in US

movable; moveable *movable* pref

Mr; Ms address men as *Mr* and women as *Ms*; use *Miss* or *Mrs* only if you know the person prefers to be so addressed; the period (punctuation) may be inserted after *Mr* and *Ms*

M.Sc. abbr for Master of Science

MS-DOS Microsoft disk operating system

msl abbr for mean sea level; also **MSL**

mucous

multi- a prefix meaning many; combines to form one word: *multiaddress, multicavity, multielectrode, multimedia, multistate*

municipal; municipality

myself often used wrongly; write "Peter and I...", not "Peter and myself"

N

NAND-gate

nano def: 10^{-9}; abbr: **n**; other abbr:

nanoampere(s)	**nA**
nanocoulomb(s)	**nC**
nanofarad(s)	**nF**
nanohenry(s)	**nH**
nanometre(s)	**nm**
nanosecond(s)	**ns** (pref); **nsec**
nanotesla(s)	**nT**
nanovolt(s)	**nV**
nanowatt(s)	**nW**

naphtha(lene)

national information infrastructure abbr: **NII**

nationwide

nautical mile def: 1853 m (6080 ft); abbr: **nmi** (pref) or **n.m.**; see **mile**

navigate; navigator; navigable

NB means note well, and is the abbr for *nota bene*; it is more common to use the word *Note*

NC abbr for *normally closed* (contacts)

nebula pl: *nebulae* (pref in Br, rec in Can.) or *nebulas* (pref in US)

negative abbr: **neg**

negligible

neighbo(u)r *neighbour* pref in Br, rec in Can.; *neighbor* pref in US; also: **neighbourhood**

nevertheless

newsgroup

newton def: a unit of force (SI); abbr: **N**; other abbr: **MN, kN, mN, μN, N·m** (newton metre), **N/m** (newtons per metre)

next write the *next two* (or *next three*, etc) rather than *the two next* (etc)

nickel

night never use *nite*; write *nighttime* as one word

NII national information infrastructure

nineteen; ninety; ninth all three are frequently misspelled

nitroglycerine

NO abbr for *normally open* (contacts)

No. abbr for **number**; omit *s* when writing a series, as in *No. 30 to 36*; see **number**

noise-cancel(l)ing *ll* pref; see **cancel**

nomenclature

nomogram; nomograph *nomogram* pref

non- as a prefix meaning not or negative, normally combines to form one word: *nonconductor, nondirectional, nonnegotiable, nonlinear, nonstop*; if combining word is a proper noun, insert a hyphen: *non-Canadian*; avoid forming a new word with *non-* when a similar word that serves the same purpose already exists (i.e. you should not form *nonaudible* because *inaudible* already exists)

none when the meaning is "not one," treat as singular; when the meaning is "not any," treat as plural: *none* (not one) *of the sites meets our needs; none* (not any) *of the receivers were repaired*

no one two words

NOR-gate

norm def: the average or normal (distribution, situation, or condition)

normalize

normally closed; normally open (contacts); abbr: **NC, NO**

normal to def: at right angles to

north abbr: **N**; other abbr:

northeast	**NE**
northwest	**NW**
north-south (control, movement)	**N-S**

northbound and *northward* are written as one word; for rule on capitalization, see **east**

notable

not applicable abbr: **N/A**

note well abbr: **NB** (derived from *nota bene*), but *Note* is more common

NOT-gate

notice; noticeable; notification

not to exceed an overworked phrase that should be used only in specifications; in all other cases use *not more than*

nth (harmonic, etc)

nuclear frequently misspelled

nucleus the plural is *nuclei* (pref) or *nucleuses*

null

number although no. would appear to be the logical abbr for number (and is pref), **No.** is much more common (the symbol # is no longer used as an abbr for number); the abbr *no.* or *No.* must always be followed by a quantity in numerals: it is incorrect to write *we have received a No. of shipments*; for the difference in usage between *amount* and *number*, see **amount**

numbers in narrative, as a general rule spell out up to and including nine, and use numerals for 10 and above; for specific rules, see pp 283 to 284

O

oblique; obliquity

obsolete; obsolescent

obstacle

obtain; secure use *obtain* when the meaning is simply to get; use *secure* when the meaning is to make safe or to take possession of (possibly after some difficulty); *we obtained four additional samples; we secured space in the prime display area*

occasional; occasionally

occur; occurred; occurrence; occurring

o'clock avoid using; see **time**

OCR optical character recognition

odo(u)r *odour* pref in Br, rec in Can.; *odor* pref in US; *odorous* has only one *u*

off- as a prefix either combines into one word, or a hyphen is inserted: *offset, offshoot, off-centre(d), off-scale, off-the-shelf*

offence; offense *offence* pref in Can. and Br; *offense* pref in US; *offensive* always has an *s*

offline

off of an awkward construction; omit the word *of*

ohm def: a unit of electric resistance; abbr: Ω or **ohm**; other abbr: **GΩ, Gohm, MΩ, Mohm, kΩ, kohm, mΩ, mohm, µΩ, uohm**; abbr for ohm-centimetre(s) is **ohm-cm**; *ohmmeter* has *mm*

oilfield; oil-filled; oilsands

omit; omitted; omission

omni- a prefix meaning all or in all ways; combines to form one word: *omnibearing, omnidirectional, omnirange*

on; onto *on* means positioned generally; *onto* implies action or movement: *the report is on Mr Cord's desk; the speaker stepped onto the platform*

one- as a prefix mostly combines with a hyphen: *one-piece, one-sided, one-to-one, one-way*; but *oneself* and *onetime*

online

onward(s) *onward* pref

opaque; opacity

op. cit. def: Latin abbr for *opere citato*, meaning the work cited; used in footnoting; now obsolescent

operate; operator; operable not *operatable*

optical character recognition abbr: **OCR**

optimum pl: *optima* (pref) or *optimums*; also: **optimal**

oral def: spoken; avoid confusing with *aural*, which refers to hearing

orbit; orbital; orbited; orbiting

organize; organizer; organization

OR-gate

orient; orientation the noun form is *orientation*; the pref verb form is *orient, oriented, orienting*

orifice

origin; original; originally

oscillate

oscilloscope slang abbr: **scope**

ounce(s) abbr: **oz**; other abbr:

ounce-foot	**oz-ft**
ounce-inch	**oz-in.**

out- as a prefix normally combines to form one word: *outbreak, outcome, outdistance*; when *out-* is followed by *of*, insert hyphens if used as a compound adjective (as in *an out-of-date list*), but treat as separate words when used in place of a noun (as in *the printing schedule is out of phase*)

outside diameter abbr: **OD**

outward(s) *outward* pref

over- as a prefix meaning above or beyond, normally combines to form one word: *overbunching, overcurrent, overdriven, overexcited, overrun*; avoid using as a synonym for *more than*, particularly when referring to quantities: *more than 17 were serviceable* is better than *over 17 were serviceable*

overage means either too many or too old

overall an overworked word; as an adjective it often gives unnecessary additional emphasis (as in *overall impression*) and should be deleted; avoid using as a synonym for *altogether, average, general,* or *total*

oxidation; oxidization *oxidation* pref in US, rec in Can.; *oxidization* pref in Br; also: **oxidize**

oxyacetylene

P

pacemaker; pacesetter

page; pages abbr: **p; pp**

paid not *payed*, when the meaning is to spend

pair(s) abbr: **pr**

pamphlet

panel(l)ed; panel(l)ing *ll* pref in Br, rec in Can.; single *l* pref in US

paper- as a prefix mostly combines to form one word: *paperback, paperbound, paperwork*; but *paper-covered, paper-thin*

parabola; parabolas; parabolic; paraboloid

paragraph(s) abbr: **para**

parallax

parallel; paralleled; paralleling; parallelism; parallelogram both *parallel to* and *parallel with* are correct

paralysis pl: *paralyses*; also: **paralyse** pref in Br, rec in Can.; **paralyze** pref in US

parameter; perimeter *parameter* means a guideline; *perimeter* means a border or edge

paraplegic

paraprofessional

parenthesis pl: *parentheses*; in Can., the term **bracket(s)** is more common

parity

particles

partly; partially use *partly* when the meaning is "a part" or "in part"; use *partially* when the meaning is "to a certain extent," or when preference or bias is implied

parts per million abbr: **ppm**

part-time

pascal def: a unit of pressure (SI); abbr: **Pa**; other abbr: **Gpa, Mpa, kPa, mPa, μPa, pPa, Pa·s** (pascal second)

pass- as a prefix normally combines to form one word: *passbook, passkey, passport, password*

passed; past as a general rule, use *passed* as a verb and *past* as an adjective or noun: *the test equipment has passed quality control inspection; past experience has demonstrated a tendency to fail at low temperature; in the past...*

pay- as a prefix normally combines to form one word: *paycheque, payload, payroll*; but *pay day*

pcb printed circuit board

PCMCIA Personal Computer Memory Card International Association

PDF abbr for portable document format

pel

pencil(l)ed; pencil(l)ing *ll* pref in Br, rec in Can.; single *l* pref in US

pendulum pl: *pendulums*

penultimate def: the next to last

P.Eng abbr for Professional Engineer

people; persons *people* pref: *all the people were present*; use *persons* to refer only to small numbers of people: *one person was interviewed; seven people failed the test*

per in technical writing it is acceptable to use *per* to mean either *by, a,* or *an*, as in *per diem* (by the day) and *miles per hour;* avoid using *as per* in all writing

percent abbr: %; use % only after numerals: 42%; use *percent* after a spelled-out number: *about forty percent*; avoid using the expression *a percentage of* as a synonym for *a part of* or *a small part*; also: **percentage** and **percentile**

perceptible

peripheral

permafrost

permeable; permeameter; permeance

permissible

permit; permitted; permitting; permittivity; permit-holder

perpendicular abbr: **perp**

persevere; perseverance

persistent; persistence; persistency

personal; personnel *personal* means concerning one person; *personnel* means the members of a group, or the staff: *a personal affair; the personnel in the power house*

Personal Computer Memory Card International Association abbr: **PCMCIA**

peta def: 10^{15}; abbr: **P**; other abbr: **PBq** (petabecquerel)

petrochemical

pharmacy; pharmacist; pharmaceutical

phase in the nonelectric sense, *phase* means a stage of transmission or development; it should not be used as a synonym for aspect; it is used correctly in *the second phase called for a detailed cost breakdown*

phase-in; phaseout (n or adj); but use two words for the verb forms: *to phase in, to phase out*

Ph.D. abbr for Doctor of Philosophy

phenolic

phenomenon pl: *phenomena*

photo- as a prefix, normally combines to form one word: *photoelectric, photogrammetry, photoionization, photomultiplier*; if combining word starts with o, insert a hyphen: *photo-offset*

pico def: 10^{-12}, abbr: **p**; other abbr:

picoampere(s)	**pA**
picocoulomb(s)	**pC**
picofarad(s)	**pF**
picohenry(s)	**pH**
picosecond(s)	**ps** (pref); **psec**
picowatt(s)	**pW**

piecemeal; piecework

piezoelectric; piezo-oscillator

pilot; piloted; piloting

pipeline

pixel

plagiarism def: to copy without acknowledging the original source

plateau pl: *plateaus* (pref in US, rec in Can.) or *plateaux* (pref in Br)

platform the underlying operating system of a computer, on which application programs can run

plug; plugged; plugging

plumbbob; plumb line

p.m. def: after noon (post meridiem)

pneumatic

polarize; polarizing; polarization

poly- a prefix meaning many; combines to form one word: *polydirectional, polyethylene, polyphase*

polyvinyl chloride abbr: **pvc**

pop-up window

portable document format abbr: **PDF**

positive abbr: **pos**

post- a prefix meaning after or behind; mostly combines to form one word: *postacceleration, postdated, postgraduate, postpaid*; but *post-mortem, post office, post-secondary*

post meridiem def: after noon; abbr: **p.m.**; can also be written as *post-meridian* (less pref)

potentiometer abbr: **pot.**

pound(s) (weight) abbr: **lb** (singular and pl); other abbr:

pound-foot	**lb-ft**
pound-inch	**lb-in.**
pounds per square foot	**psf** (pref); **lb/ft^2**
pounds per square inch	**psi** (pref); **lb/in^2**
pounds per square inch, absolute	**psia**

power factor abbr: **pf** or spell out

power house; power line; powerpack

practicable; practical these words have similar meanings but different applications that sometimes are hard to differentiate; *practicable* means feasible to do: *it was difficult to find a practicable solution* (one that could reasonably be implemented); *practical* means handy, suitable, able to be carried out in practice: *a practical solution would be to combine the two departments*

practice; practise the noun always is *practice*; the verb is *practise* (pref in Br, rec in Can.), but can also be *practice* (pref in US)

pre- a prefix meaning before or prior; normally combines to form one word: *preamplifier, predetermined, preemphasis, preignite, preset*; if combining word is a proper noun, insert a hyphen; *pre-Roman*

precede; proceed *precede* means to go before; *proceed* generally means to carry on or continue: *a brief business meeting preceded the dinner* (the meeting occurred first); *after dinner, we proceeded with the annual presentation of awards*; see **proceed**

precedence; precedent *precedence* means priority (of position, time, etc): *the pressure test has precedence* (it must be done first); a *precedent* is an example that is or will be followed by others: *we may set a precedent if we grant his request* (others will expect similar treatment)

précis

predominate; predominant; predominantly

prefer; preferred; preference; preferable avoid overstating *preferable*, as in *more preferable* and *highly preferable*

prescribe; proscribe *prescribe* means to state as a rule or requirement; *proscribe* means to deny permission or forbid

presently use with care; in US *presently* means now; in Br *presently* means soon or in good time; a better word is *immediately* (US) or *shortly* (Br and Can.)

pressure-sensitive

prestigious

pretence; pretense *pretence* pref in Can. and Br; *pretense* pref in US

prevalent; prevalence

preventive; preventative *preventive* pref

previous def: earlier, that which went before; avoid writing *previous to* (use *before*); see **prior**

principal; principle as a noun, *principal* means (1) the first one in importance, the leader; or (2) a sum of money on which interest is paid: *one of the firm's principals is Martin Dawes; the invested principal of $10 000 earned $950 in interest last year*; as an adjective, *principal* means most important or chief: *the principal reason for selecting the Arrow microprocessor was its low capital cost*; *principle* means a strong guiding rule, a code of conduct, a fundamental or primary source (of information, etc): *his principles prevented him from taking advantage of the error*

printed circuit board abbr: **pcb**

printout (n and adj); **print out** (v)

prior; previous use only as adjectives meaning earlier: *he had a prior appointment*, or *a previous commitment prevented Mr Perchanski from attending the meeting*; write *before* rather than *prior to* or *previous to*

proceed; proceeding; procedure use *proceed to* when the meaning is to start something new; use *proceed with* when the meaning is to continue something that was started previously

processor

producible

Professional Engineer abbr: **P.Eng**

program(me) single *m* pref in US, rec in Can.; *mm* pref in Br; **programmed, programmer, programming** always have *mm* in Can. and Br, and usually in US (where single *m* also is used but is less pref)

prohibit use *prohibit from*; never *prohibit to*

prominent; prominence

proofread

propel; propelled; propelling; propellant (noun); **propellent** (adjective); **propeller**

prophecy; prophesy use *prophecy* only as a noun, *prophesy* only as a verb

proposition in its proper sense, *proposition* means a suggestion put forward for argument; it should not be used as a synonym for *plan, project*, or *proposal*

pro rata def: assign proportionally; sometimes used in the verb form as **prorate:** *I want you to prorate the cost over two years*

prospectus; prospectuses

protein

protocol a term used in information technology to describe a special set of rules used to make telecommunication connections

proved; proven use *proven* only as an adjective or in the legal sense; otherwise use *proved: he has been proven guilty; he proved his case*

provincewide

psycho- as a prefix normally combines to form one word: *psychoanalysis, psychopathic, psychosis*; if combining word starts with o, insert a hyphen: *psycho-organic*

purge; purging

pursuant to avoid using this wordy expression

Q

quality control abbr: QC

quantity; quantitative the abbr of quantity is **qty**

quart abbr: **qt**

quasi- a prefix meaning seemingly or almost; insert a hyphen between the prefix and the combining word: *quasi-active, quasi-bistable, quasi-linear*

question mark insert a question mark after a direct question: *how many booklets will you require?*; omit the question mark when the question posed is really a demand: *may I have your decision by noon on Monday*

questionnaire

quick- as a prefix normally combines with a hyphen: *quick-acting, quick-freeze, quick-tempered*; exceptions: *quicklime, quicksilver*

quiescent; quiescence

R

rack-mounted

racon def: a radar beacon

radian def: a unit of angular measurement; abbr: **rad**

radiator

radio- as a prefix, combines to form one word: *radioactive, radiobiology, radioisotope, radioluminescence*; if combining word starts with *o*, omit one *o*: *radiology, radiopaque*; in other instances *radio* may be either combined or treated as a separate word, depending on accepted usage; examples are *radio compass, radio countermeasures, radio direction-finder, radio frequency* (as a noun), *radio-frequency* (as an adj), *radio range, radiosonde, radiotelephone*

radio frequency abbr: **rf**

radio frequency interference abbr: **rfi** (pref) or **RFI**

radius pl: *radii* (pref) or *radiuses*

radix pl: *radices* (pref) or *radixes*

rain- as a prefix normally combines to form one word: *raincoat, rainproof, rainwear*; exception: *rain check*

rally; rallied; rallying

RAM abbr for random access memory

ramdrive

R and D abbr for research and development

range; ranging; rangefinder; range marker

rare; rarely; rarity; rarefy; rarefaction

ratemeter

ratio; ratios

rational; rationale *rational* means reasonable, clear-sighted: *John had a rational explanation for the error*; *rationale* means an underlying reason: *Tricia explained the company's rationale for diversifying the product line*

re def: a Latin word meaning in the case of; avoid using *re* in technical writing, particularly as an abbr for *regarding, concerning, with reference to*

re- a prefix meaning to do again, to repeat; normally combines to form one word: *reactivate, rediscover, reemphasize, reentrant, reignition, reorganize, rerun, reset, reunite*; if the compound term forms an existing word that has a different meaning, insert a hyphen to identify it as a compound term, as in *re-cover* (to cover again)

reaction use *reaction* to describe chemical or mechanical processes, not as a synonym for *opinion* or *impression*

reactive kilovolt-ampere abbr: **kVAr**; the abbr for **reactive volt-ampere** is **VAr**

readability

read-only memory abbr: **ROM**

readout (n and adj); **read out** (v)

realize; realization

real time defines computer responsiveness in a human rather than a machine sense of time; insert a hyphen when two words are combined into a compound adj; **real-time chat; real-time transmission**

reboot reload the operating system; see **boot**

recede

receive; receiver; receiving; receivable

rechargeable

recipe; receipt often confused; *recipe* means cooking instructions; *receipt* means a written record that something has been received

recommend; recommendation

reconcile; reconcilable

reconnaissance

recover; re-cover *recover* means to get back, to regain; *re-cover* means to cover again

recur; recurred; recurring; recurrence these are the correct spellings; never write *reoccur* (etc)

recycle; recyclable

reducible

reenforce; reinforce *reenforce* means to enforce again; *reinforce* means to strengthen: *Rick Davis reenforced his original instructions by circulating a second memorandum; The Artmo Building required 34 750 tonnes of reinforced concrete*

refer; referred; referring; referral; referee; reference

referendum Br and US dictionaries list *referenda* as the pref pl, but *referendums* is much more commonly used and rec by CP

refuel; refuelled

reiterate def: to say again

relaid; relayed *relaid* means laid again, like a carpet; *relayed* means to send on, as a message would be relayed from one person to another

remit; remitted; remitting; remitter; remittance

remodel; remodelled; remodelling see **model**

removable

rent-a-car

reoccur(rence) never use; see **recur**

repairable; reparable both words mean in need of repair and capable of being repaired; *reparable* also implies that the cost to repair the item has been taken into account and it is economically worthwhile to effect repairs

repel; repellent; repeller

replaceable

reproducible

rescind

research and development abbr: **R and D**

reservoir

reset; resetting; resettability

resin; rosin these words have become almost synonymous, with a preference for *resin*; use *resin* to describe a gluey substance used in adhesives, and *rosin* to describe a solder flux-core

respective(ly) this overworked word is not needed in sentences that differentiate between two or more items; e.g. it should be deleted from a sentence such as: *pins 4, 5, and 7 are marked R, S, and V respectively*

restart

resume def: a personal biography; the correct spelling is *résumé* (with two accents), but the single accent (*résume*) or no accent has become standard

retrieve; retrieval

retro- a prefix meaning to take place before, or backward; normally combines to form one word: *retroactive, retrofit, retrogression*; if combining word starts with *o*, insert a hyphen: *retro-operative*

reverse; reverser; reversal; reversible

revolutions per minute; revolutions per second abbr: **rpm; rps**

rfi radio frequency interference

rheostat

rhombus pl: *rhombuses* (pref) or *rhombi*

rhythm; rhythmic; rhythmically

ricochet; ricocheted; ricocheting

right-hand(ed) abbr: **RH**

rigo(u)r *rigour* pref in Br, rec in Can.; *rigor* pref in US; *rigorous* is standard spelling in Can., US, and Br

RISC

rivet; riveted; riveter; riveting

road- as a prefix normally combines to form one word: *roadblock, roadmap, roadside*

roentgen abbr: **R**

role; roll a *role* is a person's function or the part that he or she plays (in an organization, project, or play); a *roll*, as a technical noun, is a cylinder; as a verb, it means to rotate: *the technician's role was to make the samples roll toward the magnet*

rollover one word as a n or adj; two words as a v

ROM def: read-only memory

root mean square abbr: **rms**

rosin see **resin**

rotate; rotator; rotatable; rotary

round def: circular; in Br, *round* is commonly used in place of *around*, but this is not rec in Can.

ruggedize

rumo(u)r *rumour* pref in Br, rec in Can.; *rumor* pref in US

run-off insert a hyphen when used as n or adj; use two words as a v

rustproof; rust-resistant

S

salvageable

same avoid using *same* as a pronoun; to write *we have repaired your receiver and tested same* is awkward; instead, write *we have repaired and tested your receiver*

satellite

saturate; saturation; saturable

save; savable

sawtooth; saw-toothed

scalar; scaler *scalar* is a quantity that has magnitude only; *scaler* is a measuring device

scarce; scarcity

sceptic(al); skeptic(al) *sceptic(al)* pref in Br; *skeptic(al)* pref in US, rec in Can.; also **skepticism**

schedule

schematic although really an adjective (as in *schematic diagram*), in technical terminology *schematic* can be used as a noun (meaning a *schematic drawing*)

science; scientific(ally); scientist

screwdriver; screw-driven

seam-weld

seasonal; seasonable *seasonal* means affected by or dependent on the season; *seasonable* means appropriate or suited to the time of year; *a seasonal activity; seasonable weather*

seasons the seasons are not capitalized: *spring, summer, autumn* or *fall, winter*

secant abbr: **sec**

secede; secession

second (position) as a prefix, *second-* combines erratically: *second-class, second-guess, secondhand, second-rate, second sight*

second (time) abbr: **s** (as part of a symbol) or **sec** (in narrative)

second (angular measure) abbr: ″

secure see **obtain**

-sede *supersede* is the only word to end with *-sede*; others end with *-cede* or *-ceed*

seem(s) see **appear(s)**

self- insert a hyphen when used as a prefix to form a compound term: *self-absorption, self-bias, self-excited, self-locking, self-setting*; but there are exceptions: *selfless, selfsame*

semi- a prefix meaning half; normally combines to form one word: *semiactive, semiannually* (every six months), *semiconductor, semimonthly* (half-monthly), *semiremote, semiweekly* (half-weekly); if combining word starts with *i*, insert a hyphen: *semi-idle, semi-immersed*

separate; separable; separator; separation all are frequently misspelled

sequence; sequential

serial input/output abbr: **SIO**

serial number abbr: **ser no.** or **S/N**

series-parallel

serrated

serviceable

serviceperson avoid using *serviceman* or *servicewoman*

servo- as a prefix, combines to form one word: *servoamplifier, servocontrol, servosystem*; as a noun, *servo* is an abbr for *servomotor* or *servomechanism*

sewage; sewerage *sewage* is waste matter; *sewerage* is the drainage system that carries away the waste matter

SGML abbr for standard generalized markup language

shall *shall* is rarely used in technical writing (*will* is pref), except in specifications when its use implies that the specified action is mandatory

short- as a prefix, may combine with a hyphen, as in *short-circuit, short-form* (report), *short-lived, short-term*; in some cases it may combine into one word, as in *shorthand* (writing), *shorthanded, shortcoming, shortsighted, shortwave*

shrivel(l)ed; shrivel(l)ing *ll* pref in Br, rec in Can.; single *l* pref in US

sic a Latin word which means a quotation has been copied exactly, even though there was an error in the original; e.g. *the report stated: "Our participation will be an issential (sic) requirement."*

siemens def: a unit of electric conductance (SI); abbr: **S**; other abbr: **kS, mS, μS**

signal(l)ed; signal(l)er; signal(l)ing *ll* pref in Br, rec in Can.; single *l* pref in US

signal-to-noise (ratio)

silhouette

silverplate; silver-plate use *silverplate* as a noun or adjective; *silver-plate* as a verb

similar not *similiar*

sine abbr: **sin**

singe; singeing the *e* must be retained to avoid confusion with *singing*

singlehanded

siphon not *syphon*

sirup; syrup *syrup* pref

site; sight; cite three words that often are misspelled; a *site* is a location: *the construction site*; *sight* implies the ability to see: *mud up to the axles became a familiar sight*; *cite* means quote: *I cite the May 17 progress report as an example of good writing*

siz(e)able *sizable* pref in US, rec in Can.; *sizeable* pref in Br

skeptic(al) pref spelling; see **sceptic(al)**

skil(l)ful *skilful* pref in Br, rec in Can.; *skillful* pref in US; note that this is contradictory to most *l* and *ll* situations listed in this glossary

slip- usually combines into a single word: *slippage, slipshod, slipstream*; but *slip ring(s)*

smelled; smelt *smelled* pref in Can. and US; *smelt* pref in Br

smo(u)lder *smoulder* pref in Br and Can.; *smolder* pref in US

soft key; software

solder

solely

soluble

someone; some one *someone* is correct when the meaning is any one person; *some one* is seldom used

some time; sometimes *some time* means an indefinite time: *some time ago*; *sometimes* means occasionally: *he sometimes works until after midnight*

sound- combines irregularly: *sound-absorbent, sound-absorbing, sound-powered, soundproof, sound track, sound wave*

south abbr: **S**; other abbr:

southeast	**SE**
southwest	**SW**

southbound and *southward* are written as one word; for rule on capitalization, see **east**

space- as a prefix normally combines to form one word: *spacecraft, spaceflight*

spare(s) can be used as a noun meaning spare part(s)

specially see **especially**

specific gravity abbr: **sp gr**

specific heat abbr: **sp ht**

spectro- as a prefix, combines to form one word: *spectrometer, spectroscope*; if combining word starts with o, omit one o: *spectrology*

spectrum pl: *spectra* (pref) or *spectrums*

spelled; spelt *spelled* pref in Can. and US; *spelt* pref in Br

spilled; spilt *spilled* pref in Can. and US; *spilt* pref in Br

spiral(l)ed; spiral(l)ing *ll* pref in Br, rec in Can.; single *l* pref in US

split infinitive to split an infinitive is to insert an adverb between the word *to* and a verb: *to really insist* is a split infinitive; although some grammarians claim you should never split an infinitive, many now suggest you may do so if rewriting would result in awkward construction, ambiguity, or extensive rewriting

spoiled; spoilt *spoiled* pref in Can. and US; *spoilt* pref in Br

spotweld

square abbr: **sq** or ^{2}; other abbr:

square foot/feet	**ft**^{2} (pref); **sq ft**
square inch(es)	**in.**^{2} (pref); **sq in.**
square metre(s)	**m**^{2}
square centimetre(s)	**cm**^{2}
square millimetre(s)	**mm**^{2}
curies per square metre	**Ci/m**^{2}
milliwatts per square metre	**mW/m**^{2}

standard generalized markup language abbr: **SGML**

standby; standoff; standstill all combine into one word when used as noun or adjective

standing-wave ratio abbr: **swr** or **SWR**

startup one word as n or adj; two words as a v: **start up**

state-of-the-art

stationary; stationery *stationary* means not moving: *the vehicle was stationary when the accident occurred*; *stationery* refers to writing materials: *the main item in the October stationery requisition was an order for one thousand writing pads*

statute mile def: 1609 m (5280 ft); see **mile**

statutory

stencil(l)ed; stencil(l)ing *ll* pref in Br, rec in Can.; single *l* pref in US

stereo- as a prefix, combines to form one word: *stereometric, stereoscopic*; *stereo* can be used alone as a noun meaning multi-channel system

stimulus pl: *stimuli*

stocklist, stockpile

stop- as a prefix usually combines to form one word: *stopgap, stopnut, stopover* (when used as n or adj, but two words as v); but *stop payment, stop watch*

stoppage

straightened; straitened *straightened* means to make straight; *straitened* means restricted

strato- a prefix that combines to form one word: *stratocumulus, stratosphere*

stratum pl: *strata*

structural

stylus dictionaries list *styli* as the pref pl, but *styluses* is much more commonly used

sub- a prefix generally meaning below, beneath, under; combines to form one word: *subassembly, subcarrier, subcommittee, subnormal, subpoint*

subparagraph abbr: **subpara**; abbr for *subsubparagraph* is **subsubpara**

subpixel

subtle; subtlety; subtly

succinct; succinctly

sufficient in technical writing, *enough* is a better word than *sufficient*

sulphur; sulfur *sulphur* pref in Can. and Br; *sulfur* pref in US; the prefix **sulph-** (or **sulf-**) combines to form one word: *sulphanilamide* (or *sulfanilamide*)

summarize

super- a prefix meaning greater or over; combines to form one word: *superabundant, superconductivity, superregeneration*

superhigh frequency abbr: **shf**

superimpose; superpose *superimpose* means to place or impose one thing generally on top of another; *superpose* means to lay or place exactly on top of, so as to be coincident with

supersede this is the correct spelling; see **-sede**

supra- a prefix meaning above; normally combines to form one word: *supramolecular*; if combining word starts with *a*, insert a hyphen: *supra-auditory*

surfeit def: to have more than enough

surveillance

surveyor

susceptible

switch- *switchboard, switchbox, switchgear*

swivel(l)ed; swivel(l)ling *ll* pref in Br, rec in Can.; single *l* pref in US

syllabus pl: *syllabuses* (pref) or *syllabi*

symmetry; symmetrical

symposium pl: *symposiums (pref)* or *symposia*

synchro as a prefix combines to form one word: *synchromesh, synchronize, synchronous, synchroscope*; *synchro* can also be used alone as a noun meaning synchronous motor

synonymous use *synonymous with*, not *synonymous to*

synopsis pl: *synopses*

synthesis pl: *syntheses*

synthetic

syphon *siphon* pref

syringe

syrup; syrupy

systemwide

T

tail- as a prefix normally combines to form one word: *tailboard, tailless, tailwind*; but *tail end, tail fin*

take- *takeoff; takeover; takeup*; as n or adj, these terms all combine into a single word; as a v, use two words

tangent abbr: **tan**

tangible

tape deck

target; targeted

taxable; tax-exempt; taxpayer

TCP/IP abbr for transmission control protocol/internet protocol; def: the basic communication language or protocol of the internet

teamwork

technician

Teflon

tele- a prefix meaning at a distance; combines to form one word: *teleammeter, telemetry, telephony, teletype(writer)*

telecom; telecon *telecom* is the abbr for *telecommunication(s)*; *telecon* is the abbr for *telephone conversation*

television abbr: **TV**

Telnet

temperature abbr: **temp**; combinations are *temperature-compensating* and *temperature controlled*, when recording temperatures, the abbr for *degree* (deg or °) may be omitted: *an operating temperature of 85C; the water boils at 100C or 212F*; the pref (SI) unit for temperature is the degree Celsius (C)

tempered

template; templet both spellings are correct; *template* pref in Can. and Br

temporary; temporarily

tenfold

tensile strength abbr: **ts**

tentative; tentatively

tenuous

tera def: 10^{12}; abbr: **T**; other abbr:

terabecquerel(s)	TBq
terahertz	THz
terajoule(s)	TJ
terawatt(s)	TW

terminus pl: *termini* (pref) or *terminuses*

tesla def: a unit of magnetic flux density, magnetic inductance (SI); abbr: **T**; other abbr: **mT, μT, nT**

that is abbr: **i.e.** (pref) or **ie**

their; there; they're the first two of these words are frequently used wrongly; *their* is a possessive, meaning belonging to them: *the staff took their holidays earlier than normal*; *there* means in that place: *there were 18 desks in the room*, or *put it there*; *they're* is a contraction of *they are* and should not appear in technical or business writing

there- as a prefix combines to form one word: *thereafter, thereby, therein, thereupon*

therefor(e) *therefore* pref

thermo- a prefix generally meaning heat; combines to form one word: *thermoammeter, thermocouple, thermoelectric, thermoplastic*

thermodynamic temperature the SI unit is the kelvin (abbr: **K**), expressed in degrees Celsius (C)

thesis pl: *theses*

thousand abbr: **k**

thousand foot-pound(s)	**kip-ft**
thousand pound(s)	**kip**

three- when used as a prefix, a hyphen normally is inserted between the combining words: *three-dimensional, three-phase, three-ply, three-wire*; exceptions are *threefold* and *threesome*

threshold

through never use *thru*

tieing, tying *tying* pref

timber; timbre *timber* is wood; *timbre* means tonal quality

time always write time in numerals, if possible using the 24-hour clock: *08:17* or *8:17 a.m., 15:30* or *3:30 p.m.;* 24-hour times may be written as *20:45* (pref), *20:45 hr*, or *20:45 hours*; never use the term "o'clock" in technical writing: write *15:00* or *3 p.m.* rather than *3 o'clock*

time- typical combinations are *time base, time-card, time clock, time constant, time-consuming, time lag, timesaving, time-slot, timetable, time-wasting*

tinplate; tin-plate use *tinplate* as a noun, *tin-plate* as a verb or adjective

to; too; two frequently misspelled; *to* is a preposition that means in the direction of, against, before, or until; *too* means as well; *two* is the quantity 2

today; tonight; tomorrow never use *tonite*

tolerance abbr: **tol**

ton; tonne the US ton is 2000 lb and is known as a *short ton*; the Br ton is 2240 lb and is known as a *long ton*; the metric ton is 1000 kg (2204.6 lb) and is known as a *tonne (*abbr: **t**); other terms: *tonmile* and *tonnage*

toolbox; toolmaker; toolroom

top- top-heavy, top-loaded, top-up

torque; torqued; torquing

total(l)ed; total(l)ing *ll* pref in Br, rec in Can.; single *l* pref in US

touch-tone (dialling)

toward(s) *toward* pref

traceable

trade- as a prefix combines most often into a single word; *trademark, tradeoff*; but *trade-in, trade name*, and *trade show*

trans- a prefix meaning over, across, or through; it normally combines to form one word: *transadmittance, transcontinental, transship*; if combining word is a proper noun, insert a hyphen; *trans-Canada* (an exception is *transatlantic* and *transpacific)*; *transonic* has only one *s*

transceiver def: a transmitter-receiver

transfer; transferred; transferring; transferable; transference

translator

transmission control protocol/internet protocol abbr: **TCP/IP**

transmit; transmitted, transmitting; transmittal, transmitter; transmission

transverse; traverse *transverse* means to lie across; *traverse* means to track horizontally

travel(l)ed; travel(l)er; travel(l)ing *ll* pref in Br, rec in Can.; single *l* pref in US

tri- a prefix meaning three or every third; combines to form one word: *triangulation, tricolour, trilateral, tristimulus, triweekly*

triple- all compounds are hyphenated: *triple-acting, triple-spaced*

trouble-free; troubleshoot (v); **troubleshooting**

truncated

tumo(u)r *tumour* pref in Br, rec in Can.; *tumor* pref in US; but *tumorous* has only one *u*

tune; tunable; tuneup (n or adj); *tune up* as a v

tunnel(l)ed; tunnel(l)ing *ll* pref in Br, rec in Can.; single *l* pref in US; *tunnel* has only one *l*

turbo- a prefix meaning turbine-powered; combines to form one word: *turboelectric, turboprop*

turbulence; turbulent

turn- *turnaround* and *turnover* form one word when used as n or adj, but two words as a v; *turnstile* and *turntable* always form one word; *turns-ratio* is hyphenated

two- when used as a prefix to form a compound term, a hyphen normally is inserted: *two-address, two-phase, two-ply, two-position, two-wire*; an exception is *twofold*

type- as a prefix normally combines into one word: *typeface, typeset(ting)*

tyre Br spelling of *tire* (on a car wheel)

U

UCD user-centred drive

ultimatum pl: *ultimatums*

ultra- a prefix meaning exceedingly; normally combines to form one word: *ultrasonic, ultrasound, ultraviolet*; if combining word starts with *a*, insert a hyphen: *ultra-audible, ultra-audion*

ultrahigh frequency abbr: **uhf** or **UHF**

un- a prefix generally meaning not or negative; normally combines to form one word: *uncontrolled, undamped, unethical, unnecessary*; if combining word is a proper noun, or if term combines to form an existing word that has a different meaning, insert a hyphen: *un-Canadian, un-ionized* (meaning not ionized); if uncertain whether to use *un-, in-,* or *im-*, try using *not*

unadvisable; inadvisable both are correct; *inadvisable* pref

unbalance; imbalance for technical writing, *unbalance* pref; see **imbalance**

unbiased

under- a prefix meaning below or lower; combines to form one word: *underbunching, undercurrent, underexposed, underrated, undershoot, undersigned, underway*

underage means a shortage or deficit, or too young

unequal(l)ed *unequaled* pref; see **equal**

unessential; inessential *unessential* pref

unforeseen; unforeseeable

uni- a prefix meaning single or one only; combines to form one word: *uniaxial, unidirectional, unifilar, univalent*

uninterested def: not interested; avoid confusing with *disinterested*

unionized; un-ionized *unionized* refers to a group of people who belong to a union; *un-ionized* means not ionized

unique def: the one and only, without equal, incomparable; use with great care and never in any sense where a comparison is implied; you cannot write *this is the most unique design*; rewrite as *this design is unique*, or (if a comparison must be made) *this is the most unusual design*

universal resource locator abbr: **URL**

universal serial bus abbr: **USB**

unmistakable

unnavigable

unparalleled

unpractical *impractical* pref

unsanitary

unserviceable abbr: **u/s**

unstable but *instability* is better than *unstability*

untraceable

unwieldy

up- as a prefix combines to form one word: *update, upend, upgrade, uprange, upswing;* but *up-to-date*

uppercase def: capital letters; abbr: **uc**

uppermost

URL abbr for universal resource locator

USB abbr for universal serial bus

use; usable; usage; using; useful

user-centred drive abbr: **UCD**

utilize; utilise *utilize* pref; avoid using *utilizes* when *uses* or *employs* would be a better word

V

vacuum

valance; valence *valance* means a cover over a drapery track; *valence* is an electronic or nucleonic term, as in *valence electron*

valve-grind(ing)

vari- as a prefix meaning varied, combines into one word: *varicoloured, variform*

variance write *at variance with*, never *at variance from*

varimeter; varmeter def for both: a meter for measuring reactive power; *varimeter* pref

V-chip

vdisk virtual disk

vehicle, vehicular

vender; vendor *vendor* pref

ventilator

verbatim def: written exactly as originally said

versed sine abbr: **vers**

versus def: against; abbr: **vs**

vertex def: top; pl: *vertices* (pref) or *vertexes*; avoid confusing with *vortex*

very high frequency abbr: **vhf** or **VHF**

VGA video graphics locator

vice; vise def: a clamping device; *vice* pref in Can. and Br; *vise* pref in US

vice versa def: in reverse order

video- as a prefix normally combines to form one word: *videocast, videocassette, videotape*; the abbr for videocassette recorder is **VCR** or **vcr**

video frequency abbr: **vf** or **VF**

video graphics array abbr: **VGA**

viewfinder; viewpoint

virtual disk abbr: **vdisk** (pref) or **VDISK**

vise see **vice**

visor; vizor *visor* pref

viz def: namely; this term is seldom used in technical writing

vocation; avocation *vocation* is a trade or calling; *avocation* means an interest or hobby

voice-over; voiceprint

volatile memory

volt def: electric potential or potential difference; abbr: **V**; other abbr: **MV, kV, mV, μV, nV**; also

volt-ampere(s)	**VA**
volt-ampere(s), reactive	**VAr**
volts, alternating current	**Vac**
volts, direct current	**Vdc**
volts, direct current, working	**Vdcw**
volts per metre	**V/m**

volt- combines into one word: *voltammeter, voltohmyst*

volume abbr: **vol**

vortex def: spiral; pl: *vortices* (pref) or *vortexes*; avoid confusing with *vertex*

VU-meter

W

WAIS wide area information server

waive; waiver; waver *waive* and *waiver* mean to forgo one's claim or give up one's right; *waver* means to hesitate, to be irresolute

walkie-talkie

war- as a prefix, combines to form one word: *warfare, wartime*

warranty

waste; wastage

water combines irregularly: *water-cool(ed), water cooler, waterflow, water level, waterline, waterproof, water-soluble, watertight*

watt def: a unit of power, or radiant flux (SI); abbr: **W**; other abbr: **TW, GW, MW, kW, mW, μW, nW, pW, W/m²**; the abbr for *watt-hour(s)* is **Wh** (pref) or **W-hr**; as a prefix, *watt-* forms *watthourmeter* and *wattmeter*

wave- normally combines to form one word: *waveband, waveform, wavefront, waveguide, wavemeter, waveshape*; exceptions are *wave angle* and *wave-swept*

wavelength abbr: λ

waver see **waiver**

wear and tear *no* hyphens

weather use only as a noun; never write *weather conditions*; avoid confusing with *climate* and *whether*

weatherproof

web def: the world wide web (**the web**); also **website**

weber def: a unit of magnetic flux (SI); abbr: **Wb**; other abbr: **mWb**

Wednesday often misspelled

week(s) abbr: **wk**

weekend

weight abbr: **wt**

well- as a prefix normally combines with a hyphen: *well-adjusted, well-defined, well-timed*

west abbr: **W**; *westbound* and *westward* are written as one word; for rule on capitalization, see **east**

where- as a prefix combines to form one word: *whereas, wherein*; when combining word starts with *e*, omit one *e*: *wherever*

whether; weather *whether* means if; *weather* has to do with rain, snow, sunshine, wind, etc

while; whilst *while* pref

whoever

wholly not *wholely*

wide; width abbr: **wd**

wide area information server abbr: **WAIS**

wideband; widespread

wirecutter(s); wire-cutting; wirewound

withheld; withhold

word processor; word processing abbr: **WP**; as an adj, insert a hyphen: *the word-processing software*

words per minute abbr: **wpm**

work- as a prefix usually combines to form one word: *workbench, workflow, workforce, workload, workshop*; but *work station*

working volts, dc abbr: **Vdcw**

worldwide

world wide web abbr: **www** or **the web**; all the resources and users on the internet that use the Hypertext Transfer Protocol (http)

wrap; wrapped; wrapping; wraparound

writeoff; writeup both combine into one word when used as n or adj; use two words in v form

writer see **author**

writing only one *t*

www world wide web

wysiwyg def: What You See Is What You Get

X

x- *x-axis, X-band, x-particle, x-radiation, x-ray*

Xerox

X-Y recorder

Y

y- *Y-antenna, y-axis, Y-connected, Y-network, Y-signal*

Yahoo

yard(s) abbr: **yd**

yardstick

year(s) abbr: **yr**; typical combinations are *year-end* and *year-round*

yocta def: 10^{-24}; abbr: **y**

yotta def: 10^{24}; abbr: **Y**

your; you're *your* means belonging to or originating from you: *I have examined your prototype analyser*; *you're* is a contraction of *you are* and should not appear in technical or business writing

Z

z-axis

zepto def: 10^{-21}; abbr: **z**

zero pl: *zeros* (pref) or *zeroes*; typical combinations are *zero-access, zero-adjust, zero-beat, zero-hour, zero level, zero-set, zero reader*

zetta def: 10^{21}; abbr: **Z**

zip code

zoology; zoological; zoologist

Index